Linking Practice and Theory

The Pedagogy of Realistic Teacher Education

Fred A. J. Korthagen
in cooperation with
Jos Kessels, Bob Koster,
Bram Lagerwerf, and Theo Wubbels
IVLOS Institute of Education, Utrecht University, The Netherlands

LAWRENCE ERLBAUM ASSOCIATES, PUBLISHERS
2001 Mahwah, New Jersey London

Lawrence Erlbaum Associates, Inc., Publishers
10 Industrial Avenue
Mahwah, NJ 07430

Cover design by Kathryn Houghtaling Lacey

Library of Congress Cataloging-in-Publication Data
Korthagen, F. A. J., 1949-
Linking practice and theory : the pedagogy of realistic teacher education / Fred A.J. Korthagen in cooperation with Jos Kessels ... [et al.].

p. cm.

Includes bibliographical references and index.
ISBN 0-8058-3740-X (cloth : alk. paper)
ISBN 0-8058-3981-X (pbk. : alk. paper)
1. Teachers—Training of. 2. Teacher educators—Training of.
I. Title: Pedagogy of realistic teacher education.
II. Title.
LB1707.K65 2001
370'.71'1—dc21

00-057273
CIP

Books published by Lawrence Erlbaum Associates are printed on acid-free paper, and their bindings are chosen for strength and durability.

Printed in the United States of America
10 9 8 7 6 5 4 3 2

To Ellen and Mischa

Table of Contents

Preface

> While it has been recognized for some time that many faculty institutions responsible for teacher preparation have an interest *in* teacher education but are not actively concerned *with* teacher education (Borrowman, 1965), there has been little progress in developing our collective understanding of the pedagogy unique to preservice teacher education. —*Loughran (1997, p. 4)*

THE ROAD FROM PROBLEMS TO THEORY

This book was born out of serious concern—a concern with children in schools and most of all with their teachers, who often work very hard to try and realize something good for these children.

That is how my own career in education started. In the early 1970s I became a mathematics teacher in secondary education in the Netherlands and I felt that somehow, something was terribly wrong. I had to teach children who were in an important phase in their lives—experiencing their first great love, trying to find out who they were and how to position themselves within the peer group, distinguishing themselves from important adults—in other words, an exciting, hectic, and often difficult period. I realized that to these kids school was not so much a place to learn mathematics, but a meeting place to learn about living. What could I, as a mathematics teacher, offer them of value for their lives: the principles of solving equations or the beauty of the Pythagorean theorem? I felt a bit silly, which was a feeling that was further aggravated by Paul Simon's record "Kodachrome," popular during my first year of teaching. He sang "When I think back on all the crap I learned in high school, it's a wonder I can think at all." Although I sympathized with these lyrics, at the same time I kept believing that, as a math teacher, it must be possible to offer something important to high school students.

Although I had the good fortune to start my work as a teacher at a quite progressive Amsterdam school, I was more or less shocked to discover that my colleagues were not at all concerned about such things. If I succeeded at all in starting a discussion about the goals of our work, they explained to me how important the mathematical knowledge and skills were for physics and other school subjects. Of course, that is true. Still, I felt like a being in an alien world. I started experimenting with what we nowadays would call problem-solving approaches and the development of metacognitive skills. I believed that somehow mathematics must have the potential to function as a means for developing skills that surpass the level of equations or Pythagoras, and are useful in other contexts as well. However, I felt very lonely and vulnerable on this path. The only support I found was in a book on mathematics education that I had read when certifying as a teacher. In trying to apply these ideas and approaches I met many problems, including resistance from the students to whom I hoped to offer something better. Looking back on this period now, more than 20 years later, I realize how much I needed support and guidance from an experienced teacher educator.

When I had the opportunity to get a job as a teacher educator at a Dutch teacher training college, called SOL (a Dutch abbreviation meaning Foundation for Teacher Education), I suddenly found myself amidst colleagues with the same kind of ideals. It was the time when mathematics education in the Netherlands went through an explosive development. Suddenly other people appeared to develop materials and methods that made my vague dreams come true. The so-called realistic approach toward mathematics education had just been born, which now has spread to the United States. An important starting point in this approach is the belief that children can and should develop mathematical notions themselves on the basis of practical experiences and problems. The problems are presented within a recognizable context, and are often derived from everyday situations. Emphasis is put on the practical use of mathematics, inquiry and reflection by students, group work, and hands-on activities.

The SOL team of mathematics teacher educators started to translate these ideas to the learning and teaching of student teachers, and not only in the area of mathematics. An approach was developed in which teacher education starts from practical problems and teaching experiences of student teachers, and thus from recognizable contexts. And, building on the student teachers' reflections, the teacher educators then try to develop theoretical notions about learning and teaching in such a way that the student teachers can almost immediately use these notions in practice.

The very same principles that are central to realistic math education form the core of this approach to teacher education: the development of theoretical notions on the basis of practical problems and concerns of the students, the importance of almost immediate applicability of these notions in new situations, emphasis on inquiry and reflection by the student teachers, the role of group work, and the exchange of ideas between the learners.

IS TEACHER EDUCATION REALISTIC?

I must say that I went through a shock, rather similar to the one I had experienced as a beginning teacher, when I started to discuss the realistic approach to teacher education with other teacher educators from my own country and abroad. Although many were aware of the problems of beginning and experienced teachers, they often tried to solve these problems in such a way that brought back memories of traditional mathematics education: The teacher gives a lecture on the theory and then the students apply this theory to problems, whereby they generally do not find success. Then the teacher goes over how it should be done and there is the test, which many students fail. In many places in the world at large, the situation in teacher education is similar: A teacher educator—an expert in a certain area—is in front of the classroom and lectures on recent theories in the field of learning psychology, or general education. At best, the student teachers get some assignment to try out something in practice, but very often this practice is in time far away from the lecture (even as far as months later) or the person in charge of the supervision during teaching practice does not have the slightest idea of the assignment or the theory behind it. And when the final test has come, that is when they are working as certified teachers in a school, the graduates of teacher education programs often feel they fail to pass this test. Many beginning teachers report encountering severe problems (Veenman, 1984) and often go through a very dificult period. Many research studies demonstrate the failure of teacher education to fundamentally influence teachers and improve education.

A GUIDEBOOK

Can we blame teacher educators? I do not think so. They often try very hard to make the best out of the situation but, exactly like myself, they cannot find the road toward a more effective and inspiring educational approach on their own. A teacher educator needs support from colleagues and a context in which structural changes are possible. Regretfully, the structure is often so limiting that nobody knows where to begin the journey. Still, there is a way. This book tries to show it. It is set up as a guidebook, guiding the traveler into new realms of teacher education.

I felt I would be the person to blame if I did not use my concern for students and for teachers as an incentive for writing this guidebook, in deep respect to all those people, all over the world, who are trying to make the best of education.

The book is also set up as a journey from practice to theory to practice and so on. In going from one chapter to the other, the reader will continuously commute between practice in teacher education and research on teacher education. The odd numbered chapters will deal with practice and present the basic principles underlying our approach to teacher education. The even numbered chapters deepen the odd ones by focusing on research or theoretical frameworks behind the approach; they are based more on scientific knowledge. This means that practice-oriented readers can restrict themselves to the odd chapters, which together develop a pedagogy of teacher education aiming at the integration of theory and practice, whereas the research-interested reader may wish to read only the even chapters. Although this is quite possible, I would like to emphasize that in my view both types of readers could then miss the very point, which has to do with linking theory and practice. Both practice on its own and theory alone are incomplete: I believe one can only really understand the former if one knows about the latter, and vice versa.

This is also a statement that bears on teacher education. I wish to stress that I do not believe in throwing theory out of teacher education, which seems to be one reaction in some places to the failure of teacher education. But also, I do not believe in doing the theory first and then trying to bridge the gap with practice afterward. I would prefer not to create the gap in the first place and then try to get rid of it.

In the first and introductory chapter, I describe in more detail the problematic situation in teacher education, which can be characterized by a gap between theory and practice. I analyze this problem by looking more closely at current practices in teacher education. I also prepare the reader for the rest of the journey through this book by presenting the basic ideas underlying the alternative approach this book offered herein. Chapter 1 ends with a more detailed overview of the whole of the book.

TRAVELING FURTHER

Of course, this book can only present a momentary picture of the developments in my own thinking and the progress we were able to make in some concrete teacher education programs. Looking at teacher education as a profession, I think the journey has only just begun. This book tries to offer the first building blocks of a pedagogy of teacher education. In my opinion, much more work, both research and practical work by teacher educators, is necessary before we can really consider teacher education as a professional enterprise. There is important work to be done so that future student teachers and their students can benefit from it. I hope this book may stimulate the reader to become a fellow traveler on a fascinating journey into the future.

ACKNOWLEDGMENTS

I would not have been able to write this book if I had undergone my journey alone. I have learned much of what I write about from others—colleagues, researchers, teachers, friends, and, last but not least, students. What has helped me in my learning is the use of reflection on my own experiences in teaching and teacher education and connecting these reflections with the notions these people were able to express. In other words, in my own development I was continuously commuting between "practice" and "theory." I am grateful to all my fellow travelers for helping me along this road.

Many of the ideas and principles described here have been developed by my present colleagues at the IVLOS Institute of Education at Utrecht University. Most of the examples are taken from the IVLOS teacher education program and other programs I have become acquainted with through my work as a consultant and trainer of teacher educators. Moreover, quite a number of extensive research studies have been carried out into the IVLOS teacher education program, into the processes it elicits from student teachers, and into its effects. The research findings were often very informative to the teacher educators involved and led to new developments, which then in their turn became objects of study. In that respect, this book is a product of a unique and intensive process of reflective collaboration of a whole group of people, students, teacher educators, researchers, and others. The Department of Pedagogy and Education of the University of Amsterdam gave me the opportunity to finish this book as part of my work related to the Kohnstamm-chair, which is supported by the Dutch pedagogical association VBSP. I am especially grateful to Jaap Dronkers, former chairman.

I thank all the students, student teachers, experienced teachers, researchers, and other colleagues with whom I worked during my career for what they have taught me. Special thanks go to Mieke Brekelmans, Hans Créton, Chris Day, Maarten Dolk, Truus van den Heuvel, Rob Houwen, Jos Kessels, Cor Koetsier, Bob Koster, Ko Melief, Tom Russell, Anke Tigchelaar, Ton van der Valk, Hildelien

Verkuyl, and Theo Wubbels for their important contributions. Bram Lagerwerf and Heleen Wientjes were of the utmost importance for their emotional support and careful reading of every word of this book and for bringing in new ideas. I am grateful for their commentaries, which led to essential improvements. Leen Don did a wonderful job in helping me transform my double Dutch into understandable English. I thank Marika Prak for her never-ending willingness to transform my textfiles into a readable book. I am especially grateful to Naomi Silverman and Sarah Wahlert of Lawrence Erlbaum Associates for their support. Sarah's excellent editorial work was essential in the final production of this book. And I am grateful to my partner Ellen for accepting and supporting my devotion to my work.

—Fred Korthagen

Fred Korthagen is a professor of education at the IVLOS Institute of Education at Utrecht University, The Netherlands. His address is P. O. Box 80127, 3508 TC Utrecht, The Netherlands. E-mail: F.Korthagen@ivlos.uu.nl

Credits

Chapter 1: Parts of this chapter have previously been published in: Korthagen, F. A. J., & Kessels, J. P. A. M. (1999). Linking theory and practice: Changing the pedagogy of teacher education. *Educational Researcher, 28*(4), 4–17.

Chapter 2: This chapter is a revision of Kessels, J. P. A. M., & Korthagen, F. A. J. (1996). The relationship between theory and practice: Back to the classics. *Educational Researcher, 25*(3).

Chapter 3: Parts of this chapter have previously been published in: Wubbels, T., Korthagen. F. A. J., & Brekelmans, M. (1997). Developing theory from practice in teacher education. *Teacher Education Quarterly, 24*(3), 75–90.

Chapter 4: Parts of this chapter have previously been published in: Korthagen, F. A. J. (1993). The role of reflection in teachers' professional development. In L. Kremer-Hayon, H. C. Vonk, & R. Fessler (Eds.), *Teacher professional development: A multiple perspective approach* (pp. 133–145). Amsterdam: Swets & Zeitlinger.

Chapter 6: Parts of this chapter have previously been published in: Wubbels, T., & Korthagen, F. A. J. (1990). The effects of a pre-service teacher education program for the preparation of reflective teachers. *Journal of Education for Teaching, 16*(1), 29–43.

Chapter 8: This chapter is a revision of: Korthagen, F. A. J., & Wubbels, T. (1995). Characteristics of reflective practitioners: Towards an operationalization of the concept of reflection. *Teachers and Teaching: Theory and Practice, 1*(1), 51–72.

Chapter 9: Parts of this chapter have been reprinted from : Korthagen, F. A. J. (1992). Techniques for stimulating reflection in teacher education seminars. *Teaching and Teacher Education, 8*(3), 265–274, with permission from Elsevier Science.

Chapter 10: This chapter is a revision of: Korthagen, F. A. J., & Lagerwerf, B. (1996). Reframing the relationship between teacher thinking and teacher behaviour: Levels in learning about teaching. *Teachers and Teaching: Theory and Practice, 2*(2), 161–190. Some parts of the chapter have been published in: Korthagen, F. A. J., & Kessels, J. P. A. M. (1999). Linking theory and practice: Changing the pedagogy of teacher education. *Educational Researcher, 28*(4), 4–17.

Chapter 11: A part of this chapter is a revision of: Korthagen, F. A. J. (1999). Linking reflection and technical competence in teaching: The logbook as an instrument in teacher education. *European Journal of Teacher Education, 22* (2/3), 191–207. Reproduced by kind permission of the Association for Teacher Education in Europe. Other parts of the chapter have been reprinted from: Korthagen, F. A. J. (1993). Two modes of reflection. *Teaching and Teacher Education,* 9(3), 317–326, with permission from Elsevier Science.

Chapter 12: Parts of this chapter have been reprinted from: Korthagen, F. A. J. (1993). Two modes of reflection. *Teaching and Teacher Education,* 9(3), 317–326, with permission from Elsevier Science.

1 Teacher Education: a Problematic Enterprise

Fred Korthagen

A teacher educator: "I really don't understand why my student teachers don't use the theory I taught to them. I see them have problems with their classes which could easily be avoided if only they would apply the content of my course!"

This introductory chapter describes the present problematic situation in teacher education, which can be characterized by a gap between theory and practice. This problem is analyzed by looking more closely at current practices in teacher education and the assumptions embedded therein. This chapter also prepares the reader for the chapters to come by presenting the basic ideas underlying an alternative approach to teacher education. Finally, an overview of the other chapters is presented.

1.1. INTRODUCTION

It is interesting to look back on the history of teacher education in order to see how, during the last part of the second millennium, basic ideas evolved about the way teachers should be prepared for their profession. It may help us to become aware that some assumptions have become so common that they are seldom discussed. First, three assumptions concerning the pedagogy of teacher education and the nature of teacher knowledge are discussed. Many research findings show that these assumptions create a gap between theory and practice. The chapter then focuses on this gap and the difficulty teacher educators face when trying to change teacher education practices. A new approach to teacher education is introduced, based on recent insights into the relation between teacher cognition and teacher behavior. The basic ideas underpinning this *realistic* approach are sketched. Section 1.9 presents an overview of the rest of the book.

1.2. THE HISTORY OF TEACHER PREPARATION

Let us start by looking at the period before formal teacher education started. By the end of the 19th century, teaching skills were mastered mainly through practical experience, without any specific training. Often a new teacher learned the tricks of the trade, after a study of the relevant subject matter, while acting as an apprentice to an experienced teacher.

During the late 19th and early 20th century, as psychological and pedagogical knowledge developed, academics wished to offer this knowledge to teachers in order to change education and "adapt" it to scientific insights. This is how the idea of the *professionalization* of teachers began. Indeed, as Hoyle and John (1995) point out, the availability of a recognized body of knowledge is one of the most important criteria for categorizing an occupational group as "professional" (see also McCullough, 1987).

During the second half of the 20th century, this wish to equip teachers with a professional knowledge base was stimulated by a growing desire, worldwide, to educate a broader group than the most gifted children. This democratization of education spurred on the wish for educational change, and especially to train a larger number of prospective teachers and to provide them with the necessary professional knowledge.

The general trend was to teach teachers courses in relevant knowledge domains, for example the psychology of learning. Gradually, however, it became clear that teachers did not carry much of this knowledge base into practice and more was needed. The knowledge base should become visible in the skills that teachers used in the classroom. This led to the introduction of *competency-based teacher education* (CBTE). The idea underlying CBTE was the formulation of concrete and observable criteria for good teaching, which could serve as a basis for the training of teachers. For some time, process–product research studies, in which relations were analyzed between concrete teacher behavior and learning outcomes of students, were considered a way to nurture this approach to teacher education. From this research, long lists of trainable skills were derived and became the basis for teacher education programs.

Behind this line of thought one can see what Clandinin (1995) calls "the sacred theory-practice story": teacher education conceived as the translation to practice of theory on good teaching. The desire to use as much of the available knowledge as possible has led to a conception of teacher education as a system in which experts, preferably working within universities, teach this knowledge to prospective teachers. In the best case, they also try to stimulate the transfer of this knowledge to the classroom, by skills training (which is certainly a strong characteristic of CBTE) or by assignments to be carried out during field experiences (see Fig. 1.1).

This is what Carlson (1999) calls the "theory-to-practice" approach. Wideen, Mayer-Smith, and Moon (1998, p. 167) put it like this:

> The implicit theory underlying traditional teacher education was based on a training model in which the university provides the theory, methods and skills; the schools provide the setting in which that knowledge is practiced; and the beginning teacher provides the individual effort to apply such knowledge. In this model, propositional knowledge has formed the basis of university input.

In addition, Barone, Berliner, Blanchard, Casanova, and McGowan (1996) state that many teacher programs consist of a collection of separated courses in which theory is presented without much connection to practice. Ben-Peretz (1995, p. 546) says:

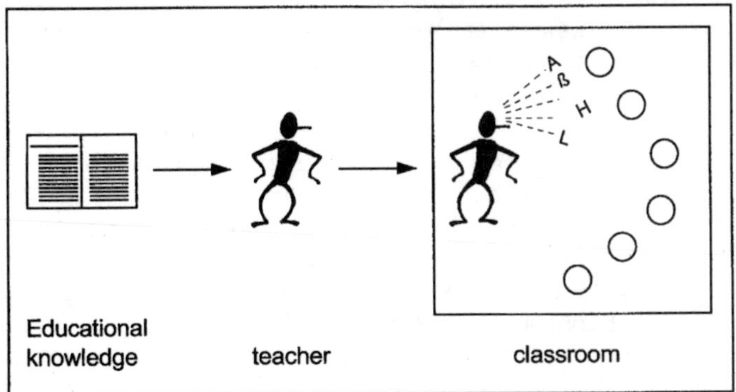

FIG. 1.1. The technical-rationality paradigm in teacher education.

> The hidden curriculum of teacher education tends to communicate a fragmented view of knowledge, both in coursework and in field experiences. Moreover, knowledge is "given" and unproblematic.

Schön (1983, p. 21) speaks about the *technical-rationality model*, which is based on the notion that "professional activity consists in instrumental problem solving made rigorous by the application of scientific theory and technique." In fact, three basic assumptions are hidden in this view (cf. Hoyle, 1980):

1. Theories help teachers to perform better in their profession.
2. These theories must be based on scientific research.
3. Teacher educators should make a choice concerning the theories to be included in teacher education programs.

The technical-rationality model has been dominant for many decades. In fact its dominance seems to become even stronger (Imig & Switzer, 1996, p. 223; Sprinthall, Reiman, & Thies-Sprinthall, 1996), although many studies have shown its failure in strongly influencing the practices of the graduates of teacher education programs. I look more closely at this problem in the next section.

1.3. PROBLEMS RELATED TO THE TRADITIONAL APPROACH TO TEACHER EDUCATION

Many researchers showed that the traditional technical-rationality paradigm does not function well. Zeichner and Tabachnick (1981), for example, showed that many notions and educational conceptions, developed during preservice teacher education, were "washed out" during field experiences. Comparable findings were reported by Cole and J. G. Knowles (1993) and Veenman (1984), who also points toward the severe problems teachers experience once they have left preservice teacher education. Lortie (1975) presents another early study of the socialization process of teachers showing the dominant role of practice in shaping teacher development.

In their well-known overview of the literature on teacher socialization, Zeichner and Gore (1990) state that researchers differ in the degree to which they consider teacher socialization as a passive or an active process. In the so-called *functionalist paradigm*, the emphasis is on the passive reproduction of established patterns, thus creating continuity (see, e.g., Hoy & Rees, 1977). Zeichner and Gore view Lacey's (1977) study of teacher socialization in the United Kingdom as an example of the *interpretative paradigm*, as it is "aimed at developing a model of the socialization process that would encompass the possibility of autonomous action by individuals and therefore the possibility of social change emanating from the choices and strategies adopted by individuals" (Zeichner & Gore, 1990, p. 330). This emphasis on the individual's choices and possibilities to change educational patterns is even stronger in the third paradigm distinguished by Zeichner and Gore, the *critical approach* (see, e.g., Ginsburg, 1988). The central purpose of critical approaches is "to bring to consciousness the ability to criticize what is taken for granted about everyday life" (Zeichner & Gore, 1990, p. 331). It will be clear that studies located within the second and third paradigm are more focused on the innovative possibilities of new educational insights brought to the schools by novice teachers. However, all studies on teacher development emphasize that it is very difficult for an individual to really influence established patterns in schools. Educational change appears to be a beautiful ideal of teacher educators, but generally not much more than an ideal. Bullough (1989) emphasizes that, in this respect, we are dealing with a severe problem in teacher education. As Zeichner and Gore (1990, p. 343) put it:

> Studies that have focused on the institutional and cultural levels of analysis have clearly shown, for example, that various ideological and material conditions within teacher education institutions, schools, and societies serve to establish limits on the range of options available to both teacher education students and teacher educators.

It is interesting to note that this problem is found in many different countries. For example, at Konstanz University in Germany, large-scale research has been carried out into the phenomenon of the "transition shock" (Dann, Cloetta, Müller-Fohrbordt, & Helmreich, 1978; Dann, Müller-Fohrbrodt, & Cloetta, 1981; Hinsch, 1979; Müller-Fohrbrodt, Cloetta, & Dann, 1978), which regrettably went largely unnoticed by the English-speaking research community. It showed that teachers pass through a distinct attitude shift during their first year of teaching, in general creating an adjustment to current practices in the schools, and not to recent scientific insights into learning and teaching. Building on the work of the Konstanz research group, Brouwer (1989) did an extensive quantitative and qualitative study in the Netherlands among 357 student teachers, 128 cooperating teachers, and 31 teacher educators, also showing the dominant influence of the school on teacher development. He found that an important factor promoting transfer from teacher education to practice was the extent to which the teacher education curriculum had an integrative design, or in other words, the degree to which there was an alternation and integration of theory and practice within the program. This important issue will be elaborated on in chapter 3, together with the causes of the failure of the technical-rationality approach.

Apart from the fact that studies into teacher development and teacher socialization show that the classical technical-rationality approach to teacher education creates little transfer from theory to practice, this approach creates another fundamental problem. Elliot (1991) states that teachers who realize they are unable to use the theory presented to them by experts often feel they fall short of living up to the expectations these experts seem to have of their capabilities. Elliot (1991, p. 45) says that "teachers often feel threatened by theory" and these feelings are enhanced by the generalized form in which experts tend to formulate their knowledge and by the ideal views of society or individuals behind their claims. As such, the technical-rationality approach implies a threat to teachers' professional status.

Indeed, what do we see happen in teacher education? Even if student teachers rationally understand the importance of theory as a means to support practice, they soon experience that they are not the only ones struggling so much with everyday problems in their classrooms that the whole idea of applying theory becomes an impossible mission. They see the same phenomenon everywhere around them in their practice schools. The only way out of the feeling of always falling short is to adapt to the common habit of teachers to consider teacher education too theoretical and useless. Then they can no longer be blamed for not functioning according to the theoretical insights; but teacher education can be blamed. It will be clear that this social game of positioning guilt with the other, too often played by teachers and their educators, is a power game with few positive outcomes. It only widens the gap between theory and practice. Elliot (1991, p. 47) concludes:

> The perceived gap between theory and practice originates not so much from demonstrable mismatches between ideal and practice but from the experience of being held accountable for them.

1.4. THE PROBLEM OF CHANGE

One thing has become very clear through a wealth of research studies: Educational change is a problematic issue. There is not only extensive literature dealing with the often unsuccessful attempts of preservice teacher educators to influence teacher behavior, but many studies on inservice teacher education and curriculum development point at the same phenomenon. It can be helpful to our purpose to discuss the problem of educational change from a broader perspective now, because the rest of this book focuses on preservice teacher education.

Holmes (1998, p. 254) sets the stage for the present discussion by stating that

> Even the strongest advocates of change concede that large numbers of change projects have gone sadly awry.

A well-known model for planned educational change is the research to development to dissemination (RD&D) model. The underlying rationale is very similar to the technical-rationality model described earlier: We have a lot of knowledge about "good education," so why not teach this knowledge to a group of teachers, and, once that has led to a successful innovation, disseminate the success? In the past, this model has often been used by policymakers, consciously or unconsciously, and has directed many attempts to change education.

After the discussion in the previous section, it will be no surprise that the RD&D model has serious limitations, as Lieberman (1998, p. 19) concludes, in her introduction to the 1998 *International Handbook of Educational Change*. She refers to an unpublished paper by Huberman in which he "critiques the RD&D model as being 'hyper-rational and technocratic,' and insensitive to the unique properties of school cultures." Day (1999, p. 15) notes that "externally imposed reform ... will not necessarily result in teachers implementing the intended changes," as "a multitude of research projects in different countries have shown." Fullan (1998, p. 227) states, "If we know anything we know that change cannot be managed.'" McLaughlin (1998, p. 83) concludes that "it is exceedingly difficult for policy to change practice." I add that this is extremely difficult for teacher educators as well.

In my view, this has to do with an aspect of change that has until now attracted relatively little attention from researchers writing about change. In fact, it is hard to find in the two volumes of the 1998 *International Handbook of Educational Change*. It is the notion that there is a world of difference between two ways in which we can use the word *change* as a verb. The first is the transitive use of the word, for example, in the sentence "I wish to change this teacher." The second is the intransitive use, as in "teacher X changes." The former use of the verb *to change* implies that there is an external pressure, however subtle, put on the teacher. The latter sentence refers to change directed by the teacher him- or herself. I agree with McIntyre and Hagger (1992, p. 271) that "teachers should develop, not that other people should develop teachers." They also state:

> "Development" takes what is there as a valuable starting point, not as something to be replaced, but a useful platform on which to build. To do so is to recognise not only that teachers do have valuable existing expertise but also that, if teachers are forced to choose, they will usually revert to their secure established ways of doing things. The metaphor of "building on what is already there" is not, however, satisfactory because it suggests adding on something separate to what is there, something extra on top. The concept of development, in contrast, implies that whatever is added, whatever is new, will be integrated with what is there already, and will indeed grow from what is there. (p. 271)

Chapter 5 discusses this issue in more depth. A major mistake when implementing innovations in education has been made by outsiders who wish to change things but who do not take into account the needs and concerns of the teachers and the circumstances in which they work. Although an author such as McLaughlin (1998, p. 72) is aware of the fact that "the presence of the will or motivation to embrace policy objectives or strategies is essential to generate the effort and energy necessary to a successful project," such a statement still looks at the problem of change from the vantage point of the outsider wishing to change teachers. Holmes (1998, p. 250) states it even more clearly:

> Despite the rhetoric, school change projects are inevitably topdown. For all the talk of democratic decision making, collaboration, and recognizing the importance of teachers, change projects are and must be implemented from the top. Occasionally, teachers may exercise the right of veto, but more usually any resistance will see them being accused of being afraid of change and defenders of the status quo, the most grievous sin in Fullan's moral code.

The problem may be that for a long time we did not know what other possibilities there were to initiate developments in education. This is clarified through Holmes' (1998) statement:

> There is an admitted problem in trying to train teachers like seals, but there is little chance of their implementing the desired changes if left alone. (p. 254)

The dichotomy between "training like seals" and "leaving teachers alone" is an example of what Watzlawick, Weakland, and Fisch (1974, p. 90) call "the illusion of alternatives": If we accept this dichotomy, then we are trapped in the idea that these are the only two possibilities. This is symptomatic of the approach toward educational change that for a long time has dominated the thinking of reformers. As Hargreaves (1994, p. 6) notes, these reformers often showed disrespect for teachers. In this book, a third possibility will be shown, which is to take teachers seriously, work with them on the basis of their concerns, and even to train them in the use of certain skills, but only on the basis of their wish to develop these skills. This means neither to train them like seals nor leaving them alone. It implies taking account of the moral purposes of teachers (Day, 1999, p. 15).

Important in the view behind this alternative approach is the emphasis on the process character of change. More than the technical-rationality approach, the realistic approach draws attention toward the process of professional development and change itself. This has been a neglected area for a long time: "There is almost a complete lack of account of how the changes come about. This is a significant deficit for those interested in teacher education because programs need to be based on an understanding of the mechanism of change rather than milestones" (Desforges, 1995, p. 388; see also Fullan & Hargreaves, 1992, p. 1). Burden (1990, p. 325) says: "There needs to be clarification of the nature of teacher changes and the process by which this change is brought about." Such a clarification is an aim of this book. One of the things that will receive much attention throughout the coming chapters is that we cannot understand teacher change if it is considered merely from a cognitive stance. Teaching is a profession in which feelings and emotions play an essential role (Hargreaves, 1998a; Nias, 1996):

> One of the most neglected dimensions of educational change is the emotional one. Educational and organizational change are often treated as rational, cognitive processes in pursuit of rational, cognitive ends.... The more unpredictable passionate aspects of learning, teaching and leading, however, are usually left out of the change picture. (Hargreaves, 1998b, p. 558)

The problem of educational change, first of all, is a problem of dealing with the natural emotional reactions of human beings to the threat of losing certainty, predictability, or stability. This affective dimension is much neglected in the technical-rationality approach.

1.5. THE DIFFICULT POSITION OF TEACHER EDUCATORS

Although the problems related to the technical-rationality approach as a means to educate teachers have been clarified by numerous research studies, it is remarkable that they have not raised more concerns in teacher educators (Korthagen & T. Russell, 1995). Perhaps an important reason for this is that the research literature shows a lack of attention for what actually goes on in teacher education (Zeichner, 1999). Researchers who do write about this (e.g., Oldfather, Bonds, & Bray, 1994, or Bullough & Gitlin, 1994) emphasize that the technical-rationality model still represents a very dominant line of thought. In Korthagen and Kessels (1999), I report about giving training courses to European teacher educators and I describe how, in doing so, I learned much about these educators' views and daily practices. This article concludes that basically the traditional view of teacher education has not changed and many of the new approaches often take the form of sophisticated procedures to motivate student teachers for the theory, support the transfer process, or bridge the gap between the theory presented and teaching practice. This underlines the power of the three basic assumptions described in section 1.2 and the fact that one often forgets that it is these assumptions that create the gap between theory and practice in the first place.

It may be dangerous to point out the failure of teacher education without emphasizing that being a teacher educator is often difficult. In the first place, teacher educators can hardly build on any pedagogical models that show them alternative ways of educating teachers. Although for many school subjects an explicit subject matter pedagogy exists, this is not the case in the area of teacher education itself. Second, the conditions under which they have to work are generally not very supportive of a change in old habits: Large enrollments and limited time for teacher educators to visit student teachers during their teaching practice are inhibiting factors (Barone et al., 1996, p. 1117). Third, in most places, there is no culture in which it is common for teacher education staff to collaboratively work on the question of how to improve the pedagogy of teacher education.

Kremer-Hayon and Zuzovsky (1995) interviewed Israelean teacher educators about their professional development. An example of one of the excerpts from these interviews illustrates the position of beginning teacher educators:

> I was very excited and flattered when I was offered the job, but at the same time full of anxiety as I had no specific preparation in the field of teacher education. My previous experience as a cooperating teacher was not sufficient. As a teacher educator I was expected to help students place their experiences in theoretical frameworks, make linkages between theory and practice, fill in gaps in pedagogical knowledge, create sequences, and suggest meanings based on sound rationales. How to do this was beyond my knowledge.

In other words, often there is no support for teacher educators in their attempts to integrate theory and practice, or more generally, in their professional learning as a teacher educator. This is an international phenomenon. Wilson (1990) notes that in almost all European Union (EU) countries, one becomes a teacher educator without any formal preparation for this profession, and often with little or no support from more experienced colleagues. Although this finding was part of a research report for the European ministers of education, the situation has not changed since 1990.

The same problem comes to the fore in the description provided by four U.S. teacher educators of their experiences on entering the profession. In the book *Teachers Who Teach Teachers* (T. Russell & Korthagen, 1995), these beginning teacher educators wrote the chapter "Becoming Teachers of Teachers: The Paths of Four Beginners" (Guilfoyle, Hamilton, Pinnegar, & Placier, 1995). Here are some excerpts:

> When I ask myself how I became a teacher educator, I am left puzzling about the first time I thought about doing that or left wondering if I ever really initiated a learning-to-be-a-teacher-educator process. I suppose, though, that I first began the process long before I became conscious of it. In the unconscious moments, I worked hard to train teachers to integrate their curricula with multicultural perspectives or gender concerns. I spent long hours designing materials to be presented to teachers for use in their classrooms. But who taught me how to do that? Really, no one taught me. I learned by watching these people around me, by reminding myself about what happened in my own classrooms with high school students, by trying to remember the stages of development and how these might fit with what I needed to do. I also learned by making errors, major errors in front of the classroom. No class at the university discussed the process of becoming a teacher educator. (Mary Lynn Hamilton, p. 40)

> As I began, I felt silenced. I came to teacher education with good credentials. Yet it quickly became apparent that my expertise would be irrelevant. Though I was an experienced adult who had been a successful teacher both in public school and at the university, I was treated as if I were a blank slate—someone who knew absolutely nothing. My senior colleagues catered to the public school's endorsement of EEI [essential elements of instruction]. While it was difficult for me to articulate clearly my own ideas of helping students learn to be teachers, these did not include teaching and enforcing this model of instruction exclusively. I wondered about Reynolds' (1992) list

> of knowledge needed for beginning teachers. I had studied the work of Schön (1983) and interpretations of how his views of professional knowledge related to development as a teacher. I wondered about "technical rationality" and reflection on practice in teacher development. There was great interest in "the knowledge base for teaching and teacher education," but I struggled to fit this perspective with my beliefs about learning to teach....
>
> When I began teaching future teachers, my image of myself was the image of a beginning tap dancer. First you get the beat, then you add fancier steps, then you add hand motions, then you pick up the cane. But I kept dropping the cane or losing the beat and ending up arms akimbo, tangled in a heap. I never saw myself getting the beat. It is ironic that I would ever think of myself in the image of a dancer because I am completely uncoordinated. I think this initial image represented the denial I felt of my own voice and talents, an incredible self focus, and my struggle to balance it all. (Pinnegar, 1995, pp. 41, 46)

Another interesting example is presented by Zeichner (1995, p. 17), writing about his own first experiences as a teacher educator:

> It became clear to me from my research on the program, and from reading hundreds of student evaluations of the seminars, that our approach of inserting critical content into the seminar syllabus was not having the impact that I wanted. Even though this critical content was part of a negotiated syllabus in which student teachers had a great deal of input into the topics included in the seminar, and although most seminar assignments were always connected to student teachers' work in classrooms and schools (e.g., doing case studies of particular children), many students still saw the seminar activities as something separate from the process of learning to teach, as just another set of academic hoops to jump through for certification.

Zeichner used his dissatisfaction with this situation to rethink the pedagogy of teacher education, thus becoming one of the very first to develop a more integrated teacher education program.

1.6. TOWARD A NEW PARADIGM

Many student teachers, graduates, and teacher educators are dissatisfied with teacher education. Barone et al. (1996) note that parents and politicians too increasingly raise doubts about the functionality of teacher education. This puts heavy pressures on teacher educators. In several countries (e.g., United Kingdom), the dissatisfaction of politicians has led to a development in which a considerable part of teacher education was moved to the schools. In reaction to the criticism on the relevance of theory as a preparation for practice (see, e.g., Sandlin, Young, & Karge, 1992), alternative certification programs have been created in which novice teachers sometimes receive very little theoretical background, and teacher education becomes more of a process of guided induction into the tricks of the trade. In many places, this trend is also influenced by the need to solve the problem of teacher shortages. Although this development may satisfy teachers, politicians, and parents, there is a great risk involved. The balance seems to move completely from an emphasis on theory to reliance on practical experience. Such an approach to teacher education, however, does not guarantee success. In fact, it has been shown that teaching experience can be a socializing factor rather than an opportunity for professional development (cf. Wideen, Mayer-Smith, & Moon, 1993). Often the process of socialization into the school context creates a dislike for reflection and theoretical deepening (Cole, 1997). The basic question, namely how to *integrate* theory and practice, has not been addressed. As G. L. Anderson and Herr (1999, p. 19) state:

> In most cases, the impulse to be more responsive [to the practitioner community] is a sincere one, but there is too often a lack of understanding of what it would mean to develop rigorous programs that placed practitioner knowledge at their center.

However, promising developments are visible. As a reaction to weaknesses of the traditional approach to teacher education and the limitations of approaches based only on practical experience, new ways of preparing teachers for their profession have emerged. For example, at many places in the United States, a trend has become visible to create so-called professional development schools (PDS), also known as professional practice schools or clinical schools (Bullough & Kauchak, 1997; Darling-Hammond, 1994; Levine & Trachtman, 1997; J. A. Ross, 1995). The idea is to develop collaborative partnerships between institute-based teacher educators and school-based teachers, sharing the responsibility for the preparation of prospective teachers. In this context, there is much attention for the role of the school in the local community, a focus on developing new teaching methods, and an emphasis on an ongoing professional development for all involved in such projects (Abdal-Haqq, 1997). Most approaches used in PDS settings are inquiry-oriented and aim at promoting reflective ways of learning. Although PDS projects seem a promising way to integrate theory and practice, case studies also illustrate the many problems associated with this approach (see Darling-Hammond, 1994). Castle (1997, p. 221) concludes that "many of the problems stem from the reality that change of this nature involves individuals and relationships."

In the United Kingdom, during the 1990s, teacher education has to a large extent moved to the schools, although the development was forced by political decisions in 1992 and 1993, which took the teacher education community by surprise (Gilroy, Price, Stones, & Thornton, 1994). Furlong et al. (1996, p. 44) discuss different forms of partnerships between teacher education institutes and schools that have emerged in England and Wales as a result of this development. They conclude that, in the majority of cases, university tutors have less opportunity to influence the character of initial teacher education as compared to the past. However, they also found that collaborative models had been developed in which teacher education faculty work together with teachers in the schools on a regular basis and in this way have increased their influence on the professional development of the student teachers. Referring to publications of those supporting the collaborative approach, Furlong et al. state that for the first time it allows for the real integration of theory and practice.

For a brief period during 1992–1993, the Australian government referred favorably to the developments in the United Kingdom and considered the idea of requiring a larger part of teacher education to take place in the schools (Chadbourne, 1997). Although Australia has until now not implemented the United Kingdom's innovations, an increasing number of partnerships between schools and university faculties of education was established during the 1990s.

Both in the PDS movement and in the more general trends to move teacher education to the schools, there are two significant aspects: On the one hand, these developments mirror a wish to ground teacher education more strongly within practical contexts, but on the other hand, teacher education faculty involved tries to avoid the risk of early socialization to traditional educational patterns. That is why these attempts at heightening the practice-relevance of teacher education are characterized by an emphasis on the need for critical reflection on current practices, and on desired changes. This means that teacher development is increasingly conceptualized as an ongoing process of experiencing practical teaching and other educational learning situations, reflecting on them under the guidance of a more experienced colleague and developing one's own insights into teaching through the interaction between personal reflection and theoretical notions brought in by teacher educators.

The idea to give reflection a central place in teacher education had already surfaced in the 1980s in reaction to the research showing the gap between theory and practice. In many teacher education programs, this idea has been implemented in the period from 1985 to 2000. Some research into strategies for promoting reflection and their effects has been published (e.g., Gore & Zeichner, 1991; Zeichner & Liston, 1987). Steps were made toward the construction of a theoretical basis for reflective approaches, for example, by formulating the cognitive psychological underpinnings, mostly in terms of constructivism (e.g., Bell & Gilbert, 1996; Oldfather et al., 1994), or sociological considerations, generally in terms of goals to strive for (e.g., Zeichner, 1983).

In the present book, reflection will be one of the central concepts and will be considered as an important means to link theory and practice. Yet, the following chapters will also discuss the fact that the foundation underlying the aim of integrating theory and practice is still weak in two respects (Korthagen & Kessels, 1999).

First, the role of theory in this approach to teacher education has not been clearly analyzed. Compared to the traditional theory as found in academic textbooks, theory takes on a completely different form in a program aiming at the integration of theory and practice. The classical form of theories, as found in the official handbooks, is empirically based generalized abstraction from practical situations. Such theories appear to be of little help to teachers, because practice is generally ambiguous and value laden (Schön, 1983), or in other words, much more messy than the ends–means models found in the official theories ("theories with capital T"). Doyle (1990) emphasizes that this is why teachers need a different kind of knowledge, which is "particularistic and situational." We could name this "theory with a small t." It has a completely different form, because it is much more aimed at possibilities for *action*. As a consequence, teacher educators

> must work against the doctrine that teachers are to be taught the results of research carried out by researchers, which I think helps to account for the widespread sense of irrelevance of courses in schools of education. (T. Russell, 1999, p. 234)

This issue will be further discussed in chapter 2.

Second, another theoretical basis for an integrative approach to teacher education is needed concerning the relation between teachers' inner processes and their external behavior. Recent insights into this relation contradict the classical view of the teacher as a rational, theory-guided decisionmaker. However, a new, comprehensive theory on the relation between teachers' inner processes and their behavior has not yet taken the place of the old view of the teacher as a rational decisionmaker. Several notions, which are remnants of an outdated view, still survive within the area of teachers' cognition, such as the concepts of "declarative and procedural knowledge" or terms like "misconceptions" of teachers. The variety of different notions and assumptions underlying new approaches to teacher education has not yet created a sound basis for further development. In this book such a basis will be presented by developing, in chapters 2–9, a view of teaching that incorporates not only the dimension of thinking, but also the emotional and volitional dimensions. In chapter 10, our view of the relation between the inner processes in teachers and their behavior will be summarized with the aid of a comprehensive model.

Thus, one of the goals of this book is to offer two theoretical bases for a new approach to teacher education, one concerning the nature of theory relevant to teachers, and the other concerning the relation between teachers' inner processes and teachers' behavior. Moreover, an attempt is made to connect these two theoretical frameworks. Reflection will be a central notion in both frameworks and will appear to help us create the connection between the frameworks.

The ideas developed in this book are to a large degree derived from theories on mathematics learning and teaching. In fact, mathematics education appears to be a domain where many problems have been first spotted (and also partly solved), which are very similar to the kind of problems teacher education faces. However, the connection between these two domains has seldom been made. Without trying to dive into mathematics education too deeply here, a short overview of relevant developments in this domain may be helpful to the development of a theory of teacher education. This is the focus of the next section.

1.7. MATHEMATICS EDUCATION AS AN EXAMPLE

For two reasons, mathematics education is an interesting field on which to build our thinking about teacher education. First, mathematics causes much trouble for many children and thus also for teachers. This implies that the need is very strong to find productive ways of helping children acquire the necessary knowledge and skills in a manner that helps them to apply what they are learning. This need has promoted the development of a theory about learning and teaching mathematics that is directly relevant to classroom practices. Second, because mathematics as a field of study can relatively easily be isolated from other knowledge domains, psychologists have been rather successful in discovering the mechanisms underlying learning.

One of the most impressive recent developments in education has been the introduction of so-called realistic mathematics education (Freudenthal, 1991; Treffers, 1987). It can be characterized by a complete break with the traditional approach, which goes from theory (principles, rules, theorems) to practice. For many years, children in mathematics classes had to learn to apply mathematical structures, developed during centuries of study in mathematics, to practical problems. Although with sufficient support they often succeeded in working their way through a series of textbook problems, in ordinary life these children were often unable to solve the simplest everyday problems, even when these problems were similar to those in the math class (Schoenfeld, 1987). In other words, a transfer problem was cleary evident in mathematics education.

Hans Freudenthal, the great mathematician and mathematics educationalist, analyzed this transfer problem and pointed out how the traditional didactic approach contradicted the essential nature of mathematics. In his view, mathematics is not "a created subject" to be transferred to children, but "a subject to be created" (Freudenthal, 1978, p. 72). When one pursues his line of thinking, mathematics becomes, or rather has always been, a *human activity* based in the reality of the world around us. (This is why he called the approach "realistic.") Activity leads to consciousness of structures underlying the problems at hand. These structures, constructed by learners, represent their idiosyncratic way of making meaning out of a problem situation. This means that these cognitive structures are closely connected to the way the learner will deal with similar problem situations in the future.

The realistic approach toward mathematics, as summarized in Freudenthal (1991), started in the 1970s in the Netherlands (Freudenthal, 1978). Through the work of the Freudenthal Institute at Utrecht University, it has now spread to many other countries as well (e.g., the United States) where it fits into ideas about changing mathematics education developed in the 1980s. An important starting point in the realistic approach is the assumption that students can and should themselves develop mathematical notions on the basis of practical experiences and problems. The problems are presented within a context recognizable for children, and often taken from everyday situations. Emphasis is put on the *practical use* of mathematics, *inquiry* and *reflection*, *group work*, and *hands-on activities*. Freudenthal (1978, 1991) characterizes the resulting teaching and learning process as one of *guided reinvention* (a term also used by Fischer & Bullock, 1984). To put it in its shortest form, the realistic approach goes from practice to theory. An interesting aspect is that the gap between theory and practice disappears, although it is better to say that it is not created by the educational process itself, as is the case in the traditional approach. In psychological terms, one can say that the intended learning processes start from "situated knowledge" (J. S. Brown, Collins, & Duguid, 1989), developed in the interaction of the learners with the problem situations, and the concrete situations remain the reference points during the learning process. This immensely diminishes the classical "transfer problem" in application situations.

In the next section, I will discuss the question what teacher education can learn from the developments in mathematics education.

1.8. REALISTIC TEACHER EDUCATION

When comparing traditional approaches to teacher education with the aforementioned example of mathematics education, there appear to be striking similarities. In Freudenthal's terms, one could say that in the traditional approach, knowledge about teaching is considered as a created subject and not as a subject to be created by the learner (i.e., the student teacher). An approach that would be more in line with Freudenthal's ideas about learning is pictured in Fig. 1.2.

According to this more constructivist view, the student teacher develops his or her own knowledge in a process of reflection on practical situations, which creates a concern and a personal need for learning. As is the case in realistic mathematics education, the emphasis shifts toward inquiry-oriented activities, interaction among learners, and the development of reflective skills.

In my work with teacher educators and program coordinators, I often hear the concern that this implies that theory will disappear from the teacher education curriculum and student teachers will have to continue to reinvent the wheel, the teacher educator's only task being to ask "what do you yourself think?" This is a caricature based on a complete misunderstanding of the processes involved in a realistic approach. During the learning processes involved, the teacher educator has an important role, also in introducing theory, although this role is completely different from the traditional role of the lecturer. The kind of support that he or she should offer has to be very much adjusted to the specific problems the student teachers are having, which requires specific professional knowledge and skills.

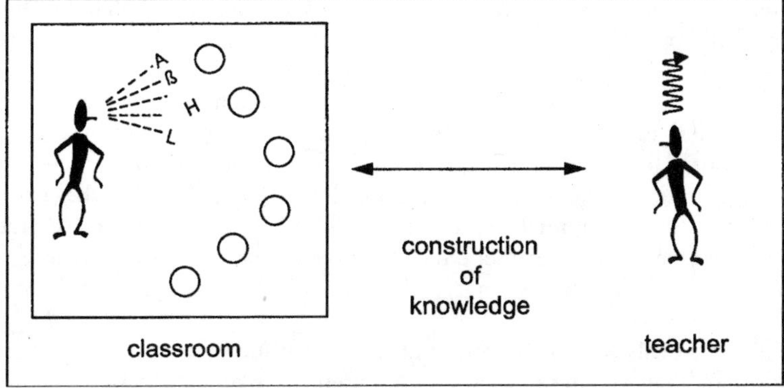

FIG. 1.2. The realistic paradigm in teacher education.

Above all, it is important to emphasize that the realistic approach to teacher education builds on a view of theory rather different from the view of theory embedded in the technical-rationality paradigm visualized in Fig. 1.1. In other words, I am talking about a completely different pedagogy of teacher education. This book offers the framework for this pedagogy of teacher education as well as an overview of the required knowledge and skills of teacher educators.

1.9. OUTLINE OF THE BOOK

I will now sketch the structure of this book. As explained in the preface, practically oriented and research-based chapters will alternate. The odd chapters are primarily written for those teacher educators who are searching for ways to narrow the gap between their work with student teachers and the practice in the schools with which the student teachers are confronted. The even numbered chapters offer the more research-based underpinnings of the odd chapters. To a large degree, they are based on several research studies carried out at the IVLOS Institute of Education. Each chapter ends with a summary and an overview of the basic concepts discussed in that chapter.

Chapter 1 already introduced a fundamental starting point of this book (i.e., that the nature of theory that is relevant for practice is completely different from theory in the traditional sense). This will be analyzed further in the second chapter. Chapter 2, which is more theoretically oriented, analyzes the gap between theory and practice, as well as the possibility to avoid this gap right from the start. My colleague and philosopher Jos Kessels and I go back to the classics, Plato and Aristotle, in order to trace the roots of current practices in teacher education. The Greek notions of *episteme* and *phronesis* appear to be helpful in developing our understanding of the nature of knowledge about teaching and the nature of learning processes of student teachers. They help us to start thinking differently about the goals and practices of teacher education.

This leads us to chapter 3, in which the alternative view of theory as developed in chapter 2 is the basis for the introduction of a new, *realistic* approach to teacher education. This approach makes it possible to diminish or even eliminate the distance between what is happening in the teacher education program and practice in the schools. A concrete example of a realistic teacher education program is described and the underlying principles are discussed and related to each other.

Experiential learning and (the promotion of) reflection on experiences are basic concepts in the realistic approach. A more theoretical analysis of these concepts will be presented in chapter 4. A phase model for reflection is introduced, which has appeared to be helpful to teacher educators and student teachers in many different countries and educational settings. Relations with the concept of action research will be considered.

Chapter 5 deals with the question of how a realistic teacher education program can be built. The principles that were presented in chapter 3 and were theoretically elaborated in chapter 4 will be used to deal with the question of what program arrangements and organizational measures can help to shape a realistic program. Chapter 5 thus offers the ground layer of a concrete pedagogy of realistic teacher education. Some examples of program elements are presented and consequences—for example, for the relations with the schools and with cooperating teachers—are discussed.

Chapter 6 presents an overview of several research studies into a realistic teacher education program and a program based on the aim of promoting reflection in student teachers. This chapter offers answers to questions such as: Does it work? What are results of a pedagogy of realistic teacher education? And what are the problems? And how do we overcome these problems?

Chapter 7 deals with a very important factor in the realistic approach: the supervisory process. How can the individual student teacher be helped to become a reflective professional and to learn how to connect theory and practice? What skills should the teacher educator possess in order to promote reflection in supervisory conferences?

Now, suppose the supervisor is indeed successful: What would one see happen in the student teacher? In other words, how would you recognize a reflective student teacher if you saw one?[1]. Chapter 8 uses the research studies discussed in chapter 6 to extract from these studies conclusions about the characteristics of reflective teachers.

The promotion of reflection cannot and should not only take place in individual supervision sessions. Chapter 9 describes methods and techniques for promoting reflection in group seminars within the teacher education institute. Some of these techniques can be used without much time investment from the part of the teacher educator.

By then, the most important building blocks of a new pedagogy of teacher education are ready. Chapter 10 is a key chapter, as many ideas from the preceding chapters come together here. It discusses the question of why realistic teacher education is more effective than traditional approaches. In previous theoretical chapters, especially chapter 6, it has become clear that it works, but now we want to know why. This requires a careful analysis of the relation between teacher knowledge and teacher behavior in the classroom. A new model for describing this relation is introduced, a model in which levels in learning about teaching are distinguished.

The next chapters deal with some concrete issues, important for the implementation of the realistic approach. Chapter 11 discusses the role of concrete techniques and instruments for promoting reflection, such as the logbook, and relates this instrument to the supervisory process described in chapter 7. It will become clear that the logbook is a very useful instrument for supporting students' learning from practice, especially if some guidelines for structuring logbook entries are used. In the same chapter, less analytical methods for reflection are introduced, such as drawing and painting or guided fantasies. The latter techniques are based on a view of reflection that takes into account the less rational processes guiding teacher behavior. Chapter 12 elaborates this broad view of reflection, thus providing an extension of the theoretical framework about reflection developed throughout the previous chapters of the book.

Chapter 13 deals with the professional development of teacher education staff, especially the question of how teacher educators can be trained to use the ideas of this book. Just like in the case of teachers, for teacher educators, knowledge alone is not enough to change their practice: The realistic approach requires specific skills, which cannot be learned from a book only. It will be no surprise that we also use a realistic approach in the way we organize training courses for teacher educators (the *congruence principle*).

Chapter 14 aims at a final reflection on the paradigm change inherent to the view of teacher education, teacher behavior, and teacher knowledge presented in this book. I will reflect on the core principles of the realistic approach and I will take a look into the future of teacher education and its links with the pedagogical mission of education. In doing so, I will outline the philosophy of education underlying realistic teacher education. I also indicate some directions in research that are necessary for the further development of the pedagogy of realistic teacher education outlined in this book. I not only believe that a fundamental change in teacher education should be supported by concrete studies into program arrangements and their effects, but also that a new type of research is needed. One might call this "realistic research."

SUMMARY

In this chapter, the relation between theory and practice was analyzed. Based on a discussion of the history of teacher education, three basic assumptions underlying traditional teacher education programs were identified:

1. Theories help teachers to perform better in their profession.
2. These Theories (with capital T) must be based on scientific research.
3. Teacher educators should make a choice concerning the Theories to be included in teacher education programs.

These assumptions form the heart of the technical-rationality model. This model has serious flaws, and creates a gap between theory and practice. An analysis of this problem from the broad perspective of "educational change" clarifies that outsiders' attempts to change education and teachers seldom succeed. What is needed for effective teacher education is a shift in our thinking about teacher change and serious attention to the professional development of teacher educators. This shift leads to a more central place for the needs, concerns, and practical experiences of student teachers, the importance of promoting reflection in student teachers, and emphasis on theory with a small t. These are basic features of realistic teacher education.

BASIC CONCEPTS

The technical-rationality model

The gap between theory and practice

Educational change

Reflection

Teachers' needs and concerns
Theory with capital T
theory with a small t
Realistic teacher education

2 The Relation Between Theory and Practice: Back to the Classics

Jos Kessels and Fred Korthagen

And he said:

No man can reveal to you aught but that
which already lies half asleep in the dawning of your knowledge.
The teacher who walks in the shadow of the temple, among his followers,
gives not of his wisdom but rather of his faith and his lovingness.
If he is indeed wise,
he does not bid you enter the house of his wisdom,
but rather leads you to the threshold of your own mind

—*Kahil Gibran: The Prophet*

In chapter 1, a distinction was made between two approaches to teacher education: the technical-rationality approach, which starts from "important Theory with capital T" and tries to equip teachers with this Theory and the related skills, and the realistic approach, which takes its starting point in practical problems met by the student teachers. The function and nature of theory is completely different in these approaches. In this more theoretically oriented chapter, we analyze the difference by building on very ancient sources, especially the work of Plato and Aristotle. We also clarify the consequences of this difference for the practical work of teacher educators.[1]

2.1. INTRODUCTION

During the 20th century, a strong inequality between theory and practice has dominated scholarly thinking. Abstract knowledge was considered to be of a higher standing and of more value than concrete skills or the tacit knowledge of good performance. Much of the educational research concentrated on theory formation—both descriptive (for explanation) and prescriptive (for behavioral instructions). Consequently, educationalists in different subjects and professions were confronted with the problem of bridging the gap between theory and practice, which is a task that never seemed to succeed. During the past few decades, this problem has been analyzed in such fields as education (Schön, Fenstermacher), anthropology (Geertz), epistemology (Rorty, Toulmin, Lyotard), and ethics (Nussbaum). In many ways, these scholars developed alternative models of knowledge. For the justification of such alternative models, several authors, especially in the philosophical domain, referred to the classical controversy between Plato's and Aristotle's conceptions of rationality (*episteme* vs. *phronesis*).

In this chapter, the characteristics of these different types of rationality are discussed, as are the consequences of the shift from an emphasis on *episteme* to more attention for *phronesis*. A revaluation of practical knowledge will be proposed, as well as an alternative view of the relation between theory and practice. In section 2.2, we will describe the distinction between *episteme* and *pronesis*, which is an elaboration of the distinction made in chapter 1 between Theory with capital T and theory with a small t. In sections 2.3 and 2.4, we will elaborate on these two types of knowledge. In section 2.5, we will look more closely at the relation between practice and these two types of knowledge. In section 2.6, we will discuss the consequences for teacher educators.

We start with an example:

> A student teacher in a university teacher education program is asked how he is doing at school. He reports to be doing pretty well: he maintains good discipline, is using several teaching methods, is trying various types of classroom organization, has made a number of tests for the students, has a good rapport with his cooperating teacher. When asked to mention some problematic points, he answers that he is experiencing difficulties in relating to individual students. Managing the class as a group is no problem, but initiating more personal contacts is hard for him. That is also what his mentor teacher has told him. This point is recognized by some fellow students, who have seen him teach before and who confirm his difficulties. The teacher of the course then asks the group what one could possibly do about a problem like this. Fellow students start giving advice: he could try walking through the class, plan his lessons in such a way that he has occasions to start up little conversations with individual students, give more individual assignments, get in touch with students after the lessons, and look into current research literature[2] for directions. The student teacher in question listens politely, but with a blank expression, indicating skepticism and resistance. He does not show any sign of recognition. At last he comments that he has heard all this before, but does not quite know what to do with this information because, "Somehow, in my case, these things just don't seem to work out.

Most teacher educators will recognize the example: A student teacher formulates a problem from practical experiences, which leads the other students or the teacher educator to come up with possible solutions, either from their own experiences or from what they have heard from others or have read about. Sometimes such a sharing of thoughts seems to help: It can generate new suggestions and ideas that are obvious once one starts thinking about them. It can also start a process of reflection about one's own behavior and how this is related to the problem. It can stimulate a student to look for instructional ideas in handbooks or even in research studies. But sometimes—more often than we wish—it does not seem to help. What seems obvious to the teacher educator is not so to the student teacher. What to us seems directly applicable in practice appears to be too abstract, too theoretical, and too far off to someone else. What to us seems evident and easy to understand does not get through to the student. No matter how carefully we consider the problem, we do not find a way into it. Or else we may seem to have found such an entrance and gotten through to the student, but afterward it becomes clear that the student has not even tried to carry out the resolution. Apparently, there is an unbridgable gap between our words and the student's experiences.

2.2. TYPES OF KNOWLEDGE

In this chapter, we will give two interpretations of the problem, leading to two different plans of action. The interpretations arise not only from different perspectives on what the student teacher needs and what it is that we, teacher educators, are meant to offer, but also spring from larger, predominantly tacit conceptions on what knowledge is and what different types of rationality exist. This is essentially a philosophical theme and a long-standing controversy as well. The discussion dates back as far as the beginning of Western philosophy, particularly to Plato and Aristotle. We will start our analysis with a rough sketch of their different conceptions of knowledge in connection with our problem. In doing this, we will, in line with Jonsen and Toulmin (1988) and Nussbaum (1986), confine ourselves to the distinction between knowledge as *episteme* and knowledge as *phronesis*. In fact, both Aristotle and Plato distinguish several other types of knowledge, for instance, craft-knowledge (*techne*), philosophic wisdom, and intuitive reason. These we will leave out of the discussion. We will concentrate on the *episteme–phronesis* distinction for clarity's sake and because, despite all the attention it has been given in the past, many people (both researchers and practitioners) find the disctinction unclear, a condition that perpetuates ineffective approaches to teacher education.

One might ask the point of considering such antique viewpoints. Are we not currently far ahead of them? If, for example, we look at Fenstermacher (1994) or Ginsburg and Clift (1990), don't we then discover that we made a lot of progress? Nowadays we can find many classifications in the literature that clarify different conceptions of knowledge: for example, public versus personal knowledge, molecular versus holistic knowledge, knowledge as given versus knowledge as problematic, knowledge by acquaintance versus knowledge by description, declarative versus procedural knowledge, knowing how versus knowing that. Haven't we made too much progress in 2,500 years to return to the very beginning of the debate? As a matter of fact, it appears not. Centuries ago, the same type of problems now confronting teacher educators were thoroughly studied by philosophers, resulting in a fruitful theoretical framework of which most modern researchers are not aware. Recently, however, some scholars have started to dig up these roots (cf.

Fenstermacher, 1994, in education; Toulmin, 1990, in theory of knowledge; Nussbaum, 1986, and Jonsen & Toulmin, 1988, in ethics). Let us see what this enterprise has to offer to our problem.

2.3. KNOWLEDGE AS EPISTEME

One interpretation of the problem runs roughly as follows. What we need to solve the problem and help the student overcome the indicated difficulty is some form of expert knowledge on the particular problem: knowledge of social skills, of ways of relating, of models of communication. This knowledge ideally is connected to a scientific understanding of the problem and shows the following characteristics. It is propositional: That is, it consists of a set of assertions that can be explained, investigated, transmitted, and the like. These assertions are of a general nature; they apply to many different situations and problems, not only to this particular one. Consequently, they are formulated in abstract terms. Of course, these propositions are claimed to be true; preferably, their truth is provable, or at least the truth is indicated because they are considered a part of a theory with which they are consistent. Because they are true, they are also fixed, timeless, and objective. And through their link with theory, they are part of the more extended domain of social science. Besides, they are fully cognitive in nature; they are purely intellectual insights, unaffected by emotions or desires. It is this knowledge that is of major importance, the specific situation and context being only an instance for the application of the knowledge. It will not be difficult to recognize these characteristics as aspects of Plato's purely intellectual forms or ideas and his mathematical knowledge-ideal, which he called *episteme*.[3]

In this interpretation, the teacher educators must, to solve the problem of the student, have this knowledge at their disposal and be able to use it in such a way that the student is really helped by it. Both requirements are, in practice, very difficult to fulfill. The knowledge is supposed to be provided by the research literature on teacher education and social science. But what knowledge is relevant in this case? That is the first problem for a teacher educator. Is it a theoretical model of interpersonal behavior, such as the model described in Wubbels and Levy (1993)? Is it Watzlawick, Beavin, and Jackson's (1967) systems theory? Is it some motivation theory from the domain of social psychology, for example, Maslow (1968)? Suppose the teacher educator takes as the relevant knowledge some elements of Watzlawick's theory, such as the distinction between the content of a message and its relational aspects and the possible contradiction between the verbal and nonverbal aspects of a message. These are general, abstract, and widely accepted distinctions with such a strong theoretical basis that they may be considered fixed truths.

Then there is a second problem for the teacher educator: How are these truths transformed into some learning process for the student that is relevant to the problem described? Should the teacher educator plainly introduce the distinctions and ask student teachers to apply them to their own behavior? Or should one try to approach the distinction inductively by asking questions about the precise behaviors of the student? Suppose the teacher's own diagnosis of the problem is in accordance with Watzlawick's systems perspective: The student's permanent need for control and the fear of disorder are part of the very cause of the situations against which the student wants to be armed; of course, dealing with these situations strengthen the student's conviction that control is indispensable and so on, resulting in the well-known vicious circle. Of course, there may be other ways of approaching and handling the problem. But whatever way the teacher educator chooses, the underlying conception of knowledge may stay the same; namely, there is a fixed solution to be found by subsuming the example under a scientific theory of effective teacher behavior. The problem is getting the student to see this.

Here we have a gap between theory and practice that hampers both the teacher educator and the student teacher. The task of the teacher educator is to try to bridge it, and, like our student teacher, the teacher educator often fails. However, in this line of thinking, this is not so much considered to be a failure of the "theory" (of the available knowledge itself), but a failure of practice (the way of handling the knowledge) or the present incompleteness of the available knowledge in the social sciences. In other words, the parallel to learning mathematics, which is so dominant in Plato's conception of knowledge, is never really abandoned: Nothing is wrong with the knowledge itself. How could it be if this knowledge is provably and objectively true, as in mathematics? The problem is in the users of the knowledge. If the teacher educator in this case could possibly have been a more ideal teacher educator, better capable of handling Watzlawick's theory, then he or she could have brought the student teacher to see the truth that he does not yet see at present.

2.4. KNOWLEDGE AS PHRONESIS

The second interpretation of our example starts from the premise that the previous account is not correct for several reasons, the central one being that there is something fundamentally wrong with such a conception of knowledge. It argues that what we need here is not scientific understanding (*episteme*), but practical wisdom (*phronesis*). This is an essentially different type of knowledge that is not concerned with scientific theories, but with the understanding of specific concrete cases and complex or ambiguous situations. The two types of knowledge differ in a few crucial aspects:[4]

First, *scientific knowledge is universal*. Whatever we know in a scientific way holds good generally. But the things that are the concern of practical prudence are variable by nature. For instance, although Watzlawick's theory may hold generally, the action that would be the right one for our student in the example to perform still "admits of much variety and fluctuation of opinion," like all fine and just actions, as Aristotle (*Nic. Eth.*, Book VI, 1141a) said. This does not mean that prudence, or practical wisdom, would not involve any general rules. It certainly does. But it must take into account particular facts as well, because it is concerned with practical activities, which always deal with particular things (Aristotle, *Nic. Eth.*, Book VI,

1141a). So having general, theoretical knowledge at one's disposal is not enough. That is precisely the problem that both the student and the teacher educator experience. They need something else to overcome it.

This something else is a knowledge of a different kind, not abstract and theoretical, but its very opposite: knowledge of concrete particulars. This implies a second difference between scientific and practical knowledge that concerns their *locus of certitude*. In the case of scientific knowledge, that certitude lies in a grasp of theoretical notions or principles. In practical prudence, certitude arises from knowledge of particulars. All practical knowledge is context-related, allowing the contingent features of the case at hand to be, ultimately, authoritative over principle (Nussbaum, 1986, p. 300). This is, according to Aristotle, why people who lack a grasp of general ideas are sometimes more effective in practice. He adds that *phronesis* requires understanding of both kinds: knowledge of particular facts and a grasp of generalities. But, contrary to the *episteme* conception of knowledge, the first is more important than the second (Jonsen & Toulmin, 1988, p. 66; Aristotle, *Nic. Eth.*, Book VI, 1141a–b). So to find a solution to the problem of our example, we may need to look for help in the concrete details of the case rather than in some theoretical domain.

Third, the two kinds of knowledge differ in their ultimate court of appeal, or *the way their certitude is finally justified*. In science, knowledge is essentially conceptual: All argumentation is governed by the basic principles, rules, or theorems to which they can be traced by way of explanation and from which they can be derived by formal deduction. In the realm of practical knowledge, the situation is quite different. Phronesis deals with the ultimate particular (*to eschaton*), and this is an object of perception (*aisthesis*) rather than episteme (Jonsen & Toulmin, 1988, p. 66; Aristotle, *Nic. Eth.*, Book VI, 1142a). In other words, such knowledge is essentially perceptual instead of conceptual. This is a crucial difference.

Let us take our example as an illustration. To choose and justify a particular course of action (either for the student teacher in his classes or for the teacher educator in the supervision of the student teacher), the ultimate appeal of *phronesis* is not to principles, rules, theorems, or any conceptual knowledge. Ultimately, the appeal is to perception. For to be able to choose a form of behavior appropriate for the situation, above all one must be able to perceive and discriminate the relevant details. These cannot be transmitted in some general, abstract form. They "must be seized in a confrontation with the situation itself, by a faculty that is suited to confront it as a complex whole" (Nussbaum, 1986, p. 301). This faculty of judgment and discrimination is concerned with the perception or apprehension of concrete particulars, rather than of principles or universals. The latter "fail to capture the fine detail of the concrete particular, which is the subject matter of choice," wrote Nussbaum (1986, pp. 300–301). Universal principles lack not only concreteness, but also flexibility, subtlety, and congruence to the situation at hand.

Aristotle uses a vivid metaphor to illustrate this point. He tells us that a person who attempts to make every decision by appealing to some antecedent general principle, kept firm and inflexible for the situation, is like an architect who tries to use a straight ruler on the intricate curves of a fluted column. Instead, the good architect will, like the builders of Lesbos, measure with a flexible strip of metal that "bends round to fit the shape of the stone and is not fixed" (Aristotle, *Nic. Eth.*, Book VI, 1137b; cf. Nussbaum, 1986, p. 301. Here and in the next paragraphs, we follow Nussbaum.) Good deliberation, like this ruler, accommodates itself to what it finds, responsively and with respect for complexity. It does not assume that the form of the rule governs the appearances; it allows the appearances to govern themselves and to be normative for the correctness of the rule.

2.5. THE MATTER OF THE PRACTICAL

One might object here that these arguments do not say anything against the value of science and episteme, against rules, principles, and theorems as forms of conceptual knowledge. For if they can be made precise and complicated enough, they will be adequate to capture in a fine-tuned way the complexities of concrete, experienced situations. But this objection misses the full force of Aristotle's criticism of universal, conceptual knowledge. In his view, practical choices cannot be completely captured in a system of universal rules. "The matter of the practical," by being variable, particular, and perceptual in nature, is essentially indeterminate or indefinite: "Let this be agreed from the start, that every statement (*logos*) concerning matters of practice ought to be said in outline and not with precision, as we said at the beginning that statements should be demanded in a way appropriate to the matter at hand" (Aristotle, *Nic. Eth.*, Book VI, 1103b–1104a). And the matter at hand, the matter of the practical, is imprecise by nature. It calls "for responsiveness and yielding flexibility, a rightness of tone and a sureness of touch that could not be adequately captured in any general description," according to Nussbaum (1986, p. 304).

We can see this need for responsiveness and flexibility clearly demonstrated in another domain, the practice of law. "All law is universal," says Aristotle, "but about some things it is not possible to make a universal statement which shall be correct" (*Nic. Eth.*, Book VI, 1137b). Therefore, the demands of justice go beyond the rules of law. Justice can be done in practice only if *nomos* (rule-governed laws) is supplemented by *epieikeia* or equity, that is, a reasonable and practical application of general legal rules (Jonsen & Toulmin, 1988, p. 68). This does not make the general statement a wrong law:

> The error is not in the law, nor in the legislator, but in the nature of the case, since the matter of the practical is essentially variable. When the law lays down a general rule, and a later case arises that is an exception to the rule, it is then appropriate, where the lawgiver's pronouncement was too unqualified and general, to decide as the legislator himself would decide if he had been present on this occasion.... The essential nature of equity is thus to correct the law in situations where it is defective on account of its generality. (Aristotle, *Nic. Eth.*, Book VI, 1137b).

If we apply this comparison to our case, we may say that it can surely be helpful to know of general rules like those of Watzlawick. But it is much more important to know enough of the concrete details of the situation. First, it has to be decided whether Watzlawick's rules are relevant at all, or if perhaps some other rules are more suited to the situation. If they are relevant, then the question is still how exactly they should be handled in a reasonable and practical way that is appropriate to the situation. Besides, it may be difficult to decide what rules are relevant here or even whether there are any general rules available at all. In all these cases, however, perceptual knowledge is the basis for a proper judgment of the situation and for an appropriate choice of behavior. Mind you, the perception that Aristotle speaks of is not just the normal sensory perception. It is the "eye" that one develops for paradigmatic or type cases. In unambiguous, paradigmatic cases, we can perceive an action as effective teacher behavior as directly as we can recognize that a figure is triangular or square: We know it when we see it. Given such perception, no further proof or theoretical justification is needed. A similar position is described by Eisner (1979, 1985a, 1985b) in terms of the development of "educational connoisseurship."

Thus, *phronesis*, practical wisdom, or perceptual knowledge, uses rules only as summaries and guides. "It must itself be flexible, ready for surprise, prepared to see, resourceful at improvisation" (Nussbaum, 1986, p. 305). An important prerequisite of this type of knowledge is that someone has enough proper experience. For particulars only become familiar with experience, with a long process of perceiving, assessing situations, judging, choosing courses of action, and being confronted with their consequences. This generates a sort of insight that is altogether different from scientific knowledge. Of course, experience is precisely what the student in our example lacks. So he cannot possibly have the corresponding sort of insight. But the point is here that such insight cannot possibly be transferred to him (or induced, provoked, or elicited) through the use of purely conceptual knowledge. There are many reasons for this, but the one that concerns us here is that conceptual knowledge is not the type of knowledge that we need most in our case. It is too abstract, too much stripped of all kinds of particulars that are predominant in concrete experience: emotions, images, needs, values, volitions, personal hang-ups, temper, character traits, and the like. The appropriate criterion for correct choice in an example like ours is not its correspondence or consistency with an abstract rule or principle (e.g., break the vicious circle that causes the problem), but instead what a concrete human being would do—the person of practical wisdom. It is the standpoint of this person that is the criterion for correct choice, not the abstract rule. Such knowledge, the standpoint of a thoroughly human being, is "not just heuristic towards a value that would be valuable without this person and his choices; it is definitive of value, and this value would not be value but for its relation to this human person" (Nussbaum, 1986, pp. 290, 311).

In fact, the difference between *episteme* and *phronesis*, between theory and practice, may be summarized in one image or one maxim: The person of practical wisdom inhabits the human world and does not attempt to rise above it (Nussbaum, 1986, p. 314). This image, as Nussbaum indicates, is beautifully depicted in Raphael's famous fresco called *The School of Athens*. At its center we see the two main contestants: Plato pointing his finger upward and Aristotle pointing to the earth.

2.6. CONSEQUENCES

Now let us return to our example and see what these considerations imply for it. First, we may conclude that the gap between theory and practice is not a problem inherent to the teaching situation. It is only inherent to our conception of knowledge as episteme. In a conception of knowledge as *phronesis*, the question of how to bridge such a gap, to connect the complexities of concrete, experienced situations to some given, abstract rules does not exist. There the central question is a different one: Namely, what is there to be perceived? What does the student perceive, what features of his experience is he aware of, and which particulars of the situation does he judge relevant? In the *phronesis*-conception of knowledge, there is no set of given, abstract rules to apply to this particular problem because the problem is (as yet) far too particular for that. There are too many details, too many idiosyncracies, and too many exceptional aspects for a general rule. So, in our example, instead of asking what could be done immediately after the student indicated his problem—which elicits the appeal to abstract rules and the offering of superficial advice—the teacher educator would rather have probed further into what the student is actually aware of, what details he sees in the problem-situation, what his own reactions were, how he felt, what he thought, and the like. This would also promote the student teacher's *phronesis*, through his observance of the intricacies of his experience.

Of course, this is not always possible, especially not in a large group in which there is little time for individual students, a risk of too much unsafety, and such. So the answers to these questions may have to be sought in private reflection, supervision, or small-group discussion. But, for the teacher eductor, in this large group situation the *phronesis* approach makes a world of difference. In this approach, it is just not one's task to bridge a gap between theory and practice as it is in the *episteme* approach. One's task is to help the student become aware of salient features of the experience. One is there to help the student see, not to teach the student a number of concepts. One is there to help the student refine his or her perception, not to provide the student with a set of general rules.[5] One is there to help students make their own *tacit knowledge* explicit (cf. Loska, 1995; Nelson, 1973, original version 1911 and 1929; Polanyi, 1967, 1978; Schön, 1987), to help the student capture the singularities of the experience, and to find the rightness of tone and the sureness of touch that only holds good for the particular situation. One is not there to lecture about educational theory, to instruct general rules, or to extensively discuss instructional principles. For "the matter of the practical" is just not helped very much by such conceptual knowledge. What it needs is the development of perceptual knowledge.

Now, this does not mean that Watzlawick's theory and rules are of no use and should be put outside with the garbage. They do have a use—although a restricted one—as a summary, a guide, or a heuristic in exploring the student's perception. But compared to the modeling instrument of *phronesis* (reflection on what a concrete person of practical wisdom would do in the problem situation), such abstract rules are a rather poor device indeed. They lack flesh and blood in a very literal sense; they do not have a face, or a repertoire of actions. They have no temperament, no personal characteristics, no history, no vices, and no virtues. They cannot be seen in action, or talked to, criticized, or admired. In short, they do not have any perceptual reality; they are just concepts, abstractions. Therefore, they cannot be identified with. That is why they produce the blank expression, skepticism, and resistance in our student. They do not have any emotional or motivational quality. And this is understandable, for, as we saw earlier, in an epistemic conception of knowledge, the will and the emotions are considered to be mere disturbances of knowledge instead of central elements of it. (As a matter of fact, the importance of this point for learning processes is not only acknowledged but also stressed by Plato. Compare *Phaedrus* 275, Letters VII, 341–344. However, in his view, this type of knowledge is only a prerequisite to a higher type that is purely intellectual. Compare Irwin, 1995, chap. 16, and Plato's *Republic*, Book VI, 507–511, and Book VII, 514–535.)

Another important consequence of the turn to *phronesis* is the following. To be able to develop this wider, perception-based type of knowledge in teacher education programs, what we need is not so much theories, articles, books, and other conceptual matters, but first and foremost, concrete situations to be perceived, experiences to be had, persons to be met, plans to be exerted, and their consequences to be reflected on. They are the sine qua non of *phronesis*. Without such perceptions, no knowledge is formed at all, no matter how beautiful the essays are that a student teacher may write (or, for that matter, researchers like us). This may perhaps seem obvious. Most teacher education programs are filled with practice periods to provide the student teachers with personal experiences and confront them with the professional "real life." But this is not what we mean by a turn to *phronesis*. Someone may acknowledge the importance of practicing periods in teacher education programs and still completely miss the point of *phronesis*. In fact, many teacher educators who stress the value of practical experience nevertheless work on the basis of an epistemic conception of knowledge; they struggle with the gap between theory and practice, they worry and puzzle about transfer problems, and they brood on how best to connect to the students' existing knowledge. This shows that they actually work from an *episteme* conception, from the tacit presupposition of the technical-rationality model that the knowledge students need is conceptual, external to them, and objective, and it somehow needs to be transmitted and it is their job to transmit it. The point of *phronesis* is that the knowledge a student needs is perceptual instead of conceptual. Therefore, it is necessarily internal to the student, that is, it is in the student's experience instead of outside it in some external, conceptual form. It is thoroughly subjective. There may be some objective aspects to it, such as Watzlawick's rules in the example, but as we have seen they are not the most efficient ones to help the student teacher. And so there is nothing or little to transmit, only a great deal to explore. And the task of the teacher educator is to help student teachers explore and refine their perceptions. This asks for well-organized arrangements in which student teachers get the opportunity to reflect systematically on the details of their practical experiences, under the guidance of the teacher educator—both in individual supervision and in group seminars. This idea will be elaborated in the next chapters.

2.7 FINAL REMARKS

One of the main problems is that most teacher educators have themselves been steeped in the *episteme* conception of knowledge. So they have always taken for granted the traditional, epistemic perspective on the relation between theory and practice. This makes it very hard to understand the full impact of the shift toward *phronesis*. For instance, one is probably inclined to ask what the role of the expert knowledge of the teacher educator is in the *phronesis* perspective. Should the teacher educator make use of his or her knowledge? The answer is simple: of course. But the question is how, and that again depends on our conception of knowledge. Let us suppose that the teacher educator is a man or woman of some practical wisdom and not only a theoretician. In other words, assume that the knowledge that makes the teacher educator an expert is itself mainly perceptual, internal, and subjective. Now, the teacher educator may besides have command of a lot of conceptual, external, and more or less objective knowledge, such as Watzlawick's rules. This knowledge can certainly be used as an instrument for exploration of the student teacher's perceptions; it can generate questions, points of view, arguments, and such. The pitfall, however, is to consider it as more than an instrument for exploration—as the thing itself that we are after, the real thing. The real thing is not conceptual knowledge, *episteme*, or Theory with capital T. It is perceptual knowledge, *phronesis*, or theory with a small t. The goal of realistic teacher education is not to make student teachers into collectors of knowledge on teaching. We want them to become good teachers. This also means that there is a second pitfall. It is the idea that the expert's knowledge can be severed from him or her, abstracted from the person, put on a blackboard in front of students, or written in a paper in a purely conceptual form, creating the impression that an insight is the same thing as the sentences to be read. We can assure you that it is not the same. In order to develop good teachers, we need another pedagogy that starts from a different view of what is important for our student teachers if we want them to become people of practical wisdom. In the following chapters such a pedagogy will be elaborated.

SUMMARY

Buiding on the work of Plato and Aristotle, we distinguished between two types of knowledge, *episteme* and *phronesis*. This provided us with an elaboration of the distinction, made in chapter 1, between Theory with capital T and theory with a small t. *Episteme* can be characterized as abstract, objective, and propositional knowledge, the result of a generalization over many situations. *Phronesis* is perceptual knowledge, the practical wisdom based on the perception of a situation. It is the eye that one develops for a typical case, based on the perception of particulars. Its value is related to the particular person using this knowledge for action.

For teacher education, the development of *phronesis*, perceptual knowledge, is most important. As a consequence, the professional learning of teachers starts from concrete experiences and their subjective perceptions of practical situations. Teacher education should aim at making tacit knowledge explicit, and not at the transmission of conceptual knowledge.

BASIC CONCEPTS

Types of knowledge

Episteme (conceptual knowledge)

Phronesis (perceptual knowledge, practical wisdom)

Tacit knowledge

3 Learning From Practice

Fred Korthagen and Theo Wubbels

> Tell me and I will forget
> Show me and I will remember
> Involve me and I will understand
> Step back and I will act
>
> —*Chinese proverb, cited in the description of an educational experiment at Aalborg University, Denmark (Kjersdam & Enemark, 1994)*
>
> *This chapter describes the Utrecht teacher education program, which is based on the realistic approach. We explore the principles underlying this realistic program, for example, the idea of building on the nonrational ways in which people process information. We then describe learning to teach as a process of experiential learning and we explain how the realistic approach to teacher education takes the nonrational aspects of teaching and professional development seriously. We also start the discussion of the role of reflection in a teacher education program that takes student teachers' experiences and their concerns as starting points for learning.*

3.1. INTRODUCTION

In the previous chapters we saw that the technical-rationality model has serious weaknesses and creates a gap between theory and practice. An alternative approach to teacher education starts from practical experiences and student teachers' perceptions of these experiences.

However, we know from the literature that the quality of student teachers' learning in practical situations—during student teaching practice and during the first years of teaching—can be questioned. As we saw in chapter 1, many studies have shown that student teachers do not use much of the theory taught in preservice teacher education. Moreover, beginning teachers often complain about the fact that, once in the school, they meet many problematic situations for which they were not sufficiently prepared. Many student teachers perceive the transition from the teacher education institute to student teaching or to teaching as a novice teacher as an emotional and disturbing period. They are confronted with a reality, responsibilities, and complexities in the classroom that they have not been aware of until then. This is often a period of severe stress and difficult problems (Veenman, 1984), described as a *reality shock* (Müller-Fohrbrodt et al., 1978) or *transition shock*

(Corcoran, 1981). Once student teachers have left their teacher education program, more progressive attitudes, acquired during teacher education, are quickly washed out by school experiences (Müller-Fohrbrodt et al., 1978; Zeichner & Tabachnick, 1981).

For example, a reflective attitude, developed during teacher education, often "disappears" during the induction period. This is illustrated by the following quotes:

> I had the experience that the capacity for reflection is pushed away when you meet a cumulation of conflicts. You feel empty. I no longer had any point of reference. And this happened although everything went very well during teacher preparation and during field experiences. (a beginning teacher in the Netherlands, cited by Korthagen, 1985, p. 14)

> I used to think I'd be this great reflective teacher. I had visions of spending time at the end of each day replaying my classes to see what worked and what didn't, etcetera but, quite honestly, by the end of the day I am so frazzled from just trying to keep up I can hardly even remember what took place only hours ago! And most of the time I am so worried about tomorrow I don't even want to think about yesterday or today.... I've taken to doing things for myself in the evenings now in order to get my mind *off* [teaching]. (a beginning teacher in Canada, cited by Cole, 1997, p. 9)

In the 1970s, the teacher education staff at Utrecht University became more aware of the problems faced by beginning teachers and the "reality shock" that followed preservice teacher education. This stimulated the wish to make teacher education more "realistic," in the sense of reducing the reality shock and confronting student teachers with the problems of first-year teaching during the teacher education program itself. At this point, the teacher educators could still offer help and could influence the learning processes of the student teachers. This is where the search for more integration of theory and practice within our program began.

The first step was to introduce more practical experiences and to make this practice more realistic. Until the 1970s, practical experiences were often not much more than observing some lessons of a teacher and perhaps take over a few lessons. Gradually, more responsibility was given to student teachers. For example, they had to teach a series of lessons and requirements were formulated concerning the total time student teachers themselves should teach. These requirements were, after some time, determined at a national level, thus giving university-based teacher education in the Netherlands a stronger basis.

After some years, the so-called Independent Final Teaching Practice (IFTP; see also Koetsier & Wubbels, 1995) was introduced into the final part of the program. In this IFTP, the student teacher gets full responsibility for a reduced number of classes and teaches without the cooperating teacher being present.

During the late 1980s and 1990s, the development finally resulted in a program in which theory and practice both have an equal and an interrelated place. We will describe this program in the next section (3.2). In section 3.3, we will discuss more of the background ideas. In particular, we will discuss the idea of taking student teachers' preconceptions into account (section 3.4) and the notion of building on less rational ways of information processing (section 3.5). This leads to an elaboration of two basic concepts: *experiential learning* (section 3.6) and *reflection* (section 3.7). The next two sections focus on promoting reflection (section 3.8) and the reasons for giving this principle a central place in our program (section 3.9). In section 3.10, we will conclude the chapter and look ahead. In that section we also present a brief outline of how these ideas will be further elaborated in the chapters that follow.

3.2. AN EXAMPLE OF A REALISTIC TEACHER EDUCATION PROGRAM[1]

In this section, we describe the teacher education program at Utrecht University.[2] This is meant to give the reader a concrete example of a realistic program as the basis for a discussion of its underlying principles.

Before entering this 1-year program, the student teachers have to do a 2-month undergraduate course, the so-called orientation program. This program helps them and their educators to discover whether it would be wise to choose a career in teaching. The studyload of the 1-year program involves 1,680 hours and includes at least 840 hours of school-connected activities and about 840 hours of on-campus activities. The school hours have to include 250 classroom hours, of which a minimum of 120 have to be taught by the student teacher. Of the 1,680 hours, they spend 300 hours on inquiry-oriented activities, divided over campus and school-connected hours. The practical component of the program includes two phases, the triad teaching practice period and the Independent Final Teaching Practice (Fig. 3.1).

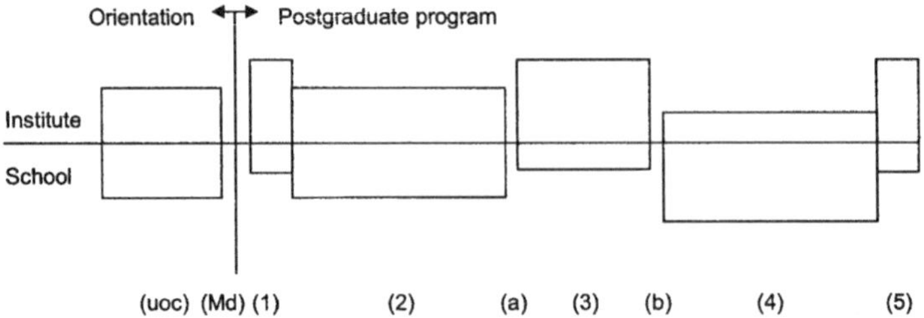

FIG. 3.1. Diagram of the teacher education program of IVLOS Institute of Education, Utrecht University. Above the horizontal line are activities on campus, below activities in school. The program starts twice a year, in August and January. The diagram concerns the course starting in January. Uoc: undergraduate orientation course, 8 weeks. Md: Master's degree. 1: Introduction, 2 weeks. 2: Triad teaching practice period, 14 weeks. 3: Reorientation period, 10 weeks. 4: Independent Final Teaching Practice, 14 weeks. 5: Concluding phase of the program, 3 weeks. a: Time off, 1 week. b: Vacation, 6 weeks.

The program is structured primarily as an alternation in blocks of one or more weeks at campus and in schools. However, during the school periods, there are also some activities at the university to optimize the integration between theory and practice.

Undergraduate Orientation Course

Some of the elements included in the introductory period program are training in observation and discussion skills and other social and communicative skills, which are important for successful progress in the postgraduate curriculum; practice in reduced teaching situations like brief lessons given to each other and role playing; reflection on the important pedagogical and subject-related principles that surface through these experiences; and visiting schools and orientation on the practice of teaching (3 days). Moreover, a teaching practice period of 4 weeks is a part of the orientation course.

1. Introduction—2 weeks. This preparatory phase is fairly short, because the students have already participated in the 2-month orientation course during their undergraduate studies.

University activities in the introduction period are meant to prepare for student teaching and include structures in which the students give small (5 to 10 minutes) lessons to each other, in small groups prepare presentations about content matter in school books, supervise group discussions, and so on. These structures lead to assignments to reflect on these experiences and to the formulation of pedagogical principles. These basic theoretical notions prestructure the student experiences in the schools. Discussion of the experiences with reflection during the introductory weeks and formulation of a phase model for reflection (to be discussed in section 3.7) prepare the students for structured reflection on their school experiences.

2. Triad Teaching Practice Period—14 weeks. The triad student teaching period is a relatively shielded teaching period during which three students work together as a group under the close supervision of a cooperating teacher and a university supervisor. The triad teaching practice includes two school periods. In the first of these (2½ weeks), student teachers teach (parts of) lessons and carry out assignments based on campus work. They gradually work up their way to a series of lessons. In the next school period (5 weeks), student teachers teach individual lessons and series of lessons and they may teach all the weekly lessons of one particular class for a few weeks.

The activities on campus between the school periods are intended for exchange and analysis of field experiences. Topics that are usually discussed include aspects of teaching methods, learning psychology, developmental psychology, foundations of education, motivation, and counseling. Also, reflection is started about the teacher's role in the department and school organization, the professional role of a teacher, and legal matters.

Supervision conferences in the triad teaching practice usually follow the specific reflection model mentioned before (see section 3.7 for a description). The supervisory discourse starts from the student teachers' experiences and their perceptions of these experiences, rather than from theories on learning and teaching from the literature. In this practice period, the university supervisor visits every triad a few times to observe lessons and to participate in supervision conferences. A frequent and intensive communication between university staff and cooperating teacher is of utmost importance for good guidance of the student teachers. Therefore, meetings are organized at the university between cooperating teachers and the university staff to discuss in collegial support groups the progress and problems of their student teachers, the best ways to supervise them, and the content of the campus activities. Moreover, most cooperating teachers follow a training organized by the IVLOS Institute of Education to help them develop the skills necessary for facilitating reflection during supervisory conferences.

At the end of this period, the student teacher is evaluated to determine his or her suitability for admission to the Independent Final Teaching Practice.

3. Reorientation—10 weeks. The triad student teaching period is followed by a reorientation period intended for reflection and the deepening of insights. Reflection on the first school experiences is central to this phase. What route of professional development has been followed until now? What does this mean for the rest of the program? For example, in this phase, the student teacher can try to gain an insight into the current state of affairs in his or her learning process by writing a paper about his or her experiences so far. The supervisor offers special tutorials and personal coaching to stimulate the student teachers to deepen their insights.

As a follow-up to the practice experience, the prospective teachers study specific issues of their concern, again supervised by the institute supervisor. They study theory behind these issues, and do research-related activities and workshops. One standard part of the program is to design and carry out one major practice-oriented research project. This project is concluded by a report and a presentation to fellow student teachers and supervisors. Some students go abroad for this project, for example, to compare Dutch education to education in other countries.

Another issue that receives considerable attention during this period is school organization, including its relations to the process of teaching a class, to educational policy, regulations, and developments on a national and international level. Again, based on the student teachers' experiences in their practicum schools, issues that are important to developing an "extended" form of professionalism (Hoyle, 1980) are discussed. This means that the student teachers are stimulated to look at their profession from a broader perspective than merely from concerns related to classroom teaching. Over the last couple of years, student teachers have studied specific issues related to school organization or educational policies in small groups and have presented their findings to their peers.[3]

4. Independent Final Teaching Practice—14 weeks. The IFTP is a continuous 3-month student teaching period, which takes place in the final part of the 1-year program at another school than the triad practicum. The student teacher functions as a regular teacher, under normal constraints and pressures, teaching all lessons of a particular subject in a number of classes. The number of classes is chosen so that from 10 to 12 hours a week are taught, which amounts to a 40% weekly teaching load. The ultimate responsibility still lies with the cooperating teacher. In addition to preparing and giving lessons, the student teacher also takes part in departmental activities and other activities within the school. In this period, the student teachers should gradually acquire a complete "starting competence" for the teaching profession, but from the outset, they have to adopt full responsibility for the classes they teach.

In the IFTP, the student teacher is supervised by means of "supervision-at-a-distance" (sometimes called "long-arm" supervision), which means that the cooperating teacher and university supervisor do not actually attend the student teacher's lessons. The cooperating teacher is responsible for supervising the quality of the work (the so-called work supervision, concretized in progress sessions), whereas the university supervisor monitors the process of professional development (the so-called learning supervision; see for more details Koetsier, Wubbels, & Van Driel, 1992). The university supervisory conferences, usually in small groups, focus on the development of student teachers' own teaching styles and their individual personal views on teaching. They also focus on the development of a reflective professional attitude. Moreover, student teachers meet on a weekly basis with their cohort group, usually at the end of an afternoon or during an evening, to share experiences, problems, ideas, and resources.

5. Concluding Phase of the Program—3 weeks. The final period is concerned with drawing up and discussing reports on and a final assessment of the program results. The conclusion includes a final report to be written by the student teacher (nowadays in the form of a portfolio), evaluations, final discussions, and an assessment of the student teachers' competence by the cooperating teacher of the IFTP and the university teacher educator.

3.3. THE PEDAGOGY USED IN THE PROCESS OF LEARNING ABOUT TEACHING

The program description in section 3.2 gives some first indications about the pedagogy used by the teacher educators at IVLOS. Practice and theory, or better practical experiences and activities at the teacher education institute, have an equal place and alternate during the 1-year program. There is a frequent "commuting" from experiences to reflection on those experiences, aimed at the development of "theory with a small t" (see chapter 1) or "phronesis" (see chapter 2): These are rather simple, but practical, principles that serve as guidelines for the perception of practice and for acting in the concrete situations at hand. During the first weeks of the program, Theory with a capital T plays a minor role, although it becomes more important about 3 months later, in the reorientation period.

Where practical experience in school is not yet available as the basis for reflection (in the introductory weeks), experiences are created in the here and now: Students give lessons to each other, supervise group meetings, and get small assignments (e.g., "formulate an exercise for the group, and introduce it within 5 minutes"). Moreover, the learning process during group seminars is reflected on, both from an individual perspective and a group perspective, so that the students' own learning about teaching is also used for learning about learning (cf. Loughran, 1997, p. 5).[4]

The program description does not reveal that the practical experiences are not used as a means to introduce theory that the teacher educators have chosen beforehand, but that the program is built on the problems the students experience and the concerns they develop through the practical experiences. In that respect, the program is concern-based. However, it should be noted that the realistic approach cannot be equated with the so-called concern-based approach to teacher education (Fuller, 1969). In this latter approach, the curriculum is grounded in research into general stages of concern development in student teachers and accordingly structured beforehand. The realistic approach acknowledges such general trends in concern development, but focuses on a more concrete level, namely, the specific concerns, questions, and problems student teachers take with them to the institute today on the basis of yesterday's experiences in the school. This implies a much greater flexibility and more limited possibilities to prestructure the program. On the other hand, years of experience with the realistic approach have helped the program staff to become able to predict rather precisely what types of problems and concerns will be generated by what kinds of practical experiences of student teachers, as well as what kind of theory can effectively be connected to these problems and concerns. The experiences that are created (e.g., the 5-minute assignments during the introductory weeks) are chosen because they almost always lead to basic concerns that otherwise would surface during the first teaching practice period, for example, concerns about taking the lead or making yourself understood.

From the very first day on, the student teachers are asked to reflect on their experiences, on the basis of their own interests and concerns. First, very simple reflection questions are used, for example, "What were the principles that you thought were most important in introducing the exercise?" Or, "From the list of important teacher skills we have now developed together, write down one thing you are already good at, and one thing you want to practice."

Group interaction or *collaborative reflection* are considered highly important in the process of developing theory with a small t. Through the interaction, individual reflection is stimulated, and when the various reflections of the individuals in a group come together, the whole is more than the sum of its parts. Together, the group members develop their own "language of practice." Here is an example. On the basis of a 5-minute exercise, a group may formulate as a principle that a teacher should both create a pleasant atmosphere and at the same time "be in control." Because these are the words of the group and not the "Theory" from a book, it is possible to push the students' reflections one step further: What do these words mean in terms of concrete behavior? The teacher educators are always striving for further specification of principles in terms of concrete skills: Each student teacher should *know* what to *do* if he or she wishes to create a pleasant atmosphere or be in control, and moreover, *be able* to do so. The latter may require skills training at the institute.

For example, further discussion in the group about the meaning of "being in control" can lead to the formulation of a concrete skill such as "establishing eye-contact when giving a direction." Only then is the knowledge that has been developed useful for practice. Next, the student teachers *practice* this skill, first within the group or in small groups. Then, as a follow-up, it is important that they practice this skill in a real teaching situation. The students formulate intentions for this before going back to their practice schools, again in concrete action terms. These intentions are the basis of their reflection afterward, when they have to critically evaluate the way their intentions have worked out.

3.4. PRECONCEPTIONS

Behind this pedagogical approach lies an important assumption. That is, it is necessary to build on the student teachers' *preconceptions* about education (Wubbels, 1992b) as they shape their perceptions of practical situations. We consider learning about teaching from a constructivist perspective (e.g., Duffy & Jonassen, 1992; Magoon, 1977; Resnick, 1983), which means that we see humans as subjects actively constructing understanding from experiences using their already existing frameworks (Posner, Strike, P. W. Hewson, & Gertzog, 1982). People continuously build their own conceptions (Groeben, 1981; Groeben & Scheele, 1977). Thus, student teachers enter teacher education with knowledge, attitudes, and beliefs that are deeply rooted in the years of experiences they had as students within the educational system (Lortie, 1975, speaks about the "apprenticeship of observation"). As Feiman-Nemser (1983, p. 152) puts it:

> Human beings have survived because of their deeply ingrained habits of correcting one another, telling each other what they know, pointing out the moral, and supplying the answer. These tendencies have been acquired over the centuries and are lived out in families and classrooms. Thus, children not only learn what they are told by parents and teachers, they also learn to be teachers.

Also, stereotyped examples of teaching shown by film and television programs may contribute to the formation of student teachers' preconceptions about learning and teaching (Lasley, 1980). These preconceptions often do not agree with the Theories we would like to teach in teacher education programs (Corporaal, 1988; Wubbels, 1992b). Preconceptions show a remarkable resistance to traditional attempts to change them (Wahl, Weinert, & Huber, 1984). Stofflett and Stoddart (1994), for example, argue that teachers' conceptions of teaching subject matter are strongly influenced by the way in which they themselves learned this subject content. They have shown that student teachers who themselves experienced learning in an active way, are more inclined to plan lessons that facilitate students' active knowledge construction. Huibregtse, Korthagen, and Wubbels (1994) showed that even with experienced teachers there is a strong relation between their preferred way of teaching and the way they themselves are used to learning: They have a limited view of the learning styles of their students and tend to project their own way of learning onto the learning of their students.

We believe that the quick "washing out of progressive attitudes" (Zeichner & Tabachnick, 1981) after student teachers have left teacher education colleges can be caused in part by too little awareness on the part of teacher educators of the conceptions student teachers hold on entering the program.

3.5. LESS RATIONAL WAYS OF INFORMATION PROCESSING AND THE ROLE OF GESTALTS

In our view, most literature on the role of preconceptions in teacher development shows a certain one-sidedness, which may be another reason for the lack of influence of teacher education programs on the student teachers' preconceptions (Korthagen, 1993c; Wubbels, 1992b). We will now discuss this one-sidedness.

In the teacher education literature, descriptions of the role of preconceptions guiding student teachers' actions tend to focus on just one type of human information processing (e.g., Hollingsworth, 1989; Weinstein, 1989). This type of information processing—mostly focused on by teacher educators—can be described as rational or logical. For example, student teachers are asked to analyze the goals of a lesson they gave, the way they worked toward these goals and the effects. The impact of such approaches on the student teachers' preconceptions is relatively low, because the situations these student teachers are confronted with during their teaching practice elicit many feelings (e.g., feelings of fear), concerns, value conflicts, and so forth, which are certainly not only rational, logical, cognitive, or conscious and easily remain outside the analysis:

> A student teacher has become rather afraid of teaching a certain class because of severe discipline problems. If the teacher educator tries to help the student teacher analyze the lesson in terms of goals, teaching activities and effects this may seem to be a "logical" approach, even having the potential to clarify the causes of the discipline problems. The question is, however, whether framing the problem in these terms matches the concerns of the student teacher. If the distance between the emotions and concerns of the student teacher and the attempted rational analysis is too large, no learning can take place. Moreover, even if a logical conclusion about concrete courses of action to take in the classroom is reached during the conversation with the student teacher, the question remains whether this will really lead to changes in the student teacher's teaching behavior.

People do not act solely on the basis of logical and rational analysis. Feelings of fear can be very influential, "washing out" any rational intentions formulated before the lesson. Very often, one sees such a student teacher fall back on very old patterns, partly influenced by survival behavior developed during the student teacher's own personal history, and partly influenced by stored images of other teachers handling severe classroom problems. Koster, Korthagen, and Schrijnemakers (1995) studied the influence of former teachers on the way student teachers teach. They showed that certain former teachers can serve both as a positive and as a negative role model to student teachers. For example, one student teacher, called Ita, said:

> When I was in the first year of my secondary school, we had a gentle and sweet teacher, who controlled the class very well. I think about her all the time. I have to be careful that students don't play tricks on me. And then I keep thinking of her. Her name is miss Hapé. (p. 161)

Although Ita may be aware of certain specific characteristics of her former teacher that she would like to copy, we believe that in a situation like this it is more adequate to say that Ita has a *gestalt* of her former teacher, consisting of not only a visual image but also of the feelings, values, and behavioral aspects linked to this image.

Koster et al. (1995, p. 162) also cite another student teacher, Jason, at the beginning of the teacher education program, talking about his former English teacher:

> We called him Mr. Elephant, because he had an enormous collection of elephants. The rugby team to which I belonged, was named "the Elephants," which shows how we thought about him. He was in that rugby team, too. We respected him. He knew how to inspire us and because of him I started to read English literature. He helped me with it and showed me how to do it. As a teacher you have to show somebody how to go about things. I want to be that kind of teacher, too. He was able to make a lesson attractive, he kept it topical, told anecdotes, and I'm going to try that too. He was inspired, he was somebody, he had character. You could also see him outside the lessons. Once I visited his home. I remember exactly the way his living room looked, very unconventional, very personal. I have that too, my living room doesn't look like an average room either.
>
> I searched and found a number of characteristics in that English teacher that appealed to me, that I wanted to develop myself. It is a kind of kinship you feel. The way he taught made it nice to be there; there was a sense of humor in the way he told things [big smile], very colorful. As I would have said then: those were the grooviest lessons I've ever had.

His story gets a remarkable "happy ending" at the end of his teaching practice period:

> When on the last day at my practice school a student stopped me and introduced me to his pal by saying "This is Jason, and he gave me the grooviest lesson of my life," it made me feel good.

Crow (1987, p. 10) presents a similar example. Coleen, a secondary student teacher says about a former English teacher:

> She was extremely knowledgeable about literature and grammar. She stimulated me to want to know more.... I wanted to read and read and understand.... She was always an English teacher and we all liked it.... She had quite an influence on me.... I definitely will use a lot of different things like she did.

D. D. Ross (1987) notes that previous teachers can also serve as negative role models. Koster et al. (1995) also found such examples of negative role models. Jeanine, a student teacher in biology says:

> I want to maintain a nice atmosphere between me and the students. I don't want a struggle like I have witnessed a lot of times when I was a student.... For example, I had an English teacher who would walk out of the classroom because she couldn't take it any more, and the next time she would bring us candy. We laughed our heads off then, but looking back I pity her. (pp. 163–164)

Such experiences made her feel that contact with students was important to her and helped her develop her ideas of how she wanted to be with the children.

These were examples of role models consciously influencing student teachers. D. D. Ross (1987) seems to believe that the use of characteristics of former teachers by student teachers for shaping their own role as a teacher is based on a deliberate process in which student teachers consciously decide on the kind of teacher they would like to become. However, Zeichner, Tabachnick, and Densmore (1987) emphasize that this influence of former teachers can also take place on a less conscious level, which is also shown by McEvoy (1986). She addressed the issue of role models in a paper with the intriguing title "She Is Still with Me." McEvoy interviewed nine teachers, of which seven could easily describe striking characteristics of impressive former teachers. Often it was a shock to these teachers to realize that they were describing characteristics that were now obvious in their own teaching, although they had not consciously been aware of the modeling process. In line with this finding, Britzman (1986) argues that it can be important to have student teachers examine the values embedded in such role models in order to avoid that they influence their teaching behavior in an unconscious way.

In sum, feelings, role models, values, and so forth may all play a role in shaping teaching behavior in the here-and-now of classroom experiences, and often unconsciously or only partly consciously. As we wish to take the role of less rational and less cognitive ways of information processing seriously, we use the term *gestalts* to indicate the internal entities that, often unconsciously, guide human behavior. With the term *gestalts*, we want to refer to the personal conglomerates of needs, concerns, values, meanings, preferences, feelings, and behavioral tendencies, united into one inseparable whole. As we saw, they often evolve as a result of a person's earlier experiences in life, for example, with other important persons in early childhood and in school.

We believe that one of the reasons that program impact is sometimes limited in scope is that the role of gestalts and less rational information processing is often neglected. We will discuss this issue in more depth in chapter 10, after further developing our framework concerning realistic teacher education.

3.6. EXPERIENCES AS A STARTING POINT FOR LEARNING

The gestalts influencing student teachers' perceptions of and behavior in practice can only become clear if there are sufficient practical experiences within the teacher education program. Thus, long student teaching periods or early entrance into the field can be proposed as contributions to a solution for the problematic relation between theoretical and practical components of teacher education (cf., e.g., Sandlin, Young, & Karge, 1992). We think that starting from practical experiences can be a viable avenue in teacher education to help integrate theoretical notions into teacher actions and to help take into account both types of human information processing. Such an approach to teacher education does, however, not guarantee success. Long student teaching periods can be a socializing factor rather than offering an opportunity for professional development. Wideen et al. (1993), for example, conclude from a review of studies on effects of teacher education programs that the student teaching experiences were so devastating that little learning seemed to take place. In the following sections and in the next chapters, we will offer suggestions for careful planning, structuring, and supervision to make practical experiences a learning experience. Before doing so, we will elaborate on the intended learning processes in student teachers.

Learning in student teaching can be seen as a form of *experiential learning* (Jamieson, 1994). We define experiential learning as the acquisition of knowledge, attitudes and skills with respect to oneself and one's environment by means of one's own observation of and participation in situations, and by systematically thinking about this under supervision (cf. Erkamp, 1981).[5] The process of experiential learning may, for example, be described by the model developed by Kolb and Fry (1975) as a cyclical process of concrete experience, reflective observation, abstract conceptualization, and active experimentation. This model, however, does not account for the nonreflective learning that is an important part of learning (Bandura, 1978; De Jong, Korthagen, & Wubbels, 1998). It suggests, on the one hand, that learning from experience is a natural, almost autonomous process leaving little room for guided learning. On the other hand, it overemphasizes the role of abstract concepts at the cost of concrete and more individual concepts, images, feelings, or needs. Moreover, "it fails to take account of the need for developmental link between cognitive, emotional, social and personal development in the journey towards expertise in teaching" (Day, 1999, p. 69). To develop teacher education programs, other descriptions of the processes during learning from experience are needed.

3.7. REFLECTION

We describe the ideal process of experiential learning as an alternation between action and reflection. Korthagen (1985) distinguishes five phases in this process: action, looking back on the action, awareness of essential aspects, creating alternative methods of action, and trial, which itself is a new action and therefore the starting point of a new cycle (see Fig. 3.2). This five phase model will be referred to throughout this book as the *ALACT model* (named after the first letters of the five phases).

Here is an example of a student teacher, Judith, going through the phases of the ALACT model, under the supervision of a teacher educator:

> Judith is irritated about a student, named Jim. She has the feeling that Jim always tries to avoid having to do any work. Today she noticed this again. In the preceding lesson the children received an assignment for three lessons to work on in pairs and hand-in a written report at the end. Today, during the second lesson, Judith had expected everyone to work hard on the assignment and to use this second lesson as an opportunity to ask her help. However, Jim appeared to be busy with something completely different. In the lesson she reacted by saying: "Oh, so again you are not doing what you should do.... I think the two of you will again end up with an insufficient result!" (*Phase 1: action*)

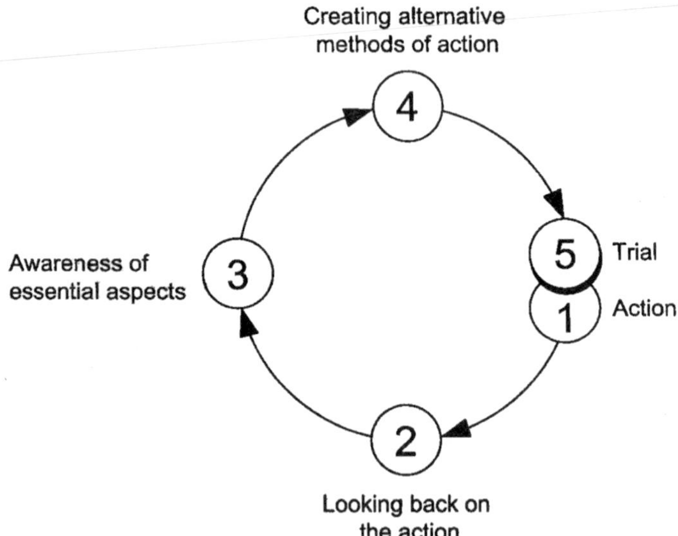

FIG. 3.2. The ALACT model describing the ideal process of reflection. In phase 3, a need for more theoretical elements can come up and these can be brought in by a supervisor, but they are tailored to the specific needs and concerns of the teacher and the situation under reflection.

During the supervision, Judith becomes more aware of her irritation and how this influenced her action. When the supervisor asks her what could have been the effect on Jim of her reaction, she realizes that her irritated reaction may, in turn, have caused irritation in Jim, probably causing him to be even more demotivated to wor1k on the assignment. (*Phase 2: looking back*)

Through this analysis she becomes aware of the escalating negativity which is evolving between her and Jim and she starts to realize how this leads into a dead-end road (*Phase 3: awareness of essential aspects*). However, she does not see a way out of the escalation. Her supervisor shows understanding of Judith's struggle. She also brings in some theoretical notions about escalating processes in the relationship between teachers and students, such as the often occurring pattern of "more of the same" (see for the underlying Theory with capital T: Watzlawick, Weakland, & Fisch, 1974) and the guidelines to de-escalate by changing this pattern and being more empathetic or by deliberately giving a positive reaction. This is the start of *phase 4: creating alternative methods of action*. Judith compares these guidelines with her impulse to be even more strict and put more constraints on Jim. Finally, she decides to *try out (phase 5)* a more positive and empathetic approach, that starts with asking Jim about his plans. This is first done in the supervision session: the supervisor asks Judith to practice such reactions and includes a mini-training in using "feeling-words." If the results of this new approach are reflected on after the try-out in the real situation with Jim, phase 5 becomes the first phase of the next cycle of the ALACT model, thus creating a spiral of professional development.

3.8. PROMOTING REFLECTION ON EXPERIENCES

In realistic teacher education, reflection is organized on the basis of the ALACT model. An *inductive* approach is followed that builds on the student teachers' own perceptions, their thinking and feeling about concrete teaching situations in which they were actively involved, and their needs and concerns. Realistic teacher education starts from student teachers' experiences and their gestalts rather than from the objective theories on learning and teaching from the literature.[6] Student teachers go to schools for observations, teaching experiences, and other assignments very early. In this way, experiences are created that can be used in the reflection process to help investigate the gestalts that student teachers have developed in experiences earlier in their lives. Next, for example, images, feelings, needs, behavioral tendencies, and so forth, triggered by small teaching experiences, can be brought into awareness, and the relation between the gestalts evoked by taking the teacher's role can be related to the student's experiences as a child in school. Through this process, inner conflicts and concerns about how to deal with teaching may surface in the student teachers. These concerns are a more productive starting point for learning about teaching than theories coming from outside the student teachers.

This does not mean that theory does not play an important role in the realistic approach to teacher education. Especially in Phase 3 of the ALACT model, where the student teacher starts to become aware of the essence of the situation he or she is reflecting on, the teacher educator can bring in theoretical elements, but they should always be tailored to the specific needs of the student teacher and the situation at hand. As explained before, this changes the nature of relevant theory: It seldom takes the form one finds in academic textbooks. (See chapter 2 for a more thorough discussion of this issue. There a distinction was made between two types of knowledge, *episteme* and *phronesis*).

Interpreting student teacher learning as learning by reflection can be taken a step further by also applying this idea to other components of teacher education, such as group seminars on campus. The realistic approach can be used at the level of a class on campus by creating an experience in that class that is the basis for learning for a whole group. One example is the idea of organizing 10-minute lessons given by student teachers to their fellow students. (See chapter 9 for other examples and a discussion of the question of how the attuning of theory to the specific needs and concerns of individual student teachers can still take place if the teacher educators work with larger groups.)

An important prerequisite for learning from experience is a feeling of safety on the part of the student teacher. Learning or professional development can be seen as a process of both personal and professional growth and it is well-known that people resist growth if the need for safety is not fulfilled (Fullan, 1991; Maslow, 1968). Student teachers, for example, are preoccupied with concerns about survival (Fuller & Bown, 1975) and this can hinder their learning about other topics. Teacher educator's empathy can help to create a safe environment. In our experience, another very powerful tool to build a positive learning climate is to reward student teachers consistently for positive elements in their performance. By emphasizing their strong points, they become more willing and able to face their weaknesses and invest their energy in risk taking actions that are necessary for improvement of weaknesses. Rewards give them the feeling that there is a positive basis from which they can work.

The *ownership* of the learning process should lie in the hands of the student teacher. Thus, he or she should be very much involved in the process of choosing suitable learning situations. In this way, the students are also prepared for deliberately finding the right balance between safety and challenge in their professional develpment after graduation. This points toward another basic teacher educator skill: the capacity for *scaffolding*. Scaffolding means offering just the degree of support and challenge to students that is necessary, while at the same time helping the student teachers develop the skill to find the right balance between safety and challenge when choosing learning opportunities themselves.

3.9. REASONS FOR PROMOTING REFLECTION IN TEACHER EDUCATION

As we explained, our choice of an approach to teacher education aiming at learning from experiences by means of reflection is, first of all, based on the results of research studies showing the failure of the traditional approach, and second, on an analysis of the crucial factors in learning processes of student teachers. There are, however, at least two more important reasons for this choice that need to be stressed here.

First, it is impossible to prepare prospective teachers for each and every type of situation they may be confronted with during their careers (Harrington, Quin-Leering, & Hodson, 1996). That is even more true in these times of fast changes: social changes, technological and scientific developments, and so on. Rogers (1969, p. 104) stated this problem very clearly:

> Teaching and the imparting of knowledge make sense in an unchanging environment. This is why it has been an unquestioned function for centuries. But if there is one truth about modern man, it is that he lives in an environment which is *continually changing*.... We are, in my view, faced with an entirely new situation in education where the goal of education, if we are to survive, is the facilitation of change and learning. The only man who is educated is the man who has learned how to learn; the man who has learned how to adapt and change; the man who has realized that no knowledge is secure, that only the process of *seeking* knowledge gives a basis for security. Changingness, a reliance on *process* rather than upon static knowledge, is the only thing that makes any sense as a goal for education in the modern world.

This means that student teachers should develop an attitude of willingness to learn from their experiences in changing circumstances. Haan (1975, p. 257) speaks of a *problem-solving attitude*: "You do not have to *know* what you must do, you should rather learn to accept the fact that every time you have to *find out what you have to do* all over again." If teachers acquire this attitude and also the necessary skills to learn from their own experiences by means of reflection, they possess a so-called *growth competence*: the ability to continue to develop when the preparation program is over. This competence can also help them to play an active role in educational change and thus promote their innovative capacity (Wubbels & Korthagen, 1990). M. Knowles (1975, p. 18) speaks about *self-directed learning*

> in which individuals take the initiative, with or without the help of others, in diagnosing their learning needs, formulating learning goals, identifying human and material resources for learning, choosing and implementing appropriate learning strategies, and evaluating learning outcomes.

Of course, the requirement that a student teacher should acquire a *starting competence* is equally important. The acquisition of a basic technical competence in teaching forms an indispensable part of the teacher education program.[7] We would like to stress, however, that reflective skills and technical competence are not mutually exclusive (Tom, 1985; Van Manen, 1977). Technical competence may even be regarded as a precondition for reflection, as a grounding in technical skills helps teachers to feel more safe and allows them to pay more attention to reflection. It prevents them from drawing the conclusion that such reflection is impractical and unhelpful for solving their problems (Hoy & Woolfolk, 1989). Thus, it is becoming increasingly clear to professionals in the field that the goal of teacher education programs should be *to develop both a starting competence and a growth competence* (Hoy & Woolfolk, 1989). This is a basic assumption underlying our framework of realistic teacher education. Of course, each of these *competences* consists of a variety of smaller *competencies*: These terms are used throughout this book in line with the view explicated by Eraut (1994, p. 179):

> We should note a useful distinction in the American literature between the term "competence," which is given a generic or holistic meaning and refers to a person's overall capacity, and the term "competency," which refers to specific abilities.

A final reason for promoting reflection in student teachers that we wish to emphasize has to do with goals of education in general. What we have just said about the fast pace of change in the world is not only relevant to teacher education, but to all kinds of education. This implies that the children that our student teachers will teach also need to be prepared for lifelong learning. Students in primary or secondary education need to develop a problem-solving attitude, to learn from their experiences, and to direct their own development. For these students, it is equally important to develop reflection skills. The congruence between the goals of realistic teacher education and a view of learning in schools emphasizing the promotion of the capacity for independent and continuing learning in children should in our view be made explicit to student teachers. It may help student teachers to see the process they are going through, including the struggles they encounter when learning to reflect on their experiences, as an important preparation for helping students in school go through the same kinds of processes. Reflection by student teachers on the ways their teacher educators model the helping process may add another dimension to learning to teach.

In section 14.4, we will further elaborate the relationships between the view of teacher education presented in this book and a philosophy of education in schools.

3.10. CONCLUSION: TOWARD A PEDAGOGY OF TEACHER EDUCATION, BASED ON EXPERIENTIAL LEARNING AND REFLECTION

This chapter introduced the basic principles of the realistic approach to teacher education, which aims to bridge the gap between theory and practice. As it takes student teachers' experiences as starting points for learning, this approach has important implications for organizing teacher education. In the next chapters (especially in the chapters 5, 7, and 9), we will further explore these consequences at three different levels: the level of the teacher educator supervising an individual student, the level of organizing and structuring group seminars, and the level of the teacher education program as a whole.

Before exploring these consequences, it may be helpful to analyze more theoretically a core concept of this book, namely, reflection. Chapter 4 is devoted to this reflection on reflection.

It may be important to state here that learning from experiences in a cyclical process of reflection is not a way of learning that many students will have encountered in schools before entering teacher education. Therefore, they may show resistance to engage in such a learning process. Regretfully, for many teacher educators, this resistance is a reason to abandon the whole idea of the promotion of reflection. However, we believe it is possible to work out a strategy of gradualness that may help to get student teachers acquainted with actively and consciously learning from their experiences. A pedagogy of teacher education in which such a strategy is used should also take into account that some student teachers are more inclined to engage in reflection than others. This seems to be another difference in the preconceptions about learning that student teachers bring to the teacher education program. According to Korthagen (1988), the first group can be called *internally oriented*, whereas the second is more *externally oriented* (i.e., they want to be guided from outside sources). This is an issue we will return to in chapter 6, because there are some interesting research results concerning these differences.

SUMMARY

Learning from practice is not always productive. The transition shock in beginning teachers is accompanied by a washing out of the theory learned during preservice teacher education and experiences of not having been adequately prepared for the problems of teaching practice. At Utrecht University, the difficult period of beginning teaching has been built into the preservice teacher education program. This program follows an inductive approach, based on a frequent commuting between experiences and reflection, and directed by the students' concerns, leading to theory with a small t. A safe learning climate is important, as well as building theory on the students' preconceptions, and on the less rational and less cognitive elements shaping teacher behavior. We use the term *gestalt* to indicate the personal conglomerates of needs, concerns, values, meanings, preferences, feelings, and behavioral tendencies guiding action.

Learning in student teaching is a form of experiential learning, which can ideally be described by the ALACT model, consisting of five phases: (1) action, (2) looking back on the action, (3) awareness of essential aspects, (4) creating alternative methods of action, and (5) trial.

Realistic teacher education aims at more than developing a starting competence: Through learning how to reflect, student teachers also develop a growth competence. In other words, they become self-directed learners.

BASIC CONCEPTS

Transition shock (reality shock)

Concerns

Preconceptions

Gestalts

Experiential learning
ALACT model for reflection
Starting competence
Growth competence
Self-directed learning

4 A Reflection on Reflection

Fred Korthagen

Life can only be understood backwards: but it must be lived forwards.

—*Sören Kierkegaard*

Reflection has become a familiar term to teacher educators, and many teacher education curricula are now based on the aim of promoting reflection. However, as soon as one starts to look more closely at reflection and the meaning of the term, confusion and obscurity arise. Therefore, the concept of reflection will now be analyzed by discussing its use in the literature and presenting a definition as well as a theoretical framework in which this definition gets its meaning. This definition states that reflection entails a process of structuring or restructuring, which will be described in more detail in this chapter. Finally, relations with action research approaches will be considered.

4.1. INTRODUCTION

During the last decades, reflection has become a basic concept in teacher education all over the world (Gore, 1987; Hatton & Smith, 1995). It has emerged as a specific topic within the general movement of "teacher thinking," which started in the 1970s. Until 1975, teachers were commonly viewed as "decisionmakers," and research into teaching dealt almost exclusively with teacher behavior in the classroom. Around 1975, the professional field showed a shift toward a perception of teachers as "reflective professionals who construct meaning" (Clark, 1986; Schön, 1983). This development was accompanied by a shift in research methods, leading to the conviction that teachers' mental structures play an important role in the teacher's functioning (see, e.g., Shavelson, Webb, & Burstein, 1986, p. 79). One of the most important functions of reflection is to help teachers become aware of their mental structures, subject them to a critical analysis, and if necessary, restructure them.

Today, almost all professionals in the field seem to agree on the fact that reflection is a generic component of good teaching. However, close analysis of teacher education practices and the literature on reflection reveals that the term has been conceptualized in many different ways (Day, 1999; Grimmett, 1988; Hatton & Smith, 1995; Tom, 1985). Often it seems that the term *reflection* is used without careful conceptualization, in a loose way, which makes it almost synonymous to "thinking":

> A teacher educator: "People make a lot of fuss about reflection. I wonder why. Haven't we always been promoting reflection in teacher education? Of course you ask a student teacher after a lesson to think about that lesson herself. And even if you don't, she will! Especially when having severe problems in the relationship with the children, the student will sometimes think about that all night! One might even wonder whether all that emphasis on reflection would not be counterproductive for such a student! I sometimes say: 'Come on, stop bothering now, let's see whether I can give you a concrete guideline to overcome these problems. Isn't that our task: to support the student teacher?'"

This creates the risk that reflection becomes a confusing concept that is simply too big, too vague, and too general for everyday application.

So what exactly is reflection? In this chapter I will discuss this issue in depth, without having the illusion that it is possible to include everything written about reflection. I will make choices and confine myself to some general lines of thinking about the concept.

Almost all researchers agree on the fact that reflection is a special form of thought (Grimmett, 1988; Hatton & Smith, 1995) and its origin can be traced back to the work of Dewey (1933), who warned against too mechanical a focus on teaching method in the preparation of teachers (see also Gore, 1987). In spite of this common origin, modern views of reflection differ substantially, if they are made explicit at all. The terms *reflection* or *reflective teaching* seem to embrace a wide range of concepts and strategies (Hatton & Smith, 1995), which differ on a number of issues, one of which is the underlying philosophy of education (Korthagen & Wubbels, 1995). Only a few attempts have been made to operationalize and measure reflection (Korthagen, 1993b). These are the issues that I will focus on in the first sections of this chapter. In section 4.5, I will present a definition of reflection underlying realistic teacher education. In the next sections, I will analyze the process of reflection in greater detail. In section 4.9, the idea to base professional learning on systematic reflection will be compared with another development in the field of teaching and teacher education, namely, the use of action research by teachers. In section 4.10, the question of whether all teachers should and can become reflective practioners will be discussed.

4.2. REFLECTION AND VIEWS OF TEACHER EDUCATION

First, let us look at what the literature says about the question of why we should promote reflection in teachers. Calderhead and Gates (1993, p. 2) state that teacher education programs based on notions of reflective practice espouse one or more of the following aims:

- to enable teachers to analyse, discuss, evaluate and change their own practice, adopting an analytical approach towards teaching;
- to foster teachers' appreciation of the social and political contexts in which they work, helping teachers to recognise that teaching is socially and politically situated and that the teacher's task involves an appreciation and analysis of that context;
- to enable teachers to appraise to moral and ethical issues implicit in classroom practices, including the critical examination of their own beliefs about good teaching;
- to encourage teachers to take greater responsibility for their own professional growth and to acquire some degree of professional autonomy;
- to facilitate teachers' development of their own theories of educational practice, understanding and developing a principled basis for their own classroom work;
- to empower teachers so that they may better influence future directions in education and take a more active role in educational decision-making.

Zeichner (1983) has clarified the relation between the concept of reflection and a number of different views on the goals of teacher education. He distinguishes four paradigms of teacher education. The first is *behavioristic* teacher education, emphasizing the development of specific and observable teaching skills that are assumed to be related to effective learning. The second is *personalistic* teacher education, focusing on the psychological maturity of prospective teachers, and "emphasizes the reorganization of perceptions and beliefs over the mastery of specific behaviors, skills and content knowledge" (p. 4). Next, Zeichner mentions the *traditional-craft* paradigm in which teacher education is viewed primarily as a process of apprenticeship. The fourth approach is *inquiry-oriented* teacher education, "which prioritizes the development of inquiry about teaching and about the contexts in which teaching is carried out" (p. 5).

Reflection plays no significant role in either the behavioristic or the traditional craft paradigm. In both these approaches, the content of teacher education can be specified and defined in advance. There is an existing body of knowledge about teaching and a given educational context. This leads to certain competencies, which the prospective teacher has to acquire. In the personalistic and inquiry-oriented paradigms, however, prospective teachers are active participants in the construction of the content of the teacher education program. Reflection is the instrument by which experiences are translated into dynamic knowledge; both these paradigms aim at an ongoing process consisting of experience, looking back on experience, analysis, and reorganization. However, the two differ in the extent to which internal or external factors are incorporated into this process. The personalistic paradigm stresses the importance of the role of personal perception (Combs, Blume, Newman, & Wass, 1974) and self-actualization (Joyce, 1975, p.

134), whereas the inquiry-oriented paradigm focuses on contextual influences on the teaching-learning situation.

The following section examines such views on the role of reflection on the basis of an overview of the ways in which reflection has been conceptualized by different authors.

4.3. CONCEPTUALIZATIONS OF REFLECTION

The literature reviews on reflection by Calderhead (1989) and Hatton and Smith (1995) are well known. They, too, point at the confusion about the precise meaning of the term *reflection* and refer to several important authors writing on the subject.

Starting with the work of Dewey (1933), we find that

> Reflection involves not simply a sequence of ideas, but a *con-sequence*—a consecutive ordering in such a way that each idea determines the next as its proper outcome, while each outcome in turn leans back on, or refers to, its predecessors. (p .4)

According to Dewey, reflection entails a *chain of thoughts*, which "are linked together so that there is a sustained movement to a common end" (p. 5). He arrives at the following definition:

> Active, persistent, and careful consideration of any belief or supposed form of knowledge in the light of the grounds that support it and the further conclusions to which it tends, constitutes reflective thought. (p. 9)

In addition, Schön (1983, 1987) distinguishes between *reflection-in-action* and *reflection-on-action*. Schön states that reflection-in-action and experimentation go together:

> When someone reflects-in-action, he becomes a researcher in the practice context. He is not dependent on the categories of established theory and technique, but constructs a new theory of the unique case. His inquiry is not limited to a deliberation about means which depends on a prior agreement about ends. He does not keep means and ends separate, but defines them interactively as he frames a problematic situation. (Schön, 1983, p. 68)

Reflection-in-action is limited to what Schön calls the *action present*: "the zone of time in which action can still make a difference to the situation" (Schön, 1983, p. 62). This is not the case in reflection-on-action, which takes place after the action itself. Reflection-on-action occurs when, during a routine action, we are confronted with an unexpected result (Schön, 1987, p. 26). This reflection-on-action can change our future actions. Schön gives the example of a person who, by reflecting on his Monday morning quarterback, plays differently in next Saturday's game

(Schön, 1987, p. 31). According to Schön, reflection-on-action implies inquiry into the personal theories that lie at the basis of one's actions.

To several authors, reflection has an emancipatory or otherwise ethical meaning. D. D. Ross (1987, p. 1) relates reflection to rationality and responsibility:

> Reflection is a way of thinking about educational matters that involves the ability to make rational choices and to assume responsibility for those choices.

Zeichner's (1983) view of reflection is strongly grounded in the work of Habermas (1973) and further elaboration of this work by Van Manen (1977). It implies the acceptance of a particular ideology, along with its accompanying assumptions and epistemology (Gore, 1987; Hatton & Smith, 1995; Wildman & Niles, 1987). Within this ideology, the emphasis is on the degree to which teachers critically reflect on the moral, ethical, political, and instrumental values embedded in their everyday thinking and practice (Liston & Zeichner, 1989; Valli, 1990; Zeichner, 1983, 1987).

Van Manen identifies three levels of reflection. At the first level (technical rationality), the dominant concern is with efficient means to attain a given objective. The rationality of the "best choice" is defined in accordance with the principles of technological progress: economy, efficiency, and effectiveness. At the second level, it is assumed that every educational choice is based on a value commitment to some interpretative framework. Reflection at this level is concerned with analyzing and clarifying individual and cultural experiences, meanings, perceptions, assumptions, prejudgments, and presuppositions for the purpose of orienting practical actions. At the third and highest level, the fundamental question is one of the value of knowledge, and reflection is then focused on the nature of the social conditions necessary for raising the question of worthwhileness in the first place. Reflection at this level involves a constant critique of domination, of institutions, and repressive forms of authority (cf. Noffke & Brennan, 1991). It calls for considerations of moral and ethical criteria, taking account of social and political contexts (Hatton & Smith, 1995).

Whereas Van Manen and Zeichner stress the importance of contextual influences on teachers' actions, Dirkx (1989) speaks of the importance of self-reflection. He does not deny the relevance of the social, political, economic, and moral dimensions of school practice, but believes these orientations are insufficient to help teachers become aware of the relational aspects of their interaction with the students. Using principles borrowed from social psychology, Dirkx's method aims at problematizing one's own feelings, thoughts, and actions in the relationship with others.

In the approach employed by Cruickshank et al. (1981), the object of reflection is the effectiveness of instructional strategies in attaining given ends. This more technical approach is most probably based on a view of the teacher as a competent, highly technical person (see Gore, 1987), although the authors also state that their aim is to develop in students good habits of thinking about teaching in order to become "wise as teachers."

Pollard and Tann (1995) combine the goal of reflecting on aims and consequences of one's own actions as a teacher and the goal of enhancing technical efficiency. In their view of reflection, both goals are important reasons for promoting reflection.

4.4. OPERATIONALIZATIONS OF REFLECTION

Only a few attempts have been made to operationalize and measure reflection. For example, on the basis of Van Manen's work, some researchers have developed systems for assessing the level of reflection of teachers. Zeichner and Liston (1987) developed their "reflective-teaching index" on the basis of the Van Manen levels. They distinguish between four levels of discourse during supervisory conferences in teacher education: (a) factual discourse, concerned with what has occurred in a teaching situation or with what will occur in the future; (b) prudential discourse, revolving around suggestions about what to do or around evaluations of what has been established; (c) justificatory discourse, focusing on the reasons employed when answering questions of the form "why do this rather than that?"; and (d) critical discourse, examining and assessing the adequacy of the reasons offered for the justification of pedagogical actions or assessing the values and assumptions embedded in the form and content of curriculum and instructional practices (the "hidden curriculum").

An operationalization concurring with the approaches of Van Manen and Zeichner and useful for the analysis of written texts is described by Hatton and Smith (1995). They analyzed the reflective writings of student teachers and distinguish between (a) *descriptive writing*, which is not reflective as it involves no attempt to provide reasons or justifications for events or actions; (b) *descriptive reflection*, which shows attempts to provide such reasons or justifications, but still in a narrative or descriptive way; (c) *dialogic reflection*, demonstrating "a stepping back" from the events or actions, leading to a different level of mulling about, discourse with self and exploration of the experience, events, and actions, using qualities of judgments and possible alternatives for explaining and hypothesizing; and (d) *critical reflection*, demonstrating an awareness that actions and events are not only located in, and explicable by, reference to multiple perspectives, but are located in, and influenced by multiple historical, and sociopolitical contexts.

There is an important difference between the work of Zeichner and his colleagues at the University of Wisconsin, on the one hand, and the approach by Hatton and Smith, on the other. In the former, certain levels of reflection are considered "higher" and "better" than others, in the latter a developmental view is proposed,

> starting the beginner with the relatively simplistic or partial technical type, then working through different forms of reflection-on-action to the desired end-point of a professional able to undertake reflection-in-action. (Hatton & Smith, 1995, p. 45)

Bain, Ballantyne, Packer, and Mills (1999) distinguish between five levels: *reporting* (with minimal transformation or added insights), *responding* (the teacher does something with the source data, but at a superficial level), *relating* (a superficial attempt to identify relationships), *reasoning* (involving a high level of transformation and conceptualization), and *reconstructing* (involving abstract thinking and generalization). Although they call them "levels of reflection," one can doubt whether the lower levels of this categorization represent any reflection at all.

It is important to mention that many attempts to operationalize reflection or reflective action have failed. Very often I receive an e-mail from someone somewhere in the world who is trying to develop an instrument for measuring reflection. After giving the information asked for, I always ask them to let me know when the attempt has succeeded. Generally, I never hear anything anymore. Indeed,

> the terms are extremely difficult to render operational in questionnaires and other research instruments. Then it would appear that it has been a considerable challenge to develop means for gathering data and analysing data so that the evidence shows unequivocally that reflection has taken place. (Hatton & Smith, 1995, pp. 38–39)

One of the major problems is that it is impossible to determine on the basis of essays written about an experience whether or not reflection-in-action or reflection-on-action has taken place, because these essays

> provide only indirect evidence of either kind of reflection, and no way of distinguishing what is being thought about *now* in contrast to *then*. (Hatton & Smith, 1995, p. 42)

4.5. TAKING A POSITION IN A CONFUSING AREA

Although this overview of conceptualizations and operationalizations of reflection is far from exhaustive, it is clear that there is no unanimity with regard to the definition of reflection. But what is even more interesting is the fact that the confusion about this definition is apparently not so much a cognitive-psychological problem as a sociopedagogical one: the different definitions of reflection are related to different beliefs about what is important in education and in teacher education (Calderhead, 1989; Hatton & Smith, 1995; Zeichner, 1983). Reflection is a normative concept, and the normative criteria involved can be characterized by means of the relations one considers important. For Dewey, the most important criterion for reflection is whether the person sees a relation between the situation the person is in and the goal he or she wants to reach. In Schön's concept of reflection-on-action, the fundamental relation that the reflecting person should see is between his or her actions and his or her framing of situations. Ross focuses on the relation between one's actions and the arguments for the choices implied in those actions. In Zeichner's opinion, relations must be established between action and ethical, moral and political principles. Cruickshank focuses on the relation between means and ends.

The fact that these differences originate in underlying views of what constitutes "good teaching" reveals that any prescriptive statement about reflection is questionable, simply because individual views on the aims of education are questionable. Prescriptive statements may be of importance to someone sharing those views, but even this is not always true because such statements often lack a sound theoretical basis: the relation between teachers' reflective skills and the quality of their teaching has hardly been studied in depth by researchers (see Kennedy, 1990, p. 850; Wubbels & Korthagen, 1990, p. 29). This issue will be further elaborated in chapter 8.

This analysis could leave us with a feeling of frustration if we are looking for an all-embracing definition of reflection. However, the picture becomes more clear when we adopt a cognitive-psychological point of view. Then we discover that much agreement is contained in the different approaches to reflection. All the authors quoted share the view that human behavior is based on mental structures and these structures are not static but, in part at least, created or altered through experiences or confrontations with situations (cf. Silcock, 1994). Moreover, they seem to agree on the fact that the mental structures guiding behavior can be influenced by reflection.

This leads to the definition of reflection used in this book: *Reflection is the mental process of trying to structure or restructure an experience, a problem, or existing knowledge or insights.* The term Schön (1987) uses for the process of restructuring is *reframing.*

I believe that most conceptualizations of reflection can be brought together by this definition, and the differences are determined by the sociopedagogical perspectives from which the intended process of structuring or restructuring takes place. The definition emphasizes the basic role of the formation of (new) mental structures in a person's learning. This makes action based on reflection fundamentally different from routine action.

4.6. DIRECTOR SYSTEMS AT TWO LEVELS

Let us now look more closely at the processes of structuring or restructuring involved in reflection.

In order to further develop the cognitive psychological framework, we can adopt a theory developed by Skemp (1979), describing the role of reflection in human behavior. This theory is an extension of the well-known TOTE model of Miller, Galanter, and Pribram (1960). TOTE stands for Test-Operate-Test-Exit. Miller, Galanter, and Pribram state that if a person experiences an incongruity between a present situation and his or her needs (this is the first test), that person can use a *plan* for action. The term *plan* refers to all organized processes in the organism that direct behavior. Such a plan is based on an internal representation of the outer world. Miller, Galanter, and Pribram use the term *image* to refer to such a mental representation of parts of the world. With the aid of the plan, the person *operates*, tests again the degree of incongruity, if necessary operates again, operates again until the test shows congruity, and then the operation is ended (*exit*).

In fact, we are talking about an elementary *feedback loop*, which makes it possible for human beings to direct their behavior. The process is pictured in Fig. 4.1 (a slight adaptation of a scheme introduced by Skemp).

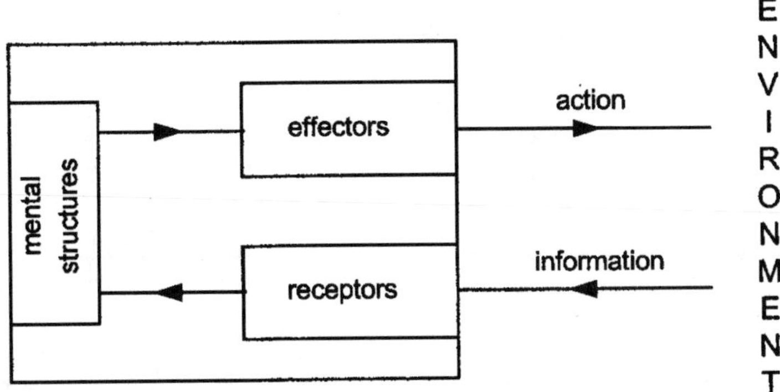

FIG. 4.1. The delta-one level: The process of interaction between a person and the environment.

The rectangle in Fig. 4.1 represents what Skemp calls a *director system*. Such a director system dealing with the interaction with the environment is called a *delta-one system* (delta after the first letter of the term *director system*). For the moment, I use the general and somewhat vague term *mental structure* to refer to the internal representations of reality helping the person to interpret information from the environment and to come up with a reaction.[1]

People can do more than just interact with the outside world. They can *reflect* on the way they interact with the world and try to improve this interaction. To put it in more theoretical terms, they then try to structure or restructure their internal representations of reality or the way they are using these representations for developing their plans or their actions. Skemp concludes that human beings have internal second-order director systems (called *delta-two systems*), which seek to improve the delta-one systems (Fig. 4.2):

As an example, let us consider a student teacher who feels she is having trouble getting her students to be quiet at the beginning of a lesson. When the lesson is over, a process can start in which she reflects on her interaction with the children. The aim of this reflection is for her to be able to perform better in the next lesson. She can reflect on her knowledge of how to get a workable atmosphere in class (reflection on her mental structures, created by former experiences and by what she has learnt during teacher education) and on questions such as whether she actually used this knowledge and, if so, how she used it and how the children reacted. The assumption is that such a reflection process is directed by an internal delta-two system using information about the way the relevant delta-one system functions and seeking to improve this delta-one system. This means that the feedback loop at the left-hand side of Fig. 4.2 represents the reflective part of the learning process. The student teacher can, for example, decide to read a book on teacher–student interac-

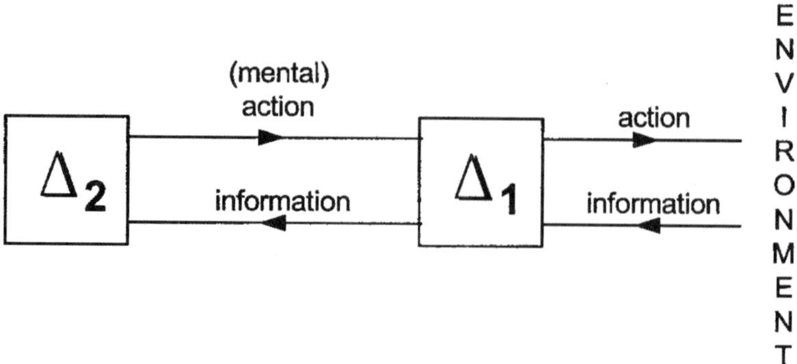

FIG. 4.2. The delta-one/delta-two system.

tion and try to enlarge her mental structure at the delta-one level. Note that her learning process (directed by the delta-two system) will be influenced by a mental structure at the delta-two level containing knowledge about and earlier experiences with learning, for example, the knowledge that a book can be helpful. Another student teacher may have a rather different mental structure at the delta-two level, containing the notion that books are not helpful in such situations. This is another way of saying that people's learning styles are different.

Skemp's idea to distinguish between director systems at two levels is in line with a distinction between two levels of abstraction made earlier by Piaget (1977).

4.7. THE RELATIONSHIP BETWEEN ACTION, LEARNING, AND REFLECTION

Skemp's model emphasizes the close relation between acting and learning. Learning improves the quality of the action, and action exposes the director systems' failings, creating learning needs. The natural order of things is therefore best described as a spiral (Fig. 4.3; see also Bruner, 1960; Dewey, 1910; Kolb & Fry, 1975).

The spiral represents the process of action, learning from that action, and thus improving on the action, and again learning, and so on. I would not want to suggest, however, that student teachers should always pass through the spiral alone, or in other words, that they should discover everything by themselves. The following three points, nevertheless, are essential.

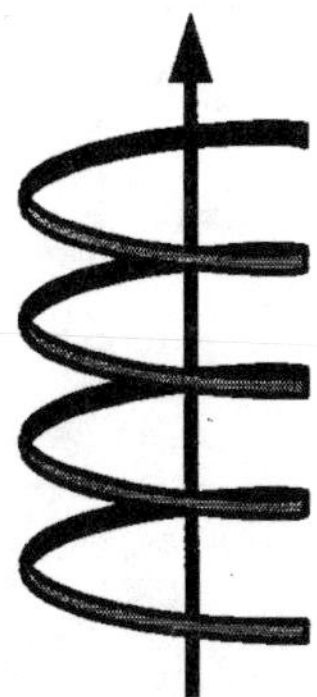

FIG. 4.3. The spiral of professional development. With every cycle, the quality of one or more director systems improves.

First, it is important that the process is based on a learning need or concern of the student teacher that has sprung from this student's own experiences; a supervising teacher educator could encourage the student teacher to have these experiences. Second, the teacher educator must build on these learning needs in such a way that the learning situation offered fits the learning objective that was set (in the student teacher's delta-two system) and lies in what Vygotsky (1978) calls the "zone of proximal development." Third, the supervisor should insure that the next phase of the spiral is entered into in time so that student teachers can apply what they have learned in real-life situations.

This is a brief formulation of a few basic teacher educator skills to be used in the realistic approach. In the following chapters, these and related pedagogical principles will be discussed in detail.

4.8. A CLOSER LOOK AT THE SPIRAL

We will now examine the spiral mentioned in the previous section more closely. I will limit myself to the learning processes that involve reflection, or in other words, learning processes in which a person consciously considers his or her delta-one level performance. As we saw in section 3.7, one complete spiral cycle comprises five phases (see Fig. 4.4).

Phases 1 and 5 show activity at the delta-one level (interaction with the environment). Delta-two is involved in the reflective Phases 2, 3, and 4. I will now discuss the separate phases individually:

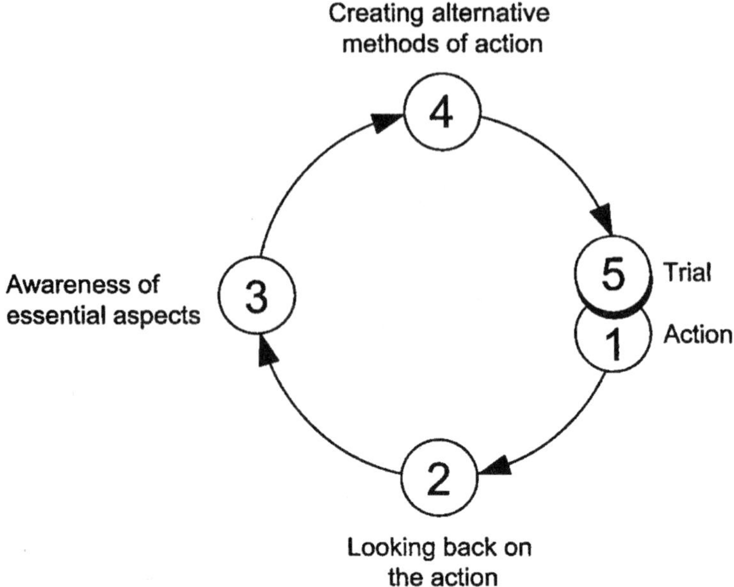

FIG. 4.4. The ALACT model describing the phases that make up one cycle in the spiral of professional development.

1. The cycle is set off by a concrete action (experience). For example, one could consider a simple action like "writing a word on the blackboard" or a more complex set of actions like "teaching a lesson in mathematics." Connected with the action is an action goal (there may even be several, and action goals are not always very clear). Delta-one is the system that is aimed at that goal.
2. After (or possibly during) the action, the process of looking back on that action can start. Generally, this happens if something puzzling or unexpected happened and an action goal was not easily reached (Grimmett, 1988, p. 6). Then delta-one's performance is being examined. This means that the delta-two director system is activated. (Example: A student teacher thinks about her way of teaching, especially about the way she explained the subject matter during the lesson.) This could lead to the next phase.
3. In this phase, certain aspects get special meaning. This often goes hand in hand with the finding of connections. The delta-one system can even be reorganized. Delta-two could, for example, imagine what

caused delta-one to fail. (The student teacher becomes aware of the fact that she took too little time to explain things.)

4. Because of this, a different approach might be chosen to be better suitable to obtain the set goal. (Example: The student teacher decides to pay more attention to the substeps in her explanation and the timing of these steps.) Delta-two could also conclude that given the current action situation, it is impossible to reach the action-goal, in other words, that the quality of delta-one is insufficient. (Example: The student teacher draws the conclusion that her knowledge of learning processes is too limited to do better.) In that case, Phase 4 can involve an extensive learning process: The delta-one system has to be expanded. Delta-two controls this improvement of delta-one.
5. Then, in a new, similar situation, another effort is made to reach the desired goal. The cycle repeats itself.

Conceivably, a feeling of confidence gradually develops that one is proficient where the action is concerned. That means the importance of the cycle diminishes until the individual is confronted with a new relevant situation in which a routine approach to the target is not possible. The principle involved is that adaptation to the environment (learning) and awareness go hand in hand.

Feelings and attitudes are important in all phases. Phase 2 (looking back) can be activated by emotional signals, for instance, a feeling of frustration that delta-one is not able to achieve the set goal. An example could be that a teacher feels frustrated about her lesson, which makes her analyze the way she teaches more closely.

Feedback from others (e.g., peers, a teacher educator, a cooperating teacher) can also be stimulating. Note the analogy with feedback from one's own director system (*internal feedback*): now others use their mental structures to provide feedback (*external feedback*).

Using ideas from chapter 2, it is important to note that the essence of Phase 3 (awareness of essential aspects) is not so much the learning of new *concepts*, but the development of better, more detailed *perception*. A greater awareness of what is happening in the situation reflected on, and in similar situations, leads to another relation with the situation. In the previous example, more awareness of the time factor in explaining subject matter, may help the student teacher to perceive, almost to feel, more easily, on the spot, when an explanation goes too fast for her students. She is then just more aware of something she was not aware of before. (In terms of chapter 2, she has further developed her *phronesis*.) Of course, "timing" or "pacing" may be an important general concept with regard to explaining subject matter, but the important thing here is that it has a specific meaning for this student teacher in this context, a meaning that is connected to a personal concern.

In Phases 3 and 4 (becoming aware of essential elements and developing alternatives), learning resistances can be very powerful. People do not like to fundamentally change their perceptions of the world: Initially, this always causes some degree of confusion and unsecurity. The underlying fear of change may not always be very clear. For example, in the aforementioned example, the learning resistance may take the form of a dislike of educational psychology. An individual could even believe improvement of his actions to be impossible. For example, if a teacher feels he or she cannot possibly pay attention to his or her explanation and simultaneously keep an eye on his or her students (something that happens regularly with beginning teachers), and if there is no obvious method to be found for the teacher to deal with that problem, then he or she shall have to accept the problem as unsolvable at that moment. It is well-known that although this process of acceptance can be painful, it eventually leads to a more realistic self-image (new knowledge about delta-one has been added to the mental structure at the delta-two level). Also, this could positively influence further learning, for instance, because learning resistances change. Sometimes this eventually renders the original problem suddenly solvable. Here we find the familiar phenomenon that sometimes the harder you try to achieve something, the more difficult it gets. (In psychology, a law says that high "arousal" improves performance, but extreme arousal has the opposite effect; see, e.g., Hilgard, R. C. Atkinson, & R. L. Atkinson, 1975.) Because this issue is especially important in the professional preparation of students, we will return to it in chapter 5. We will then also consider the fact that there are different learning styles: One person can be action-oriented, whereas another is more the thinking type. Yet another person may like to try things out, and so on. In short, people show individual preferences for different phases of the ALACT model. An important goal of realistic teacher education is to develop a balance in the degree of attention the student teacher gives to each phase.

4.9. ACTION RESEARCH

The idea to base professional learning on systematic reflection is also central to a related development in the field of teaching and teacher education, namely, the use of action research by teachers, which arose in the 1950s (e.g., Corey, 1953). The interest in action research was strongly enhanced by Stenhouse's (1975) and Elliot's (1978) work on action research and the related idea of "teachers as researchers." This development was accompanied by the introduction of action research in preservice teacher education as a means to promote systematic reflection (Beckman, 1957; Perrodin, 1959), so this chapter would not be complete without a discussion of action research.

Elliot (1991, p. 50) clarifies the close relation between action research and reflection as follows:

> Both product and process need to be jointly considered when attempting to improve practice. Processes need to be considered in the light of the quality of learning outcomes and vice versa.
>
> This kind of joint reflection about the relationship in particular circumstances between processes and products is a central characteristic of what Schön has called *reflective practice* and others, including myself, have termed *action research*.

Most researchers in the area of action research (e.g., Elliot, 1991, p. 69; McKernan, 1991) point to the work of Lewin (1947a, 1947b) as the source of modern approaches to action research. His model involves a "spiral of cycles." In recent descriptions of the methodology of action research, these cycles are generally indicated as *acting*, *observing*, *reflecting*, and *planning* (see, e.g., Grundy, 1987, p. 147, and Kemmis & McTaggart, 1981). Here we already see a close similarity to the view of reflection presented in this chapter, especially with the ALACT model.

An important argument for introducing action research in teacher education is also very much in line with my own view of the role of reflection:

> Teacher educators who have argued for the introduction of action research into the preservice teacher education curriculum have stressed the importance of establishing habits of "self-monitoring" during initial training so that teachers can enter the profession with the dispositions and skills that will enable them to continue to learn from experience and become better at teaching throughout their careers. (Gore & Zeichner, 1991, p. 119)

A second argument for the use of action research also concurs with the thinking behind the realistic approach, especially with the views expressed in chapter 2. Stenhouse's influential work on action research emerged in reaction to the development of a movement stressing the prespecification of measurable learning outcomes and the training of teachers to use specific skills in order to reach these outcomes. Stenhouse took a stance similar to the one taken in chapter 1 of this book, namely, that pedagogy is not the technical process of "transmitting" predescribed curriculum content, but involves experimentation and inquiry by the teacher. Instead of having teachers become the executors of the plans of innovators from outside the schools, he wanted them to keep control of their own work. That is why he saw action research as a better instrument to improve education, an instrument owned by the teachers themselves (teacher-based curriculum reform). In his view, educational developments could take place on the basis of experiments initiated by teachers, who could themselves gather classroom data in a systematic manner and choose their actions on the basis of their reflections on these data. As has been stressed also in the previous chapters, the kind of reflection involved should be quite different from technical means ends reasoning, but be grounded in the teacher's personal commitment:

> Inasmuch as the reflection is about choosing a course of action in a particular set of circumstances, to realize one's values, it is ethical in character. (Elliot, 1991, p. 51)

Moreover, the realistic approach is also in line with Elliot's (1991, p. 10) view of learning as "the active production rather than the passive reproduction of meaning." In fact, part of the realistic teacher education program at Utrecht University is devoted to a small research study by the student teachers of their own practice, a study often showing the characteristics of action research (see section 3.2).

However, a closer look at approaches using action research also reveals some differences with the view of professional learning proposed in this book. For example, an often cited definition of action research is that given by Carr and Kemmis (1986, p. 162):

> Action research is a form of self-reflective enquiry undertaken by participants in social situations in order to improve the rationality and justice of (1) their own social practices, (2) their understanding of these practices and (3) the situations in which these practices are carried out.

As far as this definition refers to the rational understanding, justification, and improvement of one's own practices as a teacher, it concurs with the thinking behind the realistic approach. However, the third aspect in the definition introduces something characteristic for action research, namely, the goal of improving the context of one's own teaching. Teachers involved in action research are generally supposed to contribute to changing their schools or even society as a whole:

> Action research which is educational, encourages the researcher to go beyond the constraints imposed by schools and to act for the reconstruction of educational systems. (O'Hanlon, 1996, p. 87)

As Zeichner and Liston (1987, p. 23) note, there is a metaphor of liberation underlying this goal of preparing teachers to participate as full partners in the shaping of educational policies. Although the realistic approach does not deny that this could be an important side effect of reflection by teachers on their own practice, it does not put this goal in such a central position as is common in most of the work of advocates of action research, especially those who are supporters of "critical" or "emancipatory" action research. The realistic approach, first of all, builds on student teachers' concerns, which may mean that, especially at the beginning of a preparation program, more attention goes to the issue of teacher–student interaction, with an emphasis on the relational aspect in a given context. This does not mean that teacher educators should only follow the student teachers' concerns: They can also generate such concerns, not by presenting "interesting Theory," but by first creating suitable experiences. For example, when student teachers are stimulated to follow one group of students in a school for a whole day through all their lessons, concerns about the school context and about values and norms embedded in the school culture tend to surface rapidly. The same happens when student teachers are asked to interview students at school about their images of the school, about learning, and about themselves. Such concerns then create a fruitful basis for reflection on what Zeichner (1983, p. 6) called "the examination of the moral, ethical, and political issues (as well as the instrumental issues) embedded in teachers' everyday thinking and practice." Still, it may be a long way for beginning teachers to take an active role in changing contextual influences on their everyday teaching. They should be prepared for that role, too, but the realistic approach seems to differ from some action research approaches in the sense that the realistic approach does not put this issue into such a central position. Support for this different emphasis can be found in Zeichner (1993, p. 201):

> The link with critical social science and critical theorists in universities has alienated many in the action research community in part by creating the perception that the "critical" is somehow out there above and beyond the world of practitioners in the macro-world, and that practitioners' struggles in the micro-world in which they live daily are somehow insignificant in the larger scheme of things.... I will argue ... that these separations between technical and critical, micro and macro are distortions, and that the critical is in reality embedded in the technical and in the micro-world of the practitioner.... The reality ... is that the political and the critical are right there in front of us in our classrooms and other work sites and the choices that we make every day in our own work settings reveal our moral commitments with regard to social continuity and change whether we want to acknowledge it or not.

Zeichner helps us to be aware of the fact that even within the boundaries of the microsituation, student teachers' reflection should involve the moral implications of their behavior, especially the question of whether this behavior reproduces social injustice. As such, the differences between action research and the realistic approach may be small. As I will discuss in chapter 14, where I formulate the moral basis of the realistic approach, the final goal of the realistic approach concurs with the view expressed by Gore and Zeichner (1991, p. 134):

> Our long term goal is that students will use the dispositions, skills, and knowledge gained from their teacher education program to work, in concert with others, toward the making of a more just and humane society.

4.10. FINAL REMARKS

A final question to be addressed is: Should all teachers be reflective practitioners? This question is important, because teacher educators are often confronted with student teachers who do not seem to be very much inclined to reflect, but wish to get feedback and guidelines from others. (This problem will be discussed in more detail in sections 6.5 and 11.10.) There seems to be general agreement in the literature that reflection is a generic professional disposition (Hatton & Smith, 1995; Schön, 1983, 1987; Tom, 1985). Kubler LaBoskey (1997) puts it this way:

> I was once asked by a reviewer if reflectivity ought to be a goal for all teachers. The presumption seemed to be that because it was so difficult for many to achieve, it might be an unreasonable educational aim. A colleague in a current in-service project asked me the same question just the other day. My response both then and now is: "Yes!," "Yes!" and "Absolutely, yes!" All students deserve teachers who are both willing and able to construct and examine their practice in conscientious, principled, and judicious ways.

However, if reflection is fundamental to the teaching profession, still "the problem remains of whether or not its development can be fostered in intending professionals through programs of preservice preparation" (Hatton & Smith,

1995, p. 43). My answer is the same: "'Yes!,' 'Yes!' and 'Absolutely, yes!,'" as the next chapters will show.

SUMMARY

Although reflection has become a basic concept in teacher education, the literature shows no unanimity with regard to its meaning. The different conceptualizations and rare operationalizations of reflection are related to a variety of underlying views of the goals of (teacher) education. As such, each conceptualization is questionable. However, seen from a cognitive-psychological perspective, reflection is always aimed at influencing the mental structures guiding behavior. Consider the definition used as the basis of the present book: Reflection is the mental process of trying to (re)structure an experience, a problem, or existing knowledge or insights. This reflection can take place after an action (reflection-on-action) or during the action (reflection-in-action).

The two-level model introduced by Skemp describes the relation between action, learning, and reflection. Internal delta-one systems direct the interaction with the environment, whereas delta-two director systems are aimed at improving delta-one systems (internal feedback). The feedback loop involved at the delta-two level represents the reflective part of the process. The result of the reflection can be the improvement of the action at the delta-one level. This spiral process of reflective professional development can be stimulated by external feedback from others.

The idea to base professional learning on systematic reflection is also central to action research approaches, which build on premises similar to those of realistic teacher education. Generally, these approaches put somewhat more emphasis on changing contextual factors than realistic teacher education does, as student teachers have, first of all, concerns about the interaction with the students in their classrooms.

BASIC CONCEPTS

Reflection-in-action and reflection-on-action

Director systems (delta-one and delta-two)

Spiral of professional development

Internal and external feedback

Action research

5 Building a Realistic Teacher Education Program

Fred Korthagen

Make the program follow the learning (not vice versa).

—*Donaldson & Marnik (1995)*

The basis for designing a realistic teacher education program is explored in this chapter through a more detailed look at the problem of educational change and then by formulating three fundamental learning principles and the corresponding pedagogical principles.[1] *The meaning of these principles is considered in the context of individual supervision and in the context of group seminars. Also, the consequences on the level of program organization are discussed. Finally, I look briefly at the similarity that in my view exists between student learning at school, student teachers' learning during teacher education, and teacher educators' learning.*

5.1. INTRODUCTION

As we saw in chapter 3, a well-known problem in teacher education is that many student teachers enter their preparation program with preconceptions about teaching and learning that are rooted in their experience as students. For example, many student teachers consider the teacher a "transmitter of information," although findings from educational research stress the importance of making learners active participants in their own learning process. The latter view implies that the teacher should be a facilitator of learning rather than a transmitter of information.

For quite some time, teacher educators have tried to induce changes in student teachers' preconceptions by confronting them with empirically based theories about teaching and learning. Being educators, they often devised sophisticated teaching methods to alter their student teachers' preconceptions: They used practical examples of the theories presented, gave assignments aimed at translating certain theoretical principles into practice, made use of feedback procedures, and so on. However, as we saw in chapter 1, the effects of such an approach on teaching behavior in the classroom have proved to be small. In section 1.4, the problem of educational change has already been discussed. In section 5.2, this problem will be analyzed from a psychological perspective. On the basis of this analysis, three basic principles of professional learning will be presented in section 5.3, to be translated, in section 5.4, into three basic principles of a pedagogy of teacher education. In section 5.5, I will give an example of the application of these principles within the context of a concrete curriculum element. In section 5.6, five consequences for program organization in teacher education will be discussed. Section 5.7 will be devoted to the issue of quality control and assessment. In section 5.8, I will discuss the congruence between the level of learning of student teachers and of teacher educators respectively. Finally, in section 5.9, I look at the next steps to be made in this book in order to elaborate the pedagogy of realistic teacher education.

5.2. THE PARADOX OF CHANGE

A closer look at current practices in teacher education reveals that the work of many teacher educators is led by the basic assumption that, being teacher educators, they have a better idea of what constitutes good teaching than most student teachers, and for this reason they should alter their students' conceptions. As psychotherapists have long known, the best way to prevent any change in someone is to attempt to bring about change in that person. As Cantor (1972, p. 270) puts it,

> Fundamentally the organism resists change. Once we have achieved a certain organization there is a tendency not to alter it. The organism strives to remain in equilibrium. We tend to assimilate new experience in accordance with our former habits and experience. We fight against disturbing our present wholeness.

Teacher educators appear to be faced with an almost impossible task. Not only do student teachers show a strong resistance to attempts to change their existing preconceptions, but these preconceptions also serve as filters in making sense of theories and experiences in teacher education (Hollingsworth, 1989). The resistance to change is even greater because of the pressure that most student teachers feel to perform well in the classroom. They have "concerns about survival" (Fuller & Bown, 1975); but if processes of personal change are to take place, then a climate of safety is essential (Maslow, 1968, p. 49). In stressful conditions, people try even harder to keep their equilibrium. For example, if a student teacher fails to succeed as a transmitter of information in the classroom, then he or she will often make an even greater effort to become a "better transmitter," instead of changing his or her basic conception of teaching. This is what Watzlawick et al. (1974) call the phenomenon of "more of the same."

Thus, teacher educators appear to be involved in the paradox of change: the pressure to change often prevents change. And we, teacher educators, put pressure on students in various subtle ways. For example, a seemingly harmless question such as "why did you start your lesson the way you did?" will often be—correctly—understood by the student teacher as an attempt to change him or her.

5.3. THREE BASIC PRINCIPLES IN PROFESSIONAL LEARNING

This is far from a suggestion to leave our students alone and allow things to stay the same. What I do want to emphasize is that we as teacher educators may have to change our own preconceptions about teachers' professional learning.

First of all, we should realize that student teachers may have good reasons for thinking and feeling the way they do about education, for believing what they believe, for having the ideals they have. People construct meaning through personal and social experience (Piaget, 1970). If teacher educators want to help student teachers in their professional development, they must start by trying to understand the way these students view teaching and learning, and how they have come to construct these views. This will help the educators to create new experiences during teacher education, which can lead the student teachers to question their preconceptions. But even then, change cannot be forced on the student. A fundamental change in a person can only take place if he or she desires change. This idea is the foundation of two basic principles concerning professional learning, derived from many different sources (motivation theories, constructivist psychology, psychotherapy, innovation theories, etc.):

1. A teacher's professional learning will be more effective when directed by an internal need in the learner (see, e.g., Fullan, 1991; Maslow, 1968).
2. A teacher's professional learning will be more effective when rooted in the learner's own experiences (see, e.g., Piaget, 1970; Rogers, 1969).

These principles will be elaborated on in the following sections. Before doing so, I add a third principle:

3. A teacher's professional learning will be more effective when the learner reflects in detail on his or her experiences.

This third principle is based on the notion that often the student teachers' preconceptions about teaching are implicit. As we saw in section 3.5, they may take the form of gestalts, that is, holistic constructions of reality based on experiences. They include feelings, values, and behavioral tendencies.

It is important that student teachers analyze their preconceptions about teaching and learning, thus making the implicit explicit. Only by such analysis can they discover weaknesses in their preconceptions. This, in turn, creates in them the need for further learning, which according to principle 1 is a basic factor for promoting learning.

There is another reason why the third principle is important, which was discussed in chapter 2. It is the notion that teachers' professional development is not so much grounded in knowing more, but in perceiving more in the practical context in which one has to teach. Reflection is a basic tool in developing more awareness about practical situations and, finally, while being involved in those situations. The details of this aspect of professional learning will be further discussed in chapter 10.

5.4. USING THE THREE PRINCIPLES IN A PEDAGOGY OF TEACHER EDUCATION

The three principles of professional learning share one fundamental idea: Change is seen as something that should come from within the student teacher. It is viewed as a "flux," driven by the student teacher's own needs and experiences. This process of change can, however, be encouraged by the teacher educator. Looking at the work of the teacher educator (i.e., the pedagogy of teacher education), there are three basic principles in teacher education, which complement the three learning principles mentioned earlier:

1. The teacher educator should help the student teacher to become aware of his or her learning needs.
2. The teacher educator should help the student teacher in finding useful experiences.
3. The teacher educator should help the student teacher to reflect on those experiences in detail.

These principles need not be applied in this order. Sometimes students are not aware of any learning need. In that case, it may be more desirable to start with an experience, such as a lesson given by the student to fellow students. In other cases, the student's reflection on earlier experiences can be promoted, for example, by asking the student to reflect on the characteristics of his or her favorite teachers in school and to compare those characteristics with the student's own at this moment.

Moreover, the three principles often go together. For instance, by reflecting on experiences (3) student teachers may become more conscious of learning needs (1), and by formulating a learning need (1) they often become aware of the necessary learning situation (2).

In the case of the third principle, a problem may present itself. Student teachers often lack a clear recollection of the details of a particular experience, such as a lesson they have given. For example, owing to the stress felt during the lesson, they may have forgotten what the students asked them and how they themselves reacted. Or they may not remember exactly how they explained the particular subject matter. And if there were observers in the classroom—the teacher educator, a cooperating teacher, or fellow students—their observations may be regarded by the student teacher to be "subjective"—again, in an (often unconscious) attempt to resist change.

First of all, we have to realize that such problems often indicate that the learning situation is not suited to the student teacher at this point in his or her professional development. It seems to be too threatening and a safer learning situation should be sought. However, even after relatively safe and surveyable experiences, some student teachers have difficulties in looking back on those experiences and in recalling what happened. Then the task of teacher education becomes to develop such a student's capacity for reflection.

Here technology can be helpful. Audio or video recordings of learning experiences can serve as a mirror to the student. For example, after the student teacher has taught a lesson, a recording is helpful in "reliving" the experience. It offers the opportunity to replay certain episodes as often as one likes. The student teacher may then discover details that reveal basic problems. For example, the student teacher may realize that he or she did not listen adequately to questions, or that the method for maintaining order was not as effective as he or she had hoped. This is very helpful in encouraging the development of learning needs.

Most important is what the student teachers themselves discover while replaying the tape. Just as in a regular mirror, each person sees different things, depending on the stage of the inner process of personal change. Some things are in the foreground, others are in the background, depending on the point where the student is in his or her development. (The notions of *foreground* and *background* are theoretically elaborated in gestalt psychology; see, e.g., Korb, Gorrell, & Van de Riet, 1989, pp. 7, 8, 21).

The realistic approach to teacher education is based on the aforementioned principles. The next section illustrates the principles. Before doing so, I want to emphasize that we are talking about learning processes involving much more than just cognitive aspects. When student teachers embark on a process of changing their gestalts, or start to experiment with new behavior, they are beginning to change themselves as persons. A student's view of his or her own role as a teacher and the way he or she interacts with children cannot be separated from the way he or she relates more generally to other people in his or her life. As I have stressed in quoting from Cantor's work, a certain resistance to change is inevitable. This means that the feelings and emotions involved should be given a great deal of attention by the educator. There is a danger of the teacher educator "pushing" the student who is gradually becoming aware of a learning need; the educator may be too quick to "help" the student to change things. The watchword here is "make haste slowly.". The teacher educator is the facilitator of change, but it is the student teacher who actually brings about the change. It will help if the educator remains aware of the feelings of the student, as well as his or her thinking. Trust and safety are fundamental to personal change.

5.5. AN EXAMPLE: THE ONE-TO-ONE STUDENT TEACHING EXPERIENCE

In order to illustrate the use of the three basic principles of the realistic approach, I will now examine an element of the Utrecht teacher education program known as the *one-to-one* (Vedder, 1984). It is part of the undergraduate orientation course. Teaching a whole class on a regular basis is a complex experience for beginning student teachers; it tends to foster concerns for survival and does not create the atmosphere of safety necessary to a balanced learning process. This is why the first teaching practice period has been simplified.

The arrangement can be summarized as follows. The prospective teacher gives a one-hour lesson to one high school student once a week for 7 to 8 weeks. The university supervisor and the cooperating teacher are not present during the actual one-to-one lessons, but there are supervision sessions and seminar meetings during the one-to-one period.

The lessons are recorded on audiocassettes, and are subsequently the object of detailed reflection by the student teacher. This reflection is structured by means of standard questions, which are addressed by the student in a personal logbook. These include such questions as:

1. What did you expect and how did you prepare for it?
2. What actually happened?
3. Choose some episodes from the tape and describe what you did and what the student did, what you thought and felt, and what you think the student thought and felt, and how these aspects influenced each other.
4. Try to derive conclusions from this.
5. Formulate your intentions for the next lesson.

The third question is often the most crucial one, because it focuses on the details of the lesson. For example, this might reveal to student teachers that they failed to listen to what the student was saying, or started an explanation before the problem was clear to the student. As one of my student teachers put it: "The one-to-one caused a shift in my thinking about teaching, from a teacher perspective to a student perspective."

In line with the principles formulated in the previous section, the one-to-one is designed to promote student teachers' own reflection on the essentials of their teaching and their personal learning needs. After these reflections by the student teacher, the university supervisor can offer small theoretical notions fitting in with the process the student teacher is going through. I agree with P. W. Hewson and M. G. Hewson (1989) that the student teacher should experience these theoretical notions as being intelligible, plausible, and fruitful. If these requirements are not met, then the theoretical notions are not likely to become part of the mental structures of student teachers directing their teaching. Moreover, in terms of chapter 2, the emphasis should be on *phronesis* rather than *episteme*.

Vedder (1984), who studied the effects of the one-to-one arrangement, distinguishes two main types of effect. The first has to do with the development of practical skills, which appears to be promoted by the link that has been created between theory and practice (Vedder & Bannink, 1987, p. 2). The second is related to the promotion of reflection. A major advantage of the one-to-one arrangement is the fact that it focuses the student teacher's attention on the learning process of a single student, instead of on the issue of maintaining classroom order (Vedder & Bannink, 1987, p. 10). At the same time, the student teachers become aware of their own learning processes, as documented in their logbooks. As noted before, awareness, especially awareness of the learning process of the student, and of one's own learning process, is fundamental to the process of becoming a teacher.

Of course, there may be considerable differences between student teachers in what is learned during such a one-to-one arrangement. For example, one student teacher may focus on the lack of self-confidence in the student she works with and start a search for ways of improving the child's self-image, whereas another student teacher is confronted with her tendency to explain things at a fairly abstract level and may develop the wish to include more concrete examples. This illustrates the need to plan teaching experiences as a part of a long-term development process, not consisting of separate, haphazard experiences, but deliberately chosen to be related to each other and to the needs of the individual student teacher. In other words, student teachers should get sufficient opportunity to develop their personal styles and to follow their own individual learning path. This is a necessary consequence of the choice for a realistic approach. I will come back to this issue in the next section.

5.6. PROGRAM ORGANIZATION

The previous sections draw our attention to consequences at the level of program organization.[2] For example, there are two important considerations for the kind of experiences that student teachers are introduced to. These experiences should be offered in such a way that there is a *balance between safety and challenge*, and they should be planned as part of an *individual long-term learning process*. In this section, these two aspects of the program organization will be discussed. Then I will look at the *relations between the schools and the teacher education institute*, the necessarily *integrated character* of a realistic teacher education program, and the *professional development of staff*. In section 5.7, the problem of quality control and assessment of student teachers will be discussed.

Balance Between Safety and Challenge

It has been stressed in section 3.8 that a safe climate is necessary for learning to take place. At the same time, there must be some degree of challenge in the experiences of student teachers to let these be good starting points for learning. Such challenges require assignments that create a distance between what a student teacher is already capable of and what is required. However, if this distance is too great, the challenge becomes a threat and learning is inhibited. Establishing this balance requires careful tailoring of the intended learning process of the student teacher, and thus a lot of interpersonal skills on the part of the teacher educator (to be elaborated in chapter 7).

In addition, teacher educators have the possibility to create challenges rather than threats by choosing the character of the learning experience. In a strategy of gradual immersion, experiences can be planned to have an increasing complexity and responsibility and, in student teaching, to have an increasing work load. Experiences at the beginning of teacher education can, for example, take the form of a one-to-one experience as described in section 5.5. In general, such an arrangement creates a safe and not too complex learning situation for the student teachers. If too small challenges are planned, student teachers may eventually feel that they have been insufficiently prepared to teach completely on their own, with sole personal responsibility, and thus they may encounter a reality shock. Therefore, it is important that the program has a phase in which teaching practice is as realistic as possible, without making it an experience completely identical to independent teaching: in other words, still being supervised.

In the teacher education curriculum at the IVLOS Institute of Education at Utrecht University, the program ends with the so-called Independent Final Teaching Practice (IFTP), a continuous 3-month student teaching period (already mentioned in section 3.2). The student teacher functions just like other regular teachers in the school, under normal constraints and pressures, teaching all lessons in a particular subject in a number of classes at the secondary level. The student teacher gives tests and marks and takes part in all regular activities in the school, including official meetings at the school level and parent–teacher conferences. The only differences with a regular teacher are that the teaching load is restricted to from 10 to 12 1-hour lessons and the ultimate responsibility still lies with the cooperating teacher, who also supervises the novice teacher. Again, this provides a safety net and the opportunity to tailor the balance between support and challenge to the needs of the individual student teacher. The supervision takes place by means of long-arm supervision, in the sense that the supervisor does not attend the student teacher's lessons. (The IFTP arrangement has been described in more detail in Koetsier, Wubbels, & Van Driel, 1992, and in Koetsier & Wubbels, 1995.)

Balancing Individual Long-Term Learning Processes and General Programmatic Lines

During a teacher education program, student teachers will be confronted with many different experiences. It is important that these experiences are not separate, haphazard experiences, but that for every individual student teacher they are deliberately planned to be linked to each other. The ideal learning process of student teachers is seen as a spiral process in which reflection on action leads to new actions, these actions to new reflections, and so forth. Each cycle of the spiral should be connected to previous cycles: Only then is a process of continuous professional development being created.

For example, in the IFTP the student teachers are also supervised at the IVLOS Institute, usually in small groups, by their teacher educator. These institute-based supervisory conferences focus on the long-term development of student teachers' own teaching styles and their individual views of teaching. Such supervisory conferences promote awareness in the student teachers of the thread running through their teaching experiences and reflections.

Of course, we should realize that many teacher educators, especially in North America, have to work with large cohort groups in which close personal supervision of student teachers is not always possible. As we also recognized this problem in the IVLOS program, we have developed structural methods in which student teachers do as much of the supervision as possible together. These methods of so-called *peer-supported learning* (Tigchelaar & Melief, 2000) aim at structuring the intended reflection on concrete teaching experiences (e.g., in the one-to-one arrangement or the IFTP) through a series of standard reflection questions (see chap. 11 for a more detailed discussion) to be discussed in groups of three to four student teachers. In section 9.6, we will discuss this arrangement for peer-supported learning in more detail.

Another time-saving development of the last couple of years is the use of telematics for supervising student teachers in the IVLOS program. During the IFTP, each student teacher has an e-mail link with a list-serve at the institute. The exchange of experiences, problems, ideas, and resources is very much promoted by this facility, which aims at reflective exchanges between student teachers (another example of using peer-supported learning). In addition, the teacher educator can easily join in the e-mail conversation and support the reflection process, both at the group level and by individual e-mail connections (see also section 9.6).

To help stimulate attention for the long-term learning processes, student teachers can, for example, use logbooks to document their experiences, their strengths, and their weaknesses and consequently think about their learning wishes and objectives (the use of logbooks will be further discussed in chapter 11). As already noted, every student teacher will follow an individual and highly personal learning path. This is true for two obvious reasons. First, this is a necessary consequence of the idiosyncratic character of student teachers' preconceptions, and of the competencies that they individually bring to the program. Second, I think the goals of a teacher education program always need an individual translation: There is no one way of good teaching, but student teachers must develop their own style in accordance with their personality, competencies, and biographies.

Some people may see it as a difficulty almost inherent to the realistic approach that it is hard and perhaps even counterproductive to state in advance what the student teacher's individual learning process should lead to. Perhaps this is a price to be paid for the shift toward a pedagogy of teacher education that aims at the development of knowledge, skills, and attitudes that are really being used in practice. On the other hand, years of experience with the realistic approach have helped the program staff at the IVLOS Institute to become able to predict rather precisely what types of problems and concerns are generated by what kinds of practical experiences of student teachers as well as what kind of theory can effectively be connected to these problems and concerns. This made it possible to formulate the program objectives more precisely in advance and to not only follow the student teachers' concerns, but also generate them (Van der Valk, Somers, Wubbels, & Korthagen, 1996). For example, the one-to-one teaching experience at the beginning of a program almost always draws the focus to learning and changes the exclusive preoccupation of student teachers with their own teaching. The first experiences of classroom teaching almost always promote concerns about controlling the class and maintaining discipline. These more general tendencies in student teachers' concerns open the door for group seminars on these issues, which of course should be closely related to the concrete experiences of each student teacher.

This points toward a basic requirement: A realistic teacher education program should not be the haphazard result of random experiences and concerns of student teachers. It is possible to create room for individual learning processes and to build learning about teaching on the concerns and needs of student teachers, elicited by concrete experiences, while at the same time consolidating programmatic lines that lead to predictable results. However, a shift is needed in the way teacher educators plan such a program: No longer is the program structure determined by the Theories to be presented, and by the separate modules student teachers should follow, but curriculum design in realistic teacher education starts from first determining the competencies student teachers need and then, on that basis, elaborating a long string of experiences to be created. Such a string should start from small, nonthreatening experiences in which student teachers develop their first needs and concerns about their functioning as a teacher, then reflect on their experiences and concerns, and then are helped by the teacher educator to catch a first glimpse of the competencies to be developed. Gradually, the experiences become more challenging and lead to the need to develop more complex competencies or to the need to combine several competencies at the same moment. The programmatic line is a line of experiences carefully created in order to give rise to concerns that to a large degree can be predicted and will be common for the whole group involved. Still, the program and the teacher educators should be flexible enough to deal with unexpected concerns and needs. A rule of thumb is that if the teacher educator thinks that certain theories or skills need attention, these should not be introduced in situations where the student teachers do not feel a need for them. Instead, the teacher educators' task is to create new experiences in which it is to be expected that the theories and skills aimed at match the needs elicited by the experiences. If such experiences cannot be found, teacher educators should consider the question of whether the theories and skills they have in mind are really relevant to the practitioner.

The Relations Between the Schools and the Teacher Education Institute

The need to carefully plan a series of practical experiences as the basis for the intended process of professional development shows that there should be a frequent alternation of school teaching days and meetings at the teacher education institute. Thus, a key factor in the realistic approach is the relation between the schools in which student teaching takes place and the teacher education institute. Both staff based at the teacher education institute and cooperating teachers are part of one team that supports the professional development of student teachers. Thus, as Northfield and Gunstone (1997, p. 49) put it:

> Teacher educators should maintain close connections with schools and the teaching profession.

Several measures can be taken to create circumstances favorable to the communication between school and institute. In the IVLOS program, we have cooperating teachers involved as much as possible on a level of equal responsibility in the planning of the program and in the evaluation of student teachers. They have release time for their supervision and have been trained in supervision skills. When choosing student teaching schools, the possibilities for students to experiment and the quality of internal communications within the school are important considerations.

As Bullough and Kauchak (1997) note, genuine collaboration between teacher education institutes and schools is not easy to establish. They point toward financial constraints, school and university faculty resistance to changing roles, and serious communication problems (see also Furlong et al., 1996). Moreover, according to Bullough and Kauchak (1997, p. 231),

> School and higher education institutions are both very busy places. Unless sufficient resources can be freed to provide opportunities to support the extended conversation needed to create a shared agenda and unless there is a greater commitment to stabilizing participation, separatist partnership patterns will not only persist but predominate.

Crucial elements of successful cooperation structures between teacher education faculty and school-based teachers are "shared beliefs and mutual respect for non-overlapping competencies" (Bullough, Hobbs, Kauchak, Crow, & Stokes, 1997, p. 93; J. A. Ross, 1995, p. 198). I must emphasize that the cooperation structures and procedures developed between the IVLOS Institute of Education and schools were a long time in the making and there are still great differences between schools with regard to the degree of cooperation achieved. A factor that strongly facilitated the integration between the practice component and the institute-based component of the IVLOS program was that a few cooperating teachers were given a part-time position at IVLOS and thus became faculty members (cf. Cornbleth & Ellsworth, 1994).

An Integrated Program

Using the realistic approach implies working in an integrative program. It must have become sufficiently clear that this means practice and theory should be closely connected. But there is another kind of integration that is important, namely, the integration of various academic disciplines. Usually, teacher education programs are structured in modules related to disciplines such as educational psychology, foundations of education, or teaching methods. Such a structure can promote compartmentalization of what is learned and may inhibit student teachers from integrating insights from different disciplines to solve practical problems. The realistic approach to teacher education takes the experiences of student teachers as starting points. These experiences cannot be structured according to disciplines and therefore a thoroughly consistent realistic approach leads to one completely integrated program.

Students go through the IVLOS program in cohort groups that do not follow different classes, but just one class: the program. The groups consist of students being prepared to teach at the secondary school level in the same or a related subject. Theories from different disciplines are covered in the program, but are always connected to the student teachers' practical experiences. That is why, at the beginning of the program, it cannot be said with certainty when a particular theory will be covered. The program is characterized by integration: teaching methods, general aspects of teaching, and subject matter specific elements are brought together in the program, and most importantly, they are united in the program faculty. The integration of various elements in one program has led to the decision that one staff member is responsible for the complete learning path of a group of about 10 to 20 student teachers (Tom, 1997, p. 98, advocates the same principle). This is in line with a conclusion stated by Northfield and Gunstone (1997, p. 54):

> A teacher development perspective would seem to imply a teacher education approach where the teacher educator is able to form a long-term relationship with a small group of teachers assisting them to interpret their own experiences.

In a study into the characteristics of a "high impact" program (at the University of South Florida), Graber (1996, pp. 456–457) points toward another feature of an approach based on cohort groups:

> One positive benefit of the cohort is the friendships developed among classmates, and the considerable esprit de corps that grows within the group. As a consequence, students who show initial resistance to the program orientatation often are co-opted by peers who have been persuaded.... The influence of the cohort group cannot be underestimated, particularly because it facilitates an environment in which students begin to feel part of a strong professional culture.

The IVLOS staff member who is responsible for one cohort group teaches the majority of the program, but will now and then invite experts in specific areas as guest teachers. This leads to more thematically organized seminars.

Structuring the program around themes—such as classroom management, the place of a subject in the school system, or student motivation—may also help to promote integration of knowledge from different disciplines. This kind of organization is also used in some parts of our program. However, the thematic organization can be at odds with an organization around student experiences. No matter how well experiences are prestructured, they can be unexpectedly different from what the teacher educators had intended. In such cases, the teacher educator must be ready and competent enough to change the programmed structure and adapt it to the student teachers' needs and concerns.

The Professional Development of University Staff and Cooperating Teachers

This program organization asks for very experienced teacher educators that are knowledgeable in the many disciplines contributing to the quality of teacher education. Most of the teacher educators at the IVLOS Institute originally come from the same or a related discipline background as the students of the groups for which they are responsible for (e.g., science or the humanities) and are experienced teachers. However, when they start working at the IVLOS Institute, they often lack a strong background in pedagogy, psychology, and other relevant disciplines. We therefore conduct many staff development activities, provided by experts from both inside and outside our institute, aiming at heightening their level of professionalism as "generalists." Intercollegially supported learning among staff is also strongly promoted, for example, by making two colleagues together responsible for one cohort group.

During the last few years, the training and professional development activities for teacher educators at the IVLOS Institute have also been used by many other teacher education institutes in the Netherlands and elsewhere. These kind of activities are, in my view, necessary for every teacher education program, because in most countries there is no regular education for teacher educators. The activities in the IVLOS professional training program for teacher educators are, however, not only a basis for an increase in competence of the staff, but are also intended to have the staff themselves experience the sometimes painful process of reflection. We will return to this issue, which is most relevant to the professionalization of teacher education, in chapter 13.

5.7. QUALITY CONTROL AND ASSESSMENT

Many teacher educators worry that because the realistic approach in teacher education emphasizes experiential and concern-based learning, there is a risk that important program goals will not be met. First of all, earlier chapters of this book have shown that traditional approaches to teacher education may create the illusion that everything teacher education staff consider important "is dealt with," but this does not imply transfer into practice. In that respect, stating the concern that a realistic program does not cover everything can partly be a denial of this fundamental transfer problem in teacher education, which incidentally has long existed without teacher educators being very concerned about it. However, it is justified to ask whether a realistic program does not create quality reduction. Is it possible to formulate clear criteria regarding the quality of the student teachers graduating from a realistic program? Can that be done if the program builds on experiences and student teachers' concerns that cannot be predicted beforehand? The answer is yes.

In section 5.6, it has already been stressed that realistic teacher education is not just a haphazard process. The crux of the matter is the careful planning of student teacher experiences, starting from small, not too threatening experiences, and working toward an IFTP in which the student has almost completely adopted the responsibility of the teacher. The planning of these experiences should be based on the program goals and is partly meant to elicit concerns that can lead to reflection and the introduction of important theoretical elements or the training of necessary skills. For example, the one-to-one arrangement discussed in section 5.5 is meant to stimulate concerns in the student teachers about listening to high school students and building a productive teacher–student relationship. Although it seems to be important that the student teacher become more aware of such issues, if by chance such concerns do not surface, then the teacher educator can and should create new experiences that do evoke such concerns. Thus, the teacher educator has an important role in continuously monitoring the achievement of the program goals and designing suitable experiences. In section 6.2, we will discuss the results of an external evaluation of the IVLOS program showing that this approach to designing a realistic program does indeed lead to clearly defined results.

The issue of quality control is very much related to the question of how the students in a realistic program are being assessed. In the IVLOS program, cooperating teachers serve as an important external check: They have the final say in the assessment of students' practice periods.[3] In addition, during the last couple of years, teacher education staff at the IVLOS Institute of Education have decided to further meet the concern for clearly defined program goals and quality control by introducing *portfolios* as an instrument for assessment (cf. Wade & Yarbrough, 1996). In the second half of the program, the student teachers are asked to reflect on their progress. They formulate their learning gains and their learning needs. This is compared to a list of competencies—defined by the program staff on the basis of their views of education, research on teaching, and teacher competencies formulated at a national level. This list is not used as a straitjacket (our experience is that this is only counterproductive), but rather as a mirror. The student teachers use this list to adapt their own list of what has been acquired and what is still to be learned. At the end of the program, they collect all kinds of evidence of the competencies they have mastered and put this into a portfolio, together with a reflective account of their own learning process during the program and a final self-evaluation. The portfolios they make contain evaluations of their lessons by their cooperating teacher, student evaluations, lesson plans and excerpts from logbooks, educational materials made during teaching practice periods, video recordings of lessons, and so forth. The teacher educator in charge of the student's cohort group is also the one who will be using the portfolio to come to a final assessment decision. It is our experience at IVLOS that this use of portfolios creates a happy marriage between a careful assessment procedure and the promotion of reflection and self-evaluation.

5.8. CONGRUENCE BETWEEN THREE LEVELS

This chapter points to a congruence that should exist between the way we frame the intended learning processes of student teachers and the necessary learning processes of teacher educators themselves. For example, the three basic principles of professional learning, as formulated in section 5.3, are equally applicable to both: For either student teachers and their educators, it is true that effective learning is based on personal learning needs and personal experiences and detailed reflection helps to proceed through a spiral process of ongoing development. This so-called *congruence principle* implies that a realistic teacher education program cannot be implemented by a simple top-down approach: Teacher education staff has to be given the time and support to develop such a program. Program coordinators or faculty deans should be willing to build the development of a realistic program step by step onto the concerns of the staff. Promotion of reflection of the staff on their experiences with the first steps in the direction of a realistic approach is important, as well as collaborative interactions among staff members. Most importantly, a safe learning climate for the staff is necessary, in which the willingness to learn from each other is an absolute prerequisite.

There is also another important congruence, namely, with the intended learning processes of students in schools. One important reason for changing the pedagogy of teacher education is that the realistic approach offers student teachers examples of how they can work with students in school. This is another example of the congruence principle:

> Teacher educators should treat teachers as they expect teachers to treat students. (Putnam & Borko, 1997, p. 1226)

In school, it is equally important to work on the basis of problems experienced by the students, to build theory on practical experiences, to develop a reflective attitude in the learners, to give attention to individual long-term learning processes, and so on. In fact, as showed in section 1.7, the realistic approach is strongly influenced by the realistic approach to teaching mathematics in school, as developed by Freudenthal (1991) and his colleagues of the Freudenthal Institute (see also Treffers, 1987). Freudenthal pointed to the need for learning within meaningful contexts as a prerequisite for making education relevant and fruitful. Although this view of education in schools is not a main issue in this book, which is first of all devoted to the education of prospective teachers, it will receive more attention in section 14.4.

It is not sufficient to strive for this congruence between the level of learning of student teachers and the level of learning in school: The congruence should also be made explicit to student teachers and its consequences for teaching in school should be discussed with them in detail. Moreover, a lot of guidance is necessary to help student teachers incorporate the learning principles they themselves experienced into their own teaching practice (see Wubbels, Korthagen, & Broekman, 1997).

5.9. SIMILARITIES WITH THE OXFORD INTERNSHIP MODEL

Many of the characteristics of a realistic teacher education program described in this chapter, will perhaps not sound entirely new or surprising to anyone familiar with the literature on teacher education, although the combination of principles that together help to create a realistic program may form a new synthesis. There is, however, at least one teacher education model showing almost the same combination of pedagogical principles, namely, the Oxford Internship Model, which is used in a 1-year postgraduate program for secondary school teachers in the United Kingdom. McIntyre and Hagger (1992) summarize this model in a number of principles, the most important being:

1. Heavy involvement in the teacher education program of each of a limited number of schools.
2. Extended attachment of interns to one school.
3. A closely integrated, joint school-university program.
4. A secure learning environment (including a gradual development of the tasks set for student teachers throughout the year).
5. Recognition that interns as adult learners set their own agendas.
6. Division of labor between university and school staff so that each provides the kinds of knowledge which they are best placed to provide.

McIntyre and Hagger (1992, p. 270) emphasize that their model was developed in contrast to three other models. It contrasts the theory-into-practice model because it does not start from theory or practice alone. It contrasts the apprenticeship model because "although the wisdom of experienced teachers is viewed as very valuable," it is viewed as only one source for promoting the students' professional development. Finally, the Oxford Internship Model contrasts the classical model of inservice training, which views teachers in deficit terms. A characteristic of the Oxford program is that

> It is interns' own prior experiences and commitments, their own felt needs, their own aspirations and their own understandings which determine the things they attempt to learn and the problems which they seek to resolve. (McIntyre & Hagger, 1992, p. 267)

This principle is also basic to the realistic approach and the very same differences with the three other models mentioned are also characteristic for the realistic model.

The Oxford Internship Scheme divides the learning processes of student teachers into two distinct phases (McIntyre, 1995, p. 376; McIntyre & Hagger, 1992, p. 269). The first aims at interns' attainment of the basic classroom competence necessary for certification, the second at the development of competencies necessary to be self-evaluating and self-developing teachers. These two aims are also similar to the basic goals of the realistic approach, namely, the development of a starting competence and a growth competence. A difference is that the realistic approach does not connect these two aims to separate phases. For example, right from the start of the realistic program at the IVLOS Institute of Education, the development of the reflection competence receives attention.

Principle 2 of the Oxford Model shows another difference: In the IVLOS program, the student teachers change schools after half a year. In this way, students get a broader view of education. If they stay at the same school, then they often develop the idea that secondary education equates the education at that school. Also, if they have experienced severe discipline problems in the first semester, then it is hard to change a negative pattern in the relation with classes without a change of context. More positively stated, we found that a change of practicum school gives student teachers the opportunity to make a fresh start, and it helps them to break such negative patterns.

5.10. LOOKING AHEAD: THE NEXT STEPS IN ELABORATING THE PEDAGOGY OF REALISTIC TEACHER EDUCATION

We have now laid the foundation of the pedagogy of realistic teacher education. Before diving more deeply into the elaboration of this pedagogy, it may be important to look more closely at the successes and problems in teacher education programs based on the principles of realistic teacher education, and especially at possible obstructions to student teachers' learning. For example, how do you deal with student teachers who do not seem to be reflective, those who wish to get specific guidelines and concrete help from the teacher educator, and who hate attempts to get them to reflect on their experiences themselves? These issues will be discussed in chapter 6. It may have become clear that, besides the organizational aspects described in section 5.6, there are at least two important settings in which careful elaboration of the pedagogy of realistic teacher education is necessary: Individual supervision of student teachers and group meetings at the teacher education institute are the two most frequently occurring situations in which teacher educators work with student teachers.

When looking at the first setting, it quickly becomes clear that teacher educators wanting to stimulate student teachers' learning from experience in supervisory conferences need a rich interpersonal repertoire. First of all, they must be able to ensure a safe climate. Phase 2 of the ALACT model for reflection (looking back) asks for acceptance, empathy, genuineness, and concreteness. To be able to help student teachers become aware of essential aspects (Phase 3), the supervisor needs additional, more directive skills such as the skill of confrontation. Phase 4 requires the skill to help create alternative methods of action. Such interventions, helpful for promoting reflection in supervisory conferences, deserve our extensive attention. Chapter 7 is completely devoted to it.

In order to promote reflection in individual student teachers, it may be helpful for teacher educators to know more about the characteristics of reflective student teachers. This will be the focus of chapter 8.

Teacher educators not only work with student teachers on an individual basis. Much work is done in group seminars. In this context, a central question is: How can the teacher educator promote reflection on experiences when working with groups of student teachers? For many teacher educators, this is an even more difficult situation than individual supervision. Often the context of group meetings triggers the tendency to lecture instead of to facilitate reflection in the students. Again, we are faced with a problem of educational change: In their own education, educators seldom saw good examples of how one can promote reflection in group meetings. Thus, this issue of working with groups in teacher education seminars needs extensive attention in this book. It is the focus of chapter 9.

Thus, the next four chapters elaborate on the pedagogy of realistic teacher education. After that, in chapters 10 and beyond, the discussion will be refined and deepened.

SUMMARY

Pressure to change often prevents change (the paradox of change), as concerns about survival play an important role in change processes. A student teacher's learning will be more effective when directed by an internal need, when rooted in the student teacher's own experiences, and when the student teacher reflects on those experiences in detail. Teacher educators should help create these conditions, geared to student teachers' personal learning paths, their preconceptions, needs for safety, and learning resistances. The one-to-one student teaching experience is a vehicle to start a process in which the student teacher can, within a safe and not too complex a context, develop practical skills and a reflection competence.

Important features of a realistic teacher education program are a balance between safety and challenge, the planning of experiences in balance with the students' individual long-term learning processes and with programmatic lines, strong relations between the schools and the teacher education institute, integration of theory and practice and of several academic disciplines, and staff development. These features resemble those of the Oxford Internship Model.

It is possible to combine the emphasis on experiential and concern-based learning with quality norms and a standard list of competencies, as long as the students get considerable responsibility for their own learning and their own assessment (e.g., through the use of portfolios). In this context, peers can play a valuable role.

Staff development should also follow a realistic approach (the congruence principle). There is another important congruence: Realistic teacher education prepares teachers for realistic education in schools.

BASIC CONCEPTS

Concerns about survival

The paradox of change

Learning needs

Learning resistances

The one-to-one arrangement

Balance between safety and challenge

Balance between individual long-term learning processes and programmatic lines

Generating concerns

Peer-supported learning
Relations between schools and the teacher education institute
Integrated program
Professional development of staff
Portfolios

6 Evaluative Research on the Realistic Approach and on the Promotion of Reflection

Fred Korthagen and Theo Wubbels

Lack of precision has been a source of embarrassment for the social sciences. It should not be. Paradoxically, physics is called a "hard" science because it restricts itself to the easy problems for which currently available mathematical tools are effective. Psychology, on the other hand, is called a "soft" science because it deals with reality on a level of complexity at which problems are difficult because sharp analytic tools have not yet been—and may never be—developed. It is the physicist, rather than the psychologist, who should feel uncomfortable about this division of labor.

—*Alwyn Scott (1995, p. 179)*

In this chapter we look at research studies assessing the effects of the realistic approach and, more specifically, at evaluative studies on the effects of promoting reflection in teacher education. After discussing the remarkable fact that the latter type of research is relatively scarce, we analyze the reasons for this phenomenon. Then we look at the research on the effects of promoting reflection that does exist, focusing especially on our own work in this area. One of the main conclusions is that the principle of promoting reflection does have important effects, particularly in the long run, but more attention is needed for differences between student teachers that do and those that do not already possess a reflective attitude. We also put forward some suggestions for further research and development in this area.

6.1. INTRODUCTION

Now that we have laid the foundations for the realistic approach, it is time to pose the question of what we know about the effectiveness of this new pedagogy of teacher education. There are some interesting and informative studies that address this question. These are discussed in section 6.2. However, due to the fact that the realistic approach is relatively new, evaluative studies on this approach are rather limited in number. We can also look for studies showing the effectiveness of a central principle in the realistic approach: the promotion of reflection in student teachers on their teaching experiences. Since the beginning of the 1980s, this principle has been adopted by almost all teacher educators, all over the world. However, one of the almost shocking discoveries one can do when starting to screen the international literature on the issue of promoting reflection is that there is very little research on the effectiveness of teacher education programs aiming at the promotion of reflection.

Moreover, even if we assume that promoting reflection is effective, one may well ask: effective toward what end? We are now entering an area populated more by beliefs and convictions than by proofs and empirical results. Zeichner's (1987) overview showed that the empirical data on the effects of programs and strategies designed to promote reflection were somewhat meager, and this situation has not changed very much. Many studies rely heavily on comments made by student teachers during course evaluations, as well as on self-reports, general observations, and isolated anecdotes.

In section 6.3, we will analyze the causes of this lack of sound research. In section 6.4, we will discuss a few exceptions: research studies that went a step further. In that section, we will mention some studies carried out by other researchers. In section 6.5, we will describe our own research on the promotion of reflection. In section 6.6, we will draw conclusions and put forward some suggestions for further research.

6.2. EVALUATIVE STUDIES ON THE REALISTIC APPROACH

We start by looking at a small number of studies on the effectiveness of the realistic approach. These studies have been carried out in the context of the IVLOS program at Utrecht University. During the late 1980s and the 1990s, this program, preparing student teachers for secondary education has developed more toward the approach described in the previous chapters.

A national evaluation study carried out by an external research office (Research voor Beleid; Luijten, Marinus, & Bal, 1995; and Samson & Luijten, 1996) of all Dutch teacher education programs preparing for secondary education has shown that 71% of a sample of graduates of the IVLOS program ($n = 81$) scored their professional preparation as good or very good (the two highest scores on a 5-point scale). This is a remarkable result, because in the total sample of graduates from all Dutch teacher education programs preparing for secondary education ($n = 5{,}135$) this percentage was only 41% ($p < .001$).

A fundamental question is: Does the realistic approach indeed reduce the gap between theory and practice? Several studies focused on this more specific question. In 1991, an evaluative overall study among all graduates of the Utrecht University program between 1987 and 1991 showed that 86% of the respondents considered their preparation program as relevant or highly relevant to their present work as a teacher (Koetsier, Wubbels, & Korthagen, 1997). Hermans, Créton, and

Korthagen (1993) illustrate this finding with more qualitative data of an experiment with a group of 12 student teachers strictly incorporating all the principles mentioned in chapter 5. All 12 student teachers reported a seamless connection between theory and practice, a noteworthy result, given the many research reports from all over the world showing the problematic relation between theory and practice. Some quotes from student teachers' evaluations are:

> "The integration theory/practice to my mind was perfect."
>
> "Come to think of it, I have seen and/or used all of the theory in practice."
>
> "The things dealt with in the course are always apparent in school practice."

Brouwer (1989) did an extensive study into the relation between program design and effects of 24 teacher education curricula (related to 12 different school subjects) in use at Utrecht University during the 1980s (i.e., the years in which the realistic approach started to develop). At various moments during these programs and during the first 2 years in which the graduates worked as teachers, quantitative and qualitative data were collected among 357 student teachers, 31 teacher educators, and 128 cooperating teachers. Concrete learning effects on the work of the graduates during their first year in the profession (measured by means of 14 criterion variables) appeared to depend primarily on the degree to which theoretical elements in their preparation program were perceived by the student teachers as functional for practice at the time of their student teaching, and on the cyclical alternation between school-based and university-based periods in the program, Also, a gradual increase in the complexity of activities and demands on the student teachers appeared to be a crucial factor in integrating theory and practice.

Another fundamental question is whether the professional community would consider the knowledge base offered to the student teachers at the IVLOS Institute of Education to be sufficient. Some valuable indications may be derived from two external evaluations, in 1992 and 1997, by two official committees of experts in teacher education, researchers and representatives of secondary education, instituted by the Association of Dutch Universities (VSNU). The IVLOS program received very positive assessments. For example, in 1997, the program scored "good to excellent" on 25 of 34 criterion variables, including the following important criteria: completeness and clarity of the program goals, the degree to which these goals are reached, value of program content, and professional quality of the graduates. On the other nine criteria, it received the assessment "sufficient." No other Dutch university teacher education program received such high scores.

Although the number of evaluative studies on the realistic approach is still small, we can conclude that at least there are some interesting empirically based indications that the realistic approach indeed diminishes the gap between theory and practice. Another question is whether the most important ingredient of the realistic approach—namely, the promotion of reflection on practice—is indeed a helpful ingredient. And if it is, to what purpose?

6.3. THE PROBLEM OF OPERATIONALIZING REFLECTION

A major problem in research on the effects of promoting reflection is the question of how to operationalize reflection. In chapter 4, we saw that there are many different conceptualizations of reflection. One issue on which these differ is the question of what educational aspects are worthy of reflection. As discussed in section 4.5, this question is directly related to the question of what constitutes good teaching (see also Korthagen & Wubbels, 1995). We will give an example in connection with the conceptualizations mentioned in section 4.3.

In the approach that views reflection as critical inquiry, advocated by such authors as Zeichner (1983) and Carr and Kemmis (1986), a good teacher is a critical, inquiring professional. This view is linked to a specific view of the aims of education in schools (i.e., to make students critical, responsible citizens). In a study into the quality of supervisory discourse, this view made Zeichner and Liston (1985) operationalize reflection in terms of the degree to which the critical dimension was present in the discourse (see section 6.4). It will be clear that researchers who emphasize other elements of "good teaching" will come to other operationalizations. However, if one sees good teaching as helping students to reach optimal results on tests, a completely different operationalization of reflection presents itself. Probably one would then describe reflection in terms of the degree to which the teacher systematically thinks about methods to achieve high test scores.

Perhaps the biggest problem with evaluative research in this field is that such underlying philosophies of education are seldom made explicit, which makes any claim about effects of promoting reflection questionable or at least unclear. What is needed are coherent theories in which the relation between effects of the promotion of reflection and views of good teaching are made explicit.

Another fundamental problem in researching reflection is that much of what we are attempting to measure takes place in the teacher's head. Although techniques such as stimulated recall (e.g., based on recordings of teaching activities), the analysis of supervisory discourse, or logbooks may be helpful, there is always a question concerning whether these approaches present us with valid data about what really happened inside the person. (For a further discussion of this problem, see also chapter 10.)

Now that we know how difficult any study into the promotion of reflection is, we will look at several attempts to do evaluative research in this area.

6.4. EMPIRICAL DATA ON EFFECTS OF PROGRAMS AND STRATEGIES DESIGNED TO PROMOTE REFLECTION

Zeichner and Liston (1987) discuss two studies carried out at the University of Wisconsin, which evaluated the effects on student teachers' perspectives toward teaching of a program based on the principle of promoting reflection. They conclude that the program had little effect on those perspectives. On the other hand, given the frequently noted shift from an initially humanistic orientation of student teachers to a more custodial one, "it could be argued that both Wisconsin studies indicate that the inquiry-oriented student teaching program stems the onrushing move toward a more custodial view" (Zeichner & Liston, 1987, p. 36).

Another set of studies on the results of the Wisconsin program emphasized the supervisory aspect. Zeichner and Tabachnick (1982) analyzed the various ways in which supervisors gave meaning to their work with student teachers. Of nine supervisors, only three employed a technical-instrumental approach. Given the conventional emphasis on a technical orientation in supervision, the authors feel this is a positive finding, suggesting a move toward the program's reflective orientation. Zeichner and Liston (1985) assessed the degree to which the reflective orientation was present in postobservation supervisory conferences. They used a so-called *reflective teaching index* based on the degree to which different types of discourse occur (see also section 4.4): factual (what occurred in a teaching situation or what will occur), prudential (suggestions or evaluations), justificatory (reasons for choices), and critical (the assessment of the adequacy of justifications for pedagogical activities, and the examination of values and assumptions embedded in the curriculum and instructional activities). They found that almost 20% of the time represented attention to the latter type of communication, and the conceptual levels of student teachers affected the degree of reflective discourse taking place during the conferences. The authors consider these findings an indication of a partial implementation of the program's goals.

Koskela (1985; referred to by Zeichner & Liston, 1987) studied the reflective communication in two student-teaching seminar groups in the Wisconsin program. She describes an interesting example of the way student teachers' reflections and concerns about their schools and classrooms can trigger discussions among teachers in the school about curricular policies and practices.

Considering these studies as a body, there is some evidence that the Wisconsin teacher education program was successful in attaining at least some of its goals; in particular, it seemed to help student teachers to view the student-teaching context with a more critical eye, and make them more reflective about their own role as teachers (Zeichner & Liston, 1987, p. 40). On the other hand, Zeichner and Liston also refer to research that showed the program did not succeed in its goal of promoting student teachers to act collaboratively within small groups on issues of authority and autonomy, and certain views of teachers as moral craftpersons were not implemented.

During the mid-1980s a 5-year preparation program was started at the University of Florida, based on Ross' notion of reflection (see section 4.3). Attempts have been made to investigate the developmental processes of preservice teachers in this program (e.g., Weade & Ernst, 1989), and the effects of program elements on these students (e.g., Krogh & Crews, 1989). The results emphasize such factors as the role played by student teachers' and teacher educators' beliefs and philosophies of education, which have their roots in the personal history of the individual, the influence of the school context, in particular the degree of support forthcoming from the schools with regard to the goal of promoting reflection (Kilgore, Zbikowski, & D. Ross, 1989), the need for structure in logbook writing (Krogh & Crews, 1989), and the danger that a high degree of reflectivity can lead to self-criticism and a low sense of efficacy (Ashton, Comas, & D. Ross, 1989).

The research carried out by Hatton and Smith (1995) was already mentioned several times in chapter 4. They showed that in a 4-year teacher education program at the University of Sydney, the student teachers clearly showed evidence of reflection in their final year. The most frequently occurring type of reflection in their journals was descriptive reflection, but instances of dialogic and critical reflection were also found (see section 4.4 for an explanation of these terms). Hatton and Smith noted that dialogic reflection was highly promoted through "critical friends" interviews.

6.5. RESEARCH ON A DUTCH PROGRAM BASED ON THE GOAL OF PROMOTING REFLECTION

In this section we describe our own studies into a Dutch program for the preparation of reflective secondary school mathematics teachers. This program was in operation in Utrecht, the Netherlands, from the 1970s until the mid-1980s, at a teacher education college called SOL (a Dutch abbreviation meaning "foundation for teacher education"). At the time of the research studies, it was a 4½-year program in which student teachers selected a second subject, in addition to mathematics. An aggregate of 1 year, distributed over the 4½-year period, was devoted to the professional preparation, which was strongly integrated with the subject matter component of the program.

First, in line with our standpoint described in section 6.3, we present the view of good teaching underlying this program and the view of reflection the program was based on, and then the design and results of some research studies into this program.

The View of Good Teaching and Reflection Underlying the Program

We have reconstructed the views of the staff of the mathematics department (during the period in question consisting of 10 to 13 teacher educators), focusing on secondary education (mathematics) and teacher education. For purposes of this reconstruction, we made use of document analysis (there were a great many formal and informal papers available, written by staff members), and interviews with members of staff. A verification of this reconstruction was carried out by means of a study among graduates of the SOL program, who were asked to give the characteristics of their preparation program (Korthagen, 1982). Moreover, the reconstruction of the views of the staff was translated into a questionnaire consisting of 46 statements, which were scored by the teacher educators on a 5-point scale. These checks resulted in a confirmation of the conclusions that had been drawn (Korthagen, 1988). The results of the reconstruction are described in Korthagen (1982, 1985). We will now summarize the answers to two questions: What was the staff's view on "good teaching," and what role does reflection play in that view?

The replies given by the individual staff members to these questions were strongly influenced by the context of Dutch secondary school mathematics education, which in the 1970s saw a surge in the direction of realistic mathematics education (as described in section 1.7). This entails the use of concrete problems and real-world contexts. Students are taught to translate a problem from reality into a mathematical model, to apply mathematical techniques within that model, and then to translate the mathematical solution into the best possible solution in the real world. Students are thus required to analyze, to distinguish between matters of major and minor importance, to structure, to combine theory and practice, and to devise creative alternative solutions and methods of problem solving. Collaborative learning and metacognitive strategies are of prime importance here, and are given explicit consideration. (For more details of this development toward realistic mathematics education, see Freudenthal, 1991, and Treffers, 1987).

This process-oriented view of mathematics education was not without its influence on the thinking of the teacher educators in the SOL mathematics department. In retrospect, we can say that their outlook was characterized by the following statements:

1. Good education is *learning oriented*: It focuses on the learning process of the student; the teacher is the facilitator of that process.
2. One of the main tasks of the teacher is to present *real and concrete problems*, which the student then approaches by means of *analysis*, *structuring*, and the *testing of alternative solutions*.
3. Education should devote considerable attention to *problem-solving*, *collaborative learning*, *metacognitive strategies*, and *learning how to learn*.
4. The ultimate goal of good teaching is the promotion of *conscious and strategic learning* and *problem solving*.
5. The process toward more independent learning by the student requires a *strategy of gradualness* in which the student is given more responsibility for the learning process.
6. The relationship between the teacher and the student is a *helping and cooperative relationship* in which the teacher offers a climate of *security* and *challenge*, and only as much *structure* as each individual student needs.
7. Teachers should be able to *analyze and develop their interpersonal relationships* with the students, with a view to attaining the ideal helping and cooperative relationship.
8. Teachers should be capable of committing themselves purposefully, consciously, and methodically as an *instrument* in the teaching and learning situation.

9. Teachers should themselves be able to *deal with mathematics in a conscious and systematic way.*
10. Teachers should be aware of *contextual influences* on their interpersonal relationships with the students, especially the influence of the school context.
11. Teachers should be conscious of their *own strong and weak points*, and *direct their own development* in the direction of the 10 principles formulated earlier.

It will be clear from these 11 principles that the fostering of a reflective attitude and the promotion of the ability to analyze, to structure, and to devise creative solutions were among the basic educational goals both for students in mathematics classrooms in secondary education and for prospective teachers. As regards the student teachers, these goals were pursued not only in the mathematics component, but also in the professional preparation component of the program. The aim was to produce student teachers ultimately capable of independently using the ALACT model (Fig. 3.2). The process described by means of this model may be seen as the SOL conception of the process of reflection. The crux of this process lies in Phase 3 of the model, where a mental structure is formed, or an existing mental structure altered. (Compare the definition of reflection introduced in section 4.5.)

Thus, in the view of the SOL teacher educators, reflective teachers are capable of tracing the ALACT cycle for all aspects of the teaching and learning situation, but focusing on reflection on mathematical situations, interpersonal relationships in the classroom, and on their own development as a teacher. During the preparation program, student teachers should develop a reflective attitude, thus fostering a growth competence.

Program Content

The emphasis in the program was on systematic reflection about one's thoughts, feelings, attitudes, and actions in everyday teaching situations. The final goal was that the student teachers learned to reflect without the help of the supervising teacher educators and to make use of external feedback from students or other teachers, adjusting where necessary their own subjective view of reality. An important program characteristic was that the student teachers learned to reflect before embarking on student teaching. The first period of student teaching can be one of extreme stress in which the prime concern is simply to "get through." This is not an auspicious moment for learning the art of reflection. The idea was that prospective teachers must already have at their disposal sufficient powers of reflection to enable them to evaluate the influence of such personal concerns on the way they themselves function in the classroom (cf. Goodman, 1985). This means that in the first year of the program, other experiences were used for reflection. First of all, there was a special practicum in which the student teachers learned to reflect on their own thoughts, feelings, attitudes, and actions in everyday relationships with their fellow students. This practicum also contained exercises aiming at the promotion of social skills, such as empathy, expressing feelings, and so on.

The mathematical and the professional components of the program were closely linked. The processes involved in learning the mathematical content in the program were also used as objects of reflection. The student teachers were encouraged to reflect both on the subject content and on the way they helped or cooperated with their fellow students. At regular intervals, the students were asked to hand in written reports on the way they worked on a particular mathematical problem. In this way, not only the mathematical product was stressed, but also the mathematical inquiry process. At secondary school, students are often given the impression that the important thing in solving mathematical problems is to produce the right answer. It is for this reason that the teacher educators preferred problems to which more than one solution is possible, or for which no cut-and-dried solution exists. This makes it more interesting to compare solutions and the ways in which the various students tried to tackle the problem. As regards the student teachers' reflection on their working and learning methods, the program did away with the idea that mathematics is primarily a mental exercise. Feelings and attitudes quite naturally come to the fore in such aspects as the fun of problem solving, an aversion to a particular problem, the experience of sinking one's teeth into a problem, the pleasure of working together, and the excitement when something finally "dawns." The student teachers were asked to reflect on such aspects. It is extremely important for prospective teachers to recognize the significance of the more emotional aspects of the learning process.

Throughout the program, there were several points at which the student teachers were allowed a choice. On the pedagogical side, for instance, they had a say in the general curriculum, and in the mathematics courses they were often given a choice of materials. There is a close link between learning to reflect and learning to choose: Pondering past or future choices compels the prospective teachers to reflect on their own goals and attitudes. Individual interviews and the students' logbooks, to which the supervisors would add their comments, encouraged the student teachers to reflect on the various choices open to them, and helped them to develop their own style of teaching.

It was not until the second year that student teachers actually became involved in practical teaching. The first stage was helping individual secondary school students (a one-to-one arrangement similar to the arrangement described in section 5.5). This eliminated the problem of controlling a whole class and gave the student teachers enough safety to devote their full attention to individual learning processes and pedagogy. Here, too, the use of the logbook and college-based supervision were important in stimulating reflection.

The first classroom experience took place at the end of the second year. A primary school class (11- to 12-year-olds) was divided into three (or two) groups. During a period of 6 weeks, each student teacher worked with his or her own group of approximately eight children from 1 to 1½ hours a week. The cooperating teacher was not present. The group of two or three student teachers teaching children from the same class was supervised by a teacher educator. This supervision was based on the students' logbooks and the supervisor did not visit the school, which means the student teachers were given a large measure of freedom and responsibility. This helps the prospective teachers to find their own personal style of teaching and, more important, it stimulates reflection on personal style and growth. In the third and fourth years, the student teachers worked with whole classes at the secondary school level and were supervised by cooperating teachers. To provide effective supervision, these teachers were trained in specific helping skills, the most important being the ability to set aside their personal beliefs about teaching and to help the student teachers to develop their own beliefs.

Four Research Studies

We carried out four research studies within the framework of the program already described. These will be discussed in brief in the present section.

Study 1: An Overall Evaluation. The first study (1982) was set up as an initial overall evaluation of the program. It consisted of a written survey of 116 graduates of the SOL and 13 student teachers on the point of graduating, supplemented by interviews with 10 of them. The most important questions in the questionnaire were: What have you learned during your teacher education period? What do think was lacking in your teacher education program? (For details of this study, see Korthagen, 1982, 1985.)

On the first question, more than half of the respondents spontaneously mentioned learning results in the field of reflective teaching and directing one's own development. However, many teachers, especially those working in lower vocational schools, reported difficulties in controlling the class and in handling motivation problems.

An important research finding was that the respondents differed in their appreciation of a reflective way of learning. We called the reflective ones *internally oriented* student teachers. These are students wanting to use their own knowledge and values to structure problems and experiences themselves. (Note that this is in accordance with our definition of reflection; see section 4.5.) *Externally oriented* student teachers ask for guidelines and structuring from outside (e.g., from the teacher educators).

Study 2: A Longitudinal Study. The phenomenon of internally and externally oriented student teachers prompted our decision to carry out a second study, this time with a longitudinal design. This study was initiated in 1984. We followed a group of 18 students during their teacher preparation, using questionnaires, interviews, and video recordings of supervisory conferences. In addition, we regularly interviewed their teacher educators and asked them to fill out questionnaires about the student teachers. (For more details of this study, see Korthagen & Verkuyl, 1987, and Korthagen, 1988.) This study again brought to light a difference between internally and externally oriented student teachers. To illustrate this difference, we will give some examples of statements by respondents, taken from Studies 1 and 2.

The respondents with an internal learning orientation made the following statements when asked what they had learned during their training:

- I have learned to reflect on my teaching. I think this is important because I think it can be helpful when I am teaching on my own. How can I correct myself? What did I do well? What did I do wrong? Why? I think that the ability to do this can be important in difficult classroom situations.
- I have learned to learn, as best I can, from my experiences.
- I have learned to look at my mistakes and to improve myself.
- I have discovered that it helps, and that it is necessary to keep asking myself why I do things in a certain way.
- I have learned to evaluate myself.
- I think the most important thing I've learned is to look at myself, to solve problems by myself, or at least to work out the first steps toward solving a problem.
- I have learned to act self-reflectively, to regularly look back on the way I function as a teacher, and to attach to these actions both conclusions and guidelines for the future.

Externally oriented respondents made the following statements on the program:

- There are too many things you have to find out for yourself.
- It should be clearer what you are supposed to learn, when something is good enough, what is right and what is wrong.
- Those teacher educators are always asking questions.
- You have to keep telling them what your opinion is, and what you are thinking or feeling.
- Too much has to come from the group, and there is not enough explanation.
- There is no structure.
- I would rather have had a course with the ordinary things you come across every day, like refusing to work, cribbing, and cutting classes.
- How do you deal with situations that have to do with a lack of motivation on the part of the students?

The study revealed that, in some cases, there was a "clash" between the implicit conceptions of learning on the part of the teacher educators (strongly based on the notion of reflection) and the learning orientations of the student teachers. One danger in a teacher education program based on the goal of promoting reflection is that it is most beneficial to those who are already fairly reflective (internally oriented) (cf. Calderhead, 1989, and LaBoskey, 1990).

The longitudinal study showed that after 1 $^1/_2$ years, most of the externally oriented student teachers in the research group of 18 had left the program. Although this was often due to poor results in mathematics, a major motive for the decision to drop out appeared to be the lack of desired structure (Korthagen, 1988). Of the 18 student teachers in the group, 8 gave up their studies before the end of the second year. It is likely that some of these students would have benefited from an even more gradual introduction to the reflective approach than the teacher education staff already used.

Study 3: The IEO Test. After distinguishing between internally and externally oriented student teachers, we devised a questionnaire to measure these learning orientations of teachers and prospective teachers. It is known as the IEO test for internal/external orientation (Korthagen, 1988, 1993a). There are two versions of this test: one designed for student teachers in the initial stage of the preparation program, and the other intended for teachers or student teachers who have already done some classroom teaching.

Version 1 consists of six subscales, concerned with internal (I) and external (E) learning orientations in the following domains: (S) the prospective teacher him- or herself, (F) the fellow students, and (M) the subject matter in the program (mathematics). (See Table 6.1.) A pilot study had revealed that the learning orientations of student teachers may differ in these domains (see Korthagen & Verkuyl, 1987, for more information).

Version 2 of the IEO test (for teachers or student teachers with teaching experience) consists of eight subscales, namely, two scales (for the degree of internal orientation and the degree of external orientation) for each of the following domains: (S) the teacher himself or herself, (P) the students in the school, (M) the subject matter at school (mathematics), and (C) the school context. In both versions of the IEO, test items are scored by the student teachers on a 5-point scale (ranging from 1 = "strong disagreement" to 5 = "strong agreement").

Version 1 of the test was administered to 138 first- and second-year mathematics students in the SOL program and in two other colleges of teacher education. (For more details of this study, e.g., the use of two different types of items, see Korthagen, 1993a. The main conclusions are summarized here.)

The reliability of the 6 subscales was reasonable (Table 6.2). Fewer than 1% of the interitem correlations was over .70, and the highest was .76. We may conclude from this that the IEO test is a reliable instrument. However, a recognized disadvantage of this type of questionnaire is the fact that there may be a discrepancy between what someone writes down and his or her actual preferences.

We used the IEO test to determine whether the SOL mathematics students did indeed acquire a more pronounced internal learning orientation in the course of

TABLE 6.1

Three Representative Items from Each Scale of the IEO Test (Version 1), Translated from Dutch

No.	*Item*	*Scale*	*Type*	*M*	*SD*
47	I ask myself "Who am I?"	SI	b	3.23	1.26
57	I think about my own development.	SI	b	3.33	1.15
60	I reflect on myself.	SI	b	3.60	1.10
18	I appreciate it when people tell me how I can improve my conduct.	SE	a	3.81	0.88
31	I want people to tell me what I am doing wrong.	SE	a	3.75	0.95
40	I like it when others comment on my conduct.	SE	a	3.55	0.89
25	I am interested in my fellow students.	FI	a	3.64	0.89
42	I try to get to know my fellow students	FI	a	3.53	0.90
54	I am interested in the problems of my fellow students.	FI	b	2.72	0.98
33	I am interested in tips on the best way of working with my fellow students.	FE	a	3.23	0.95
35	I consider it important to receive information from a supervisor about my way of dealing with my fellow students.	FE	a	2.92	1.09
43	I think it is important to be given suggestions for better ways of co-operating with my fellow students.	FE	a	3.17	1.00
30	I can spend hours working out a mathematical problem.	MI	a	3.29	1.42
51	I try to solve mathematical puzzles in my spare time.	MI	b	2.53	1.12
53	I sometimes go on thinking about mathematical problems that have come up.	MI	b	3.12	0.97
4	I like to have the support of others when I am working on mathematical problems.	ME	a	3.65	1.02
26	I like to work on mathematical textbooks in which everything is explained step by step.	ME	a	3.64	1.16
32	I like it when someone shows me how to solve a certain type of problem.	ME	a	3.56	1.00

TABLE 6.2
Reliabilities of the IEO Scales ($n = 138$)

	Scales					
	SI	*SE*	*FI*	*FE*	*MI*	*ME*
Number of items	11	10	10	10	10	10
Cronbach's alpha	.87	.77	.87	.81	.85	.80

their studies. By means of a *t* test, we compared the SI, FI, and MI scores of the 37 SOL students majoring in mathematics with those of 55 students of the other two colleges also majoring in mathematics. The choice of mathematics majors is important here, because at the SOL, it was only the majors who were taught according to the principle of promoting reflection. This was not an explicit goal in the mathematics department of the two other colleges.

SOL students did not score significantly higher on the three internal scales than the students of the other teacher colleges. It is important to note that the group studied consisted of first- and second-year students. Any results of the promotion of reflection may be expected to be realized gradually. It was for this reason that we also compared the scores of first- and second-year SOL students on the internal scales. No significant differences were recorded on the FI and MI scales, but on the SI scale (reflection on self), second-year students scored significantly higher than first-year students ($p = .02$, on a one-tailed *t* test). However, second-year students of the other colleges also scored significantly higher on SI than first-year students, although the difference was somewhat less marked (Table 6.3).

We also used this study to determine how the extent to which student teachers are internally or externally oriented in the domains "self," "fellow students," and "mathematics" is correlated to the variables age, previous schooling, and gender. Older students appeared to be less inclined to reflect on their relationships with their fellow students ($r = -.29, p = .01$). We found a tendency of student teachers with a relatively high level of previous schooling to be less externally oriented with regard to the teaching of mathematics ($p = .02$). These results are in accordance with the established fact that as one approaches adulthood, the peer group becomes less important, and the fact that in pre-university, higher vocational, and higher general education, students are expected to be capable of studying on their own. It was noteworthy that there proved to be almost no relationship between age and an internal learning orientation with regard to oneself ($r = -.03$).

It was also interesting to note that women scored significantly higher than men on the FI scale ($p = .02$) and significantly lower on the MI scale ($p = .05$). Apparently, prospective women teachers say they are inclined to reflect more on their relationships with their fellow students than do their male counterparts, and they are less inclined to solve mathematical problems on their own. In other words, in their learning, women seem to be more socially oriented. This finding is in line with research results in the field of gender differences in general. Miller (1976), for in-

TABLE 6.3

Scores of First-and Second-Year Student Teachers Majoring in Mathematics

		First Year		*Second Year*			*P*
		n	M	n	M	t	(1-tailed)
All students	SOL	26	3.32	11	3.82	2.04	.02
	Other colleges	18	3.20	37	3.56	1.74	.04
Men	SOL	13	3.32	8	3.80	1.47	.08
	Other colleges	12	3.18	23	3.46	1.00	.16
Women	SOL	12	3.30	3	3.85	1.31	.11
	Other colleges	5	3.44	14	3.73	0.98	.17

Note. A number of subtotals do not tally, due to missing data.

stance, mentions females' greater concern with social harmony and smooth interpersonal relationships (their greater "social orientation"). The significantly lower MI score (and a nearly significantly higher ME score) could be explained by the often heard expectation that women have lower self-esteem than men, which could mean that the differences on MI (and ME) are due to the self-report technique used. However, Maccoby and Jacklin (1975), in their thorough overview of research on this subject, found almost no gender differences in self-esteem. Other explanations could be that females are supposed to be more willing to disclose their weaknesses than males (Van der Meulen, 1987), emphasize academic achievement less than males (Flaherty & Dusek, 1980), or are generally more sensitive to evaluative feedback (Roberts & Nolen-Hoeksema, 1989). These explanations support the hypothesis that we should devote more attention to the preference of prospective women teachers for external guidance in the learning of subject matter. Here one must be careful to avoid gender role stereotyping. Long-term strategies should be used in the development of learning conceptions and learning orientations to counteract gender differences. Eccles (1985) points out that girls' good grades in mathematics are often attributed to hard work, whereas boys' good results are credited to talent and an interest in the subject. Teachers can be influential in establishing views among children about the effect of talent on results. This could be a major factor in building up student confidence in the effect of internal direction in learning, something that is not only important for girls.

Study 4: A Comparison of the Effects of Two Teacher Education Programs. Finally, a fourth study was carried out in which graduates of the SOL program were compared with graduates of another, more subject matter oriented program (Wubbels & Korthagen, 1990). The graduates of the SOL program (n = 37) and of the other program (n = 36) had been teaching between 1 and 10 years. They were compared with regard to their reflective attitude, using the IEO test (the internal scales of the second version), their inclination toward innovation, their job satisfaction (both of these measured by means of a teacher questionnaire), the quality of the interpersonal relationships with the students in their classes as measured through these students' perceptions, and the adequacy of the teachers' perceptions of these relationships as measured by determining the difference between the students' and the teacher's perception of those relationships. This study demonstrated no clear evidence of effects of the program on teachers' reflective attitude and inclination toward innovation.

Although this is perhaps partly due to the already mentioned problem of finding an adequate operationalization of reflection, this result is of course somewhat disappointing, given the close relation between these variables and the program goals. On the other hand, a noteworthy result was that graduates of this program performed better on several variables—quality of interpersonal relationships, adequacy of perception of these relationships, and job satisfaction—than graduates from a more conventional program, based primarily on subject matter knowledge, and these effects were significant for those teachers who graduated more than 2 years before. This seems to support the idea that the effect of a program designed to promote reflection will mainly surface in the long run, an idea that has also been put forward by other authors, for instance, Zeichner (1987, p. 573) and Zeichner and Liston (1987, p. 36). Study 1 showed that even teachers who acquired a strong inclination toward reflection during the preparation program did not benefit much from this attitude during the initial period of their teaching careers. In an evaluation of the program 1 year after graduation, a teacher (already cited in section 3.1) not only stressed his learning results in the field of reflection, but also revealed:

> I had the experience that the capacity for reflection was pushed away when meeting a cumulation of conflicts. You feel empty. I no longer had any point of reference. And this happened although everything went very well during teacher preparation and during field-based experiences.... But the ability to face problems returns. I am growing again. I just stood still for a while.

This example is similar to other stories reported by the graduates of the SOL program. Korthagen (1982, 1985) considers this as an indication that the competency for reflective teaching tends to disappear during the first year of teaching. However, this competency seems to return after about half a year. It then served to enable the graduates of the Utrecht program to use their experiences, including those from the first difficult period, to make deliberate choices in behavior. Lost ideals then got a new chance as well, as many of the respondents reported. The results of Study 2 were in line with this finding: When the teachers in this longitudinal study were in their first year of teaching, they showed the same decrease in reflection about the relations between their ideals and everyday teaching practice, but at the same time they were very aware of this phenomenon. These graduates of the SOL program seemed to use a strategy of both temporary adjustment to established patterns of school practice and waiting for the moment they saw a chance to realize their "latent" ideals. On the basis of such results, we are inclined to assume that the ability to reflect tends to pass through a so-called *latency period* of about half a year.

As far as we know, the effects of the ability for reflection on teachers' development later in their careers have not yet been studied. However, based on the literature, the hypothesis can be inferred that this ability may counteract the phenomenon of teacher burn-out. For, as Schön (1983, p. 61) says, the more routine the activities of practitioners become, the more acute is the danger that they no longer think very much about what they are doing; ultimately, they will lapse into patterns of behavior that can no longer be corrected. One can assume that routine actions can easily lead to boredom and a feeling of being burned-out. The ability to reflect can help teachers to keep an interest in their work and to maintain a reasonable level of job satisfaction. As we noted in our description of Study 4, our findings seem to confirm this hypothesis.

6.6. CONCLUSIONS AND SUGGESTIONS FOR FUTURE RESEARCH AND DEVELOPMENT

When reflecting on the research described earlier, the following conclusions and possibilities for research and development present themselves.

Studies on the realistic approach as a whole are relatively scarce, but the few studies that have been carried out show that the gap between theory and practice is diminished and graduates of a realistic teacher education program are much more positive about their preparation for the profession than teachers generally are.

Our search for studies into the effects of an important ingredient of the realistic approach—namely, reflection—led to a disappointing discovery. The different conceptualizations of reflection and reflective teaching that researchers use are generally too vague to be used as the starting point for curriculum development in teacher education. Much clarification and elaboration of the concept of reflection in relation to underlying philosophies of education are needed. This will help us to move beyond vague discussions and beliefs about the benefits of teacher education programs designed to promote reflection, and instead, to build our theories on empirical data concerning the degree to which program goals are being reached. This requires not only careful operationalization of the concepts of reflection and reflective teaching, but also sophisticated research methods. This is no simple task, considering the fact that much of what we are attempting to influence takes place in the teacher's head. The few existing studies devoted to the effects of programs and strategies designed to promote reflection have produced some evidence of favorable influences on certain aspects of teachers' functioning; however, they also indicate that student teachers' learning conceptions and contextual influences on teacher education have a limiting effect on the potential of those programs.

In our view, effect studies should focus on the question of which program characteristics and program elements are responsible for which effects, and thus on the important practical question of which strategies employed in the preparation of more reflective teachers appear most promising. In order to assess relations between program characteristics and learning outcomes, we also need longitudinal studies focusing on the developmental processes of teachers, both during their preparation and after (cf. Wubbels & Korthagen, 1990; Zeichner, 1987). Such studies can throw more light on the hypothesis that the effects of programs aimed at promoting reflection may not be evident until after the first few years of teaching experience. In this kind of research, differences between individual student teachers, such as differences in learning orientations, should be taken into account.

We believe that contextual influences on teacher development should be an important issue in the research on reflective teaching (see also Wildman & Niles, 1987; Zeichner & Liston, 1987). It will be necessary to investigate ways of altering the context of student teaching, for instance, in so-called professional development schools (see section 1.6). This requires a kind of action research carried out by teams of teacher educators in collaboration with teachers and researchers. This type of research will be discussed in chapter 14.

An important conclusion of our own research studies on the promotion of reflection is that a more gradual approach to reflection may benefit more externally oriented students. It may be advisable in the initial stages to offer these students the external structure they prefer. We refer to this as a strategy of gradualness (also advocated by Hatton & Smith, 1995). Otherwise, the externally oriented students' feelings that they do not really benefit from their studies can become a self-fulfilling prophecy (see also Korthagen, 1988, and Korthagen & Verkuyl, 1987). The teacher educator can help externally oriented student teachers by not expecting them to be able to figure out everything for themselves right from the start, and by giving them concrete instructions, offering them choices, and providing sufficient feedback. The use of logbooks (to be discussed in chapter 11) provides opportunities to give student teachers individual feedback on their learning process; this may be especially helpful for externally oriented student teachers. "Make haste slowly" is the watchword here, because:

> An emphasis upon reflection too soon in their preparation may be alienating to neophytes. It can become difficult to sustain, for student teachers may see it as a rather esoteric and useless diversion from mastering the technical skills and content of teaching which they regard as essential, especially early in their training. (Hatton & Smith, 1995, p. 36)

Hatton and Smith (1995, p. 36) also point to the problem that reflection is not generally associated with working as a teacher:

> Teaching is often seen to be primarily about the immediate present and instant pragmatic action, while reflecting is perceived as a more academic pursuit.

Having student teachers reflect on short lessons to their fellow students (lessons of about 10 minutes) is in the beginning more effective for the promotion of reflection than asking them to analyze longer lessons or lessons given to students at school and focusing on issues that are not their first concern.

In addition, we feel that student teachers should be made explicitly aware of the issue of learning orientations. Gibbs (1983), for example, advocates a structural method by which students reflect on their understanding of learning processes and study projects and discuss these within a group. Such approaches are extremely useful in teacher education. Benefits can be felt on two levels: first, in the teaching–learning processes taking place within teacher education, and second, in the schools in which the student teachers will ultimately be teaching. It is important for prospective teachers to realize that their students, too, will have different learning orientations, which may be influenced by the education they receive.

SUMMARY

The small number of research studies into the effectiveness of realistic teacher education provide indications that it reduces the gap between theory and practice. Research on the effects of promoting reflection, an important ingredient of the realistic approach, is relatively rare. Moreover, as conceptualizations of reflection depend on underlying philosophies of education, claims about effects of promoting reflection are sometimes questionable. However, a few research studies carried out in the United States and Australia do show positive effects on supervisory discourse and journal writing, although school contexts often have a limiting influence. Our own research studies showed effects on the quality of graduates' interpersonal relationships with students, adequacy of perception of these relationships, and job satisfaction. These were mainly long-term effects. During their first half year of teaching, graduates initially seem to go through a latency period in which the ability to reflect disappears.

Our studies also revealed differences in program appreciation by students related to student teachers' learning orientations. Internally oriented student teachers are inclined to reflect on their own, whereas externally oriented students wish to get more concrete guidelines and feedback. This difference was further investigated by means of the IEO test, which showed correlations with age, previous schooling, and gender. A strategy of gradualness is important to take the needs of externally oriented student teachers into account.

We need more effect studies relating program characteristics to learning outcomes. Longitudinal studies can provide more insight into the influence of learning orientations and context on teacher development.

BASIC CONCEPTS

Teacher–student interpersonal relationships
Job satisfaction
Learning orientations (internal and external orientation)
Strategy of gradualness
Latency period

7 Helping Individual Student Teachers Become Reflective: The Supervisory Process

Fred Korthagen

> The sage has no mind of his own
> He takes as his own the mind of the people
>
> —*Lao Tzu: Tao te ching*
>
> *In this chapter, individual supervision of student teachers is discussed. Basic to the realistic approach to teacher education is the promotion of reflection on concrete teaching situations, with the student teacher's personal perception of these situations as the starting point of the reflection process. Several issues are dealt with in this chapter: How can a teacher educator or school-based supervisor facilitate this process? What supervision skills are helpful? How are these skills related to the phases of the ALACT model?*

7.1. INTRODUCTION

In this chapter I will discuss the process of helping student teachers reflect on their experiences, with the emphasis on experiences in teaching practice.

Previous chapters have already clarified what the "ideal" process of reflection could look like (see sections 3.7 and 4.8). To describe this process, the ALACT model has been introduced, consisting of five recurring phases:

1. Action
2. Looking back on the action
3. Awareness of essential aspects
4. Creating alternative methods of action
5. Trial

The final goal of promoting reflection, in my view, should be that the teacher is able to go through the cycles of the ALACT model independently. In other words, it is not sufficient in teacher education to have student teachers reflect, but it is necessary that they learn how to reflect on their own, without the help of a supervisor.[1] This equips them with a so-called *growth competence*: the ability to continue to develop independently when the preparation program is over (see also section 3.9). Here the word "independently" does not mean "individually." Independent learners are able to direct and monitor their own development and to do so in collaboration with others. They are also able to ask for help based on an awareness of their own learning needs and the phases successfully completed, as well as of the moments in which they need support or feedback.

In this chapter, the emphasis is placed on the question of how the goal of making student teachers more reflective can be realized by the process of supervision or mentoring. (The term *mentoring* is more common in European countries. In order to simplify the terminology, throughout this chapter I will only use the word *supervision*, with which I also intend to refer to mentoring.) In chapter 9, I will also discuss the role that peers can play in the promotion of reflection.

7.2. A STRATEGY OF GRADUALNESS

Student teachers who are not used to an approach based on the promotion of reflection are often typically less than willing to take responsibility for their own learning. Combs et al. (1974) and Rogers (1969) point to this passive attitude in many learners, and Cantor (1972, p. 111) vividly voices the attitude of students:

> Here we are. Talk to us and we'll do what we're supposed to do. Only please let us alone. Don't pick on us; don't ask any embarrassing questions. Just talk, we'll take notes. Let us know when the exam comes around. We'll do a bit of cramming, go through our notes of your answers and we'll pass. Only please don't bother us. We don't know the stuff. That's what you're here for. Tell us.

Combs et al. (1974, p. 35) notes that

> Because of their past experience, they [students] have usually been thoroughly brainwashed into the belief that they are not learning anything unless they are being given more facts.

The resistance to other ways of learning can obstruct growth. This is why I now briefly repeat a few important notions about working with student teachers that were discussed in the previous chapters. In my view, they are conditional to any approach aiming at the promotion of reflection.

First, a strategy of gradualness is important (see section 6.6). Indeed, the prospective teacher should acquire the ability to reflect on his or her own, but the teacher educator must offer sufficient *structure* to make learning possible. The student teacher should not be forced to find out everything without help. Initially, the teacher educator can give concrete assignments, indicate possible choices, give feedback, and offer the help that is—implicitly or explicitly—asked for by the student teacher. Gradually, more decisions can be left to the student teacher, although the teacher educator has to consider individual differences.

The process of learning how to reflect starts with reflection on simple and brief experiences, for example, the situation of explaining a relatively simple concept or principle to one's fellow students.

We also discussed the importance of a balance between safety and challenge (section 5.6). Learning contracts and monitoring schedules are useful aids in creating the balance he or she needs (Gibbons & Philips, 1979). After a while, students can also share the responsibility for the evaluation of their own achievements. In fact, an increasing emphasis on self-evaluation is basic to the development of a growth competence. But gradualness is always the guiding principle.

Finally, the more theoretical insights to be developed during the supervisory process need to be helpful to the student teacher, and therefore should be linked to the students' own needs, concerns, perceptions, and reflections. In terms of chapter 2, this means that the supervisor should aim at the development of *phronesis* (theory with a small t), rather than *episteme* (Theory with capital T).

Keeping these points in mind, the supervisory process will now be discussed.

7.3. THE HELPING PROCESS: SUPERVISING THE SPIRAL OF PROFESSIONAL DEVELOPMENT

The ultimate goal of supervision is making the student teacher capable of going through the ALACT model autonomously: By continuously and consciously learning from his or her own experiences, he or she will become a better teacher.[2] How can the supervisor (who may be a teacher educator or a cooperating teacher) assist the student teacher in learning to reflect?

To begin with, the two-way division Carkhuff recognizes is important for the understanding of what is involved when one cycle of the spiral is being passed through:

> The helping process may be divided into two principal phases: (1) the downward or inward phase and (2) the upward or outward phase or the phase of emergent directionality. During the initial phase the goal of helping is to learn not only the nature of the individual's problems but also how the helpee views himself and his world. During the latter phase the goal is to establish and operationalize a constructive direction or problem resolution for the helpee. (Carkhuff, 1969b, p. 28)

In the ALACT model, Phases 2 and 3 are the inward phases in which the reflection on a situation takes place. Phase 1 (and 5, which is in fact Phase 1 of a next cycle) is the outward phase, directed at acting, prepared by the outwardly oriented Phase 4. What happens in Phase 4, namely, developing alternative methods of action, could be called *anticipation* rather than reflection because the focus is already shifting toward the future action.

In both parts of the cycle, the supervisor should keep abreast of what happens to the student teacher and should only "take over" those functions the student teacher cannot deal with without help. In fact, the supervisor should only act when the student teacher asks him or her to, or when its is clear that the student teacher gets stuck in a particular part of the spiral. Here are two examples:

1. A student teacher has given a lesson to her fellow student teachers, the supervisor being present. Immediately after the lesson the student teacher asks her fellow student teachers and the supervisor for feedback. In such a situation there is a risk that the student teacher hardly gets around to looking back on the lesson herself (phase 2). This could eventually result in her becoming entirely dependent on others for the improvement of her teaching. The supervisor could therefore intervene, for instance, by asking the student teacher to first look back on her lesson herself. It depends on the student teacher whether the supervisor should perhaps assist her further by asking guiding questions, like "what did you do," "what did you feel," "what did you think," "what did you want," and so on.
2. Another student teacher appears to have problems with maintaining discipline in the classroom. He asks the supervisor for advice.
   The first pitfall for the supervisor is that it seems that the student teacher is asking for a solution (which is of course understandable), at a stage when the problem is not yet altogether clear. Why is it that the student teacher cannot maintain discipline? Does that apply to all classes? What exactly shows that the student teacher cannot maintain discipline? How does the student teacher feel about the problem? What are things that go well in his lessons?
   Such questions can lead to an awareness of essential aspects of an initially vaguely formulated problem. The supervisor tries to help the student teacher formulate the actual problem more clearly (phase 3). Only then is it meaningful to go over to phase 4 (developing alternatives to the approach). Here a second pitfall for the supervisor comes to light. The supervisor possibly considers one particular solution as the obvious one and has trouble not volunteering it. However, it often appears that the student teacher is quite able to think of a solution once he or she has the problem in focus! But even if that is not so, the supervisor should at least stimulate student teachers to think about solutions for themselves. If a student truly appears not to be able to get through this phase 4 on his or her own, only then can the supervisor take over.

These examples illustrate that being aware of the phases of the spiral can support the supervisor in his or her helping capacity. So "helping to learn" can be interpreted as "helping the student teacher pass through the spiraling development process." Combs et al. (1974, p. 26) put it like this:

> The teaching of methods has long been regarded as a prime function of teacher education. Indeed, there are some who have complained of a preoccupation with methods. The self-as-instrument concept of professional training, however, places a different

> emphasis on the matter. The teacher-education program must help each student find the methods best suited to him, to his purposes, his task, and the peculiar populations and problems with which he must deal on the job. This is not so much a matter of *teaching* methods as one of helping students *discover* methods. It is a question of finding the methods right for the teacher rather than right for teaching.

The latter statement again points toward the need to develop theory (with a small t) that is relevant to this specific teacher, in this specific situation, at this specific moment.

As the ultimate goal of realistic teacher education is that student teachers should learn to be their own supervisor, the supervisor must also make student teachers aware of the spiral process described by the ALACT model. Of course, for this to succeed, a student has to have gone through the cycle several times with some success, preferably in quite different learning situations; otherwise, there are no experiences to reflect on.[3]

It is helpful to have student teachers write down before the supervisory session their own reflections, as well as the questions they have arrived at, because this is another way of making them more aware of their own process. During the supervisory conference, these notes can be explicitly positioned in the ALACT model. (In chapter 11, this issue will be elaborated by discussing the role of the logbook in the reflection process and the role of *meta-reflection*: reflection on one's own reflection.)

7.4. BASIC SUPERVISORY SKILLS

I interpreted the supervising process as "helping a student teacher go through a spiraling development process." This gives us the opportunity to discuss the helping skills the supervisor should possess in more detail. In this section, some basic skills that are relevant for the whole process are described. The next sections look at the supervisory skills important for each of the separate phases of the ALACT model.

Determining What Kind of Help Is Needed

A first, obvious, basic skill involves determining what phase the student teacher is in. Here are some examples:

Situation A:

When a student teacher is clear about what she wants to learn and how, she is apparently fairly capable of going through the spiral autonomously. The supervisor should ask himself or herself whether any help is needed. At the most, it could be meaningful to show the student teacher possible alternatives (phase 4).

Situation B:

However, in reality it is hardly ever this perfect. For instance, a situation could exist in which the student teacher knows roughly what she wants to learn, but cannot make it concrete (for example a student teacher who says she wants to learn to "explain things well"). This looks like the situation discussed in section 7.3 (example 2), in which the problem was insufficiently clear to enter the phase of developing alternative methods of action. For supervisors to apply the principle that they are there to help the student to learn, they must realize that student teachers must first learn to specify their problem. The supervisor in this example should help the student teacher do this. The emphasis will be put on helping with phases 2 and 3.

Situation C:

Another possibility is that a student teacher has no learning goal at all. She might want to learn something, if only she could see what would be useful to her. This might offer a point of departure: the student teacher must be helped to find meaningful goals (phases 1 and 2 are emphasized).

These examples show that the helping supervisor actually uses a kind of decision model shaped as shown in Fig. 7.1. Only if it is evident in which phase the student teacher has arrived can one help adequately.

Before examining which helping skills are particularly important for each phase, the matter of possible approaches to learning needs some attention.

Approaches to Learning

In Phase 1 (action), one does not have to think exclusively about very practical, action-oriented affairs like, for instance, "teaching." A more cognitive approach to Phase 1 is also possible; reading an article, for instance, can be an action phase leading to reflection and to the formulation of a learning need. In short, in each different phase there are various ways to approach the learning process. Four dimensions can be distinguished: wanting, thinking, feeling, and acting (although this is a distinction one can never make quite sharply). The first dimension is most important as it directs the learning process: What is it the person wants to learn, or wishes to change, or has a concern about? This is the dimension behind the decision model in Fig. 7.1. Let us assume that this dimension has been adequately dealt with. What is the procedure then? Using the three situations (A, B and C), I will briefly illustrate how the other three dimensions can represent different approaches to the learning process.[4]

In situation A, the student teacher knows what she wants to learn and how she wants to do it. As already mentioned, the supervisor can perhaps point to alternative methods (if the student has not yet considered them). For example, when a student teacher wants to learn how to make good use of the blackboard and is reading about it (a cognitive approach), the supervisor could tell her about the possibility of (additional) practicing by using the blackboard and reflecting on her experiences with it (approach from the action dimension). It may also be helpful to ask her how

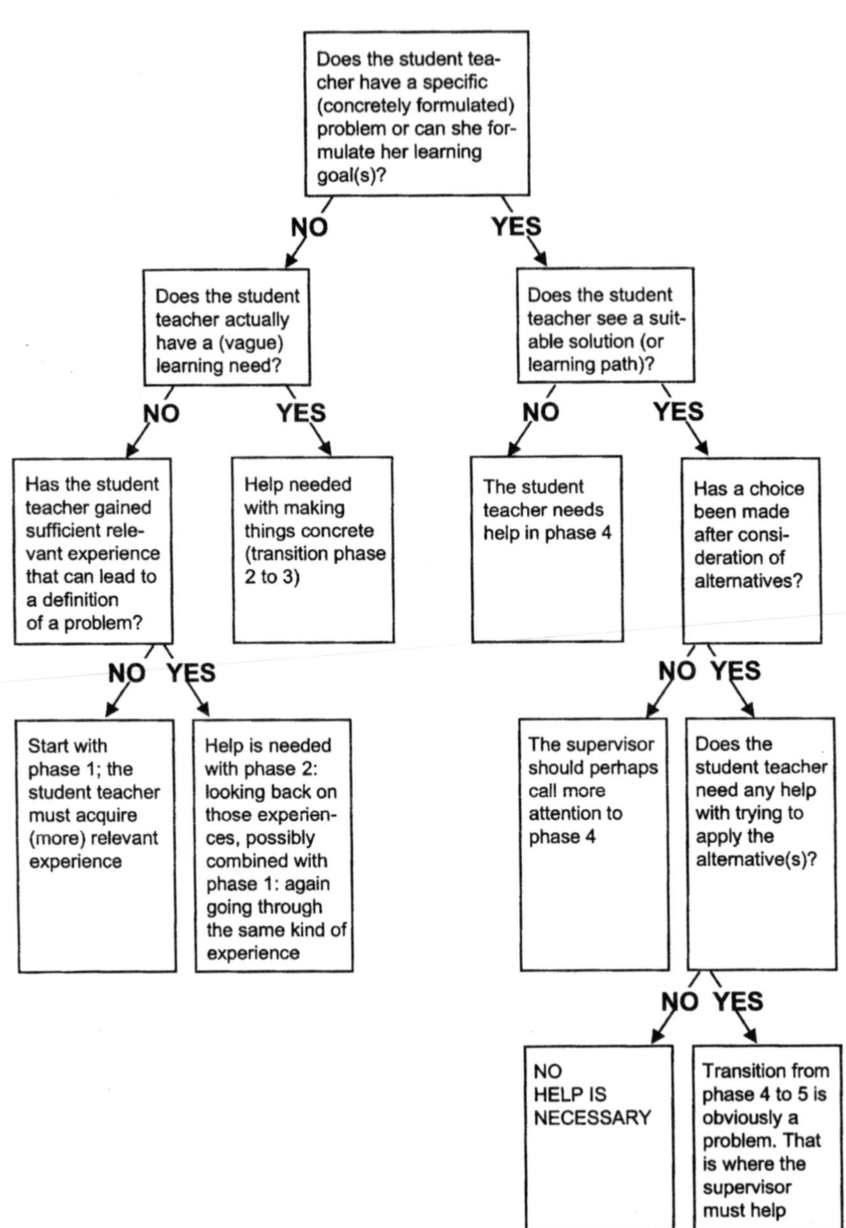

FIG. 7.1. A decision model for the supervisor.

she feels about her problem and how she would like to feel about using the blackboard (feeling dimension).

In situation B, where the student teacher has to specify her learning goal before she can learn efficiently, the supervisor can point to the different ways of achieving it. The student teacher who wants to learn to explain things well is possibly directed by feelings of insecurity. In order to specify the student teacher's learning goal, it is necessary to clarify those feelings and the situations in which they occur (approach from the feeling dimension). A more cognitive approach could be that the student teacher studies an overview of several pedagogical theories and then considers which theory she would like to study in depth and learn how to implement. In an action approach, situations could be created in which the student teacher has the role of "explainer." Reflection on those situations can help formulate problems and set up a "development program" for the student teacher.

In the same way, in situation C (the student teacher does not know what she wants to learn) the supervisor can provide different approaches to Phases 1 and 2 (which the student teacher can apply simultaneously). The student teacher can begin by reading a book on teaching (more cognitively oriented); at the same time, she could consider what she likes to do, what frightens her, or what she tries to avoid (more affectively oriented); or she can start by just doing some "work" (e.g., tutoring) and then try to find a possible learning goal (action-oriented approach).

This does not mean that the learning situation should just be adapted to the student teacher's learning style. As learning styles are often the result of earlier experiences, one could learn to make use of learning approaches other than the approach one is inclined to use. However, the supervisor would have to take into account that learning resistance could occur.

To avoid complications, the issue of different learning approaches will not always be explicitly mentioned in the following sections. Yet this aspect of the learning process does play a large part in the separate phases of the ALACT model that will be discussed.

7.5. HELPING WITH PHASE 1 (ACTION)

Phase 1 has been characterized as a phase of action. Helping with Phase 1, therefore, means that one has the student teacher undergo concrete experiences.[5]

Numbering the phases from 1 to 5 has the disadvantage that one is likely to forget that Phase 1 is not necessarily the first phase of a learning process. After all, the process is spiral shaped, so Phase 1 is often the fifth phase of a previous cycle. So when a student teacher needs help with this phase, the supervisor should think about what action situations the student is ready for.

Let me give an example. In every teacher education program, some experiences with explaining subject matter are obvious examples of Phase 1. In this there is a range of possibilities: The experience can be explaining something to one of the fellow students, to an entire group of student teachers, to one child (e.g., in a tutoring situation), or to an entire class. One can also vary the subject matter's degree of complexity for each of these possibilities. Which situation suits a student teacher best depends on what he or she has already lived through.

This does not mean that the student teacher should always start with the least complicated situation. The student teacher may then hardly feel that there is a problem; then there is no need for learning. Particularly in view of the idea that learning needs should come from student teachers themselves, it can sometimes be a good start to let student teachers experience problems with explaining things in a rather difficult situation. After that, a simpler situation (e.g., having to explain the same topic to a fellow student) may be better suited for further learning.[23] The previous situation can be regarded as an illustration of two supervisory skills that are important in Phase 1: building on the student teachers' learning needs, and making student teachers sensitive to new learning goals. They can be summarized as *helping to continue the learning process*.

7.6. HELPING WITH PHASE 2 (LOOKING BACK)

Before, the learning and acting spiral was divided into inward-directed and outward-directed halves. Helping a student teacher with Phases 2 and 3 is, therefore, about stimulating student teachers to think about themselves and reach conclusions. In this respect, the transition from Phase 1 to Phase 2 is a fundamental one: It marks the start of an inward-directed part of the learning process. Phase 2 is concerned with the student's reflection on his or her way of acting, thinking, wanting, and feeling. Now the student will find him- or herself somewhere between "safety" (the need to preserve the existing internal psychological order) and "growth" (expanding one's possibilities). Maslow (1968, p. 49) states: "Safety needs are prepotent over growth needs." So in Phase 2 of the spiral, those supervising skills that contribute to the student teacher's feeling of safety are especially important[7]:

> A crucial relationship dimension is that of *trust-distrust*. Helpees are willing generally to accept help from people they trust. The helpee must have confidence in the helper and must be able to believe what he says in order for trust to develop. (Brammer, 1973, p. 49)

Now, which supervisory skills are essential to the creation of a safe atmosphere? Those who try to answer that question with the help of the literature meet a vast diversity of theories and terminology.

Rogers (1969) basically recognizes three central skills: *acceptance*, *empathy*, and *genuineness*.[8] In Brammer (1973), several dozen skills can be found. Egan (1975) and Carkhuff (1969a, 1969b) adopt a middle course as far as the skills they mention are concerned.

On inspection of what the different authors mean by the skills they mention, there are many similarities, even if they use a different terminology. For instance, many skills that Brammer describes can be regarded as further specifications of those mentioned by Rogers. As Egan (1975, p. 3) remarks, the helper's degree of experience will determine to what extent he will benefit from a far-reaching specification of subskills or a general outline:

> While this proliferation of stages and skills is bewildering to the novice, the detail and specificity are very stimulating to the experienced helper.

Within the scope of this section, I will discuss one by one what I believe to be the most important skills.

Acceptance

Student teachers should feel accepted as a person, even if they do not live up to the expectations the supervisor or they themselves had before. Acceptance of the student teacher includes accepting his or her needs and possibilities as established facts and also that the student teacher is not judged as a person. This acceptance must be clear to the student teacher. Consider an example:

> A student teacher appears to have a strong resistance to anything that reeks of social skills, expression of feelings and the like. Mathematics fascinates him and though he wants to know about learning processes in connection with teaching, he is only interested in the cognitive aspects.

The supervisor can generally deal with this student teacher in two ways. One way, which is seldom effective in such a case, is to try to direct the student teacher to the area of social skills and feelings he has neglected. For instance, in the supervisory discussion after the student teacher has taught a class, the supervisor can alert him to moments during the lesson when aspects from this area played a part. The student teacher will, however, soon regard this as a judgment: He might read it as something like, "There is something wrong with you; you don't amount to much in a certain area and that has to change soon." The student teacher could start to feel less and less secure and "close up." Here we see the paradox of change (section 5.2) in operation: Pressure toward change hampers change. This approach could even cause the student teacher to develop a greater resistance to the area of interpersonal relationships than before. How the student teacher will react depends on his relationship with his supervisor. If he feels that the supervisor does not accept him and there is a risk of a negative assessment, then he might start to put on an act in order to "survive" and he might, for example, pay lip service to the importance of his interpersonal relationships with the children in his class and to the role of feelings.

In opposition to this nonaccepting approach, there is another possibility in which the supervisor accepts the student teacher, including his resistance to certain things. In the supervisory session, the supervisor will not direct attention to those aspects the student teacher disregarded during his lesson. He will consistently keep his role as helper in mind and support the development process the student teacher goes through. Supervisors with little or no experience with a consistently applied nondirective approach often have trouble imagining that it is exactly this approach that stands a good chance of eventually causing the student teacher to explore the area that he wanted to avoid. The explanation, again, is that safety needs must be met, before growth can be possible. If the student teacher is allowed to reflect on his experiences freely and without judgments given by the supervisor, then he will be given the chance to become even more competent in the cognitive aspects that he regards important, and at the same time encounter the limitations that these bring with them. This could get a new learning process started in the student teacher, which this time is directed by his own learning need (in terms of section 4.6, by his own delta-two system). Furthermore, he can hold on to the knowledge and skills he acquired at the cognitive level. There is a good chance that the student teacher will choose a cognitive approach to learning about feelings and social skills: Given his own preconceptions about learning, he will probably start by *thinking* about feelings and social skills and not by *feeling* or *doing/acting*. In my experience, whether he will eventually get to that will again depend on the supervisor's acceptance.

Empathy

Rogers understands empathy to mean the skill to understand the other person "from the inside" and to communicate that understanding. Empathy aims at what Boud, Keogh and Walker (1985) call "attending to (or connecting with) feelings." I will again give an example. A student named Susan says:

> What really bothers me is that I cannot truly devote myself to the discussion of genetics. I wonder if I am really motivated to be a teacher, and that with the final exams coming up.

One could react empathetically:

> (Supervisor 1): You are worried that your limited interest in the discussion of genetics might be a indication that you should choose a different occupation?

If, because of this reaction, the student teacher feels understood, this could have a very stimulating effect. There is a good chance that she will continue to reflect on her experiences and perhaps her suitability for the teaching profession.

For the sake of contrast, consider some other possible reactions:

> (Supervisor 2): What kind of problems do you have with genetics, Susan?

This is clearly not an empathetic reaction, because the actual message Susan has sent has not been given back to her. In fact, it could be a helpful reaction to stimulate Susan to make her problem explicit—but only after a climate of understanding and trust has been created.

> (Supervisor 3): During the teaching practice period, many student teachers struggle with the question of whether they want to teach.

This supervisor generalizes the problem and shows insufficient understanding for the fact that this problem is very real to *Susan* at this particular time, and it is indeed a problem for *her.*

> (Supervisor 4): Don't you see, Susan, that your lack of dedication to the subject genetics is simply another way of putting the same problem we have been talking about? You still adopt an attitude of wait and see, and you refuse to take the responsibility for your own work.

Here we see a helper who tries to look "intelligent".... As Rogers (1969) emphasizes, this way of reacting is fundamentally different from empathetic understanding:

> This kind of understanding is sharply different from the usual evaluative understanding, which follows the pattern of, "I understand what is wrong with you." When there is a sensitive empathy, however, the reaction in the learner follows something of this pattern: "At last someone understands how it feels and seems to be *me* without wanting to analyze me or judge me. Now I can blossom and grow and learn." (pp. 111, 112)

Brammer (1973, p. 30, 31) also raises this issue:

> The helper gets into the internal frame of reference by listening attentively and asking himself several questions. "*What* is the helpee *feeling* right now: *How* does he view this *problem*? *What* does he see in his *world*"? If the helper is thinking from an external or diagnostic frame of reference, he is asking "why" questions as, "*Why* is he so upset," "What is *causing* the problem?" He also makes judgments such as "He's *upset* and seems to be in bad shape; I've got to help him." The external frame, then, is the helper's attempt to understand the helpee from an observer stance using an intellectual problem-solving framework.

Brammer then refers to research showing that effective helpers use an internal rather than an external frame of reference.

The idea that one can help someone else merely by restating (in a few words) what the other has already expressed causes surprise in many who have no experience with it. Apart from the fact that this is not actually as easy as it seems (it is very hard to put your own thoughts and feelings aside for a while and to think completely from the other person's frame of reference), experience is the best proof that this way of helping exerts a powerfully stimulating influence.

Nevertheless, the model formulated in section 4.6 offers an explanation for this phenomenon. Ideally, functioning persons have the use of a well-developed delta-one and delta-two system and are therefore able to correct themselves. Reflection is characteristic for the functioning of the delta-two system: The person thinks about his own thinking, feeling, wanting, and acting. For this, one is required to "distance" oneself from one's own delta-one systems; this will always be difficult and learning resistances (of which one is not always aware) will often hinder it. In fact, an empathetically reacting helper takes over a part of this job; the helpee does not have to rely on his internal reflection, but the helper is a kind of external mirror.[9]

Genuineness

The supervisor should certainly not pretend to accept or understand when in reality he or she does not. The fact is, the most important thing in helping is for the helper not to hide behind a professional facade but to come across as a real person, with feelings and thoughts of his or her own. This is called genuineness, or realness.

Spontaneity is an important aspect of genuineness. Another is *congruence*: What the supervisor does (says) should correspond with what he or she thinks (feels). A supervisor who says to a student teacher: "What you are saying is quite interesting" with a bored expression on his face does not make a very credible impression. Clearly, double signals like that will make the student teacher feel unsafe: Does the supervisor mean what he or she says? What is going on behind that guise?

Lack of genuineness can also appear when the literal message is inconsistent with what is really meant. A supervisor who claims what the student is telling is very interesting, but then quickly switches to another subject, will not come across as very genuine. This could make the student feel unsafe and he or she will certainly not feel invited to explore his or her feelings any further.

In a developing helping relationship, genuineness can grow into *self-disclosure*: The supervisor can introduce his or her own experiences. However, the supervisor should carefully consider whether the student teacher really benefits by it: Does the self-disclosure relate to the student teacher's frame of reference? If so, self-disclosure can intensify the helping relationship.

Concreteness

The supervisor must stimulate the student teacher to carefully consider *concrete* feelings, thoughts, needs, and actions. The supervisor must help prevent student teachers from losing themselves in generalities or vague formulations. Let me give another example:

> Student teacher: It is always hard to know right from the start the kind of things that can happen in a lesson. It is impossible to predict everything.
>
> Supervisor 1: Did Peter's reaction to your question take you by surprise?

Compare this to the following reaction (after Egan, 1975, p. 103):

> Supervisor 2: Children often react unpredictably.

The goal of concreteness is that the student teacher is stimulated to make things concrete, to zoom in on his or her behavior in and thoughts about the situation, and the feelings and needs that accompany them. One should, however, realize that a tendency to talk in abstract and vague phrases could indicate learning resistances in the student teacher. As already remarked with regard to empathetic understanding, one should first make sure there is an atmosphere of trust before the student teacher can be stimulated to make his or her problems concrete.

The questions in Fig. 7.2 can be helpful in promoting concreteness.

Finding answers to all of these questions is often difficult. The questions on the right-hand side are often problematic to student teachers: Sometimes they have no idea about their students' thinking or feeling. Of course, that is a good starting point for discussing the question of what the student teacher could do in the next lesson to find answers.

The important final step in Phase 2 is connecting the answers to questions 1–8, or in other words, analyzing the circular process going on between the teacher and the students. For example, how did the student teacher's own feelings influence his or her actions during the lesson, how did these actions influence what his or her students felt and wanted, how did that influence their behavior, what was the effect of that behavior on the teacher's feelings, and so on. In this way, the essential aspects of the process during the lesson become clear, which brings the reflection into Phase 3. An example of this kind of reflection in Phase 2, leading to awareness of the circular process between a teacher and a student, was described in section 3.7. In section 11.5, I go more deeply into the question of how student teachers can learn to use the "9 areas" of Fig. 7.2 to learn to bring concreteness into their analysis of classroom situations on their own, without the help of a supervisor.

7.7. HELPING WITH PHASE 3 (AWARENESS OF ESSENTIAL ASPECTS)

If all or many of the aspects in Fig. 7.2 have been dealt with, then Phase 2 (looking back) slowly evolves into Phase 3 (becoming aware of essential problems). In Phase

0. What is the context?	
1. What did you want?	5. What did the students want?
2. What did you do?	6. What did the students do?
3. What were you thinking?	7. What were the students thinking?
4. How did you feel?	8. How did the students feel?

FIG. 7.2. Concretizing questions for phase 2 of the ALACT model.

3, the supervisor skills discussed in the previous section are still important, but some other skills start to play a part too.

Confrontation

This time I will begin with some examples of supervisor reactions:

1. You would like to be able to make clearer rules, but you never get around to actually doing it?
2. What you are saying sounds like you are angry and at the same time I can see you smile.
3. You tell the students that you are not only interested in the answers to the problems, but that the way they solve them is at least as important. Still, when marking the tests you only looked at the answers.
4. You feel like you are putting your back into it. Yet I see an attitude of "wait and see" in you, for instance in your reaction just now.

The supervisor can confront the student teacher with discrepancies between his or her ideal and the real self (Example 1), verbal and nonverbal expressions (Example 2), what the student teacher says and what he or she does (Example 3), how the student teacher sees himself and how the supervisor perceives the student teacher (Example 4), and so on.

Confrontation is directly connected with feedback: The supervisor gives (external) feedback on issues where the student teacher's director systems are apparently not able to give (internal) feedback.

In several places in the literature, *criteria* are mentioned that feedback must meet in order to be effective. This is a brief summary:

- Feedback must apply to the other's observed and apparent (sub)-behavior and not to his personality. For instance, make clear that when you give negative feedback, you are not blaming the feedback recipient as a person.
- Feedback must be a description, as opposed to an interpretation of or a judgment on the behavior. (For example "I see you lower your eyes," and not "You are shy.")
- This description involves the behavior *you* observed, how *you* experienced it and what *your* reaction to it is. So it is always a subjective description.
- Feedback must be specific and not general; it must deal with concrete, specific and clearly described behavior.
- Feedback is more effective when the time lapse between the behavior and the feedback is as brief as possible.
- Feedback must give the recipient the opportunity to do something with the information. So it is useless, as well as frustrating, to remind someone of something he cannot change (for example: you are so small).

- Limit the feedback to information only, and do not give advice on what the feedback recipient should do with that information. Only then do you give him/ her the freedom to correct his/her behavior, or not.
- The feedback should be given at the moment that the feedback recipient wants it; when the feedback has no other value than that the supplier can ventilate his or her information, it can easily have a destructive effect.
- The feedback must be formulated in such a way that the recipient feels invited to respond.

If the student does not feel safe, then a confrontation has very little effect. It usually only strengthens learning resistance. *Confrontation should therefore be accompanied by acceptance, empathy, and genuineness*.

It is also true for those skills that will be discussed later on that they can only be effective in a learning situation that the student teacher considers safe. Another way in which safety can be promoted is by emphasizing strong points and strengths that have become clear in Phase 3, especially if a student teacher is very negative about him- or herself.

Generalization

Making things concrete can lead to taking a closer look at problems of which the student teacher was initially only vaguely aware. But at the same time, it incurs the risk that the interrelation between those problems can no longer be seen. For instance, it might happen that a problem is linked by the student teacher to only one particular situation, although the problem has significance for the student's overall performance. Because of this, it is important that the supervisor helps the student teacher to connect isolated instances of knowledge and experience:

> (Supervisor): It seems to me that all these things are related to making demands of students?

Using Experiences in the Here-and-Now

In making things concrete as well as in confrontation and generalization, the current supervisory discourse can play a special role. By involving a consideration of the actual interaction between the student teacher and the supervisor, the student teacher is able to reflect on one particular, topical situation in which the supervisor is also closely involved. This kind of making things concrete can possibly lead to confrontation (look at Examples 2 and 4 under confrontation). In addition, the number of situations that the student teacher reflects on is increased, which makes generalization easier.

A student who deals with the issue of "taking the initiative" could, for example, sometimes be helped by reflecting on the way he takes the initiative in his exchange with the supervisor. A student who would like to get a better grip on feelings could practice by becoming aware of the feelings she has during the supervisory session.

Helping to Make Things Explicit

Language plays an important role in the support of thinking (Vygotsky, 1978). Making a problem or learning feel concrete, possibly *writing* it down, helps to continue learning. In terms of section 4.6, one can regard making things explicit as making the delta-two level come down to delta-one level: What has been made clear at the delta-two level becomes tangible, manipulable. The supervisor must, however, take care that the student teacher takes the first step in making a problem or learning needs explicit!

Then the supervisor may connect the formulation of the problem or learning need with *theory*. Chapter 2 stressed that this should be theory with a small t: In the middle of the process of going from one action phase to the other and trying to solve their problems in the classroom, student teachers are generally not yet motivated for the "big Theories." What certainly is helpful are small principles that help the student teacher to perceive more in the situation he or she is struggling with and that support action. It is important that these principles remain close to what the student has already become aware of. (See the example of the supervisor who mentions the principle of "more of the same," in section 3.7). In Phase 4, these theoretical principles may be complemented with concrete suggestions for action.

In the training courses for supervisors we organize (described in chapter 13), participants often express their concern that merely adding small practice-relevant principles in this phase lowers the academic level of teacher education. However, what is often forgotten is that the intended learning process of the student teacher is a spiral process and Phase 3 returns many times. Not only does this deepen the student's reflection and the theoretical principles that the supervisor can bring in, it also opens the door to a more theoretically oriented period in which the student reads about the issues dealt with during supervision. The big difference between this realistic approach and an approach starting from the Theory with capital T is that the systematic use of the ALACT model promotes more meaningful learning of theory: Theory can be connected by the student to concrete experiences and concerns of his or her own.

7.8. HELPING WITH PHASE 4 (CREATING ALTERNATIVE METHODS OF ACTION)

Once a problem or learning need has become clear and explicit, a need for solutions, or a "learning path," becomes visible. To begin with, the supervisor must take care that after helping with Phase 3, he or she does not automatically continue to help. Often it turns out that the student teacher is quite capable of helping him- or herself through Phase 4. In other words, the student can find solutions by him- or herself once the problem is clear (cf. Fig. 7.1). If that is not the case, and if the student teacher realizes that he or she is looking for solutions to a problem but is not able to find them, then the supervisor can possibly introduce ideas. The supervisor can also make sure the student teacher does not choose the first possible solution, but also considers alternatives (weighing pros and cons). With this, the *risk factor* is not to be neglected: It might be advantageous for the student teacher to first try out a solution that holds little risk, and possibly, after the student teacher has gained some self-confidence, other more risky alternatives. Of course, when alternative solutions are explored, *learning resistances* play a part: The student teacher will perhaps hardly accept or not accept solutions that he or she considers very risky alternatives.

This last fact again indicates that in this phase *acceptance*, *empathy*, and *genuineness* are still important to the supervisor. This also applies to *concretizing, generalizing* (this time with regard to alternatives), and *confrontation* (this time, e.g., confronting the student teacher with discrepancies between ideal solutions and what is really feasible). The *here-and-now* can also offer ideas for solutions. For instance, when the student teacher's problem is that he has difficulty taking the initiative, ways could be found for him to improve on that in the supervisory sessions. Finally, *helping to make* alternative solutions *explicit* can be important in supporting thinking about and making choices. In short, every supervisory skill that was necessary in the previous phases still remains important.

Actually making a choice between the formulated alternatives can sometimes be difficult for the student teacher. Here again, the supervisor's acceptance and empathy are important, as is confrontation. The following is an example of a supervisor reaction in such a situation:

> It is hard for you to finally decide how you are going to go about it in tomorrow's class, isn't it?

A final guideline for the supervisor may be to help the student teacher *generalize* the solutions under discussion. Often solutions discussed in the context of a specific lesson, or principles within these solutions, can be used more often in other lessons too, for example:

> Supervisor: Is this a principle you think you can use more often in your lessons?

Indeed, it is important to help enlarge the student teacher's repertoire of pedagogical approaches. It is not only today's or tomorrow's lesson that is important, but most of all the ability to be able to choose adequate solutions in any lesson.

In Fig. 7.3, a number of guidelines or "checks" for Phase 4 are summarized, based on Brammer (1973) and Egan (1975). Some of them have been discussed in this section, others are new but speak for themselves.

I mention again (see also section 7.4) that when a *learning need* has become apparent in Phase 3, Phase 4 can consist of thinking of *learning paths* and choosing the most suitable one(s). One could say that a byway to the cycle has come to exist temporarily, consisting for instance of studying a textbook or entering a special training program (see Fig. 7.5).

Guidelines for Phase 4: creating alternatives

1. Is the student sufficiently involved in the search for alternatives?
2. Does the student formulate the alternatives?
3. Are the alternatives concrete enough?
4. Are they realistic? (in terms of ability and risk taking)
5. Are the possible effects examined?
6. Can the alternatives be generalized to other situations?
7. Did the student finally choose from the remaining alternatives?

FIG. 7.3. Creating alternatives.

7.9. HELPING WITH PHASE 5 (TRIAL)

Now Phase 5 will be discussed. In fact, the remarks already made in "helping with Phase 1" apply here as well. After all, Phases 1 and 5 are not fundamentally different in nature, it is just that the student teacher has developed somewhat during the learning process in between Phase 1 and 5. An important aspect is that learning from experience should not become a haphazard process: The ALACT model is not intended as a description of isolated cycles, but as a spiral. Thus, a supervisor should try to prevent the student from regarding Phase 5 as the final phase. It is important that it is regarded as intermediate. The supervisor should also take care that the student teacher is not overly occupied with short-term goals in his or her own learning process (Combs et al., 1974, p. 35). Furthermore, it must be promoted that the goals the student teacher sets do go beyond the limits of the kind of education he or she knew as a child in school. By offering suitable action situations, the supervisor can make the student teacher sensitive to other learning goals.

7.10. SOME ADDITIONAL SKILLS

In this section, some supervisory skills will be discussed that are not especially linked to a specific phase of the helping process.

The Skill of Keeping Silent

The supervisor should only help when it is really needed. He or she should make sure that student teachers are allowed to think for themselves and to help themselves. That is why it is necessary that the helping process is *restful*. *Periods of silence* can be beneficial: They give the student time to get down to reflection and take a few mental steps that could conceivably take the student longer than they would the supervisor.

For most supervisors, keeping silent is more difficult than it seems. Almost everyone is influenced by the traditional image of an active teacher, dealing with the subject material and everything else within a limited time span (and so hurry!) (Cantor, 1972, p. 173). This is not the ideal image of a supervisor. In supervision, the pace should be based on the student teacher's needs.

Emphasizing Strong Points and Taking Advantage of Them

Striving toward making the student aware of a problem or learning need is essential in helping with Phases 2 and 3. However, it can be very frustrating to be continually confronted with your problems and failings. Students must be able to retain their faith in themselves. A lot depends on the way the student's problems are handled:

> There is a world of difference, however, in a program that begins by giving the student a feeling that his self as it stands is enough for now and can be helped to become adequate, or a program that diminishes and degrades the self by continual harping on its insufficiencies. Acceptance of self, as any psychotherapist is aware, is essential to personality change. One can only progress from where he is. He cannot start from where he is not. So it is necessary that professional students begin with the feeling, "It is all right to be me," and "This self with which I begin can become a good teacher." (Combs et al., 1974, p. 118)

So, the supervisor should also help the student teacher to become aware of *strong points* (see also Cogan, 1973). Making things concrete, confrontation, and generalization could be helpful with this too! The fourth phase in the cycle can then become one of searching for possibilities to further explore such a strong point.

Helping Learning to Learn

As previously noted, the ultimate purpose of helping to learn is for the student teacher to learn to pass through the learning and acting spiral autonomously, and in this way acquire a growth competence. Carkhuff (1969b, p. 35) formulates it like this:

> The goals of the helping processes, then, are facilitative communication and constructive action both as an individual relates to himself and to others. Consistently constructive action is not possible without the fine discriminations of sensitive understanding; consistently sensitive understanding is not possible without the learning that comes from the feedback of action. In healthy people understanding is simultaneous with action, and the achievement of this balance is the ultimate goal of the helping process.

This leads to the formulation of the final important skill the supervisor must have: He or she must be able to make student teachers aware of their own learning process and of its spiraling nature. Learning itself should be the subject of reflection every once in a while (*meta-reflection*). This simply means the student teacher passes through the spiral again, but the subject of reflection is not some action but the learning (Fig. 7.4).

During learning to teach, a good alternation between acting and learning from that acting is very important. This is true on the delta-two level as well: The supervisor must make sure that learning and learning to learn are well alternated. This is important for several reasons. First, student teachers can then acquire more (delta-two) knowledge about their own learning. Second, reflection on their own learning can stir up positive *feelings*: when a possibly difficult, painful learning process is over, reflection can make clear that the goal has been reached or has come within closer range. This reflection may also make student teachers aware of the fact that, for the most, they have been able to bring that about themselves. Such observations can arouse positive feelings that influence the student teacher's *attitude* toward learning. That may be a far more important result than the learning of knowledge:

> As the student engages in this process of becoming aware of his own need to know, expressing that need, acting on it, and learning relevant concepts as a result, he senses a growing belief about himself that he is able and that he is becoming an increasingly effective instrument with which to achieve his purposes. This growing self-concept as teacher, coupled with the increased understanding, which is its major component, leads to the desire for more learning. (Combs et al., 1974, p. 143)

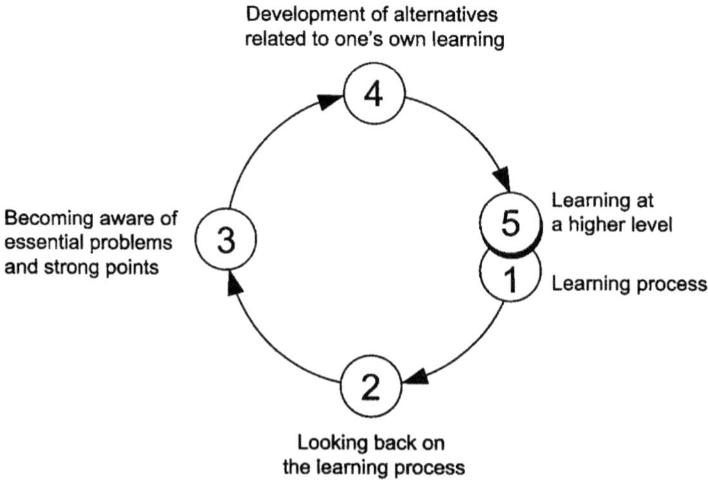

FIG. 7.4. Learning to learn.

It is not always easy to motivate students to learn about learning to teach. They are often inclined to focus on their teaching only. Paying attention to learning to learn is only possible when students are not faced with too many problems in their teaching; otherwise, these problems will drain away all their attention.[10]

Once the student teacher has become aware of how his or her own learning process is evolving, then the supervisor can more easily clarify (and bring up for discussion!) his or her own role in helping.

7.11. FINAL REMARKS

To conclude the discussion of helping skills, a few remarks are important. First, it is useful for a supervisor to note in which phase of the cycle the student usually needs help. It is striking how a student often runs aground in the same phase, even if the learning situations are different. Some students continue to have difficulty reflecting on their actions. Others think about their experiences but repeatedly fail to make their problems concrete. For yet another group this is no problem, but it may be difficult to think of solutions or to actually try out solutions. If the supervisor detects a pattern like that in the student teacher's learning problems, then this can further support the helping process (e.g., because the supervisor makes the student aware of the pattern).

Finally, I would like to emphasize strongly that I have described the helping process from the vantage point of a model. Of course, reality never quite corresponds to this model. For instance, the five phases of the cycle will not always follow each other neatly, but the learning process will proceed much more erratically. Nor is it uncommon for a cycle to stop at Phase 3, at becoming aware of a problem. Some problems cannot always be solved in a way that fits the student teacher (at that point in time). Then it is necessary for the student teacher to accept the problem. Consider an example:

> It is obviously difficult for me [student teacher] to make demands of students; that is something that does not suit me very well.

Such a process of acceptance is usually very painful for the person involved (the self-image is affected). A continued grim search for solutions can only obstruct this process. It is more appropriate to use the supervisory skills of Phases 2 and 3, acceptance (by the supervisor!), empathy, making concrete (in what kind of situations does the problem occur), generalization (is there a connection between different problems of the student teacher), and so on.

This concludes the description of individual supervisory processes, aiming at the promotion of reflection. Now, suppose the supervisor is indeed successful: What changes would one see in the student teacher? How could one recognize that the student teacher has indeed become a reflective practitioner? Those are the issues of the next chapter.

SUMMARY

This chapter dealt with the supervision of individual student teachers. Following a strategy of gradualness, they can not only be stimulated by a supervisor to reflect according to the ALACT model, but also learn to use this model independently, and thus acquire a growth competence. In order to help student teachers acquire this growth competence, it is important to determine what kind of help is necessary in which phase and not to help too much. The supervisor should also be aware of the variety of possible approaches to learning: approaches using the cognitive, affective, and behavioral dimension. The dimension of "wanting" is most important, because personal learning needs direct the learning process.

The supervisory skills important in each phase of the ALACT model and the basic concepts of the chapter are summarized in Fig. 7.5.

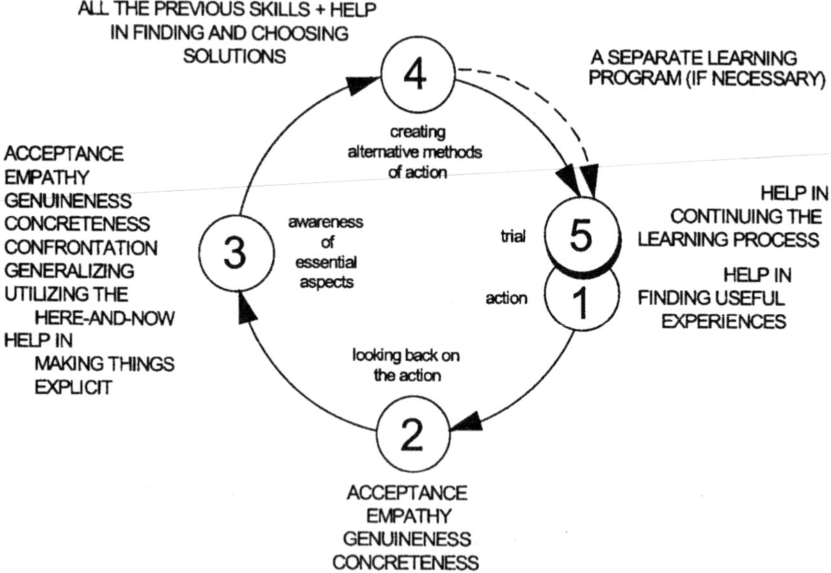

Basic skill: DETERMINING THE STUDENT TEACHER'S POSITION IN THE CYCLE PRINTED ABOVE.

Additional skills:

a. KEEPING SILENT

b. EMPHASIZING AND TAKING ADVANTAGE OF STRONG POINTS

c. HELPING WITH LEARNING TO LEARN (PROMOTING AWARENESS OF THE MODEL AND AUTONOMOUS USE OF THE MODEL).

FIG. 7.5. Helping to learn, an overview.

8 Characteristics of Reflective Teachers

Fred Korthagen and Theo Wubbels

Reflective abstraction is the driving force of learning.

—*Fosnot (1996, p. 29)*

In this chapter we use the data from the four research studies described in chapter 6 to empirically answer the question of what characterizes a reflective teacher.[1] *We saw in chapter 4 that any conceptualization of reflection depends on the underlying view of "good teaching," so we start by describing the context of the SOL teacher education program, in which the research studies were carried out. The studies reveal a number of characteristic attributes and correlates of reflectivity, thus offering building blocks for a theory in which empirically based relations are established between good teaching, the concept of reflection, and characteristics of reflective teachers.*

8.1. INTRODUCTION

The promotion of reflection in student teachers is fundamental to the realistic approach. In the previous chapter we looked at many details of the process of helping a student teacher become reflective. Now, suppose teacher educators are successful in this process, and a teacher leaves a teacher education curriculum as a "reflective practitioner." What would that mean? How would you recognize a reflective teacher if you saw one? In this chapter we address that question. We will also look at the question of whether a reflective teacher is a better teacher, and what "better" means in this context.

The search for characteristics of reflective teachers requires some care. As we saw in chapter 4, we can talk about the *structure* of the reflective process without reference to its goals, but it is impossible to talk about the final *value* of reflection without being clear about one's view of the goals of education: Whether we consider something as a good example of reflection depends on what we find important in "good teaching":

> The theoretical framework for reflection adopted by a particular program will depend upon its purposes and focus, and therefore in turn upon the assumptions about teaching and teacher education upon which these are based. (Hatton & Smith, 1995, pp. 35–36)

For this reason, two questions must be answered before we can meaningfully describe the characteristics of reflective teachers:

1. What do we consider as good teaching?
2. What is the role and nature of reflection in that view of good teaching?

The answers to these questions are crucial to an investigation of the central question of this chapter:

3. What are the characteristics that distinguish reflective teachers from their less reflective colleagues?

As the answers to Questions 2 and 3 depend on the answer to Question 1, we have to specify the educational context within which we are trying to determine the characteristics of reflective teachers. We will answer the questions within the context of the SOL teacher education program in the Netherlands, on the basis of the research studies carried out there. These studies have been described in section 6.5. There we also described the view of good teaching of the SOL teacher educators. In other words, in section 6.5 we gave the answer of the SOL staff to our first question. The second question will be dealt with in section 8.2. In section 8.3, we will get to the core: the answer to the third question, based on empirical material gathered in 10 years of research on the SOL program. We will formulate four attributes of reflective teachers. During our research, we also found some indications that certain teacher characteristics are correlated to reflective capacities and attitudes, and a number of these correlates will be described in section 8.4. In section 8.5, we present additional comments on the reported research. In section 8.6, we draw conclusions.

Before we start, let us repeat once again the following in order to avoid any possible misunderstanding: In attempting to define guidelines enabling us to recognize a reflective teacher, we will confine ourselves in this chapter to the kind of reflective teacher as identified by the SOL program. In that respect, our discussion is an example of the type of discussion that in our view should occur within the context of any teacher education program taking the promotion of reflection seriously.

8.2. THE ROLE AND NATURE OF REFLECTION IN THE CONTEXT OF THE SOL VIEW OF GOOD TEACHING

In section 6.5, we formulated 11 principles of good teaching that together characterize the SOL view. Summarizing these principles, we can say that, in the view of the SOL teacher educators, reflective teachers have the capacity to trace the ALACT cycle for all aspects of the teaching and learning situation, but focus on reflection on mathematical situations, interpersonal relationships in the classroom, and their own development as a teacher. During the preparation program, student teachers should develop a reflective attitude, thus fostering a growth competence.

The contents of the SOL program put special emphasis on learning to act in, and reflect on, a great variety of situations, either independently or in collaboration with others. Thus, student teachers were confronted with a great many teaching situations, cooperative assignments, and interpersonal problems, as well as mathematically oriented problems.

The fostering of an inquiry-oriented attitude and the promotion of the ability to analyze, to structure, and to devise creative solutions were among the basic educational goals, both for students in mathematics classrooms in secondary education and for prospective teachers. As regards the student teachers, these goals were pursued not only in the mathematics component, but also in the professional preparation component of the program.

The process described by the ALACT model may be seen as the SOL conception of the process of reflection. The crux of this process lies in Phase 3, where a mental structure is formed, or an existing mental structure is altered. In our reconstruction of the way the SOL staff viewed the concept of reflection, we arrived at the definition of reflection, introduced in section 4.5: Reflection is the mental process of structuring or restructuring an experience, a problem, or existing knowledge or insights.

8.3. CHARACTERISTIC ATTRIBUTES OF REFLECTIVE TEACHERS

We can refer to the four research studies carried out within the framework of the SOL program as the initial overall study (Study 1), the longitudinal study (Study 2), the IEO study (Study 3, into internal and external orientations in learning), and the comparison study (Study 4). (See section 6.5 for the details of these studies.) From the longitudinal study, we selected two student teachers who in comparison with the others made the greatest number of statements, which on the basis of our definition of reflection displayed the major attribute of a "reflector":

Attribute 1: A Reflective Teacher Is Capable of Consciously Structuring Situations and Problems, and Considers it Important to Do So.

We coded these reflectors as R1 and R2. They finished the program in less than 5 years. We will illustrate this attribute by means of several of their statements during the interviews.

Interviewer (in the second year):

"Do you consider the process of reflecting on yourself just as important as the teacher educators here?"

R1: "Yes, I do think it's important. Later, when you're teaching, it doesn't make any difference how much math you know, if you can't maintain discipline in the classroom. To do that it's important to learn how to stop and think: why did things go wrong, and what did I do that I could have done differently? That's why I think it's so important to stop and think about yourself."

In an interview at the end of the course, the same student teacher said:

"During a lesson you just react to the situation, do whatever occurs to you. Later, thinking back, I want to work it out for myself. Not just ask someone else's opinion. I feel sort of like, well, I could have figured that out for myself, and then I don't like hearing it from someone else. Or else later you think, what I really meant was such and such, because he didn't understand why I reacted the way I did. Once I've got it all clear in my head, then I wouldn't mind hearing it from someone else, if they were there at the time. And if I have an idea about what went wrong, but I'm still not sure, then I'd like to hear what a more experienced person has to say. So first I need to be clear in my own mind what happened, and decide whether I'm satisfied with the way I reacted, and after that I'll listen to what someone else has to say about it."

And here is an excerpt from an interview with R2:

Interviewer: "Suppose you've just finished a lesson that didn't go too well. What do you do afterwards?"

R2: "I try to figure out for myself why things went wrong. By thinking back, trying to remember what went wrong, what I did, what I was trying to do. What was all right, what wasn't. I try to find a solution - I'm so sure of myself that I think I can! If it were during my student teaching period, and I couldn't figure things out for myself, then in the end I'd ask for help. I know, because during the student teaching period I really had problems when I was teaching. First I spent a week mulling it all over in my mind, trying to decide what to do. Finally I went to see the cooperating teacher. I know I tend to be too self-confident, always thinking I can figure things out for myself."

From the group of 10 student teachers who continued their studies, we selected one individual whom we considered less reflective. The view of this student (coded as L) was quite differently:

Interviewer (a year and a half into the course): "As I understand it, the teacher educators want you to reflect on yourself."

L: "In what way?"

Interviewer: "By thinking about on your own functioning, how you work on math, the relationship with your fellow students, with your students. Does that sound familiar to you?"

L: "Oh, you mean what was on the questionnaire? No, I never really noticed."

Interviewer (at the end of 4½ years): "Suppose that during a field experience you had a class that didn't go well. What would you do afterwards?"

L: "I'd talk about it with other student teachers. Ask about other ways of dealing with the problem."

It will be clear from the previous statements by the student teachers R1, R2, and L how, in selecting the reflectors, we operationalized the characteristic "structuring the situation yourself." We verified our choice of these three student teachers by having an independent researcher evaluate all 10 student teachers on the basis of the interviews. She was asked to rate the degree of internal orientation in the domains "oneself," "fellow students," and "mathematics" for every student teacher on a 5-point scale. The two reflectors we selected had the highest total scores (R1: 13, and R2: 14). The lowest score (10) was registered for three individuals, among them the student teacher L.

A second check was performed by calculating the mean of all the scores on the internal scales from the IEO test that had been administered every year during the longitudinal study. Figure 8.1 gives the scores for the 10 student teachers. The respondents selected on the basis of high reflectivity rank 1 and 3, respectively, whereas the less reflective student teacher recorded the lowest score. These results reinforced our confidence in the previous labeling of R1 and R2 as highly reflective and L as a less reflective student.

The excerpts from the interviews with R1 and R2 reveal another characteristic of the reflectors:

Students	1 R1	2	3 R2	4	5	6	7	8	9	10 L	Mean
Mean reflection score	4.1	3.7	3.6	3.6	3.5	3.5	3.5	3.4	3.4	3.2	3.5

Figure 8.1 Mean of all the scores recorded on the internal scales of the IEO test by 10 student teachers during the longitudinal study.

Attribute 2: A Reflective Teacher Uses Certain Standard Questions When Structuring Experiences.

Structuring always takes place from a certain perspective. This perspective is translated into one or more questions: what happened, why did it happen, what did I do wrong, what could I have done differently, and so on? We believe it is important that student teachers are taught to deal with such questions during their training. The specific questions selected for such training will reflect the educational views in which the course is rooted. Thus, in the SOL program, a great deal of attention was given to the way the teacher's actions during the lesson influence the interpersonal relationship with the students.

Attribute 3: A Reflective Teacher Can Easily Answer the Question of What He or She Wants to Learn.

The structuring of experiences and situations can also be directed towards one's own *learning process*, as formulated in principle 11 in section 6.5. We found that the capacity to structure one's own learning manifests itself most clearly in the fact that reflectors are less dependent on the teacher educators when it comes to choosing learning goals. A few examples from the interviews follow here:

> R1: "... like during the first short field experiences. You become aware of certain problems, you start to think of certain things as important, and that's when you're able to say: that's what I want to learn. I like the structure they use in the mathematics department, where you start off with little things, and later on you're able to formulate real learning goals, and to start working on them."
>
> Interviewer: "Can you decide for yourself how you want to learn something? Or do you need a teacher educator to provide suggestions?"
>
> R1: "I'd prefer to figure out for myself what I want to learn, and decide how I want to learn it, because you know better than anyone else what the best way of learning is for you. I would read something on the subject, try out a few things myself, not too much at first. No, I don't think I really need a teacher educator to help me. If a teacher were to offer unsolicited advice, I'm not sure whether I would appreciate it. No, I don't think I would."
>
> Interviewer: "If you look at your own development as a teacher, and then consider the future, what would you like to learn, or learn to do better?"
>
> R2: "Classroom work could be more structured, more under control. Sometimes I get the impression that I don't have everything in my grasp. I know what's going on in class, at least for 20 of the 30 students, but the other 10... Sometimes they escape me, and I want to get hold of them too (...) And devote more attention to a quiet atmo-

sphere in the classroom. I try to do that by speaking directly to individuals wherever I can. Asking a group at the back of the class that's getting a bit noisy to come to the front, and talking to them there, instead of reprimanding them by raising my voice. Or separating groups, usually boys and girls who are just beginning to get interested in each other. At that age, that always leads to whispering, clowning, and a lot of noise."

By way of contrast, here is an excerpt from an interview with the less reflective student teacher (during the last stages of the preparation program):

Interviewer: "Would you know an answer if I asked you: what do you want to learn?"

L (after being quiet for some time): "I guess I'd like to learn more in practical situations."

Interviewer: "Is it a difficult question for you?"

L: "Yes, it is a difficult question. Maybe later, after I've done some teaching, there will be situations that I find difficult. But I'll manage. I have no idea what else I should learn. I just have to get on with the work."

Attribute 4: A Reflective Teacher Can Adequately Describe and Analyze His or Her Own Functioning in the Interpersonal Relationships with Others.

Of the various possible objects of reflection, the SOL program focused on the student teacher's own performance in the interpersonal relationships with others (in particular, students and fellow teachers). According to the SOL view, good teachers are able to analyze their performance in the interpersonal relationship with others (see section 6.5, principle 7). Thus, they reflect in particular on interpersonal relationships. Concerns about the relationships with students are not usually apparent until a later stage in the professional development (Fuller & Bown, 1975). This was confirmed by the results of our longitudinal study (Study 2), which showed that attention shifted from "concerns about survival," to "teaching situation concerns," and "concerns about the students." Attribute 4 was apparent from Study 1, where reflective graduates voiced such views as:

- During my training I have examined, often in depth, my own performance. I have decided for myself exactly how I help others. I have taught myself to develop, and learned to think about myself with respect to certain theoretical frameworks, in relation to myself as well as to others. This ability is quite well developed, and it is of great help to me as a starting teacher.

- At the SOL I learned to look at myself, to see what effect my behavior has on the children, and to be consciously involved in the situation of the moment. This attitude has gradually become second nature to me.
- (On the influence of the program) You gain insight into your own performance, what you do and don't do in a group, and how others see your actions. This way I've gained a much clearer picture of myself, and this helps me to determine my attitude in the class. It also makes itself felt in contacts with colleagues and the school management.

In Study 4, we also collected quantitative data showing that SOL graduates with more than 2 years' experience have a more adequate perception of their own performance in their interpersonal relationships with the students than experienced graduates of another, more subject-oriented preparation program (Wubbels & Korthagen, 1990). In two classes taught by each teacher, the students' perception of the functioning of the teacher in his relationship with the students was measured by means of the Questionnaire on Teacher Interaction (the QTI; see Wubbels & Levy, 1993). The teacher also filled out the QTI for the two classes, indicating how he or she perceived his or her own performance in the class. For each class of a particular teacher, we calculated the sum of the absolute differences on the eight scales of the QTI between the average student score in that class and the teacher score. This "difference score" is an indication of the degree to which the teacher can adequately reflect about his or her performance in their interpersonal relationships with the students. The averages of the difference scores in the group made up of SOL graduates, and the group made up of graduates from the other program, were compared by means of a *t* test. These scores did not differ significantly in the case of teachers with 1 or 2 years of experience. Among those who graduated more then 2 years before, however, there was a significant difference: The discrepancy between teacher and student perceptions of the teacher–student relationship was significantly smaller in the SOL group than in the control group. The scores were 3.1 and 3.8, respectively, on a 5-point scale ($t = 2.2$, $p = .02$, effect size about .5 standard deviation). We concluded that the teachers who graduated more than 2 years before from the SOL had a more adequate perception of their interpersonal relationships with students in the classroom than the teachers in the control group who also had more than 2 years of experience.

8.4. CORRELATES OF REFLECTIVITY

In this section, we will present a number of aspects that, on the basis of the four studies, may be considered correlates of reflectivity. These aspects are, in some cases, the consequences of the characteristic attributes and, in other cases, the antecedents. They may even be related to the attributes in a circular manner in that they reinforce a characteristic attribute and are, in turn, reinforced by it. The correlates are, however, not a generic aspect of reflection.

Correlate 1: Reflective Teachers Have Better Interpersonal Relationships with Students Than Other Teachers.

According to this correlate, reflective teachers are more capable not only of adequately analyzing their interpersonal relationships with students (attribute 4), but also succeed in making those relationships better.

In Study 4, the interpersonal relationships of SOL graduates were compared with graduates of another preparation program. Judging by the students' perceptions, measured by means of the QTI, the SOL graduates scored higher on all the scales that are positively linked to cognitive and affective learning outcomes.[2] This was reported in one measure on which the SOL graduates scored significantly higher than the other graduates ($t = 1.9, p < .05$, effect size .6 standard deviations). This difference was above all a long-term effect, that is, the difference was not significant for teachers who had graduated less than 3 years before. (See Wubbels & Korthagen, 1990, for more details.)

Correlate 2: Reflective Teachers Develop a High Degree of Job Satisfaction.

The comparative study (Study 4) also showed that teachers who graduated from the SOL 3 or more years before had a significantly higher level of job satisfaction than teachers in the control group who had likewise graduated 3 or more years before (means of 3.9 and 3.3, respectively, on a 5-point scale, $t = 2.4, p < .01$, effect size .6 standard deviations). The difference was not significant for teachers who graduated less than 3 years before.

We propose the following theoretical explanation for the correlation between reflectivity and job satisfaction. As Schön says (1983, p. 61), the more routine the activities of practitioners become, the more acute is the danger that they no longer think very much about what they are doing. We believe that teachers who get into this kind of rut will ultimately lapse into patterns of behavior that can no longer be corrected. This can lead to boredom, which can result in a low level of job satisfaction.

Correlate 3: Reflective Teachers Also Consider It Important for Their Students to Learn By Investigating and Structuring Things Themselves.

It would appear that teachers who consider reflection important for themselves also stimulate their students to reflect. The following statements made by student teachers involved in the longitudinal study illustrate this point:

> R1: "There's one thing that I think is especially good. In class when someone has a question, you don't just give the answer, or part of the answer. You help them to think

again, or ask another question which will get them on the right track. That's what I liked about my student teaching. Whenever a question was asked, I'd think 'now don't just tell them the answer. Stop and think how to get them to figure it out for themselves.'"

R2: "During teaching practice I noticed that if you make your students think, they make much faster progress. Just writing down more examples on the blackboard isn't going to help them much. If you let them work it out for themselves, it may take twice as long, but the second, third and fourth time it'll go ten times as fast. And in the end you get much better results. I'm convinced that it not only works in theory, but in practice too. I do it without even thinking."

By way of contrast, we will give the views of the less reflective student teacher recorded during the longitudinal study. In his opinion, the SOL did not put nearly enough emphasis on group teaching, explaining a point to the class as a whole:

L: "It's only when there are problems that he [the teacher educator] gives you a clue, and even then you have to figure out the rest yourself."

Interviewer: "Would you like to teach that way?"

L: "No, I don't think so."

Correlate 4: Reflective Student Teachers Have, Earlier in Their Lives, Been Encouraged to Structure Their Experiences, Problems, and So on.

This correlate became obvious from the interviews. The reflective respondents often indicated they had been through a difficult period in their lives, or had been confronted with powerful cultural differences. As an example, let us look at the words of a very reflective graduate of the SOL program whom we interviewed in Study 1. He talked about the extreme stress he had experienced as a starting teacher:

And yet it's difficult to prepare yourself for such stress during your training. If you've never experienced a situation of great stress in your private life, where it's you against the rest, then you don't have any idea what it's like.

Similar views were voiced by reflective student teachers in our longitudinal study (Study 2):

Interviewer: "Are you the sort of person who reflects on himself?"

R2: "Well, I was more or less forced to. I was out of work for two years, and then when I got back in the running ... that sort of makes you stop and think about yourself."

Interviewer: "And how about the subjects?"

R2: "Yes, especially pedagogy. Like for kids from lower social classes."

Interviewer: "Why does that interest you?"

R2: "Well, I come from a working-class background. My parents are just ordinary working-class people. I went to a pretty fancy school, and that meant that I was part of a group that wasn't entirely accepted."

This same sort of personal confrontation with a different cultural background was recounted by another reflective student teacher:

R1: "Most of the teachers here have a fairly open attitude, but even so they sometimes make certain comments. I'm a Christian, and people can make very insulting and hurtful remarks about the Christian faith that are absolutely untrue. They paint a kind of caricature of a group of people, to make them look ridiculous. Then I just withdraw into a sort of shell. If I had a problem, I would never go to a teacher like that, because he's destroyed my confidence in him. And that's a shame, because most of the time I know that the teacher is really OK, he just doesn't know what he's doing to other people."

For purposes of comparison, we also present the view of the less reflective teacher from the longitudinal study:

Interviewer: "Strange, isn't it, that you weren't that interested in the reflection practicum in your first year?"

L: "That's probably because of the way things were at home. We never talked much, and you certainly didn't put forward any opinions. And when you get here, and all of a sudden people start expecting you to have opinions of your own, then it's really hard. In my first year it just didn't work; I dreaded all those discussions. Very gradually things have improved, and I've managed to change the way I feel, but it took a long time."

Thus, it is important for teacher educators who aim to promote reflection to realize that in many cases reflective teachers in our studies seemed to be already reflective before they started their training. As we concluded earlier (see section 6.5, and for more details, Korthagen, 1988), a preparation program aiming at the promotion of reflection would seem to be most beneficial to those student teachers who are already somewhat reflective.

Correlate 5: Reflective Teachers Have Strong Feelings of Personal Security and Self-Efficacy as a Teacher.

The relation between reflection and self-efficacy has a theoretical basis. Reflection is a form of metacognition, which has been shown to be positively related to self-efficacy (Bandura, 1982; McCombs, 1988). It is well-known from the work of developmental psychologists that reflection may form a threat to the self-image. Laying your own performance open to inspection makes you vulnerable and threatens your survival within your own inner reality. Thus, for reflection, high degree of self-efficacy is necessary. This is illustrated by the following statements from the interviews in the longitudinal study:

> R1: "In the course of my training I've gradually become more sure of myself. I don't know whether it has to do with the course or not. I find it much easier to speak up. In secondary school, if there was something I didn't understand, I'd go home and try to work it out. I did that the first couple of years here too, but now I put on the brakes, and just say that I don't understand. Three out of four times you discover that you weren't really concentrating, or that it was some minor point that you missed. But sometimes it's a good thing you put on the brakes, because there are a lot of others who don't understand either, or because I missed a couple of essential steps. I'm not hesitant about doing that any more. I think that the same thing is true in classroom situations. Your first student teaching period, you're explaining something and you think, let it go for now, and check again in a couple of minutes. But now if you're explaining something, you say 'Jane, would you mind putting that diary away for now?' and just go on talking. You look to see if they do it, and if necessary you tell them a second time. Whereas in the beginning you'd just let it go."

> R2: "I think being articulate and sure of yourself are closely related. These are things that I still think about, that are a kind of central principle running through my training. I try to go through things systematically, and I feel sure of myself when I'm able to put something into words. I know that I'll learn how to do it in the end, but now I'm starting to grasp certain things, so that the pieces are starting to fall into place."

For purposes of comparison, here is the story of our less reflective student teacher:

> L: "I often feel as if I don't really have anything to contribute. When I start to say something I think, no, that's not really important. And then later when someone else says the same thing, it gets used after all. A lot of the time there's a thought circling around in my head, but I just can't get it out....
>
> In the group I found it very difficult to talk, especially about myself. I'd start to perspire, and I hated it. It's still not easy for me, but it's a lot better now. It's as if they expect it of you; they don't say so, but you can feel it. Everyone talks about their own feelings, so why shouldn't I?"

As Lucas (1996, p. 33) states:

"... you need to have courage to engage in (at least certain approaches to) reflection."

This may be an aspect of reflection that needs more attention on the part of teacher educators (cf. Cole, 1997).

Correlate 6: Student Teachers with Teaching Experience Who Have a High Degree of Self-Efficacy Focus in Their Reflections About Their Teaching on the Students. When They Have a Low Sense of Self-Efficacy They Focus on the Self.

An analysis of the quantitative data suggests that when the prospective teachers have teaching experience, the relation between reflection and self-efficacy is somewhat more complicated. For more experienced student teachers, there seems to be a link between self-efficacy and the object of reflection. Student teachers who emphasize their own functioning when they reflect about their teaching have a relatively low sense of self-efficacy. If they emphasize the students in their reflections, then they have a relatively high sense of self-efficacy. This hypothesis about the relation between reflectivity and self-efficacy is based on the results of both the longitudinal study and the comparison study, which are presented in Fig. 8.2. Self-efficacy was measured with an adaptation by Brekelmans (1989) of a questionnaire of Cloetta and Hedinger (1981).

There appear to be consistently positive correlations between the degree of self-efficacy and the internal scale "students" of the IEO test: The more self-confident teachers are, the more inclined they are to reflect on their students. For the internal scale "self" of the IEO, these correlations are usually negative: The more self-confident teachers are, the less inclined they are to reflect about themselves. These findings are in line with results found by Ashton et al. (1989). For the other domains (mathematics, school, etc.), the correlations are near zero. These results would seem to make sense, as high concerns for the self can indicate a lower quality

	comparison study		longitudinal study			
	n=72		3rd year *n*=10		5th year *n*=10	
	self	students	self	students	self	students
self-efficacy	-.04	.31**	-.75*	.14	-.37	.57

Figure 8.2 Correlations between the self-efficacy scale and the internal scales of the IEO test for the domains "self" and "students". *p<.05 **p<.01.

of interpersonal relationships in the classroom, and thus a lower sense of efficacy. If these interpersonal relationships are positive, then teachers can allow themselves to reflect more on their students.

Correlate 7: Reflective Teachers Appear to Talk or Write Relatively Easily About Their Experiences.

The reflective teachers and student teachers in our studies appeared to talk and write easily. In the longitudinal study (Study 2), the answers of the two reflectors (R1 and R2) to the open questions in the interviews were approximately twice as long as those of the less reflective student teacher, who said that he had never been much of a talker (see his statements under Correlate 5). In the comparative study (Study 4), we asked graduates of the SOL program and of another program to mention a number of characteristics of their preparation program. Graduates of the SOL program gave twice as many characteristics (on average, 4.6) as did the graduates from the control group (on average, 2.3).

8.5. A FEW COMMENTS

In the present section, we first mention some relations between reflectivity and other variables that we expected, but for which we have not obtained confirmation. We also discuss the validity of the IEO test. Finally, we will examine differences between teachers in different stages of their career.

Age

In Study 3, we found no strong correlations between age and reflectivity for the domains "self" and "mathematics," as we had expected on the basis of indications in Study 1. As mentioned in section 6.5, there was a negative correlation, however, between age and the internal orientation regarding fellow students ($r = -.29, p < .01$). Thus, older student teachers are somewhat less inclined to reflect on their fellow students and their relationships with them.

Previous Schooling

On the basis of the results of Study 1, we had hypothesized to find that student teachers who had a higher level of schooling were more reflective. In Study 3, however, this relation could only be demonstrated for reflection on mathematics. An analysis of covariance with previous schooling as factor and age as a covariate showed a significant main effect of the factor previous schooling on the scale "external orientation regarding mathematics" ($df = 4, F = 2.93, p < .02$). When the student teachers' level of previous schooling is high, they are slightly less externally oriented in the domain of mathematics.

Inclination Toward Innovation

In our comparative study, we found no indication of a link between reflectivity and inclination toward innovation, as we had expected. Such a link has been suggested by Zeichner (1983, p. 6), and Zeichner and Liston (1987). It is possible that the difference (discussed in chapter 4) between the operationalization of the concept of reflection in the SOL program and that in the Wisconsin program have resulted in fundamental differences. In any case, we know of no empirical results that show that the Wisconsin operationalization of reflection is correlated with an inclination toward innovation.

The IEO Test

It must be observed that in our comparative study (Study 4), we were not able to demonstrate that SOL graduates score significantly higher on the internal scales of the IEO test than the graduates in the control group. On the other hand, we have many other indications that SOL graduates are indeed more reflective (Wubbels & Korthagen, 1990, p. 41). We believe that the present form of the IEO test is not as adequate as we would like it to be. To begin with, the IEO test suffers from the familiar drawback of many attitude tests, namely, that respondents are asked to indicate how often or in what way they usually do something. Obviously, this does not have to agree with what they actually do. Moreover, it is conceivable that distortion occurs when respondents are influenced by a comparison of their own reflective orientation with a norm that says how reflective they ought to be. That norm is no doubt influenced by the teacher education program, and such influence may affect one student teacher more than another.

For these reasons, we believe the results recorded for Study 3 should be interpreted with some caution. The same holds true for the attributes and correlates: Further research is needed before we can speak of firm conclusions.

Reflectivity and the Reality Shock

Finally, our results indicate that the view of reflection as a purely rational process is too limited. Emotions and attitudes play a crucial role (cf. Correlates 5 and 6). We are convinced that the stimulus to engage in reflection is almost always rooted in a need to get a better grasp of the situation. However, when fear of the situation becomes too great, as often happens during the "transition shock" (Corcoran, 1981; Müller-Fohrbrodt et al., 1978), reflection may disappear altogether (see also sections 3.1 and 6.5).

Our longitudinal study of the development of student teachers in the SOL program also provided indications of a relapse, a lessening of the ability to reflect, when an individual actually enters the teaching profession. And yet in Studies 1 and 2, we found indications that the capacity for reflection returns after about 1 year. As mentioned in section 6.5, this would seem to point to the existence of a *latency period*. The comparative study (Study 4) confirmed this hypothesis. It appears that at the beginning of their professional career, there were almost no differences between the graduates of the SOL program and those of the program that was more oriented toward subject matter. After a few years, however, the SOL graduates have a more adequate self-perception (attribute 4), better interpersonal relationships with their students (Correlate 1), and a higher degree of job satisfaction (Correlate 2). All in all, there is sufficient reason for researchers in the field of reflective teaching to distinguish between student teachers, teachers in the initial stages of their teaching career, and experienced teachers. This may sharpen the results presented in this chapter, because in the previous presentation of our findings no such distinction has been made between these different groups of teachers.

8.6. CONCLUSIONS

Based on the SOL conception of reflection, we found four characteristic attributes of reflective teachers and seven correlates. These are important findings, for example, in the light of the philosophy of education of the SOL program described in section 6.5. Concerning at least four of the educational principles underlying this teacher education program, we can conclude that reflective practitioners indeed meet the ideals of the SOL staff. These principles are:

- Teachers should be capable of committing themselves purposefully, consciously, and methodically as instruments in the teaching and learning situation.
- The relationship between the teacher and the student is a helping and cooperative relationship in which the teacher offers a climate of security and challenge, and only as much structure as each individual student needs.
- Teachers should be conscious of their own strong and weak points, and direct their own development.
- Teachers should be able to analyze and develop their interpersonal relationships with the students, with a view to attaining the ideal helping and cooperative relationship.

In this respect, reflective teachers can be considered "better" teachers.

The findings from our studies are also important because they show a direct relation between reflectivity and teacher performance, which is seldom supported by empirical research. On the other hand, we did not have strong evidence of a *causal* relationship. It may, for example, be that there is an underlying factor making teachers both more reflective and better at the characteristics already described, or even that better functioning in the relationship with students makes teachers more reflective.

Overall, this chapter offers a number of initial building blocks for a theory in which empirically based relations are established between a definition of reflection, characteristics of reflective teachers, and principles of good teaching. These building blocks have arisen from the SOL definition of reflection. We believe that also for other conceptualizations of reflection a great deal of empirical research will be needed to leave behind the vague notions and beliefs about the benefits of reflective teaching and the effects of programs designed to promote it.

SUMMARY

On the basis of research, we formulated four characteristic attributes of reflective teachers, based on the SOL conception of reflection:

1. A reflective teacher is capable of consciously structuring situations and problems, and considers it important to do so.
2. A reflective teacher uses certain standard questions when structuring experiences.
3. A reflective teacher can easily answer the question of what he or she wants to learn.
4. A reflective teacher can adequately describe and analyze his or her own functioning in the interpersonal relationships with others.

We also found seven correlates of reflectivity:

1. Reflective teachers have better interpersonal relationships with students than other teachers.
2. Reflective teachers develop a high degree of job satisfaction.
3. Reflective teachers also consider it important for their students to learn by investigating and structuring things themselves.
4. Reflective student teachers have, earlier in their lives, been encouraged to structure their experiences, problems, and so on.
5. Reflective teachers have strong feelings of personal security and self-efficacy as a teacher.

6. Student teachers with teaching experience who have a high degree of self-efficacy focus in their reflections about their teaching on the students. When they have a low sense of self-efficacy, they focus on the self.
7. Reflective teachers appear to talk or write relatively easily about their experiences.

Some of these findings can be interpreted as warnings to teacher educators. For example, an emphasis on reflection may be more beneficial to student teachers who are already pretty reflective, and to student teachers with a relatively high sense of self-efficacy.

In order to answer the question about whether reflective teachers are better teachers, more empirical studies are needed linking views of good teaching and conceptualizations of reflection to teacher characteristics.

BASIC CONCEPTS

Standard reflection questions

Personal security and self-efficacy

9 Working With Groups of Student Teachers

Fred Korthagen

What is good, Phaedrus,
And what is not good—
Need we ask anyone to tell us these things?

—*Robert Persig, Zen and the Art of Motorcycle Maintenance*

A characteristic of the realistic approach is for teacher educators to work with student teachers on the basis of their practical experiences. This is often done in groups of student teachers, because reflective interactions among students deepen the learning process. Consequently, in this chapter, the realistic approach is situated within the setting of group seminars in teacher education. First, a five-step procedure is discussed for working with practical experiences and integrating these with theoretical elements. Then four specific techniques are described for promoting reflection, which can be used in group seminars. An overview is presented of findings regarding the use of these techniques. Finally, further possibilities are discussed—for example, the step toward peer-supported learning, a structure within which student teachers learn to supervise each other.

9.1. INTRODUCTION

In chapter 7, the process of promoting reflection in individual supervision has been described. Of course, teacher educators do not always have the time to work with student teachers on an individual basis. Moreover, group settings are even essential for promoting reflection: By sharing experiences, teachers are stimulated to structure these experiences and, by comparing their own analyses of practice with those of others, they may discover other possible ways of framing their experiences. They can also ask for and get feedback from peers. In sum, reflective interactions among student teachers deepen the intended process of professional learning (*collaborative reflection*). Northfield and Gunstone (1997, p. 49) state:

> Learning about teaching is a collaborative activity and teacher education is best conducted in small groups and networks with ideas and experiences being shared and discussed.

Bell and Gilbert (1996, p. 57) discuss the consequences of constructivism for teacher development and conclude:

> Social interaction–for example, in dialogues, accounting and narratives–promotes learning of socially constructed knowledge, personal construction of meaning, and the reconstruction of social knowledge.

However, it is remarkable that, although the promotion of reflection is generally accepted as an important goal in teacher education, there is a lack of descriptions of techniques or activities that can be used in seminars to promote reflection in groups of student teachers. Most program descriptions (e.g., Feiman, 1979; Zeichner & Liston, 1987) are quite general, and provide no detailed information about activities encouraging prospective teachers to subject their teaching practice to a critical analysis (a positive exception is Harvard, 1994). However, just putting students together is not sufficient to promote learning from practice. As we saw in the previous chapters, the presentation of theory to groups of student teachers may not help either. So the question remains: What can be effective ways of promoting reflection in groups and of linking practice to theory?

The ALACT model could again be of help here, because it describes the ideal reflection process in terms of cycles consisting of five phases. However, the ALACT model does not yield a direct answer to the question of what teacher educator interventions are helpful to promote the intended spiral development in student teachers within the context of group meetings. This question will be dealt with in this chapter, which is comparable to chapter 7 in its focus on teacher educator interventions. However, the present chapter deals with promoting reflection in groups, whereas chapter 7 focused on promoting reflection in individual supervision.

In section 9.2, a five-step procedure will be described, which offers guidelines for working with groups of student teachers bringing in practical experiences. The procedure can, for example, be used in group seminars organized around teaching practice periods. Ideally, the student teachers come back to the institute after some experience, have a group meeting under the supervision of the teacher educator, go back to their practice schools, come back again, and so on. Such an arrangement is called a commuting model (Van der Valk et al., 1996). But even if there is little "commuting," it may be important for teacher educators to be able to link teaching practice periods with theory. In section 9.3, the five-step procedure described in section 9.2 will be illustrated using the transcript of a real seminar.

After that, in section 9.4, four concrete techniques for promoting reflection will be discussed, which can even be used in very large groups (e.g., up to 200 people). In section 9.5, research findings in using these techniques are reported. In section 9.6, a logical next step will be discussed in making student teachers independent learners: Through a structure of *peer-supported learning*, student teachers can learn to supervise each other. In section 9.7, some conclusions will be drawn.

9.2. A FIVE-STEP PROCEDURE

We have developed a five-step procedure to structure learning by reflection in group seminars in teacher education (Hermans, Créton, & Korthagen, 1993). This five-step procedure may help teacher educators who wish to take their students' experiences seriously and build theory on practice. The five-step procedure is a pedagogical structure, a method to promote learning. As such, it differs fundamentally from the ALACT model, which also has five phases, but describes the ideal learning process of a student teacher. There is a connection because by applying the five-step procedure, teacher educators can stimulate student teachers to pass through the phases of the ALACT model:

1. In the first step, student teachers get assignments *prestructuring* the experiences that they will have. These could be both experiences in class, at the institute, or in teaching in a school. Ideally, these assignments are based on a concern or learning need of the student teachers. For example, they may be concerned about motivation problems with students at school. An assignment can then be to try and map the motivation of high school students from an interview with one or more of them. One could say that during this prestructuring step, the student teachers receive "glasses" to look through when at school.
   It can be necessary to prepare the intended experiences by skills training on campus. If the student teachers lack experience with questioning other people on issues, they can practice conducting a 7-minute interview with a fellow student on what he or she wants to learn from the seminar. The questioning techniques can then be reflected on in the group and further training, let's say in using more open questions, can then be part of the prestructuring phase.
2. In this step, the student teachers go to a school to have *experiences*—in this example, interviewing high school students. The crucial element in this step is that these experiences create more specific concerns and elicit gestalts (see section 3.3) in the student teachers serving as the starting point for the next steps.
3. In the third step, the experiences are reported back by the student teachers so that the teacher educator, together with the student teachers, can *structure* the experiences and the elicited gestalts by clarification, classification, and generalization. As we have seen before (see, e.g., section 4.5), structuring is an essential part of the reflection process. The students' reports can take the form of presentations in much detail with the help of video recordings, or it can be a more overall exchange within the group on the basis of questions of the teacher educa-

tor. The aim of structuring is to bring order into the "chaos" of the different experiences that the students have had.
It is important for the teacher educator to realize that although "motivation" and "interviewing" were presented as points of attention, the student teachers' attention may be drawn by a completely different issue. For example, they may have started to become concerned with the behavior of high school students. The essence of the realistic approach is that the teacher educator then takes these concerns as the starting point for the structuring process. This implies that in such a situation the teacher educator must be willing to put aside the program he or she had prepared for the meeting. To put it a little less mildly: The induced experiences were not the most suitable ones to prepare for the intended program.

4. After (usually a wealth of) experiences have been structured, it is possible to *focus* on some aspects of these and the elicited gestalts and analyze them in greater detail. It is possible to focus on many different things, such as commonly perceived learning needs of the student teachers (e.g., how to create safety in an interview with a child?), essential aspects or generic features of the concept under study (e.g., what kinds of motivation can be distinguished?), the gestalts embedded in the student teachers' reports on their experiences (e.g., gestalts about students of this age), the relation of these gestalts to the experiences (e.g., how did the student teachers' gestalts about children of this age influence their questioning?), student teachers' strengths and weaknesses in relation to a particular competency (e.g., how competent are you in being empathetic?), what they have learned, what their learning aims are for the next weeks, and so on.
Careful application of the realistic approach requires that in choosing from all these options, the teacher educator tries to follow the concerns and gestalts put forward by the student teachers.

5. Already during the previous step, the teacher educator may not only label experiences or things student teachers have said on a more abstract level, but can also point to theoretical interpretations and connections between different categories and causal relationships. The presentation of theoretical concepts and principles is Step 5. It is important to emphasize that preferably the form of theory in this step is not as usually found in books (e.g., theory emphasizing descriptions of theoretical constructs and conceptual networks or research reports): The theoretical elements presented should still be directly connected to the student teachers' experiences or future plans. In terms of chapter 2, theory in Step 5 takes the form of *phronesis* instead of *episteme*. Step 5 is called the step of *introducing theory with a small t*.

In order to offer the students more background, the teacher educator may of course also add Theories (with capital T) from the literature in a more traditional form, such as a chapter on motivation in a book on educational psychology (this is called *episteme* in chap. 2). The introduction can, for example, be in the form of a short lecture or a written presentation. If a standard text is used, then it will usually be necessary to make explicit what the connection is between the theory and the experiences of the student teachers. Sometimes, however, it may even be better to stick to the theory with a small t, linked to the student teachers' own practical experiences, and skip the introduction of more formal scientific theories. Later, in chapter 10, we will analyze more thoroughly why it is often better not to include too much Theory with capital T in this step. Chapter 10 will also provide us with guidelines for deciding about the degree of emphasis on Theory that is fruitful at a certain stage.

Then, of course, the cycle repeats itself and a new step of prestructuring can start. Often Steps 4 (focusing) and 5 (theory with a small t) almost automatically lead to Step 1 (prestructuring): That which has been the focus today becomes the issue to be practiced in tomorrow's teaching experience.

For an overview of the five-step procedure, see Fig. 9.1.

9.3. AN ILLUSTRATION OF THE FIVE-STEP PROCEDURE

In this section, the five-step procedure will be illustrated by means of an excerpt from a 2-hour seminar given at the IVLOS Institute of Education at Utrecht University.[1] The participants were members of a so-called inservice group, consisting of student teachers who after graduating in their subject matter studies, had a brief 1-week training at IVLOS before they began teaching at a school for secondary education. Such teachers work roughly half the number of hours involved in a full-time appointment. Although unqualified, they teach independently from the start, and the cooperating teacher who is responsible for supervising their work is not present during their lessons. In addition, the student teachers spend 2 days a week at the in-

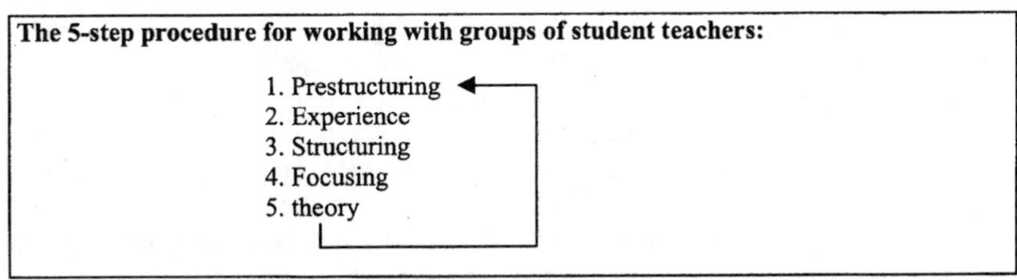

FIG. 9.1. Overview of the five-step procedure for working with groups of student teachers within a realistic approach.

stitute. An institute day consists mainly of an exchange of experiences; various themes are covered, all of which are keyed to the questions and experiences of the student teachers. They indicate which particular subjects they are interested in, and theme sessions are then planned around the chosen topics. For example, one theme that was brought up after they had been teaching for about 4 months was the after-class talk with a student who had been "troublesome" during a lesson. The student teachers indicated that they found such talks difficult. Concerns of this nature are quite common among beginning secondary school teachers, who are confronted with problems affecting the atmosphere in the class. Most are not yet able to prevent such problems from arising, and one of the instruments to improve the atmosphere in the class is a private talk with individual students or small groups of students. If properly conducted, these talks can bring about a considerable improvement in the relationship between teacher and student. Because the distance between them is smaller, the teacher often finds the atmosphere less tense and confrontational than a discussion with a large group of students. Moreover, such talks can also be used for metacommunication (i.e., discussing the way teacher and students communicate with one another in the classroom); in this way they have proved helpful in altering undesirable patterns in the teacher-student relationship (Watzlawick et al., 1967).

The greater part of the institute work that takes place within the framework of in-service teacher education is carried out by one regular teacher educator. He or she is responsible for those components in which the student teachers exchange experiences, arrive at solutions for their problems, acquire theoretical insights, formulate personal learning goals, and indicate their preferences for the form and content of the training provided by the institute, according to their own school experiences. If there is a specific subject that the regular teacher educator feels less qualified to discuss, then he or she asks a guest teacher educator specializing in that subject to deal with that component.

When the chosen topic was the after-class talk, a guest teacher was invited. After a brief personal introduction, this teacher educator began the seminar as follows:

> Important phases in reflection consist in looking back and becoming aware of exactly what the difficulty is *for you*. Often this results in a highly personal answer. And I think that might be a good starting point for this meeting. I'd like each of you to consider just what the crux of the problem is when you think about these after-class talks. I'm not looking for general or abstract answers that are valid for everyone. I want to know how you feel yourself. A good exercise in reflection is to try to see how concisely you can formulate the answer. Give me just one sentence that says "That's it! That's the problem for me." You may not be able to do that yet, but perhaps you could give me some idea of the area that's giving you trouble. Something like "When I think about these talks, this or that problem or difficulty comes to mind" or, conversely, you think of aspects that you enjoy. I'd like to ask you to concentrate for a minute and then write down, in one sentence, "What comes to mind when I think about after-class talks."

This is Step 1, *prestructuring*. The attention of the student teachers is directed toward what is to come and they are stimulated to select a focus for themselves within the theme of "after-class talks." In this particular case, the assignment led to a brief round of exchanges, which included concerns about how to motivate students, how to deal with resistance, how to reduce the distance between teacher and students, how to resolve a conflict with a student, how to learn to put your problems into perspective, and the question of how seriously to take a student.

Then two sessions of role playing were staged (Step 2: *experience*). One of the student teachers played the teacher, the other a student. These sessions, which lasted from 5 to 10 minutes, were conducted according to specific role descriptions, and formulated in such a way that certain conflicts and breakdowns in communication were bound to occur.

The role descriptions provided before the first talk are summarized here. The other student teachers were asked to observe the role playing while keeping in mind their own particular problem or focus (formulated in Step 1).

The role-playing instructions

The instructions for the first talk state that the student in question is in grade 9. The student's school performance is erratic, only just sufficient for a passing grade in the student teacher's subject, a tendency which is also seen in other subjects. According to the teacher, the student is capable of much better work, and the colleague teachers confirm that with a bit more effort, he could probably reach a high level. In class today, the student was not paying attention and was continually fooling with a pocket calculator. The decision to ask the student to remain after class was triggered by the following incident. It was clear that the student had not done his homework. Moreover, he was constantly talking to his neighbors next to him and behind him. When asked about a point that had just been explained, the student was unable to answer the—very simple—question. It was at this point that the teacher asked him to stay after class for a talk (during the lunch break).

The descriptions of the role of the teacher and the role of the student depict the same situation from two different viewpoints. In that of the student, there is a good reason for not having done the homework, while the student also finds this teacher's lessons extremely dull. The role description of the teacher emphasizes that this student has the capacity to do much better work, but displays extremely irritating behavior.

The role playing is discussed according to a fixed pattern (Step 3: *structuring*). First, the student teacher who played the role of the teacher talks about his experiences during the role playing, with special reference to his own problem issue. Then, the other student teachers contribute their own observations, and the person who played the student says how he felt about the experience.[2]

We are now going to take a closer look at the discussion of the first role-playing session, because it provides an illustration of Steps 3, 4, and 5. In this session (Step 2: *experience*), the teacher's role was played by a student teacher named Brigit, who had formulated her problem point as follows:

I've had a couple of talks where the student just says what he thinks you want him to say. He's polite and agrees with you, so he can get out of there as fast as possible. I keep wondering what's going on in his head. Have I really accomplished anything? How can you tell?

She says that she experienced the role play—in which she played the teacher and another student teacher played the student—as very true to life, because it illustrated her own problem. Several excerpts from the follow-up discussion are given here:

Teacher educator: "Okay, Brigit, what did you think of it?"

Brigit: "I have a feeling that there's a barrier that I'm trying to overcome by getting him to calm down, to begin with, just to sit down. I said something like: Concentrate on me, and try to understand that I really want to talk to you. But it was difficult because he actually had a good argument: he's not actually failing the subject. I wanted to say something about his attitude in the classroom, the fact that he's always looking around and that he distracts the others."

Teach. ed.: "So in the first place you were trying to calm him down?"

Brigit: "Well, I wanted to start by making it clear that there's a problem, not only during this lesson, but all the time. I want to tell him that I think he is smart enough for the assignments, but that I don't understand why once in a while he doesn't do it."

Teach. ed.: "Do you feel that your strategy has been successful up to now?"

Brigit: "Not really. I don't feel as if I've gotten through to him. It could take me the whole break.... No, somehow or other I've got to find a way to get my point across. Maybe I should just ask him point blank: What do you think of the subject I teach, what is it like for you sitting in my class, how does it make you feel?"

Teach. ed.: "There's something you said that I think is really important: I can't get through to him." [And he draws an arrow on the blackboard from teacher to student.]

Birgit: "I can't even make a dent."

Teach. ed.: "You can't make a dent. There is an interesting rule about making a dent. It says that the harder you try, the less you succeed."

Brigit: "Yes."

Astrid: "There also an old saying about catching more flies with honey than with vinegar, or something like that."

Teach. ed.: "Oh, yes, that's pretty much the same thing, isn't it? Okay, so the harder you try to catch your fly with vinegar ... the harder you try to get through to him, the more difficult it becomes. [The teacher educator writes all this down on the blackboard.] How can you tell that it's getting more difficult?"

Brigit: "You mean a certain stage when he begins to disconnect? I can't get him to stay seated, I can't get him calmed down. And he doesn't take me seriously."

...

Teach. ed: "Astrid concentrated on the issue of resistance and reducing the distance between her and the student. I have an idea that that could have a lot to do with what we're talking about here."

Astrid: "Yes, I definitely saw an attempt, even non-verbally. She really tried to sort of reach out to him, across the table. And he kept moving further and further away from the table.... You let him eat his sandwiches. That was a good idea. You were trying to let him know that you understood that he was much more interested in the lunch break than in a talk with you."

Teach. ed: "Yes, I'd like to look at that point, because it's important: showing people that you understand their problem, what concerns them. [The teacher educator writes on the blackboard: 'let the other see that you understand his problem'].... This probably isn't the first time that you've talked about this, since I know that your group has already had quite a bit of discussion technique when discussing peer-supported learning: trying to empathize with the other person, put into words what the other is thinking and feeling. That's what we mean by discussion technique, isn't it?"

Group: "Yes."

Astrid: "Letting the other person know that you've been listening."

Teach. ed: "Letting the other person know that you've been listening. [The teacher educator writes this on the blackboard.] Of course, you can do that literally, but sometimes you can do it by 'listening between the lines,' so to speak, or trying to see what's on his mind. Putting that into words is one way of reaching someone, because then the other person feels that you understand him. That's exactly the opposite of using *your* message to try to get through to someone. Here, you're trying to pick up the message the other person is sending and using it to make contact ..."

What the teacher educator is doing is, first of all, making use of the principle of tuning in on the concerns and gestalts of the student teachers. In his own words (recorded after the meeting):

> I didn't know the group, so I considered it even more important to use an inductive approach: let the group make the first move, and then introduce a few elements of theory, trying to find the spot where the energy is. And what I was really interested in was discovering their concerns, experiencing them. Finding out what was going through their minds when they thought about the subject, what they saw as the problem? That helps me to understand their language and use that as a starting point. That's why I almost always start with a reflection assignment: think about a recent example of the kind of talk we're focusing on here and formulate what you see as the problem. I remember that I also tried to make the link back to a previous occasion, when a student teacher gave a lesson on reflection, but that resulted in a few glassy-eyed looks.

It will be clear from this explanation why the teacher educator began the meeting as he did. He was trying to find out what was in the minds of the student teachers by asking them what the crux of the problem was for them personally, so that he could key his remarks to their individual concerns. During the introduction, he immediately tries out various approaches in an effort to discover the concerns of the student teachers and how they cope with those concerns. He refers back to a shared experience (discussion on reflection in which the phases of the ALACT model had been presented), asks them to indicate their own problems in the area, and then requests that they make them more concrete (e.g., "For me, the core of the problem is ..."). This produced a statement for each student teacher, which he then translated into an observation assignment for the role-playing sessions. In this way, he ensured that all the individual concerns of the student teachers were addressed during the discussion. This is an example of how Step 1 (*prestructuring*) can prepare the way for Step 3 (*structuring*). The teacher educator used the concerns of the student teachers as a point of departure for the final component of the meeting, the exercises based on individual concerns. Somewhat to his disappointment, his effort to create a link with an earlier lesson on reflection made it clear that the student teachers did not have any real sense of involvement with the theme of reflection. As a result, he felt that it would not be fruitful to explore that relation any further. Here it is important to note that he did not attempt to force the discussion in a direction where the interest and energy of the student teachers apparently did not lie.

During the summing-up round, Brigit had formulated her problem with one of her students as follows: "I keep wondering what's going on in his head. Have I really accomplished anything? How can you tell?" Now we see the teacher educator using various ways of connecting up with what is bothering Brigit and how she feels about the problem. First, he lets Brigit describe how the talk with her student went. While she is talking, he backtracks to make sure he understands what she was trying to do (i.e., "So in the first place you were trying to calm him down?"), and then asks her whether her strategy was successful (i.e., "Do you feel that your strategy has been successful up to now?"). At that point, Brigit comes up with a more precise description: "I don't feel as if I've gotten through to him." As a kind of check, the teacher educator writes the sentence on the blackboard, and Brigit responds with "I can't get through to him." Here we see Step 4: *focusing*.

The teacher then tries to formulate a general rule: The harder you try, the less successful you are. This is Step 5: *theory with a small t*. In his own reflection on the course of this group meeting, he later indicated that during the preparation for this meeting he had planned on introducing communication rules. One such rule emphasizes the importance of "less of the same during an escalation" (Watzlawick et al., 1974, p. 116). The teacher educator gives an example of a related rule, which says that more of the same has no effect, and may even be counterproductive. In any case, it does nothing to help you accomplish what you are trying to do. It would be better to try less of the same, or even something totally different.

Brigit's statement that she "can't get through to him" bears a close resemblance to what Astrid said during the summing-up round: "I want to break down his resistance, and reduce the distance between teacher and student." Then we see how the teacher educator tries to connect with Astrid's gestalts by relating Brigit's experience and observations to those of Astrid. He then turns to the group as a whole and, as he formulates the rule, he goes back to related experiences in the past where the rules also played a role.

In this way, the teacher educator recommends these rules to the student teachers, making use of their experiences in the role-playing session, and the gestalts that this calls up. The most important skills he uses here are addressing both the group and the individual, listening, asking questions, and getting them to make their remarks more concrete, and then checking back to make sure he has correctly understood them. In the first place, he is trying to be receptive to what is occupying the student teachers. Through his approach and his relationship to the student teachers, he models the attitude and the skills that form the central theme of this meeting, that is, afterschool talks with students as a means of improving the teacher–student relationship.

In view of Astrid's reaction, the teacher educator felt that it might be helpful to examine her concern. She came up with a formulation of the rule that says more or less the same thing. Apparently, Brigit does not take the teacher educator's suggestion any further, falling back on her original version. It is possible that her main concern is slightly different. This illustrates how difficult it can be to find precisely the right approach for each individual student teacher, and help him or her a step further.

The teacher educator is more successful in finding the right approach when he introduces the second principle ("show that you understand the other person's problem"), and tries to create a link with a topic that has probably been dealt with earlier in the course. To that end, he has the student teachers formulate how they talk about empathy, and then writes down their exact words. But he also adds something to what they already know: He links this term to a new experience that was part of the role playing. This term was probably known to the student teachers only in the context of peer-supported learning (a regular component of the teacher education program; see section 9.6). It is made applicable to the afterschool talks with students. Now the secret of linking up with the concerns and gestalts of the students is to go just a bit further than where they are, and then to get them to move forward along with you. During the introduction of the first rule, the teacher educator probably succeeded in getting Astrid to move forward, but he may have lost Brigit. When the second rule was introduced, the transcript does not indicate whether he succeeded in getting the student teachers to move forward.

In any case, the teacher educator tried to optimize the link between himself and the student teachers by deliberately refraining from presenting them with a Theory with capital T. Instead, he gave them phronesis (theory with a small t): simple concrete principles that are very close to their own experience and help them to perceive the situation in such a way that it helps them to decide how to act. Using everyday words (show that you understand the other person, let the other person know that you heard what he said, etc.), he tried to get across to them the theoretical notions "acceptance" and "empathy." This is in line with the guideline formulated by McIntyre and Hagger (1992, p. 272):

> Teachers' professional development must stem not only from their own energy and motivation but also from their own understandings of their existing practices.

It is characteristic of the realistic approach used in this example that although the teacher educator had prepared a number of theoretical notions, he made limited use of them. In effect, he used only those concepts that coincided with the reflections of the student teachers on their experiences. We also saw that at times he adapted or revised those notions to fit in with the gestalts of the student teachers. The fact that the teacher educator decided not to put forward a number of theoretical principles because they did not appear to be appropriate at that particular moment is an essential component of his strategy. For example, he chose not to discuss the concept of the self-image of the student (a topic he prepared) on the grounds that the student teachers were apparently more concerned about their own "survival" and their own behavior than about improving the self-image of their students. It is a logical consequence of the aforementioned that the teacher educator must accept that he will not always be able to make use of all his "beautiful theories." There may be a temptation to quickly reel off yet another rule on the basis of a superficial link with the experience under discussion. In most cases, this is a waste of energy.

A disadvantage of this method is that it may be some time before certain theories are dealt with. The guiding principle is that it is useless to discuss a theoretical point unless there are experiences that give rise to concerns and gestalts to which it can fruitfully be linked. At the same time, by helping to create the appropriate experiences, the teacher educator can steer the concerns put forward by the student teachers. The training component dealt with here is a case in point: The role playing was prestructured (by means of the role descriptions given by the teacher educator) in such a way that themes like getting your message across, resistance, empathy, and so on, were likely to be put forward.

The discussion thus far has illustrated of the five-step procedure. The description of the concrete group meeting shows how the basic principles of the realistic approach are applied:

1. The teacher educator helps the student teachers to become aware of their learning needs.
2. He creates useful experiences in the here-and-now.
3. He helps the student teachers to reflect on these experiences in detail.

These three central principles were introduced in chapter 5. The third principle is important, because it helps the student teachers to perceive more in practical situations, which is considered more important than knowing more about such situations. In fact, the idea is that the development of conceptual knowledge (episteme, or Theory with capital T) follows the development of more detailed perceptual knowledge (phronesis, to be improved by theory with a small t). In other words, learning about teaching should, in my view, start with becoming aware of one's gestalts by reflecting on these gestalts in detail, before the step toward concepts and relations between concepts is made. (This is a central theme in the next chapter).

In the reflection process, the reader can recognize the phases of the ALACT model: After looking back on the situation (Phase 2), some essential aspects are formulated (Phase 3), and alternative methods of action are put forward (Phase 4). The phase of trial (Phase 5) will not only take place when the student teachers have their next real after-class talk: In the second part of the group meeting, the teacher educator created brief role plays in which each student teacher got an opportunity to practice.

The example also shows the importance of the group setting. First, it makes role playing possible, and thus concrete experiences in the here-and-now. Second, it stimulates discussion about these experiences, an important ingredient of promoting reflection.

9.4. FOUR CONCRETE TECHNIQUES

There are other, more specific techniques that also help to stimulate reflection in groups. Four of these will now be introduced. The idea behind these techniques is that prospective teachers often enter a preparation program with gestalts that need to be restructured to be able to adopt new educational theories. Let us take as an example a student teacher who regards teaching as "telling facts to students," perhaps because of her own experience as a student at school, or perhaps because other ways of viewing teaching would make her uncertain and afraid of losing control of the class. The educational literature emphasizes such other views of teaching, based on the important role of learner activities and the promotion of understanding of relations within the subject matter. How could a teacher educator, within the context of a group seminar, promote the restructuring of the student teacher's gestalt of teaching and promote the internalization of empirically based educational theory? It will be clear that this is no simple task confronting teacher education, because people's mental structures generally resist change (Turk & Speers, 1983) even when confronted with incompatible information (Fiske & Taylor, 1984, p. 171).

The basic assumption underlying the techniques described is that the effectiveness of the process of trying to (re)structure one's experiences (the process named reflection) will be determined by the degree to which the relationships within one's gestalts are considered. As already announced at the end of section 9.3, this assumption will be more theoretically elaborated in the next chapter. In the example of the student teacher who considers teaching as "transmission," she could, for example, try to formulate the relation between her teaching activities and the cognitive and affective processes in the student. I believe that without such reflections by student teachers, educational theories taught in teacher education programs have little chance of becoming guidelines for student teacher behavior in the classroom.

Thus, each of the four techniques is based on the idea of encouraging student teachers to analyze relationships, either within their gestalts of teaching and learning or between their gestalts and their actual behavior.

The Wall[3]

This technique aims at formulating the relations between different educational goals or values, which often remain implicit if the student teachers' gestalts are not reflected on. Each student teacher in the group receives a number of paper "bricks" with statements about educational goals or values. Some of the bricks are blank and have to be filled in by the prospective teacher. The assignment is to build your own "teaching wall"; the bricks are placed with the most important principles at the bottom and the others on top (Fig. 9.2). The wall is glued onto a piece of paper. The student teacher can also draw a "waste-paper basket" in which useless bricks are deposited.

This is the first step in a process of reflection on one's goals and guiding principles in teaching. A comparison of the various walls constructed by the members of the group stimulates the student teachers to give voice to their own views, but also to reflect critically on those views.

As some of the bricks are filled in beforehand, teacher educators are able to channel the discussion toward topics that they think are important and reflect educational theory. For example, as in the IVLOS program, considerable significance is

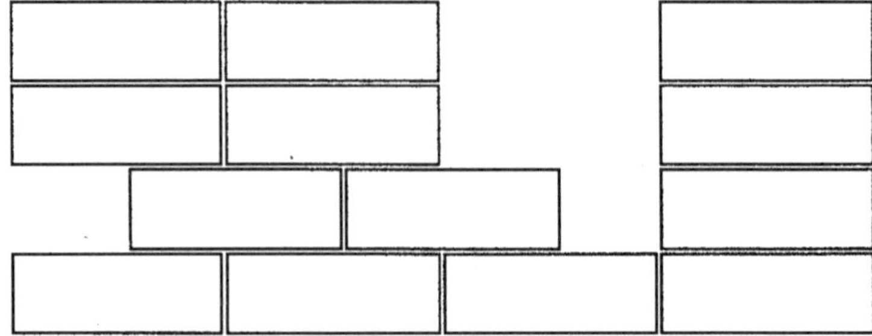

FIG. 9.2. A wall.

attached to process goals in education. Often, bricks are used with such statements as "students should learn to reflect on their work," "it is important for children to become self-confident," but also "I want to prepare the students for their examinations" and "students should listen to me." Other examples of bricks are the following: it must be quiet in the classroom; the students should see relations between subject matter and everyday life; the students should develop a critical attitude toward social issues; and students should be given a sense of the "beauty" of the subject matter.

It is helpful to use one or two subject-specific bricks, especially bricks containing a basic goal that is conditional on other subject-specific goals. In the field of mathematics, for instance, this could be "learning to solve quadratic equations." Such subject-specific bricks help to integrate general pedagogical thinking and subject-specific views.

Columns

This technique is designed to promote reflection on the relations between educational goals and actual teaching behavior. Each student teacher chooses one class he or she often teaches. Where possible, these classes of the student teachers should preferably be on the same grade level, or of similar subject matter. Four columns are drawn on a large sheet of paper (Fig. 9.3). In the first column, the student teacher enters a general goal he or she thinks is important in education. This goal can be selected from the "wall." In the second column, the student teacher writes a specific goal for the next series of lessons in that class, derived from the general goal in the first column. In the third column, the student teacher puts down a further specification of the goal to be achieved in the next lesson. The fourth and last column is filled in after the lesson. A particular piece of interaction is entered—say, from an audio recording of the lesson—which shows how the student teacher went about achieving the goal. It is emphasized that this last column should show evidence that the students really achieved the goal described in the third column.

Back on campus, the student teachers show to each other their columns, discuss them, and prepare the columns for the next lesson, which are written below the previous ones. This often results in changes in the third, second, or even the first column: The realization that there may be a conflict between one's goals and one's actual teaching can lead student teachers to alter their view on education or their own role in the teaching–learning process. The teacher educator or fellow students in the group can be helpful in finding ways to overcome obstacles that prevent the student teacher from achieving the formulated goal. This often requires a careful formulation of long- and short-term strategies.

The whole process toward which this activity is directed is illustrated by the successive rows referring to the various lessons. I often ask the student teachers to write down their rows and columns on a large sheet of paper, which makes it easier to present their "story" to their fellow students. These fellow students are then stimulated

general educational goal	goal for the series of lessons in class ...	specific goal for lesson # *n*	particular episode from lesson # *n*

FIG. 9.3. The columns.

to ask "why questions" over and over again, thus forcing the person telling the "story" to make his or her ideas as explicit as possible.

The Repertory Grid

This technique involves relations between teacher behavior and student characteristics, as perceived by the student teacher. The activity is based on Kelly's (1955) technique for inquiring into the constructs people use when dealing with their environment. Repeatedly, each student teacher receives three cards, each containing the name of one high school student (Fig. 9.4). These students are all in the same class, well known to the student teacher. Without thinking about it too long, the student teacher must choose one of the three students whom he or she thinks is different from the other two. Next, the teacher must formulate the characteristic, or construct, describing the difference. In this way, a list of personal constructs is generated. The repertory grid technique helps teachers to discover the ways in which their behavior is shaped by subjective perceptions of high school students.

For this activity, it is advisable to divide the group of student teachers into pairs. One shuffles the cards and offers three of them to the other student teacher. The first student teacher also writes down the construct mentioned by his fellow student. Then the cards are shuffled once again, and so on. When a list of about 10 constructs has been drawn up, the two student teachers change roles.

It may promote the reflection process to realize that all the characteristics are at one pole of a dichotomy, which is why I also ask the student teachers to name the opposite of each characteristic on their list. It is important the student teachers formulate the characteristics and their opposites in their own words, because the strength of the method is in the fact that these self-chosen terms have a particular significance to the individual.[4]

In order to reflect on the relations between the student teachers' lists of constructs and their teaching behavior, they are asked to explain how they think their reactions to students with the various characteristics differ. This question becomes especially interesting when they start to compare their reactions to students with

Jim	Selina	Helen

FIG. 9.4. Three cards in the repertory grid procedure.

opposite characteristics, which can lead to critical reflection on their behavior and the underlying teaching strategies. An example is given in section 9.5, where some results are discussed.

Arrows

This technique focuses on relations between goals, student characteristics as perceived by the student teacher, and teaching strategies. The activity "arrows" may be seen as an integration of the wall and the repertory grid and should be introduced after these techniques, because it can then build on the previous results.

For this exercise, paper cards and arrows are used. A particular student characteristic, say, "dependent," is taken together with an educational goal that one finds important, such as "seeing relationships between the subject matter and everyday life." Both are written down on separate cards. Then a paper arrow is placed between the two cards and the student teacher has to fill in the strategy he or she would use in order to attain that goal in the case of a student with that specific characteristic (Fig. 9.5).

The same question can also be asked with respect to the opposite characteristic: for example, how do you work toward the goal of seeing relations between subject matter and everyday life with an "independent" student? This procedure is repeated several times, using various other goals and student characteristics. Group discussions on the strategies formulated will, of course, promote further reflection. The student teachers are then challenged to discover the teaching strategies of their fellow students by asking questions about the how and why of the strategies written on the arrows and questions about the advantages of the strategies when compared with alternatives. In fact, this is the most important part of the technique, because it often leads to the restructuring of the student teachers' strategies or their gestalts about high school students, student learning, or teaching.

9.5. A STUDY OF THE EFFECTS OF THE FOUR TECHNIQUES

The techniques described were gradually developed over a period of several years, in which they were used in many groups of student teachers, as well as in professional training groups of teacher educators. I decided to investigate these tech-

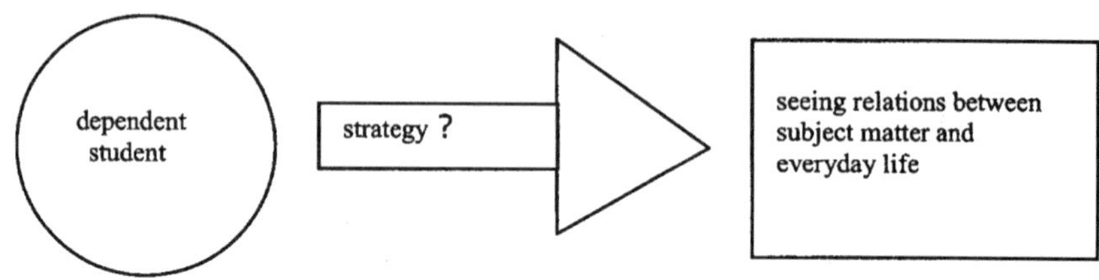

FIG. 9.5. Working with the "arrows" technique.

niques more thoroughly in a group of student teachers in a teacher education program at a Dutch university. The group consisted of 18 student teachers of a variety of subjects, such as economics, biology, mathematics, and history (but excluding languages). I studied the results of the techniques, and examined in depth the accompanying learning processes in a smaller sample of five student teachers. This smaller sample was chosen not because it was representative, but rather for practical reasons: It included two mathematics and three biology students, who had been supervised and taught as a group throughout a large part of the program. Although there is no reason to assume that these student teachers were not individually representative, I must point out that this group was characterized by an atmosphere of safety and mutual concern, which was undoubtedly beneficial to the work involving the techniques. As the effects of these techniques will invariably depend on such factors, and on the individual teacher educator using the techniques, the goal was not to prove that the techniques work or show how impressive the results were, but to investigate how they work and whether they are capable of changing mental structures, in particular with regard to the four relationships formulated earlier.

The "wall" technique was used in the group of 18 student teachers right at the start of their teacher preparation program, which is a 1-year program, following a 4-year subject-oriented university curriculum. The wall was repeated in the smaller group of five student teachers after 6 months, about 400 hours of study on campus and 400 hours of field experience. The students themselves had by then taught for about 80 hours in secondary school classes.

The "columns" technique was used in the first and second month of the program, during the first field experience of the small sample of five student teachers, which was a one-to-one teaching experience: For 6 weeks, each student teacher worked with one high school student for 1 hour a week, and reflected on these lessons with the aid of audio recordings of the sessions. The audio recordings resulted in verbatim transcripts of small episodes from the lessons in the fourth column. The student teachers' learning processes during this stage of the program were assessed with the aid of interviews and group discussions. Like the wall, the columns assignment was repeated after 6 months, at which time the Individual Final Teaching Practice period started, during which the student teachers work as regular teachers of two secondary school classes (i.e., without the cooperating teachers or fellow students being present and with full responsibility for such matters as grades, parental contact, etc.). For purposes of the columns assignment, the student teachers had to choose one of these two classes.

At this stage, the "repertory grid" and "arrows" were introduced in both the larger and the smaller group of student teachers. Interviews and group discussions were used to assess the learning processes induced by these techniques.

The four techniques were also evaluated by means of a questionnaire using open questions, asking for cognitive and affective learning outcomes and for criticism. I will now present the results of this study.

The Wall

In working with the wall, the student teachers were found to have no difficulty in choosing those bricks matching their views on education and discarding the others. Arranging the bricks to form a wall was more difficult. It led to considerable reflection, because one cannot place one brick on top of another without manifesting certain ideas about relations between the various goals and values. When asked about the reasons behind their choices, the student teachers clarified their teaching strategies in a more explicit way, using sentences like "In order to reach goal X you need principle Y, and it is only later on that you reach Z, which I think will more or less solve itself." The arrangement of the bricks, together with such statements, often showed that there was one central underlying principle guiding the student teachers. In the small sample, the five student teachers formulated these principles as follows:

- education should be directed towards promoting processes in students rather than towards products;
- it all boils down to a good atmosphere in the classroom;
- first of all, you have to be able to make the subject matter clear to students;
- there should be a proper balance between the demands made on the students and good teacher–student relationships;
- there must be a clear understanding about rules and discipline.

At the very beginning of the preparation program, there were obviously more differences than similarities between the walls and the views on education expressed by the different student teachers. This supports the assumption that student teachers enter the program with quite different gestalts about teaching and learning.

An important discovery was that the guiding principles behind the students' walls were essentially the same the second time they made their walls (i.e., 6 months later). This is noteworthy, because in the meantime these student teachers had gained quite a bit of teaching experience; as explained, they had taught secondary school classes for about 80 hours and all of them had been allowed by their schools to take responsibility for two classes, which means they were thought to have acquired the necessary basic competence as teachers. In addition to their field experiences, they had also had about 400 hours of study on campus, in which emphasis was put on the relation between educational theory and practice, including much discussion about the way several educational goals might be translated into practice. This finding is in line with conclusions from other research about the stability of student teachers' conceptions about teaching and learning (cf. Calderhead & Robson, 1991).

The questionnaire showed that the student teachers' assessment of the wall was favorable. Typical answers to the question "What did you get out of it?" were "I learned a lot from thinking about which things should take priority," and "It was an incentive and a help, and made it easier for me to think about my views on teaching."

Columns

The most obvious result of the columns activity was that it made the student teachers look at their teaching goals and behavior more closely and more critically. This revealed things that had been implicit before. To take an example, the questionnaire produced statements, like:

- It is surprising to see that sometimes you choose goals that are unrealistic. When it becomes clear from the last column that you aren't going to reach your goal, you can choose a more realistic one.
- When your goal is not achieved, you start to make concrete plans to try to do better in the next lesson.
- It gives me a means for monitoring my progress.

The student teachers' columns showed that the technique had helped them to differentiate between general goals and subgoals. A common observation made by the student teachers was that they had discovered that stating a goal is one thing, but a lot of thinking, planning, and careful evaluation is needed in order to realize it. Moreover, they were confronted with the fact that realizing a goal involves more than just a few comments during a lesson.

I had the impression that use of the columns technique after the wall elicited more critical reflection on the student teachers' goals than the wall by itself. The columns confront student teachers with the question of why they do what they do and why other actions are not taken, although one might expect these actions on the basis of the student teachers' goals. Here is an example:

> One student teacher observed that what he was doing in the classroom did not really match his own goals, but that he was influenced far more by the need "to teach as other people think you ought to teach." This discovery made him look more critically at his cooperating teacher, whom he had originally admired somewhat uncritically. It helped him to go his own way. The student was so pleased with the "columns" technique that he kept making his columns throughout the whole year of teacher prepa-

> ration. Each weekend he evaluated his week of teaching, and adjusted the first three columns on the basis of the concrete classroom experiences which appeared in the fourth column. He reported that it helped him to find his own teaching style.

This is an example of the qualitative and quantitative changes in the relations in the student teachers' mental structures that seemed to take place—changes that I saw in almost all of the student teachers that were involved. Gestalts, which beforehand unconsciously directed their behavior, became conscious and in that way could be critically examined and sometimes changed. I observed that the "why questions" from their peers were very influential in promoting processes of reframing. As already mentioned, more research is necessary in order to find more evidence of this observation. In such research, pre- and posttests seem to be necessary, but the question is how to administer a pretest without already inducing reflection.

The Repertory Grid

When this technique was used in the small group, it produced a great deal of joking and giggling, although the student teachers went about their task very seriously. It appears that the technique confronts student teachers with their own conceptions of students, and with the often idiosyncratic constructs they use. This may cause them to feel somewhat ashamed. The students had only a few constructs in common, such as "clever," "interested," "diligent," and "lively." Some rather personal constructs were mentioned, such as "crazy," "plays the marimba," and "uses her looks."

The formulation of the constructs helped the student teachers to become aware of their subjective view of high school students and their preferences with regard to young people in general. The discussion about the ways in which the student teachers react to students with different characteristics was especially interesting in a comparison of the interactions with high school students with opposite characteristics. This helped the prospective teachers to reflect on the question of whether their behavior was adequate. This may be illustrated by the following example:

> One student teacher formulated the construct "interested-uninterested," and reported that she kept looking for stimulating examples and activities for the uninterested students. However, she did not make the same effort in the case of interested students: "I just start the ball rolling and expect them to take it from there." Reflection on these two different types of teaching behavior made her see that there was a danger that the uninterested students might become more and more dependent on the teacher's inspiration. The interested ones on the other hand, could become less motivated because of the lack of stimulating and challenging activities. This discovery created a moment of confusion, in which the adequacy of her strategy was being questioned by the student teacher herself.

Such a situation, when the status of existing ideas theory is lowered, is an ideal starting point for a discussion of principles from theories on motivation. I believe that this kind of theory is more likely to become part of the student teacher's mental structures after this type of analysis of her own teaching behavior than it is without such reflection.

Arrows

It seemed that in many cases the arrows activity was the first time the student teachers had ever thought in a critical and analytic manner about the relation between individual student characteristics, educational goals, and their own teaching behavior. Such probing into the reasons for their behavior makes explicit gestalts and teaching strategies that student teachers seemed never to have reflected on before. This may be inferred, for example, from the observation that the student teachers often had difficulty in formulating their teaching strategies in the case of one certain type of high school student and one basic goal from their wall. As one student teacher put it: "I discovered that I am so pre-occupied with trying to come across well, that everything else sort of gets forgotten." For others, the arrows activity helped them to differentiate between their strategies for different students. Although I have no clear evidence to this effect, I had the distinct feeling that before this activity they saw the class more or less as an entity, with very little differentiation with regard to goals and teaching strategies. The arrows technique can also deepen the student teachers' strategies. One example of this is the case of a student teacher who formulated his arrow between the student characteristic "rude" and the goal "learning to interact with other students in a respectful manner." He was already using the strategy of giving the class feedback about the way he perceived the students' conduct in concrete situations, but while formulating this strategy, the student teacher became aware of the fact that he should do this in a more respectful (less rude) way.

Group discussion about the arrows resulted in a collaborative search for solutions to special situations, in learning from each others' strategies and, last but not least, in doubts about one's own strategies and the gestalts behind them. As said, such doubts can be important starting points for the next step in a learning process in which the student teacher feels a natural need for educational theory. My own strategy, then, was to offer this in the form of theory with a small t, in close relation to the special situations with which the student teachers had to deal.

9.6. GROUPS REFLECTING ON THEIR OWN

Techniques such as the wall, the repgrid, arrows, and columns have the advantage of strongly promoting reflection, and at the same time diminishing the amount of time and attention needed from the teacher educator. This shows that the promotion of reflective learning from real experiences need not always be a time-consuming enterprise. This is important because many teacher educators, especially in North America, have to work with large cohort groups in which close personal supervision of student teachers is not always feasible.

A logical next step is that student teachers learn to promote each other's reflections so that the teacher educator's presence is not needed. To this purpose, two of my colleagues have developed a structure named *peer-supported learning* (Tigchelaar & Melief, 2000). It is now used by almost the entire staff of the IVLOS teacher education program, with very positive results. As McIntyre and Hagger (1992, p. 276) state:

> Collegiality has been demonstrated to be a critical factor in helping individual teachers to develop their classroom practice.

Within the setting of a whole cohort group, the student teachers are trained in using the ALACT model, not only for structuring their own reflection but also to help each other reflect. This means that they learn how to use many of the supervision skills described in chapter 7.[5] In small groups of about three, they practice these skills. And during teaching practice periods these groups of three meet on a regular basis for peer-supported learning. Each small group is required to write brief reports on their meetings, in which they both evaluate the process of peer-supported learning, and describe the content discussed in their small group. In the reports, they can also put forward issues on which they wish to receive further support from the teacher educator. Every 2 weeks, there are meetings of the whole cohort group facilitated by the teacher educator. These group meetings are partly devoted to further training in supervision skills, in order to support and further develop the processes of peer-supported learning. In addition, on the basis of the problems and concerns that formed the content of the supervision sessions in the small groups, themes and issues are discussed in the whole group. This is where the teacher educator again takes the role of supporting the professional development of the student teachers, other than through developing their competency to support each other. The teacher educator can introduce new content, based on the issues raised in the reports of the small groups.

Through this structure, a balanced sharing of the responsibility for professional learning is created between the teacher educator and the student teachers. The structure has many advantages. First, it further strengthens the capacity of student teachers to take responsibility for their own learning. An important aim behind the structure is also that it prepares them for peer-supported learning during the rest of their careers, thus creating a counterbalance to what Feiman-Nemser and Floden (1986) call the highly individualistic and noncollaborative culture of teaching. As Putnam and Borko (1997, p. 1247) state:

> Just as students need to learn new ways of reasoning, communicating, and thinking, and to acquire dispositions of inquiry and sense-making through their participation in classroom discourse communities, teachers need to construct their complex new roles and ways of thinking about their teaching practice within the context of supportive learning communities.

The process of learning how to support each other's reflection also promotes the students' insight into the ALACT model and thus their individual competency for reflection. Another advantage is the fact that, after an initial investment, the structure saves time for the teacher educator. Fellow students can become valuable supervisors, thus taking over part of the role of the teacher educator (cf. Hawkey, 1995, and Little, 1982). Moreover, through the reports of the small groups, the teacher educator receives concrete information about the learning processes going on and the concerns and problems that surface with the student teachers. This helps the teacher educator in choosing the topics to be dealt with in the group meetings and increases chances that these topics will be experienced as relevant by the student teachers. Finally, many of the supervision skills the student teachers acquire during their preparation for peer-supported learning are just as important in their guidance of their own students in school.

A development of the last couple of years is the use of a *listserve* (or WebCT) to enable the student teachers to communicate by e-mail during their teaching practice periods (Admiraal, Lockhorst, Wubbels, Korthagen, & Veen, 1998). Especially in cases where the student teachers do their teaching practice in schools far removed from each other (which is often the case during the Individual Final Teaching Practice period, see section 3.2), this is an excellent means to create possibilities for exchange. Moreover, the teacher educator can easily monitor the e-mail conversations, and, if needed, react to them, either with the purpose of improving the process of peer-supported learning, or for supporting student teachers clearly in need of specific help. A study into the effects of this form of *teleguidance* in the IVLOS teacher education program has shown that student teachers appreciate the opportunity to share experiences by e-mail, but their reactions to each other are often quite brief and remain stuck at a level of emotional support. In order to have them deepen their reflections, both their own and those of their fellow students, vis-à-vis meetings seem to be necessary (Admiraal et al., 1998).

9.7. FINAL REMARKS

The whole chapter points toward the fact that reflection and learning from experience is deepened by interaction among learners. Although this book emphasizes the need to build the pedagogy of teacher education on the individual concerns of student teachers, realistic teacher education does not aim at merely individual processes. On the contrary, the promotion of reflective interactions among student teachers is an essential feature of the approach. This chapter has demonstrated that it is not only possible to take individual concerns and problems seriously within group settings, but that the application of specific group techniques and procedures also deepens the individual processes.

Now that we have dived so deeply into the practical work of the teacher educator with student teachers, both at an individual level (in chapter 7) and at group level (this chapter), it is time to describe an underlying theoretical framework with regard to professional learning and the relation between teachers' mental structures and behavior. The principle of "making implicit relationships explicit" is an essential ingredient of this framework, and will be the main focus of the next, more theoretically oriented chapter.

However, before making this step, it is important to end this one by emphasizing once more that the methods of working with groups of student teachers described here require skills and attitudes in the teacher educator, which point toward the need of professional development programs for teacher education staff (an issue to be discussed in more detail in chapter 13). Especially if one is used to lecturing, it is a giant leap to really connect with the concerns of student teachers, to create useful experiences instead of introducing "important" Theory, and to help student teachers reflect on their gestalts. In my experience, one of the greatest difficulties is to let go of the seemingly strong grip and safety well-prepared theoretical lectures offer to the teacher educator: One has to learn to live with the unexpected, to improvise, to make use of several theoretical backgrounds, and to translate them into concrete helpful guidelines for action. And all this can only be successful if one is really willing to relate to student teachers in a personal way—to connect with them—by being acceptant, empathetic, and genuine.

SUMMARY

In this chapter, a five-step procedure to promote reflection in groups was presented. The steps are prestructuring, experience, structuring, focusing, and theory. The use of this procedure was illustrated by means of a transcript of an authentic group meeting within a teacher education program. The description clarified how the principles of the realistic approach can be applied in practical situations in teacher education, for example, how theory can be built on student teachers' concerns and on the gestalts elicited by their practical experiences.

Also four specific techniques were introduced (the wall, columns, repertory grid, and arrows), which aim at reflection and can be used by student teachers without much intervention on the part of the teacher educator. Thus, they can even be used in very large groups. The techniques help student teachers to reflect on their gestalts and teaching strategies, and on the constructs they use in their perception of students. Each technique focuses on special types of relations within the student teachers' mental structures, their perception, and teaching behavior. Under the influence of the techniques, these mental structures often change from unconscious gestalts to more conscious cognitive schemata. This change process is very important, because it makes critical reflection and reframing possible.

A study into the functioning of the techniques showed that they promote lively group discussions about teaching practice, and create a need in student teachers for educational theory. However, the study also showed that basic elements in student teachers' gestalts, especially basic values, are hard to change.

Both the five-step procedure and the four techniques can be seen as representative of the principles of realistic teacher education. They try to build on student teachers' concrete experiences and the concerns developed through these experiences, they try to make student teachers more aware of these concerns, and they stimulate reflection using peer interaction. The description of the five-step procedure and the four techniques also showed how the process of promoting reflection often boils down to "making implicit relationships explicit," especially the implicit relationships within student teachers' unconscious gestalts guiding their actions.

Finally, a structure was described for promoting peer-supported learning within small groups, in which it is also possible to make use of e-mail exchanges between student teachers. Through this structure, another fundamental step is made toward helping student teachers become independent learners. It is also a solution to the problem that careful individual supervision of student teachers often takes much time.

BASIC CONCEPTS

Five steps: (1) prestructuring, (2) experience, (3) structuring, (4) focusing, (5) theory

Techniques for reflection in groups (the wall, columns, repgrid, arrows)

Making implicit relationships explicit

Peer-supported learning

10 Teachers' Professional Learning: How Does It Work?

Fred Korthagen and Bram Lagerwerf

> Introducing the new scholarship into institutions of higher education means becoming involved in an epistemological battle. It is a battle of snails, proceeding so slowly that you have to look very carefully in order to see it going on. But it is happening nonetheless.
>
> —*Donald Schön (1995)*

Having described theory and practice of the realistic approach to teacher education, it is now time to analyze the core of the process of teachers' professional learning. First, a new conceptualization of the relation between teachers' inner processes and their behavior will be presented. We will distinguish between three levels of teacher knowledge: the gestalt level, the schema level, and the theory level. The processes of gestalt formation, schematization, and theory-building will be analyzed and the three levels will be illustrated by means of excerpts from interviews with teachers and nonteachers. Following a theoretical reflection on the proposed view of learning about teaching, its implications for teacher education and research on teaching will be discussed. One of our conclusions will be that the theoretical model developed in this chapter offers an explanation of the gap between theory and practice as well as directions for solutions.

10.1. INTRODUCTION

As Munby, T. Russell and Martin (in press) note, the search for a scientific basis for teacher education has led to a considerable growth in the research on the nature of teachers' knowledge. Many different notions can be found in the professional literature, such as "declarative and procedural knowledge" (Peterson & Comeaux, 1989), "personal theories" (Carter, 1990), "images" (Calderhead & Robson, 1991; Elbaz, 1983), "practical and formal knowledge" (Fenstermacher, 1994), and "craft knowledge" (Calderhead, 1991; Desforges & McNamara, 1979). Moreover, several forms of constructivism have become part of our professional thinking. Researchers within the constructivist paradigm emphasize that teachers can learn to construct meaning in a conscious and systematic way (Calderhead, 1989). In many cases, this process can and should lead to a reframing of their experiences (Korthagen, 1992; Schön, 1987).

In spite of the considerable growth of research concerned with these topics, certain basic questions about the nature of teachers' knowledge still remain unanswered (Bennett & Carré, 1993, p. 12; Calderhead, 1988). Desforges (1995, p. 386) complains that

> work in the field of learning to teach has produced some interesting descriptions of changes in teachers' skills, beliefs and practices but has rarely been able to explain these changes in terms of a theory of learning or a theory of teaching.

Munby et al. (in press) state that "the nature and development of that knowledge is only beginning to be understood by the present generation of researchers in teaching and teacher education." For example, how do images relate to more logically structured knowledge? Can these two types of knowledge coexist, even when they are in effect contradictory? How do images develop and change? What does it mean to "reframe" experiences, and last but not least, how does knowledge, in whatever form, relate to feelings and actions?

The reason why these questions are so complex has much to do with the nature of teachers' professional knowledge. This knowledge cannot easily be separated from other knowledge, such as commonsense knowledge about how people relate to each other. Nor is there any unique, generally accepted hierarchical ordering of concepts about teaching.

These characteristics of knowledge about teaching are fundamentally different from those that characterize knowledge in the field of mathematics, where it appears to be relatively easier to develop theory about knowledge development. As far back as the 1950s, the Dutch mathematics educator Van Hiele and his wife, Van Hiele-Geldof, developed a model that distinguishes several levels of mathematical thinking, and accounts for the relations between those levels.[1] In this chapter, we will show that this model can be translated to the more complex situation of learning about teaching, offering us a framework for answering many of the questions already stated.[2] To be more precise, the aim of the present chapter is to introduce a model of levels in professional learning that builds on the Van Hiele levels. We have included in this model the emotional, volitional, and action-related components of human functioning. In that respect, we wish to take Hargreaves' (1998a) view seriously that teaching is not just a cognitive process.

Our presentation of the model is somewhat unconventional in that it does not start from a theoretical framework, but rather concludes with an attempt to develop one. In section 10.2, we present an overview of the basic ideas underlying this chapter. These are elaborated in the sections 10.3, 10.4, and 10.5. In section 10.6, the model of levels in knowledge about teaching is illustrated by means of empirical data. In section 10.7, we take a closer look at the relations between the levels. Section 10.8 offers a reflection on the theoretical basis of the proposed model, placing it within a broader field of theories on human behavior. In section 10.9, we discuss the implications of the model for framing the relation between teacher thinking and teacher behavior, for teacher education, and for research. In this section, we also demonstrate that our model offers an explanatory model for a variety of concepts and principles in the field of learning to teach, such as "reflection" (Calderhead 1989; Zeichner, 1983), "reframing" (Schön, 1987), "concerns" of student teachers (Fuller & Bown, 1975), the "washing-out" of teacher education during field experiences (Zeichner & Tabachnick, 1981), "conceptual change" (Hewson, Zeichner, Tabachnick, Blomker, & Toolin, 1992), and "knowing-in-action" (Schön, 1987). We believe that our model goes to the heart of the problem commonly referred to as the gap between theory and practice in teacher education by demonstrating that this problem is an artifact of the way the process of professional learning has often been conceived in the past. This leads to section 10.10, in which we reframe the previous chapters of this book with the aid of the level model.

10.2. THREE LEVELS IN LEARNING

We will start with an example:

> A student in primary school writes "12 + 9 = 22." Seeing this, the teacher, Mrs. Wilson, immediately reacts by saying: "That's wrong. You know that 12 + 8 = 20, so 12 + 9 = 21."

Let us analyze this situation. First, most educators will agree that the teacher's reaction is not entirely adequate. She made no attempt to discover how the child arrived at the answer of 22; she did not stimulate the child's reflection on the way he had solved the problem; and she did not help him to develop his own strategy for dealing with this type of problem. This increases the likelihood that the child will make the same type of mistake next time. Moreover, most educators will consider this situation as an excellent starting point for a classroom discussion, thus involving more children in the reflection on the exercise and creating possibilities for a positive use of the interaction between the students.

Nevertheless, Mrs. Wilson reacted the way she did. How can we, as educators, explain this reaction? For many years, the dominant view of teachers as thinkers and decisionmakers led researchers to believe that the teacher has a theory about this type of situation, interprets the situation on the basis of this theory, and rationally arrives at the decision to react the way she did. If we ask the teacher to explain her behavior after the event, we indeed expect her to give an explanation of this type, an explanation that displays a chain of perception, interpretation, logical thinking, decision making, and acting. However, we venture to question whether this is an adequate account of what was really happening during the split second before her reaction.

First, we believe that in a case like this, which Dolk (1997) calls an immediate teaching situation, it is almost impossible to separate perception, interpretation, and reaction from one other. They all take place within that same split second, and together they form a unity that is rooted in many earlier experiences in the teacher's life. Had we not asked her for an explanation, the way she reacted would probably have remained at an almost subconscious level; she would feel that this was the "natural" way to react to such a situation. The term "natural" may hark back to situations in which she herself was a student and the way her own teachers reacted to her mistakes.

Second, we do not believe that the internal process taking place within the teacher is an exclusively cognitive process. Without trying to present an exhaustive list of possible origins of the teacher's behavior, we can quickly see that the following aspects may play a role:

- *feelings*: for example, irritation that Jim is still making mistakes.
- *former similar experiences*: for example, with Jim or with other children who keep making mistakes.
- *values*: for example, the teacher may find it important that children in this grade are capable of performing additions up to a hundred without making mistakes.
- *role conceptions*: for example, the conception of a teacher as someone who "transmits" correct answers.
- *needs or concerns*: for example, the wish to get through the lesson quickly and give more attention to the subtraction problems she had in mind.
- *routines*: for example, the routine of quickly correcting a wrong answer as a means to circumvent a problem.

All these thoughts, feelings, values, conceptions, and so on, together create the personal meaning of the situation for Mrs. Wilson and lead almost automatically (i.e., with very little conscious awareness) to her reaction, which is rooted in earlier, similar experiences. We will be referring to this phenomenon by stating that a certain gestalt is triggered in the teacher (i.e., a unity of perception, internal processing and a tendency to behave in a certain way).

This alternative analysis of the example is not intended as a rejection of the first, classical analysis. It may be that the description of the process in terms of a chain consisting of perception—interpretation—thought—action is more accurate in cases where the teacher is operating on a fairly conscious level, especially if there has been a small moment of *stop-and-think* (Schön, 1987) before she reacts. However, we believe that in most situations during a lesson the notion of "immediate teacher behavior"—in which thinking, feeling, attaching meaning, and acting form one inseparable whole—leads to a more accurate description of teacher behavior. A similar position is taken by Eraut (1995) in his analysis of teacher behavior and teacher reflection. He also stresses the influence of the available time on the "mode of cognition." In the present chapter, we not only wish to introduce this distinction between two types of information processing during teaching, we also discuss the question of how these types relate to each other.

The *formation of gestalts* is a very common type of learning. We talk about learning, because once a certain gestalt is triggered in a person, a similar gestalt will more easily be triggered in another situation with the same characteristics. In many situations, the formation of gestalts is the end of the learning process, because there is no need for more.

Occasionally, learning goes further and "background knowledge" develops. This is the case when the teacher feels the need to reflect on a gestalt triggered by a situation (Van Hiele, 1973, p. 142), for example, when the teacher wishes to explain what he or she was doing and why, or tries to confront his or her view with ideas of others. We call this process *schematizing*. The resulting schema describes the gestalt in more detail, and in a more generalized way (i.e., more separate from the concrete experiences that elicited it). This does not mean yet that the teacher is in the stage of *theory building*. With the term "theory," we refer to a logical and consistent network of axioms and definitions, leading to certain consequences for teaching. For example, if Mrs. Wilson starts to accept the constructivist axiom stated in section 10.1, then she may logically come to the conclusion that students need practical experiences on which to reflect themselves in order to develop understanding, and that her natural tendency to correct a student may thus be counterproductive. This is what we call *theory building*.

Gestalt formation, schematizing, and theory building are three fundamentally different stages in the process of becoming acquainted with a field. We will now go into the details of each of these stages.

10.3. GESTALT FORMATION

Gestalt formation processes start very early in life:

- *Example 1*
  In the contact between a baby and his mother, a rather stable gestalt is created in the baby. This gestalt contains the way the mother looks at the baby, her loving words, the warmth of her body, the smells associated with her, the comfort she brings, the replete feeling which follows feeding and a behavioral tendency, viz. the tendency to move towards the mother. This gestalt is completely different from the one that is elicited in the baby's father when he meets the mother. The father has different needs and consequently his experiences with her are different.

Through the various experiences of life, gestalts are elicited in people. These gestalts are closely tied to the concrete situations through which they are triggered. In similar situations, these gestalts are recreated and help us to find our place in the here-and-now.

Here are two other examples of familiar gestalts:

- *Example 2*

A notion of learning is very common in people's lives. We are all familiar with everyday phrases like:

- My dog has learned to bring me the newspaper.
- I have learned that it is not always good to say what you think.
- I am learning how to use the computer for writing letters.

Again, most people will feel no need for a definition of learning. It is enough for them to use an implicit gestalt of what it entails. This gestalt is not only of a cognitive nature. It encompasses feelings, needs, values, and previous experiences with learning. This appears to be sufficient for most communication situations in which the word is used.

- *Example 3*
  The same is true of teaching. It is something that everyone has had some experience of, generally in the sense of being taught. Even when the term is not made explicit, most people will think of a teacher as someone who is standing in front of a classroom, explaining something. This is the way teachers are pictured in films and plays, and when children "play school." If a student writes "batery" instead of "battery," it is considered "normal" for the teacher to correct him. Often strong feelings or values are part of the gestalt triggered by a teacher or by a teaching situation.

The examples also show that the same type of gestalt may be connected with different situations. A variety of experiences that feel similar create a similar gestalt, for example, a positively colored gestalt related to "learning." On the other hand, a specific learning situation may still trigger a different gestalt. For example, if someone has had many problems with his or her computer, then the situation of having to learn to use a new word processor may elicit a gestalt composed of awful images, nasty feelings, and an action tendency to withdraw from the situation.

One characteristic of gestalts is that they are elicited in situations where the person has some kind of need or concern. This is most clear in the example of the baby. A gestalt of learning and teaching develops in a school child when the child has to deal with what is going on in the classroom. The need or concern not only triggers the process of gestalt formation, it also colors perception by focusing the attention: Some things in the environment become important, others are disregarded; what is important is what helps to satisfy the need. Moreover, our feelings at the moment of the formation of the gestalt may remain connected with the gestalt when it is triggered in future situations. A gestalt of learning may be connected with a feeling of "hard labor."

Another characteristic of gestalt formation is the fact that underlying concepts or rules are seldom made explicit. And when they are, this consists of no more than a vague sketch formulated in a few words. These words are used quite casually, compared with the way an expert on the topic would define the concepts or rules.

Gestalt formation is the process in which a situation triggers a unity of needs, thoughts, feelings, values, meanings and action tendencies, generally based on previous encounters with similar situations. Gestalts are elicited by certain relevant characteristics of the situation, i.e., those characteristics that help to satisfy a need. They constitute the feelings which belong to previous similar experiences. Generally gestalts function in an unconscious and unintentional way. Language plays a minor role in gestalt formation; people use words that seem self-evident to them.

10.4. SCHEMATIZATION

In everyday life, gestalts are generally sufficient to allow people to make use of past experiences when faced with new situations. Sometimes, however, a certain problem—or simple curiosity—may prompt people to think again about their gestalt. They may feel the need to recognize, describe, and name some characteristics of it. That need may be utilitarian, as in the case of a teacher thinking about a way of motivating an uninterested student to work on an assignment. It may also be elicited by purely intellectual curiosity. Behind such needs one can generally discern a certain need for control over situations: It is easier to control something you understand. Often this type of understanding is based on little more than a quick generalization, along the lines of "correcting a child helps to prevent problems." Note that such generalizations are not necessarily in line with the way an expert in the field would view the situation.

We will now look at an example of such a process of schematization:

> When a student teacher starts to look more closely at *learning*, she may discover that it is actually quite an interesting topic. In the process of learning, a person acquires something, but this "something" can be any one of a wide variety of things. One can acquire a physical ability, like skiing, or the ability to speak French, or knowledge about solving mathematical equations. One can even learn to become friends with someone who at first seemed unsympathetic. And how do people acquire these abilities? What is it in human beings that makes this possible? And does the process of learning differ according to what is being learned and by whom? Sometimes people seem to have learned something, but confronted with an unfamiliar situation, it looks as if they have lost this capacity.... The concept of "transfer" seems to support our understanding of this phenomenon.
>
> There is much to know about learning for the interested student teacher, but this does not yet mean that she has a "theory" about learning.

During the schematization process, the person develops a mental framework of concepts and relations between these concepts. This implies that the resulting schema is of a much more cognitive nature than a gestalt:

> In the same way one can form a schema about "teaching." While few people would have any particular need to look more closely at teaching, those involved in teacher education will be inclined to take that closer look. They will realize that there is no teaching without a learner. From a common gestalt in which teaching is seen as "explaining" or "transmitting knowledge," it is only one step to the idea that "good teaching" means "efficient knowledge transmission."

This is, indeed, the idea that many student teachers bring with them to teacher education. Educators, however, often regard this as a misconception. We consider it a fundamental mistake to try and offer student teachers an alternative conception in the hope they will then use this in their teaching practice. At best, they will be capable of formulating the alternative conception. In practice, however, they will unconsciously act on their own gestalt of teaching, which remains unaffected because it is rooted in lifelong experiences as students. In effect, what they need is *sufficient new experiences to help build alternative gestalts*. Through reflection on such new gestalts, student teachers can develop their own conscious and alternative conceptions of teaching. Only if the new experiences are appropriate will this new conception match their educator's view. We will return to this important issue in section 10.9, where we discuss the consequences of our analysis of professional learning.

It is characteristic of these examples of schematization that they involve the development of new concepts (e.g., learning styles, transfer, steps to be taken during teaching, etc.) and the relations between concepts. This means that certain characteristics of gestalts become conscious and details are perceived within these gestalts. Just as in the case of the formation of gestalts, this process is supported by experiences with concrete examples. The person's needs play a central role in focusing the attention on certain details.

The schematization process can often be encouraged by talking about what one is seeing, thinking, and doing and by looking more precisely at what was self-evident. A discussion within the group after a lesson given by one student teacher for the others may be helpful in developing a schema about teaching. Here it is important that the students feel free to say things in their own words. At this stage, pressure to put things into expert language is counterproductive, because the student teachers' language then remains separated from the gestalt guiding their actions. On the other hand, a group of individuals working together may experience a need for words to express what they all feel to be important. In such situations, more technical terms, used by experts in the field, can gradually be introduced.

After some time, the schematized knowledge related to an area can often become self-evident and the schema can be used in a less conscious, intuitive way. It is as if the whole schema has been reduced to one gestalt. Van Hiele (1986, p.46) calls this *level reduction*. We give an example:

> Before entering teacher education, a student teacher reacted automatically to a student who wrote down "12 + 9 = 22" by pointing out his mistake. During teacher education she went through a process of change by experiencing in a variety of situations the fact that knowledge transmission is not actually very effective. She became aware of the importance of creating experiences for children, and promoting their reflection as a prerequisite for their learning. In supervision and during group discussions she developed a schema about teaching and learning of which she is consciously aware. In this schema notions like "experience" and "reflection" play a central role. Having taught for a time on the basis of this schema, she again reacts "automatically" to a student who writes "12 + 9 = 22," but this time her reaction is to ask him how he can check his work. In the concrete action situation her schema now functions as if it were a gestalt: she uses it almost unconsciously.

Thanks to level reduction, the relevant schemata need less attention. This allows the individual to concentrate on other things.

> Schematization is rooted in a need for more clarity. It is a long-term process, during which a gestalt is reflected on and acquires more "interiority" (Skemp, 1979). This means that gradually more elements in the gestalt are distinguished and named, together with relations between those elements. The person's needs play a central role in focusing the attention on certain elements. Formulations are shortened and symbolized, a process requiring a considerable capacity for abstraction, as the concrete situations in which the gestalt was elicited become less important.
>
> The result of the schematization process is a schema that, when employed in a new situation, offers far more possibilities for conscious actions than the original gestalt. This schema may comprise all kinds of detailed subschemata and may itself be part of one or more larger schemata.
>
> The learner can schematize by reflecting on the gestalts formed during previous or present experiences in the course of a search for more clarity.
>
> Schemata offer people the possibility to justify what they are doing, to take responsibility for their actions, and to check their work.

10.5. THEORY BUILDING

Someone who has drawn up a rich schema may feel a need to *explain* its structure, to establish the logic of the schema, and to make that logic explicit. This need is most likely to arise in cases where logical mistakes involve a potentially high risk, or the schema has become so complex that the person is unable to continue learning or working without a logical ordering of the material. Consider the following:

> For example, a teacher who is experienced and who has developed a schema about learning (including such concepts as experience, knowledge, skills, transfer, reflection, and the relationships between those concepts) may develop an interest in the logic behind her schema. She may start to search for one or two basic principles on which to base the other concepts and relationships in the schema in a logical way. She may end her search by accepting the constructivist principle that everyone constructs personal meaning on the basis of his or her own experiences; from now on she may see this as the fundamental principle on which a whole theory of learning can be built, a theory which explains most of the relationships in her schema, for example the relationship between the concepts "knowledge" and "transfer."
>
> This teacher will probably feel the need to look at *teaching* from her new perspective on learning. If teaching is meant to promote learning, then suddenly it is no longer such a self-evident phenomenon.... On the one hand, the teacher will now have a

better understanding of what is helpful in the process of trying to transmit knowledge to students; on the other hand, she may well begin to question whether her view of teaching as the transmission of knowledge is still valid. Finally, she may start to redefine teaching as the facilitation of learning. At that point, two schemata (one about learning and one about teaching) fit together, forming a single theory; she will probably call this "a theory about learning and teaching." From now on, teaching and learning are two sides of the same coin. Note how far removed this view is from the original—more or less separate—gestalts of learning and teaching she may have started with (compare the examples in section 10.3).

The step between knowing the characteristics of certain situations and providing a logical explanation for those characteristics (properties), as well as the connections between them, can lead to what we call a *theory*. During schematization, gestalts are described in words and pictures. Logical arguments, however, cannot be expressed in pictures; in theory building, everything must be put into words, and this can easily result in all sorts of *uncertainties*, which promote the search for the "logic behind the story." Consider two examples:

- Someone may have learned something, even though he or she is unable to express it in words. Is it possible to give an exact description of the difference between the situation before and after someone has "learned" something?
- Is it possible to integrate the behaviorist and the humanistic view of learning in one theory?

Questions like this lead to definitions, which to the layperson appear labored and artificial. For the person on the street, the definition of learning found in scientific books does not seem to have much to do with his "learning" today that Central Park starts at 59th street.

Theory building originates in a need for order in and verification of the schemata constructed. It involves the logical structuring of schemata. Essential is the formulation of starting points, definitions, and logically derived propositions: now everything must be expressed in words, which may lead to a reassessment of the content of the concepts and relations within the schemata.

It is not always desirable or possible to make the transition from schemata to theory. In everyday situations, schemata, or even gestalts, are generally sufficient. Only if there is a special wish—for example to become an expert in a particular field or to develop more certainty about an important issue—will the need arise to understand the logic behind things. Such a need can be stimulated by opportunity and the time to become thoroughly acquainted with a subject before being required to formulate logical theories. Educators often forget how much time and energy they themselves have devoted to thinking about teaching and learning, and how much their own learning process was stimulated by an internal learning need (often more of an intellectual than a practical need). It is understandable that they should wish to shorten the time it takes their students to reach the level at which they themselves function. However, in striving to do so, they often hinder the intended process, as we will see in section 10.9.

10.6. ILLUSTRATION OF THE THREE LEVELS, BASED ON EMPIRICAL EVIDENCE

In this section we present a few excerpts from interviews, as empirical illustrations of our analysis. We use the word "illustrations," because it is too early to talk about a formally tested theory on levels in teachers' professional learning. We used several different types of interviews. In addition, we chose different types of respondents: laypeople, high school students, student teachers, beginning teachers, and experienced teachers. For our present purpose, we present data from a type of interview we developed on the basis of research designs used by other researchers in this field, such as Carter, Cushing, Sabers, Stein, and Berliner (1988) and Copeland, Birmingham, DeMeulle, D'Emidio-Caston, and Natal (1994). In these interviews, the respondents watched classroom vignettes on video and were subsequently questioned about them. The three cases described here are drawn from semistructured interviews about a 5-minute video recording showing a discussion between a small group of high school students and their biology teacher about a test many students had failed:

Respondent 1: A 13-year-old high school student

Interviewer: "Can you tell me what you've just seen, in one sentence?"

Student: "A teacher who has a talk with students about a test they failed."

Interviewer: "What do you think about that talk?"

Student: "Well, I think, that teacher, he ... It is indeed kind of dry material. If you would have a book that has pictures and good, readable pieces of text in it. Isn't that much nicer to study than when a teacher tells you about things in class you have to memorize right away?"

Interviewer: "So you're saying: I understand what those students are trying to say."

Student: "Yes. In our class we always have practicals and nice pictures and stuff, and then it's easy. You know right off how everything is put together and how it works, just from looking at those pictures."

Interviewer: "What do you think about the talk?"

Student: "You know, teachers always think: this is my subject and you have to start three days in advance and this, that and the other. But we get other assignments too, you know! We might well have two more tests to study for before that one, and that's it then. Then it's really impossible to study for all of them days in advance."

Interviewer: "So what you're saying is: some of the problems those students mention are well-known to me. What do you think of the teacher in that talk?"

Student: "That teacher puts it all down to pace, but pace has nothing to do with it! If you explain everything well, use good pictures to go with it, and you just understand everything, you could make it as fast as you like." (...)

Interviewer: "And what did you think of the talk?"

Student: "Well, I think things didn't get any clearer for the students. I mean, if they studied as hard as they could this time, then I think they'll probably fail the next test, too."

Interviewer: "Is there a logic to what you're saying?"

Student: "I don't know."

Interviewer: "I mean: could you make a sentence that goes like: "if this, then that"?"

Student: "Well, if teachers would explain things better and be clearer and draw easier pictures, then that'd mean the grades would go up."

Interviewer: "Do you know any theory about this?"

Student: "No?" [The student seems to be surprised by the question.]

Although the interviewer makes several attempts to focus on the discussion itself, the student is hardly aware of the structure in the communication on the video. Instead, she has focused her attention on high school students' problems and teachers' classroom behavior. These issues apparently reflect her "concern," shaping her perception of the video. With regard to these issues, she seems to have a kind of schema with concepts and relations, even a logical relation.

However, as far as the communication structure on the video is concerned, we are inclined to conclude that she is at a gestalt level: There seems to be one overall idea that characterizes the conversation for her, which is something like: Such a conversation does not help and is irritating. This is only verbalized after repeated inquiry. The student does not seem to have many concepts at her disposal to describe this gestalt in more detail. It is typical for the gestalt level that the phenomenon is self-evident for the person. This seems to be the case here: The student seems to think that this is just the way teachers talk. This example shows how cultural factors shape students' perception and is an illustration of the complex interplay between cultural, social, and psychological factors in the gestalt formation process. It is also the reason why we started with the example of a nonteacher: We found that, as soon as people start to think seriously of becoming a teacher, their reflections on the video are more focused on the teacher–student interaction and its limitations:

Respondent 2: A postgraduate student teacher in chemistry

Interviewer: "Can you sum up what you have just seen in one sentence?"

Student: "A lecture, he was giving a lecture, pure and simple. He was trying to find the reasons to explain to the students why they'd failed the test. He's already analyzed it completely, he knows exactly what the problem is. That's fairly obvious. It was a lecture I saw."

Interviewer: "What makes you say that? Why is it a lecture?"

Student: "He was talking for a fairly long time. At a certain point he's listing the things he thought had caused the students to flunk the test. The fast pace, outside pressures. He didn't allow the students to speak very often, either. The students tried to several times, by saying: "Yes, but don't you think it could've had something to do with the way you teach?" Well, of course that wasn't it, obviously. That didn't fit in with his explanations. Those were not the problems he foresaw. It was more like a one-way transfer of what was really at the bottom of it. And as for the students' role in it, there hardly was any."

(....)

Interviewer: "Do you know more about this type of situation, in terms of the words you use, like lecture, one-way transfer?"

Student: "I perceive it as a lecture, because that's how I experienced lectures at university. That's what a lecturer is there for, he transmits his views on a particular subject and you really just absorb that and maybe you put it to use at a later stage. There is no interaction, really. Also, I could appreciate where those students were coming from. Because that is how you often feel, that the teacher really knows best, because of his experience."

Interviewer: "When I ask you, what do you know about these things, I am referring to educational and pedagogical knowledge too. What is your reaction to that?"

Student: "When I look at a situation like this one, I'm thinking: they'll leave in a minute, but they haven't achieved anything. They've discussed the problem, but whether they'll actually be able to do something about it, that wasn't the issue here.

So, I think that in that respect, he didn't make the most of the discussion. It was an exchange of ideas, more than anything. The students came to him with a problem, but he didn't solve it for them. At the end he just goes: "Well now, you'll start to study a couple of days sooner, you'll put in more time. And this time, don't just put it off till one day before the test." You see, he claims that is what happens 99% of the time. And then their simple admission that they're just not going to do that. The discussion hasn't changed anything."

Interviewer: "Do you know any educational or pedagogical theory that could apply to this situation?"

Student: "No, you're right, I don't know much about that."

We conclude that this student teacher has reached a schema level with regard to the communication between a teacher and his students in which some first logical relationships are discernible. The elements of the schema are concepts like "lecture" and "one-way transfer." A logical relation seems to be: If a teacher employs one-way transfer in this way, then a problematic situation like this will not change much. We conclude from the last part of the interview that this student teacher has not yet reached the theory level.

Respondent 3: A professor of education

In the first part of the next interview, the respondent describes his thoughts on what he saw on the video. Basically, he feels that the students in this situation analyze the problem differently than the teacher, and the teacher tries to explain that his way really is the right way to do it. In answer to the question "What do you know about this kind of situation?", the respondent refers to publications by Gordon on teacher–student interaction and Leary on interpersonal behavior and theory of discussion techniques.

Interviewer: "Summarizing the things you brought up in answer to my question about what you know about this kind of situation, I heard you mention Gordon, a number of his principles, like "whose problem is this," you refer to discussion techniques, you comment briefly on the fact that there's little or no communication in this situation, you mention Leary, you regard it from a Leary point of view, you picture a Leary-rose [the model for mapping behavior, developed by Leary], you thought about what you could do about it, and then you observe that this'd be probably very hard, since this type of thing is usually very deep and fixed. It is rather a lot of different subjects you mention there. Is there any logical structure behind that multitude of things? Is there a logic which ties it all together?"

Professor: "If I start with non-communication I'd probably be able to draw circles and arrows or something to connect it to the other concepts." [He starts to make a drawing, see Fig. 10.1] "Leary is one way to study that communication; Gordon provides another way to look at it, and I should add here that I usually tend to use this to look

FIG. 10.1. The professor's drawing.

at classroom situations and that I apply that to discussion situations outside the classroom situation. And of course they're closely related, because of escalating processes, for one thing, symmetrical communication and complementary relationships, things like that. This makes up one theory, and then you have ..." [he is elaborating the drawing].

Interviewer: "You're referring to this as a theory?"

Professor: "You can combine this into one theory, I think that in my head this might be something in the shape of one theory, more or less...."

Interviewer: "You say that was not on your mind when you were looking at the video, but could you describe it ..."

Professor: "Guidelines, like if this man really wants the students to start now, make them start studying for the next test earlier, he'd better do things differently, that type of thing crossed my mind constantly, but I couldn't simply add them here [in the drawing], this is more like a sort of overall network of concepts. There's bound to be some logical structure in there, but I can't see that now."

There is no doubt that the professor has reached theory level with regard to the theories he mentions, because he has written books on some of them. In the interview, he tries to find logical relations between these separate theories. The theories and theory-elements seem to play a role in the way the professor interprets the vignette, but not so much at a conscious level. He is more focused on finding practical guidelines for action. He reports that only afterward, during the interview, he becomes aware of the connection between these guidelines and the theories. We are inclined to regard this as an example of a reduced theory level. This seems to be characteristic of every situation in which a respondent who has reached the theory level is asked to reflect on a practical situation: It appears that in such cases the connection with practice can only be established through level reduction.

10.7. A CLOSER LOOK AT THE RELATIONS BETWEEN THE THREE LEVELS

In this section we discuss a few aspects of the three-level model in more detail, thus enriching our framework. In particular, we focus on the relations between the three levels.

The Development of Teachers' Mental Structures

We will now try to formulate the essence of level transitions. As we have seen, gestalt formation is the most common type of learning. Sometimes the learning process goes further. Occasionally, there is a need to understand what it is that makes different objects or situations "the same." This, too, reflects a need to grasp some aspect of reality. In such cases, it is necessary to establish the characteristics of one's own gestalt. This means that a mental structure (schema) is formed consisting of elements and relations between these elements (Van Hiele, 1986, p. 50). The gestalt gets more "interiority" (Berliner, 1987; Skemp, 1979) and becomes both conscious and more static. In order to do this, the person must *reflect* on his or her own gestalt. The greater the quality and quantity of the elements in the schema and the relations between them, the richer the schema.

Once a person has reached the schema level, he or she may feel the need to distill from the multitude of elements and relations within a schema the essence of that schema. By adopting, say, a constructivist theory on learning, one can derive many principles from one or more basic assumptions. This makes the world just a bit easier to understand. The ability to *clarify* and *verify* by means of logic is another way of increasing our grasp of the world. If we look more closely at what is going on at this theory level, we may then conclude with Van Hiele (1973) that the network of relations (the schema) has been reordered in such a way that a small number of relations form the core from which the others can be logically derived. In other words, relations are created between the relations within the existing schema. The relations of the old network become the nodes of a new one.

Reflection

In order to promote the transition to a new level, the person must think about the knowledge he or she has already acquired or the experiences he or she has undergone, and strive to introduce into them a new structure. This is precisely how we defined reflection in section 4.5. In chapter 4 we showed that, on the one hand, researchers in the field of teacher thinking and teacher education use different conceptualizations of the concept of reflection, and these differences draw on various views of the goals of education and the role of the teacher. On the other hand, a common characteristic of all conceptualizations of reflection is the fact that the reflecting person structures or restructures his or her already existing knowledge or experiences. The educational views behind the different conceptualizations of reflection are the perspectives that determine the favored way of structuralization. The three levels and the related processes are summarized in Fig. 10.2.

Level Reduction

Concepts and relations that have been formed mentally can be concretized by writing them down, drawing them, or explaining them verbally; this makes them more tangible and more manageable. In this way, a theory or a complex schema can begin to function as a gestalt. The person can use it almost "automatically." This is known as *level reduction* (Van Hiele, 1973, p. 101; 1986, p. 53). Level reduction allows the actor to give more attention to other things. A second and more important function of level reduction is the fact the person can use his or her knowledge to guide action, without reflecting during the action (see the example of respondent 3 in section 10.6). This principle is related to our belief that it is gestalts that direct most of the teacher's behavior in the classroom (see also Korthagen, 1993c; Wubbels, 1992b). The phenomenon of level reduction concurs with Berliner's (1986, 1987) model of professional growth in which the expert level is the level at which the professional can act fluidly on the basis of an intuitive grasp of the situation.

Characteristics of the Three Levels

How can we determine the level a person has reached with respect to a certain subject, say, "the rectangle" or "learning"? On the basis of the aforementioned discus-

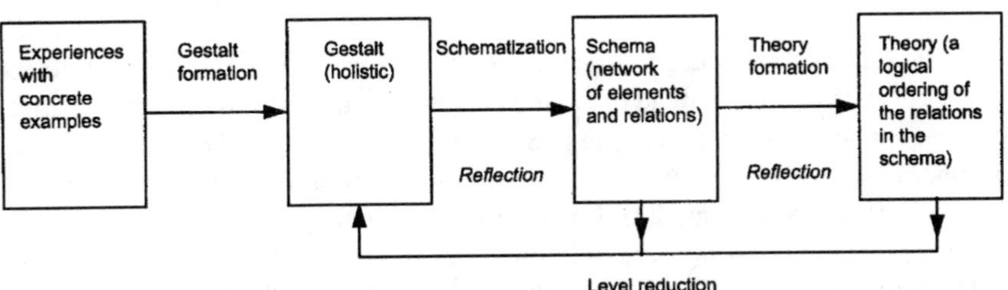

FIG. 10.2. Phases in the process of learning with regard to a certain domain and the accompanying levels.

sion, we know that an important indicator is the way the person responds to the question "what is . . . ?" Someone at the gestalt level may say "something like . . ." and give an example. If we ask someone at the gestalt level "what is learning," we might expect him to answer "learning to ski, for example" (i.e., he gives a personally relevant example). Someone at the schema level will enumerate properties, for example, in the case of "learning," characteristics of learning. Someone who has reached the theory level is able to give a definition. According to Kuhn (1977), there are at least five characteristics of a "good" theory: It is accurate (i.e., consistent with known data), it clarifies a broad range of data, it is both internally consistent and consistent with other accepted theories, it is simple (i.e., it brings order to a variety of isolated phenomena), and it is fruitful (i.e., it generates new results).

The differences will be even more marked when subjects are asked "why this is so." The person at the gestalt level will be surprised at the question and say something like "that's just the way it is." A person at the schema level will be able to produce an example showing that the particular properties he or she mentioned are indeed present. The individual at the theory level will be able to come up with a logical argument demonstrating that the definition is both necessary and sufficient.

It will be clear that the three levels differ substantially from one another. The gestalt level is closely related to sensory perception in the concrete situation in which a particular experience took place. In other words, at the gestalt level, we have *situated knowledge* (Borko & Putnam, 1996; J. S. Brown et al., 1989), which is tied to concrete situations and their context. At this level, we are dealing, by definition, with undifferentiated, unexplicated, holistic representations of situations. (As Van Hiele, 1973, p. 142, says, "The image is a symbol for a great deal which is not expressed in words.") At the schema level, experiences or situations are no longer perceived as a whole; instead, the focus is on individual elements, properties, and relations. It is at this level that language is first used to name these elements, properties, and relations. At the theory level, the relations of the schema become the elements of a network of logical relations. If-this-then-that arguments are used to clarify experiences or situations.

The Relation with Phronesis and Episteme

Most practitioners' schemata are very much colored by the wish to know how to act in particular situations, instead of having an abstract understanding of these situations. As explained in chapter 2, this purpose leads to the need to be able to perceive the important features of practical situations and thus to the development of phronesis (theory with a small t). Indeed, teachers' schemata often show more of a phronesis than an episteme type of knowledge.

The knowledge at the theory level is typically epistemic. This knowledge is helpful to understand a certain class of situations on the basis of a logical framework, an understanding that is different from the ability to act in those situations. The latter requires level reduction.

Continuity and Discontinuity in Learning

It is important to note that a level transition entails more than just generalization or abstraction. Someone functioning at the gestalt level, with respect to a particular subject, sees the concept differently from someone functioning at the schema level. This causes many problems in the communication between experts and laypeople. A level transition is an essential qualitative change in the internal representation of a situation or object in the external world.

As the learning process progresses, we see a more gradual development within a single level. The gestalt level, for instance, initially is closely related to one or more concrete objects or situations. As the person gains more experience with a greater number of related examples, a more abstract gestalt of these examples is gradually formed. This development from concrete to abstract at the gestalt level is a prerequisite for a level transition. One cannot become aware of the essential properties of a phenomenon or class of objects (schematization) until some abstraction has taken place.

At the schema level, there is a similar gradual development, in this case from a simple network of connections to a more complex structure. The development of a rich schema is a prerequisite for a correct transition to the theory level; only after one has come to recognize a multitude of relations is it possible to distinguish basic characteristics and others following logically from them.

To summarize, there are different processes involved in the development of teacher knowledge: gradual developments within a single level, and transitions from one level to another (Fig. 10.3). In level transitions, we are dealing with discontinuous processes, because the question being asked changes fundamentally. During gestalt formation, one is (often unconsciously) focused on how to act in certain situations; in schematization, one is consciously striving to bring clarity to the gestalts; and in theory-building, the aim is to introduce logical order into the schemata. This distinction between gradual and discontinuous transitions echoes that made by Rumelhart and Norman (1981) between *accretion*, the gradual increase in information within existing schemata, and *restructuring*, which involves "the creation of new schemata" (Rumelhart & Norman, 1981, p. 45; see also Vosniadou & Brewer, 1987).

Subjective Theories

One problem that may arise is related to the fact that people often feel the need for a logical explanation before a sufficiently rich schema has been formed. They apply "local" logical structures to the schema, and this sometimes blocks correct theory building. For example, a teacher who starts off with a view of teaching as knowledge transmission may develop a network of if–then relations concerned with "effective knowledge transmission." The more powerful such mental networks are, the more difficult it will be to help the teacher reframe his or her thinking about teaching. In line with Mandl and Huber (1983), we call these local orderings *subjective theories*.[3]

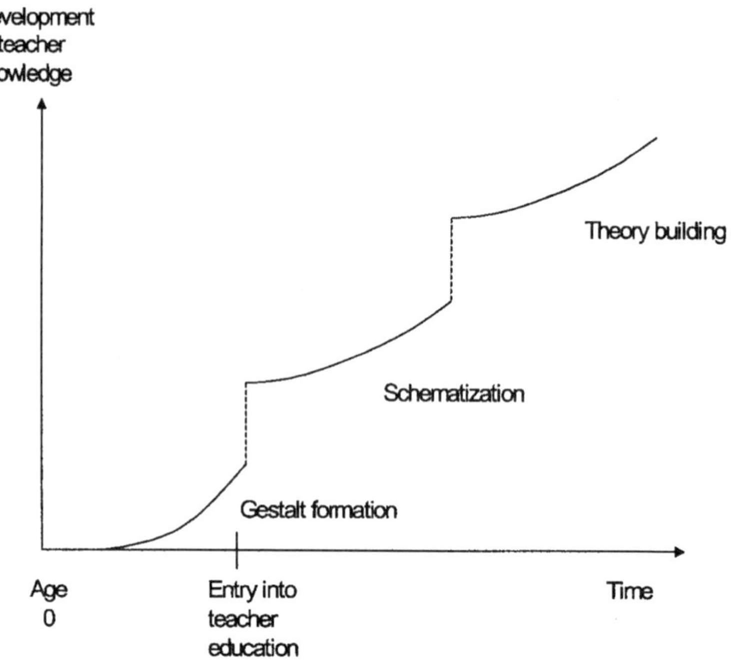

FIG. 10.3. The development of teacher knowledge within a certain domain, for example, "teaching."

For instance, a subjective theory of a teacher might be: "If a student does not understand my explanation, then I have to explain it again." Such a local ordering can hinder an overall ordering congruent with current theories on learning (Theories with capital T).

10.8. THE THEORETICAL BASIS OF THE THREE-LEVEL MODEL

Having arrived at this point, the reader may be wondering about the theoretical basis behind our model of levels in professional learning. What is the logic behind all that we have said? What are the underlying assumptions and how can other principles be derived from these assumptions? In other words, can we reach the theory level with regard to the model?

Starting Points

Our starting points, the axioms of our model, are derived from what is known as the action–theory paradigm (Groeben & Scheele, 1977), influenced by the cognitive shift in psychology (cf. Mayer, 1981). The first starting point is that people's actions are based on personal *goals*, goals of which they are not necessarily aware (Skemp, 1979, p. 2). This can also be expressed in terms of needs: Human action is aimed at the satisfaction of personal needs (Maslow, 1968). It should be noted here that action includes not only "interaction with the environment," but also mental action, such as the structuring of experiences in our heads.

The second starting point of the action–theory paradigm is that an individual's actions are directed by mental structures (e.g., stored experiences, knowledge, beliefs, etc.) and, moreover, these mental structures are constantly being developed and adjusted (Groeben & Scheele, 1977). This latter assumption also forms the basis of *constructivism* (Fosnot, 1996; Sigel & Cocking, 1977; Von Glasersfeld, 1990).

These two starting points—actions are based on individual needs, and there is an interaction between an individual's mental structures and the objects and situations in the environment—are closely related. All human beings have a basic need for a grasp of their environment; without it, they are helpless and entirely at the mercy of that environment. Mental structures help us to achieve that grasp, and enable us to place situations and objects. Note that as a consequence the characteristics of these mental structures are more or less determined by the need that triggered their development.

We have borrowed from gestalt psychology the notion that the most elementary way individuals acquire a grasp of their environment is through the formation of gestalts, which often unconsciously or semiconsciously help us to see objects or situations as an entity and to respond to them as such (Ellis, 1950). For immediate teaching situations, this means that the many and multifaceted conditions and events embedded in a given situation are combined into one holistic perceptual identity.

The Social Context

This implies a complex interplay between social, cultural, psychological, and physical factors. First, the knowledge imbedded in gestalts is linked to concrete situations previously encountered by the person (often very early in life) and colored by the subjective and value-laden experiences of such situations. This is in line with Van Manen's (1990) conception of the interplay of a situation and the person experiencing that situation and the role of context in that experience (cf. Carter & Doyle, 1996; Clandinin, 1985). For example, in Mrs. Wilson's situation described earlier, negative experiences with classroom discussions may shape her present behavior.

Following the work of authors such as Vygotsky (1978) and Giddens (1984), we can look at the role of context from a broader sociocultural perspective. For example, it is possible that Mrs. Wilson is strongly influenced by her need to get through the lesson quickly, which may in turn be influenced by pressures put on her by a prescribed and overloaded curriculum. This may in turn reflect a macro social-economic emphasis on productivity, and diminishing consideration for the value of care in human relationships. As H. Berlak and A. Berlak (1981) pointed out, the teaching profession is filled with such dilemmas between conflicting values, goals, conditions, and personal needs of the participants in classroom interactions. To give an example of the latter, Mrs. Wilson may also be influenced by her feeling Jim's resistance toward being asked to reflect on his own thinking, which again may result from his cultural background.

However, being "in action," Mrs. Wilson will not have the time to reflect on such important, but numerous and very complex, relations between the various factors imbedded in the situation: Foremost, she has to act, and a gestalt of the situation helps her in doing so.

Images

Other authors use the term *image* to refer to the holistic perceptions guiding behavior (e.g., Connelly & Clandinin, 1984; Denis, 1991). "Images stand for perceptual events in the close but conventionalized way that a picture stands for the pictured object" (Bruner, 1964, p. 2). These images are not only visual, but can also contain imprints from other sensory perceptions (Dennett, 1991; Johnson, 1987). However, there are two problems with this term, causing us to prefer the term *gestalt*. First, Calderhead and Robson (1991, p. 3) point out that "the concept of image is a fairly crude one that has not been very precisely defined either in cognitive psychology or in research on teaching." Indeed, the term is used for different phenomena, for example, both in the sense of a context-bound, concrete mental picture of a certain situation and in the sense of a general view of teaching or education, thus coming close to the concept of a metaphor. Second, the term *image* seems to refer to something visual, and it is important to include imprints from other sensory perceptions (Dennett, 1991) and behavioral tendencies. For the purposes of a further development of our model (which implies the necessity to formulate basic notions precisely), we believe that gestalt is more suitable. In line with gestalt psychology, we use it to refer to a holistic unity elicited in the teacher by a concrete here-and-now situation (within a certain context), often within a split second. As Korthagen (1993c) notes, "In a gestalt the person's needs, values, meanings, thoughts, feelings and actions are all united into one inseparable whole." (See also Huibregtse et al., 1994.)

Is the Three-Level Model a Theory?

Is the network of relations described in this section a theory? We do not think so, at least not if we define theory in the sense we did earlier. It is more like theory in development, consisting of more than just local logical orderings, but still in need of more empirical support and elaboration. That is why we used model rather than theory.

Our attempt to develop the model builds heavily on two foundations. The first of these is the *Van Hiele model*. It has been empirically tested in school subjects like mathematics and chemistry, but not extensively in the area of teacher knowledge.

Moreover, there is an important difference between Van Hiele's model and our own. Van Hiele, too, distinguishes between three levels, but the first level (called the *ground level*) is much more formulated in terms of visual aspects and does not include all the dimensions we incorporate in our definition of a gestalt. This has to do with the fact that the Van Hiele model was developed within the context of geometry education. In this respect, our gestalt-schema-theory model is an extension of the Van Hiele model.

Second, our theory-in-development builds on gestalt psychology, which is no longer an integral part of mainstream cognitive psychology. Although Anderson's (1980) well-known handbook on cognitive psychology included a chapter on mental imagery, in recent years cognitive psychologists have focused more on what we would call the schema level than on less conscious aspects of learning. They have also appeared to be more interested in cognitive rather than affective aspects (Pintrich, 1990), and more in products of learning (e.g., the structure of a person's schema) than in long-term learning processes (Freudenthal, 1991, p. 87). Nor has the role of gestalts or images in the creation of meaning been discussed in any of the standard texts on semantics in the 1980s (Johnson, 1987). During the 1990s, we have seen slightly increasing interest in so-called implicit learning (i.e., learning resulting in knowledge that is difficult to express in words). (For an overview, see Berry & Dienes, 1993; Epstein, 1994.)

Although our attempt to build a theory of teacher learning builds on these other two frameworks, it also represents a new synthesis. As such, it requires more empirical support and more elaboration of the relations within the network we have constructed.

We find additional support in the work of a number of creative researchers who in the past dared to propose somewhat original views of human functioning. One of these is Watzlawick (1978), who maintains that the combination of previous experiences and our knowledge of everyday life results in what he calls "world images." Building on discoveries in the field of psychotherapy and brain research (e.g., Bogen, 1969; Gazzaniga, 1970), he makes it plausible that the representation of reality in mental images takes place primarily on the right-hand side of the brain (see also Korthagen, 1993c; Wubbels, 1992b). Although it has since been shown that the organization of the brain is much more complicated (see, e.g., Bryden, 1982), the view suggested by Watzlawick is helpful in coming to terms with the processes described earlier. A typical feature of images (in our terms gestalts), and the right half of the brain associated with it, is their *analog* nature. The schema level and the theory level, by contrast, are associated with the left-hand side of the brain and are characterized by the use of *digital* structures. Although Watzlawick relies on theories that enjoy empirical support, Wubbels (1992b) rightly points out that Watzlawick's theory has not itself been proven.

Support for the connection between certain neurophysiological processes and image formation as we conceive it can be found in D. I. Lawson and A. E. Lawson (1993) and Kosslyn, Van Kleeck, and Kirby (1990). Barlow (1990) notes: "Neurons respond selectively to just the characteristics of the image that the gestalt school drew attention to." Indeed, the application of the well-known gestalt laws (e.g., the law of closure; see also section 10.9) to processes in teaching appears to deepen our understanding of phenomena in educational contexts (see Dolk, Korthagen, & Wubbels, 1995, for an elaboration).

The gestalt level can be considered the psychological counterpart of the observation made by Damasio (1994, pp. 83–84) that behavior is grounded in many parallel systems in the human body and emotion is linked with the primary decision-making process. According to Damasio, the idea that our behavior is based on information located in a single "Cartesian theater" is an illusion (cf. Edelman, 1987). Damasio (1994, pp. 97–98) emphasizes that images play an important role in our functioning as human beings and are closely related to dispositional neural patterns. He points out (p. 240): "The present is never here. We are hopelessly late for consciousness." Gazzaniga (1999, p. 73) points toward the same phenomenon: "Major events associated with mental processing go on, measurably so, in our brain before we are aware of them."

Another author whose work shows similar lines of thinking is Johnson (1987). His book *The Body in the Mind* starts with a discussion of the present crisis in the theory of meaning and rationality. He points to the total absence of adequate studies on what he calls *image schematic structures*, which are of a nonpropositional, analog, and figurative nature. Johnson's argument begins by showing that human bodily movement, manipulation of objects, and perceptual interactions involve recurring patterns without which our experience would be chaotic and incomprehensible. He calls these patterns "image schemata" and argues:

> These are gestalt structures, consisting of parts standing in relations and organized into unified wholes, by means of which our experience manifests discernible order. When we seek to comprehend this order and to reason about it, such bodily based schemata play a central role. For although a given image schema may emerge first as a structure of bodily interactions, it can be figuratively developed and extended as a structure around which meaning is organized at more abstract levels of cognition. (Johnson, 1987, pp. xix–xx)

Support for the existence of a theory level in experienced teachers can be found in Copeland et al. (1994), who discovered that teachers with more experience and expertise identified more causal relations when viewing a video recording of a classroom episode.

10.9. IMPLICATIONS

In this section, implications of the three-level model are explored, for the relation between teacher thinking and behavior, for teacher education, and for research.

Teacher Thinking and Teacher Behavior

The relation between teacher thinking and teacher behavior has been one of the major issues in the literature on teaching and teacher education during the past few decades (cf. Carter, 1990). What is interesting in the context of this chapter is the question of whether teacher behavior is actually guided by rational thought. Many publications on the role of teacher routines (e.g., Clark & Yinger, 1979; Halkes & Olson, 1984) stress the fact that the automatic or mechanical performance of acts is characteristic of a good deal of teacher behavior (see also Unwin & McAleese, 1978, p. 677). Carter (1990, p. 297) concludes that teachers' actions seem to be governed largely by rules and routines, with decision making in a studied, deliberative sense taking a minor role in their interactive thinking. Elbaz (1991) notes that teachers' knowledge is nonlinear, holistic, imbued with personal meaning, and largely tacit. Sternberg and Caruso (1985, p. 148) argue that unreflected "tacit knowledge" is a key factor in one's success or failure as a teacher. According to T. Russell et al. (1988, p. 67), "professional knowledge consists of more than that which can be told or written on paper." Concluding, we agree with Clark and Lampert (1985) when they say that we are beginning to appreciate that strictly logical thinking is often not the most appropriate tool for solving the problems that teachers confront in classrooms.

Denis (1991, p. 171) argues that "images seem to play an important role in the regulation of behaviors by which individuals act on the world and perform transformations" (see also Kaufmann, 1985). He refers to the concept of "operative images" as proposed by Ochanine (1978), which stresses the regulatory function of imagery in human action. Denis continues by stating that "imagery is considered to be a privileged form of representation in that it provides individuals with an internal model of the world, a model that is built up from action and is designed to organize action" (p. 171). This causes us to believe that unreflected teacher behavior is guided by what we call gestalts. This assumption is also based on an important organizing principle of gestalt learning theory, called *closure*. In their perception of the world, human beings tend to complete incomplete information. A well-known example is that if parts of a picture are missing, then we still "see" those parts. If a song on the CD player suddenly stops, we "hear" the next part of the song in our head. Early research in gestalt psychology showed that a certain tension is created by unresolved, incomplete experiences (Rickers-Ovsiankina, 1928; Zeigarnik, 1927): Our organism tends to do something in order to release this tension. The theory on gestalt therapy extends this principle to interpersonal relationships: People strive for closure of the gestalts triggered in them by interpersonal situations (Korb et al., 1989, p. 9). Past experiences determine the gestalt and thus the completion process; we tend to "re-act" (i.e., repeat the action that completed the situation or situations we encountered earlier). For example, if, as a child, we had to deal with an authoritative father and solved problematic situations by withdrawal, this may have become our action tendency in any conflict situation. This is why we have included "actions tendencies" in our definition of a gestalt.

Research on *metaphors* used by teachers when describing their classroom role supports this view of the role of gestalts in teacher behavior (Bullough, J. G. Knowles, & Crow, 1991; Créton, Wubbels, & Hooymayers, 1989; Munby & Russell, 1989; Tobin et al., 1990): teachers tend to interpret classroom situations with the aid of rather stable, semiconscious metaphors, and act accordingly. We find other support in the finding of Carter et al. (1988) that expert teachers viewing a series of classroom slides, reacted quickly to visual stimuli indicating to them whether or not students were "working well" (a basic gestalt for teachers!). Korthagen (1993c, p. 310) summarizes our view as follows: "It is our hypothesis that during teaching certain cues from the environment activate a gestalt, triggering an immediate interpretation and reaction. In this way logical analysis can be circumvented, making it possible for teachers to deal with a great many different stimuli at the same time" (cf. Day, 1984; Doyle, 1979).

This is not intended to reject the possibility of *reflection-in-action* (Schön, 1987), which often takes place when, during routine procedures, the teacher is suddenly confronted with an unexpected result (Schön, 1987, p. 26). However, we believe that teachers reflect only a limited number of times during a lesson, although they make hundreds of smaller and bigger decisions in the less conscious way described earlier. After the lesson, they may use *reflection-on-action*, as Schön calls it, to become more aware of the way their gestalts influenced these decisions. Chapter 11 describes a number of techniques that can help the teacher to do this.

Our analysis has an important consequence, namely, that at first the process of theory building is often not helpful to the teacher's functioning in the classroom. Only after level reduction from the theory level to the gestalt level has taken place can the new organization of the teacher's knowledge directly influence his or her unreflected behavior, and lead to what Schön (1987) calls "knowing-in-action." This means that teacher education should pay much attention to the practicing of theoretical insights to such a degree that the resulting behavior becomes almost automatic, and can take place without much reflection. Still, we should keep in mind that teacher educators should not overestimate the role of theory, and it is better to focus on the sound development of already existing gestalts. We will now elaborate on this.

The Gap Between Theory and Practice in Teacher Education

Our model of teachers' professional learning has important implications for teacher education, especially for the well-documented failure of teacher education to influence teachers' practices (see chapter 1). If one reads Johnson's account of what he sees as a fundamental crisis in theories of meaning and rationality, then it is no wonder that current views on this problem in teacher education show the same denial of the role of experience-based gestalts. As so often happens in situations where a certain scientific paradigm is dominant, researchers in the field of teaching and teacher education tend to interpret the gap between theory and practice in teacher education in terms of this paradigm, seeing it as the problem of improving the transfer of theories presented in teacher education (*episteme*) to teaching practices, or, in other words, as the problem of promoting the "application" of existing knowledge (Berry & Dienes, 1993, p. 130). We agree with Louden (1991) that this view is based on a fundamental misunderstanding about teachers and teaching. The gap between what is taught in teacher education and the way teachers actually teach in schools is an artifact of this view. Learning about teaching is a process of developing adequate gestalts and not a question of learning to apply theories from academic textbooks. Student teachers entering preservice teacher education programs have years of life experience, including thousands of hours spent in education as students (Lortie, 1975; Zeichner & Gore, 1990). Because of these experiences, certain gestalts are triggered by educational situations. These gestalts filter everything offered to them in teacher education (Stofflett & Stoddart, 1994; cf. Bullough et al., 1991). If they enter the program with a view of teaching as the transmission of knowledge, then theories building on other views will be only partially incorporated into these gestalts, and thus into their behavior in the classroom. This is an explanation for the "washing-out" effect that Zeichner and Tabachnick (1981) found when they looked at the influence of teacher education on practice. For example, in a study on the effects of the SOL mathematics teacher education program (described in chapter 6), Wubbels et al. (1997) showed that the constructivist view presented in this program resulted only in the teachers' use of more differentiated examples while explaining mathematics, and not in attempts to build on students' notions.

Our model emphasizes that learning about teaching is not only a cognitive process, but is influenced by feelings (cf. Hargreaves, 1998a, 1998b) and by personal needs. The most important need of beginning teachers is to survive in the classroom (Fuller & Bown, 1975; Katz, 1972). This elicits gestalts related to keeping a grip on the class, including experiences with authoritarian teachers who kept the class under control by means of strict disciplinary measures. Such gestalts are not compatible with theories of teaching and learning in which the teacher plays a less dominant role. The idea of building on students' ideas promotes feelings of anxiety: How can one handle the class during the complex process of communicating about meanings? In other words, even if teacher educators wish to build on the gestalts of beginning teachers, they face the problem that the gestalts related to the need for survival are not a particularly auspicious basis for schematization and theory building in the direction these educators have in mind. Together with our assumption that gestalts form the basis for teacher behavior, this implies that it is almost impossible for expert theories on teaching and learning to have much influence on student teachers' behavior in the classroom during the initial stage of a teacher education program. Any attempt to use exercises and training elements after the introduction of theory, with the aim of promoting the transfer to practice, is like starting with the walls of a house and then laying the foundation. It amounts to turning the world upside down, which Freudenthal (1991) calls an *antipedagogical inversion.*

The Realistic Approach

We believe that our analysis of the levels in learning about teaching not only explains the failure of most teacher education programs, but also offers a theoretical foundation for the realistic approach to teacher education. What is needed for a process of schematization in the direction that teacher educators prefer is the organization of sufficient suitable experiences, which are tailored to the needs and concerns of student teachers and at the same time prepare the way for the intended process of schematization (Note that this is not yet theory building!) and opportunities for reflection on those experiences.[4] The term "suitable" means there is a reasonable chance that during the experiences needs and gestalts related to those needs are triggered that can be further elaborated in a way that comes close to what the educator has in mind. This always implies some degree of uncertainty: A teacher educator can never be sure what the experience brings about in the student teacher. This means the educator cannot plan the program completely beforehand, although the experience of the teacher educator will of course make the outcome of certain types of experiences more predictable. For example, experiences with classroom teaching at the beginning of a program almost always elicits gestalts concerning "survival" and "classroom discipline." A program that builds on the model of levels in professional learning should always be flexible: What second experience is suitable for a student teacher depends on the outcome of his or her reflection on the first experience, and so on.

By suitable, we also mean that, if appropriate, the experience is challenging enough to offer opportunities for a confrontation with gestalts that the educator would like to change. If, for example, a student teacher has a rigid view of teaching as knowledge-transmission, suitable experiences would be those that offer the student teacher an opportunity to discover that the transmission did not work. As already noted, such an unexpected result promotes reflection, which can lead to a so-called lowering of the status (P. W. Hewson & M. G. Hewson, 1989) of gestalts, schemata, or subjective theories. This, in turn, creates in the student teacher a need for "conceptual change" (P. W. Hewson et al., 1992; Wubbels, Korthagen, & Dolk, 1992), thus promoting a process that Schön (1987) calls *reframing*. Suitable experiences may be experiences in the role of a teacher, but also one's own experiences as a learner in the teacher education program. The latter type of experience has the added advantage that it does not focus on gestalts about survival as a teacher, so that the relation between learning and teaching can more easily be reflected on by the student teachers.

It is important to keep in mind that early practical experiences with classroom teaching in a preservice program often serve to strengthen traditional views of teaching and learning (Feiman-Nemser & Buchman, 1986; Korthagen, 1985). As pointed out in section 5.5, in the IVLOS teacher education program, the first practice teaching period (6–8 weeks) is often organized as a *1-to-1 experience*: One student teacher gives one high school student a 1-hour lesson each week. The lessons are recorded on audio cassettes, and are reflected on by the student teacher, who keeps a prestructured logbook. This arrangement appears to be very suitable in the sense elaborated earlier: The student teachers are confronted with the way their implicit gestalts about learning and teaching are working out within a fairly simple and nonthreatening situation. As one of our student teachers characterized the experience, "It brought about a shift in me, from a teacher perspective to a student perspective."[5]

As noted before (e.g., in section 9.7), in such an approach to teacher education the professionalism of teacher educators is completely different from that of a traditional lecturer. Most of all, realistic teacher educators need to have the capacity to skip the theory for a while, to create suitable learning experiences, and to promote reflection on these experiences. This is no simple task given the traditional practices in many schools. On the one hand, the experience should be as real as possible (i.e., the student teacher must be able to consider it as directly relevant from a professional standpoint), while, on the other hand, premature socialization into traditional practices should be avoided. Moreover, the experience should not be too threatening, otherwise the start of the process leading from gestalt formation to schematization will be blocked by the wrong gestalts, namely, those triggered by survival needs. Chapter 13 is devoted to the development of the skills teacher educators need to work in this way.

Implications for Research and the Body of Knowledge on Teaching and Teacher Education

Although in this chapter we have garnered a great deal of support for our analysis of teachers' professional learning, as a theory it is still in the developmental stage, and will require further confirmation within different contexts. Because the implications as described could cause a fundamental, almost paradigmatic change in teacher education practices, further research is urgently needed.

The ideas expressed in this chapter may also lead to important consequences for research itself. The principle of level reduction calls into question the validity of the "stimulated recall" technique, in which a person explains what went on in his or her head during a certain teaching episode, while seeing or hearing a video or audio recording of that episode. There is a problem with this research technique because if during teaching someone uses knowledge at a reduced level, then the gestalt nature of such knowledge is distorted by the technique. The impression is created that the knowledge was consciously present at a schema or theory level at the moment of teaching, which may not be the case. Moreover, as Argyris and Schön (1974, p. 7) noted, people often explain their behavior by means of "espoused theories" that may not be compatible with the real sources of their behavior. As they say, an individual may or may not be aware of this incompatibility.

10.10. REFRAMING THE PREVIOUS CHAPTERS

In the previous chapters, we have already given many concrete examples of the way the intended process from gestalt formation to schematization can be fostered. We will now reinterpret some of these examples with the aid of the model on levels in teachers' professional learning.

The ALACT model (see section 3.7) starts with a phase of concrete action so that the relevant, action guiding gestalts are triggered, which then can be reflected on in Phases 2 and 3 of the ALACT model. Phase 3, awareness of essential aspects, is an important step in the process of schematization. The whole of chapter 7, in which we described the individual supervisory process in relation to the ALACT model, can be seen as a description of what is needed in order to help a student teacher become aware of his or her gestalts and to promote schematization on the basis of that awareness.

In section 9.2, we summarized a five-step pedagogical procedure to work with groups of student teachers on their practical teaching experiences, consisting of five phases: (1) prestructuring, (2) experiences, (3) structuring, (4) focusing, and (5) theory. Its essence is that, through suitable experiences, adequate gestalts are formed that afterward are used as the basis for schematization by means of reflection. In Step 5, it is important for the teacher educator not to push too hard toward theory building. Van Hiele (1986) has pointed out how the step toward a higher level is often easier after a certain period of time. It is as if some maturation has taken place, even though the schema was not activated in a conscious way: After some time, a fresh look at what we already know makes it easier to restructure our knowledge. This implies that if there is an important place for real theory in the academic sense at all (e.g., theory on constructivist approaches or motivation), it is often at a much later stage in teacher education, especially after the preservice period. Then, too, it is important to build schemata and theories on adequate experiences and to give due attention to the promotion of level reduction by providing varied opportunities to practice what has been learned.

It is important to note that both the ALACT model, which describes the intended learning process in an individual, and the five-step procedure, which is a pedagogical procedure for working with groups of student teachers, are cyclical: After any progress in the learning process, the newly gained knowledge should be connected to new experiences in practice in order to foster level reduction.

If we look at the four techniques described in the second part of chapter 9 (the wall, columns, the rep-grid and arrows), we can see that these techniques are also ways to make unconscious or semiconscious gestalts explicit, and second, to promote further analysis of elements constituting these gestalts as well as the relations between these elements, thus fostering schematization.

In conclusion, we have demonstrated that our analysis has the potential to consolidate a number of separate theories and principles used in teacher education into a single framework. Harvard (1994, p. 155) notes that there is a need for a general model of learning linking experiences to the thinking and learning processes of student teachers. The three-level structure described in this chapter is meant to offer such a model. This framework may be an important building block for further development of the body of knowledge in the field of teaching and teacher education. It may help us to overcome the stage of local orderings of psychological phenomena within teacher education (Pintrich, 1990, p. 849) and ultimately arrive at a theory level in our thinking about teacher education.

SUMMARY

There is an enormous body of literature on teacher knowledge, but relatively little is known about the development of such knowledge. In this chapter, we reframed most of the principles outlined in the previous chapters by introducing a comprehensive model describing professional learning. The model consists of three qualitatively different levels:

1. *The gestalt level.* If a person reacts without much thinking (in immediate teaching situations), the reaction is generally based on unconsciously triggered needs, values, meanings, feelings, and behavioral inclinations, which together form an inseparable whole called a *gestalt.* This is an extrapolation of the classical gestalt concept, which was mainly used to describe the organization of the visual field. This extrapolation is based on the fact that the classical gestalt laws (e.g., the law of closure) appear to be applicable to the functioning of teachers. Gestalts are very much colored by the needs of the person in the situation triggering the gestalt.
2. *The schema level.* If the actor reflects on the situation and the actions taken (this reflection may take place "in-action" or afterward), and on similar situations, he or she may develop concepts, characteristics, principles, and so on, helpful in describing practice. Still, in order to be functional for practical use, the resulting schema should be of a *phronesis* rather than an *epistemic* character. If someone wishes to develop a more theoretical understanding of a range of similar situations, then this will lead to an emphasis on *episteme*, and possibly on to the next level:
3. *The theory level.* This is the level at which a logical ordering is constructed in the knowledge formed before: The relations within one's schema are studied or several schemata are connected into one coherent theory. This conceptual knowledge is helpful to *understand* a certain class of situations on the basis of a logical framework, an understanding that is different from the ability to use this knowledge for *acting* in those situations. For this, level reduction is necessary.

The three-level model concurs with theories on teacher images, the role of metaphors, implicit learning, the development of meaning, and with neurophysiological theories. It has serious implications for our view of the relation between teacher thinking and teacher behavior and of teacher education, as it points toward the limited role of Theory in teachers' functioning, the important role of needs and feelings, and the necessity to create suitable experiences to promote professional learning.

BASIC CONCEPTS

Gestalt and gestalt formation
Schema and schematization
Theory and theory building
Immediate teaching situations
Closure
Level reduction
Images
Metaphors
Implicit learning
Suitable experiences

11 Specific Instruments and Techniques for Promoting Reflection

Fred Korthagen

The relation between thought and word is a living process: thought is born through words.

—*Vygotsky (1986, p. 255)*

This chapter is devoted to instruments and techniques for strengthening the relation between student teachers' experiences in practice and their reflections about this practice. One of the most important is the logbook. This chapter describes ways of shaping the logbook, for example, by means of standard questions to structure the student teachers' reflections. I will also analyze the relation between reflection and improving interpersonal classroom behavior. Finally, techniques and instruments are presented that use more holistic ways of reflecting on practice.

11.1. INTRODUCTION

By now, the practical and theoretical foundation has been laid for the realistic approach in teacher education. The previous chapter provided an overall synthesis of many of the elements put forward in chapters 1 through 9. In the present chapter, the focus shifts to a very concrete issue: What instruments or techniques can the teacher educator use to strengthen the relationship between student teachers' experiences in practice and their reflections on this practice? In chapter 9, four techniques have already been discussed (the wall, columns, repgrid, and arrows). In the present chapter, a broader range of instruments and techniques will be described.

One of the instruments for promoting reflection advocated by many researchers and teacher educators (e.g., Zeichner, 1987) is the *logbook*. However, I know of no well-documented description of the use of the logbook within a systematic approach that links the promotion of reflection to the process of developing concrete teaching competencies[1]. The aim of the first seven sections of this chapter is to present such a description, focusing on the integration of the development of reflective skills, based on clear criteria, and competencies related to the building of adequate interpersonal relationships with students in the classroom. The latter competencies are seen as fundamental to the creation of a classroom atmosphere that supports learning. I will describe how the logbook can be used in a stepwise approach aimed at helping student teachers to become self-directed learners who are able to analyze and surmount the problems they meet in their interpersonal relationships in the classroom, in other words, teachers with a *growth competence* (see section 3.9).

In section 11.2, some of the difficulties will be discussed that teacher educators may encounter in student teachers if they want to develop this growth competence. Section 11.3 will be devoted to the question of how a structured approach in using logbooks may help to overcome these difficulties. The role of the teacher educator in the introduction of this structured approach is discussed in section 11.4. In section 11.5, the core problem is analyzed: How do you link reflection and classroom behavior? Section 11.6 describes a concrete case: By means of concrete and authentic logbook entries, I will show how the structured use of logbooks can indeed shape the way a student teacher frames his or her own behavior in practice. When using logbooks, it is important to now and then give feedback to student teachers, for example, by means of written commentaries. Section 11.7 presents some examples of how this can be done.

Section 11.8 is a brief intermezzo in which a shift is made from the more technical-analytical way of reflecting, characteristic for logbook writing, to a more holistic approach to reflection. Examples of holistic instruments and techniques are presented in section 11.9. Finally, in section 11.10, I will look at the question of how to use logbooks or more holistic instruments and techniques for reflection with students who are less inclined to reflect.

11.2. DIFFICULTIES IN PROMOTING A GROWTH COMPETENCE

Central to this book is the conceptualization of the process of reflection in terms of the ALACT model (see Fig. 3.2). In effect, the ALACT model is a kind of ideal in that it is more prescriptive than descriptive. Although from time to time everyone reflects more or less systematically, student teachers sometimes find it difficult to reflect independently and adequately. A number of the most common difficulties are listed here.

1. Some student teachers expect their teacher educators to simply tell them what they are doing right and what they are doing wrong, and to offer the appropriate solutions and guidelines. (In sections 3.10 and 6.5, such student teachers were named "externally oriented.") This expectation is not in itself surprising, but if student teachers become dependent on help from outside, then they will not learn to reflect on their own teaching (i.e., become more internally oriented), which is important for acquiring a growth competence.
2. Many student teachers who are capable of reflecting on their teaching go off in search of a solution (Phase 4 of the ALACT model) before they

have a clear understanding of the problem. For example, if a student teacher discovers that the students do not have a good grasp of the material presented in the previous lesson, then he or she may decide that from now on it would be better not to cover as much ground in a single lesson. It will be clear that this is not necessarily the right solution, because the root of the problem may lie in the way the material was presented or the motivation of the students.

3. Initially, many student teachers are extremely self-centered. They focus on their own behavior (i.e., Am I doing it right? How should I tackle the problem?), and have fewer concerns that are related to their students (i.e., What are my students like? What "past history" do they bring with them? How do they experience my lessons?).
4. Some student teachers are happy to have found one solution to a problem. The professional, by contrast, is expected to have developed a whole repertoire of approaches from which to choose, depending on the particular situation.
5. There is often very little continuity in the learning process of the student teacher. For example, after the first lesson, he or she may concentrate solely on the best way of beginning lessons, whereas after the next lesson, the student teacher reflects on some conflict that arose, and so forth. However, it is important that after the second lesson in this example the student teacher also reflects on how the beginning of the lesson went this time, and in particular how the new resolves worked out. In this way, Phase 5 of the ALACT model does indeed form the beginning of a new cycle, resulting in the intended spiral-shaped learning process. If this is not achieved, then there is a danger that the learning process will become random and uncoordinated.

In view of these difficulties, it is important that teacher education devote systematic attention to learning how to reflect. First, let us look at the way the logbook can be used as a means to this purpose.

11.3. SHAPING THE LOGBOOK

A logbook is a notebook in which student teachers record their own reflections on a particular lesson or meeting with the teacher educator. However, although the literature indicates that the logbook is helpful in encouraging reflection, it is not always clear exactly how the logbook functions in *learning* to reflect, in other words, how it develops student teachers' capacity for reflection and helps them to surmount difficulties such as those mentioned in section 11.2. Having student teachers keep a logbook is not in itself sufficient, and may even be counterproductive, as inadequate routines can be reinforced. The important thing is the question of how student teachers can learn to reflect better through the use of a logbook.

To answer that question, it is important to establish what exactly the student teacher should be entering in the logbook. Then I will examine the question of how student teachers can learn to make the best possible use of their logbook.

Content

The more concrete the event on which the student teacher is asked to reflect, the greater the chances that the student teacher will actually learn from it. This means that when a student begins his or her reflection on a lesson with a remark like "Things went pretty well today" or "I was sort of tense today," he or she should realize that the next step is to present examples that will concretize the general impression. One or two of these concrete situations can then be systematically examined in the logbook,[2] for example, on the basis of standard questions that promote reflection. Such questions are presented in Fig. 11.1. To a large extent, these questions were determined by the decision to combine learning to reflect with learning about interpersonal behavior in the classroom. Obviously, it is not my intention to make such a list into a kind of straitjacket. It simply provides suggestions designed to encourage the student teachers to gradually extend their repertoire of reflection questions.

Meta-reflection

If student teachers are to acquire growth competence, then it is also important that from time to time—say, after a series of lessons—they reflect on their own develop-

Reflection questions

Phase 5 of the previous cycle (= phase 1 of the present cycle):
1 What did I want to achieve?
2 What did I want to pay particular attention to?
3 What did I want to try out?

Phase 2 (looking back):
4 What were the concrete events?
- What did I want?
- What did I do?
- What did I think?
- How did I feel?
- What do I think that the students wanted, did, thought, felt?

Phase 3 (awareness of essential aspects):
5 What is the connection between the answers to the aspects mentioned in question 4?
6 What is the influence of the context/the school as a whole?
7 What does that mean for me?
8 What is the problem (or the positive discovery)?

Phase 4 (alternatives):
9 What alternatives do I see? (solutions or ways to make use of my discovery)?
10 What are the advantages and disadvantages of each?
11 What do I resolve to do next time?

FIG. 11.1 Questions for promoting reflection according to the ALACT model.

mental process. This means reflecting on the series of reflections that have already taken place: in effect, *meta-reflection*. Elliot (1991, p. 65) states:

Reflective teachers would do well to engage in a little meta-reflection on how they deliberate about what to do in a particular situation.

In section 7.10, I explained that this meta-reflection can be based on an adaptation of the ALACT model (see Fig. 7.4). This leads to questions such as the following:

- What did I want to learn?
- How have I tried to learn this?
- What learning moments can be distinguished?
- How did I learn then?
- How did I feel about this?
- What helped me to learn, and what interfered with my learning?
- Which problems and strong points do I see in my own way of learning?
- Which alternatives do I see for my way of learning?
- What resolutions for the coming period of learning now present themselves?

As a result of such meta-reflections, student teachers may be prompted to steer their own learning process in a more conscious manner. In addition, through such meta-reflections, student teachers may be more inclined to accept the rough spots that are an inevitable part of any learning process. In retrospect, it is often clear that such difficult moments heralded the beginning of a breakthrough in the learning process.

11.4. THE ROLE OF THE TEACHER EDUCATOR

Earlier, I described the ideal use of the logbook. In this section, I will be examining the question of how educators can help student teachers to approach that ideal. First, consider an important preliminary remark. The ultimate aim is to teach students to use the logbook as an aid in reflecting on their own lessons. However, the period during which the student is actually teaching is probably the worst suitable time for learning to reflect (Korthagen, 1988). Student teachers are confronted with a great many concerns at once, and it is well-known that, at this time, so-called concerns about survival (Fuller & Bown, 1975) play an important role. Because reflection requires time and a certain measure of peace and quiet, it would be unreasonable to expect the student teacher to systematically learn to reflect at such a time. This means that reflection must be learned beforehand. And even then, there is often a relapse in reflection capacity when student teachers are faced with the necessity of taking responsibility for one or more classes.[3]

However, we also saw (in section 6.5) that there are indications from research that after an initial slump, the reflection capacity developed during a preservice program is recovered (see also Korthagen, 1985). For example, in section 6.5, a research study was mentioned that demonstrated that this is so in the case of reflection in the area of interpersonal teacher behavior.

The student's reflection competency must be developed as soon as possible, and this means in the earliest stages of teacher education. It is preferable not to immediately confront the student teacher with the spiral-shaped model or the lists of possible reflection questions, but rather to start off at a more leisurely pace. As a teacher educator working with a group of student teachers, I generally open with a talk that goes more or less as follows:

> This course is structured quite differently from what you were used to during your academic career. In our group sessions I will not be dealing with a lot of theory. But we will be *doing* a great deal, and the aim is to learn from these "do activities." This learning requires effort on your part; above all, it means that you will have to stop and consider what it is you have learned. Otherwise, there is a danger that a month or so from now you won't even remember what you learned during the first few weeks.
>
> We do this for a reason. "Learning from practical experience" is the most crucial characteristic of teacher education. In fact, it is what practice teaching is all about. And we have discovered that it is possible to learn how to get the most out of your experiences. So in the next few weeks we are going to practice "learning from practical experiences," in this case, from our experiences within the group.

Then I explain the role of the logbook and give the students a number of simple questions to serve as guidelines. Although initially I do not make this explicit, these questions are designed to prepare students for Phases 2, 3, and 4 of the spiral model. These are questions, such as (a) What happened/What did we do today?, (b) What do you consider important?, and (c) Which resolutions or learning wishes does this give rise to?

Experience has shown that it is easiest for student teachers to form an impression of what reflection is when they start off slowly in another respect as well, namely, by initially reflecting on short, surveyable situations or clearly defined issues. These might include a brief 10-minute lesson for fellow students, a 15-minute discussion centering on a particular exercise, the first 5 minutes of a group session, the characteristics of their best secondary school teacher, and so forth. I have obtained good results by stopping the proceedings of the first campus-based seminars from time to time to allow students to write in their logbooks. At the next session, these entries can then be discussed in the group, for instance, by asking students what they wrote about in their logbooks. Such a discussion should be kept brief and casual, so that it does not become overly serious. It is often a real eye-opener for students when they realize that such aspects as their own behavior or their role within the group are also worthy of consideration. This often leads to a discussion on the use of the group as "exercise material" for interpersonal behavior (e.g., with respect to taking the initiative, adopting an active listening attitude, etc.) in combination with the reflections in the logbook.

Gradually, I phase out the writing breaks, and point out to the student teachers that they are now expected to write in their logbooks at home. For a time I continue to use this method, and every once in a while I ask the group how they are doing with their logbooks. One of the main advantages of this is that it gives them an opportunity to share their worries about whether they are "doing it right."

After a few sessions, it is announced that the logbook reports of that day will be used for discussion. The following day they are xeroxed and compared in subgroups. I ask the students in each group to make suggestions for improving the usefulness of the logbook. (This is killing two birds with one stone, because they will later be required to initiate just this sort of discussion with their students in school.)

This is followed by a plenary discussion on writing in the logbook, in which I elaborate on the remarks I made on the first day (e.g., by introducing the ALACT model). It is helpful to keep in mind the advice given by Hatton and Smith (1995, p. 37):

> Likely reactions to demands for reflection require some attention. Responses on the part of students might include feelings of vulnerability which follow from exposing one's perceptions and beliefs to others, especially if the locus of control is not seen to be with the individual, who may tend to self-blame for any perceived weaknesses uncovered through reflection (Wildman & Niles, 1987). Such possibilities support a case for collaborative rather than individualistic approaches to reflection, so that a structure is provided within which students can work together as "critical friends."

In section 9.6, such a structure was described: In the IVLOS program, the process of learning to reflect is very much embedded in what we call "peer-supported learning," a structure in which students reflect on practice in small groups and learn to stimulate each other's reflection.

One exercise consists of asking students to note the phases of the spiral model (2, 3, 4) in the margin of their fellow students' logbook reports. I point out that individuals differ in the amount of attention they give to the various phases, and it may be important for them to broaden their natural repertoire in this respect. Thus, this stage of the course actually involves meta-reflection, although this is only possible after students have gained sufficient experience in reflecting.

I usually add a few leading questions for Phase 2, such as: What was I thinking? What was I feeling? What did I want? What did I do? What do I think the others were thinking, feeling, and wanting (possibility for concretization: What concrete behavior do you base your answer on?)?

Gradually, we can work toward a longer list of reflection questions (e.g., the questions in Fig. 11.1). Again, it must be stressed that I try to keep the list from becoming a straitjacket.

But we are not finished yet. During the teaching practice periods, it is important to go back to the theory of reflection constructed thus far, and to encourage students to practice meta-reflection. Otherwise, all they have learned about reflection may easily be lost.

11.5. AN OPERATIONALIZATION OF THE AIM "LEARNING TO REFLECT" IN RELATION TO THE DEVELOPMENT OF ADEQUATE INTERPERSONAL TEACHER BEHAVIOR

The list of reflection questions provides the educator with a good diagnostic measure of how far the student teacher has progressed in reflection competency. Depending on which aspects the student teacher is accustomed to include in his or her reflection and which he or she usually skips, the educator can emphasize the student's strong points and carefully try to reinforce the weaker points, for example, by suggesting new reflection questions. In this way, the aim "learning to reflect" is made more concrete and measurable.

The core of reflection on a situation lies in Phase 3, which is characterized by awareness of the essential aspects. This awareness should develop by means of Phase 2 (looking back). In my experience, students find the transition from Phase 2 to Phase 3 the most difficult. When faced with new classroom situations that they initially experience as difficult, they tend to remain dependent on a supervisor for a fairly long time, relying on this supervisor to provide insight into the processes going on during their lessons.

And yet the learning process of student teachers can be accelerated by making explicit what is involved in an analysis of these processes. I explain to them that there is no sense in trying to capture the essence of a situation (Phase 3) before the "boxes" of Fig. 11.2 have been "filled in." (Figure 11.2 is almost identical to Fig. 7.2; cf. section 7.6.)

Experience has shown that student teachers often find it difficult to fill in the boxes on the right-hand side, particularly in the early stages of the program. They have no idea what their students were thinking or how they felt. This, of course, offers a perfect opportunity to talk about how they might find the answers to these questions during their lessons. Student teachers are quick to realize that a lesson involving "one-way traffic," whereby the information goes from teacher to students, is not ideal for this purpose. I point out the various opportunities the teacher has to

0. What is the context?	
1. What did I want?	5. What did the students want?
2. What did I do?	6. What did the students do?
3. What did I think?	7. What did the students think?
4. How did I feel?	8. How did the students feel?

FIG. 11.2 Concretizing questions for phase 2 of the ALACT model.

carry on mini-discussions (5 seconds to about 1 minute) with individual students while the class is working on an assignment.

In this way, the aim of learning to reflect goes hand in hand with the aim of learning to activate the class. This means that learning to reflect is integrated into other aspects of teacher education.

The question on filling in the nine boxes returns as often as necessary until the student anticipates the question and fills in the boxes in the logbook. In addition, I gradually make explicit what the following step is, namely, "drawing arrows" between the different boxes (e.g., as indicated in Fig. 11.3).

Here follows an example of how this arrow diagram might arise. A student teacher feels unsure about his or her authority in the classroom, and fails to take the necessary measures to keep order. He goes on talking, which gives the class the impression that the teacher does not have the necessary authority. The students start acting up, and this causes the teacher to become even more unsure, stumble over his or her words, and so on. This is an example of a so-called *circular process*, which in its simplest form is shown in Fig. 11.4.

As Watzlawick et al. (1967) explain, there is usually little to be gained by inquiring about the origin of such processes, because the participants always think that it was the other party who "started it." What is important for student teachers is to recognize such circular processes, which take the form of either negative or positive "spirals." They should know that any strong feeling after a lesson can be considered as a signal that a circular process took place, and this process can be brought to awareness by a search for relations between the nine boxes. Of course, it may be helpful to address the problem of escaping from a negative spiral. One of the few possibilities, aside from changing the context, can be found in box 2 of Fig. 11.2: The student teacher can break through the pattern of "more of the same" by changing his or her own behavior. Another possible approach is metacommunication (i.e., talking about the problem); however, for inexperienced teachers, this may create new pitfalls. (See, for more elaboration of these principles in relation to classroom teaching, Wubbels, Créton, & Holvast, 1988.)

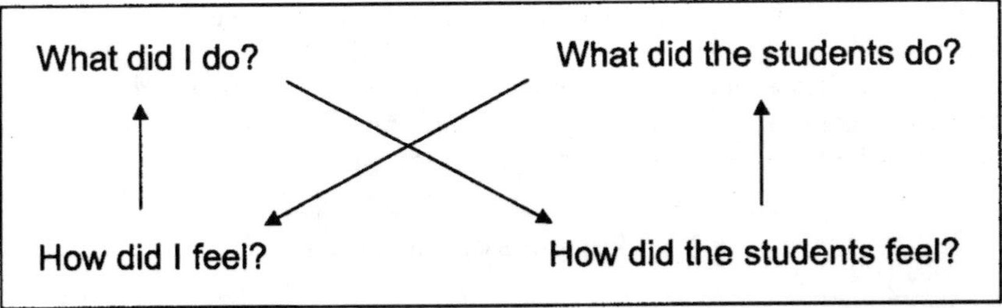

FIG. 11.3. Finding relations between "the boxes."

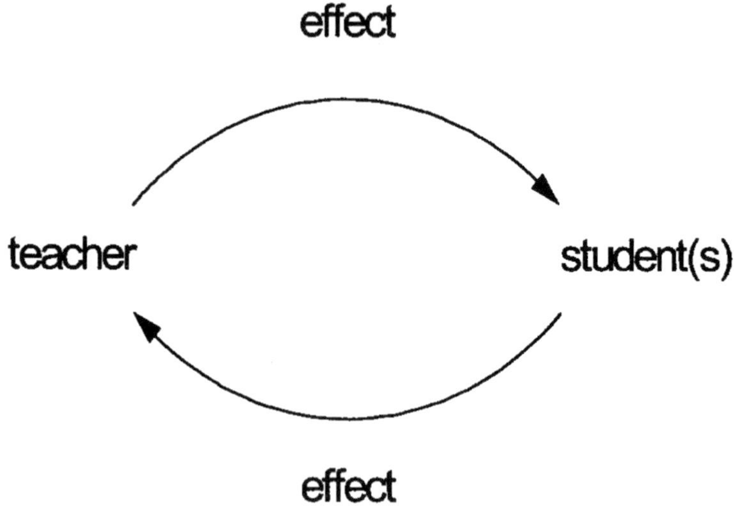

FIG. 11.4. The circular process between the teacher and the student(s).

Back to the matter of learning to reflect. Learning to draw arrows between the boxes may be seen as the ultimate goal of the process of learning to reflect in the preservice program. Most student teachers are amazed to see that inevitably "drawing the arrows" clarifies the "underlying" problem that they experienced in the classroom. Furthermore, in the course of the developmental process described earlier, they also begin to realize that their own actions and those of their students are guided much more by their feelings at a particular point in the lesson than by any thoughts or ideas they might have had before the lesson began. In this way, the central role played by feelings in teaching and learning is touched on in a natural way, as part of the process of learning to reflect.

When student teachers have reached the point where they are able to independently analyze a problem that presented itself during a lesson in terms of circular processes, to find a solution for the problem and to apply that solution, then it is justified to say that they have acquired a growth competence. Ideally, student teachers should be capable of completing the intended reflection process during the lesson itself (*reflection-in-action*; see Schön, 1987), but I believe that at the close of a preservice program, it may be seen as an accomplishment if they are capable of such reflection in between two lessons (*reflection-on-action*).

11.6. THE CASE OF JOHN[4]

Consider a concrete case of a student teacher, named John. He is a student at a teacher's college in the south of the Netherlands, preparing for secondary education. He wrote the following reflection on a lesson in his logbook:

The class started in a very noisy and unruly atmosphere. In my opinion this was caused first by the fact that Ajax [a Dutch soccer team] was playing that day and second because I was wearing a suit. (Special shoes, white socks, black trousers, belt, necktie, tie-clip and a bright yellow jacket). The atmosphere did not improve a bit during the lesson. The students were practically not listening to me. One of them even talked back at me. At that point I had to restrain myself from scolding at this student. After the lesson I summoned some students. I was also extremely annoyed with the fact that the antisocial behavior of my students did not make it possible for me to go through the whole material. Only one of the students participated actively in that class. It was George, and I could fall back on him several times for answering some of my questions.

During that lesson there were 19 students in the classroom: 5 boys and 14 girls. Even now I would say that the attention per student was unbalanced, because a number of students were spoiling the atmosphere. One of them (a girl) even refused to listen to me. I had to restrain myself from scolding at her.

I had planned my class as follows: register the absent students; check who did the homework; make the intro (describing real-life situations); read aloud the theory; give examples and/or ask questions; discuss the assignments of lesson 19; assign new homework. I wanted to reserve the last minutes of my class for communicating the test results. As regards the assignments, I managed to get as far as task 2a. Looking back to my planning, I still think it was a good one. With regard to my teaching methods I could not make any variations either. The antisocial behavior of my students was the reason for this. During that class I intended to use: blackboard, overhead projector and face-to-face tuition.

If I look back on the way that lesson took place, I think that the students have hardly assimilated anything from the material, because all I could teach was about one and a half sheet of text and one and a half assignment. They most certainly know by now that they found a good way to make me (almost) loose my composure.

This lesson has taught me that I should not make the introduction of the lesson too long, and that I should not enter into too many details. Furthermore it taught me that I should keep a better eye on my students.

When John discussed this lesson with his teacher educator, he was reminded of the ALACT model and helped to analyze the situation with the use of the nine boxes. This changed his reflection rather fundamentally, as is shown by the following logbook entry that was written after the supervision:

Phase 1:

During this class I intended to teach lesson 19 from the "Percent" textbook. Furthermore, I wanted to reach some objectives that I had formulated for my students and for myself. You will find these objectives in the teacher preparation form at the back of this report.

In this lesson I intended to pay special attention to several points of interest that had come up during the previous lesson (interaction, differences in intonation, and noting down the homework on the blackboard).

I wanted to see if I could describe several practical situations related to the theory in my intro.

Phase 2:

I wanted to start the lesson in a nice way. I thought that I could do this by describing a number of real-life situations. I did this in the form of a narration, while I was walking up and down in front of the class. Anyway, the events I was describing were situations that I had experienced myself during the previous Friday.

I thought that the way in which my students behaved during that class was just a coincidence and that it would change in a couple of minutes. This, however, did not happen. On the contrary, it became worse. I also thought that the students would experience the way I was holding my intro as a nice change.

During that lesson I felt awfully ragged by my students. At a certain point I got really angry. That was when a girl refused to listen to me.

The students did not want to sit still for one minute during that lesson; they wanted to go straight away to find a TV where they could watch the match between Ajax and Gremino, which was supposed to start at 11.00 a.m. They did their best to sabotage my lesson, so that they could go and watch the match. I think they felt let down because I had told them they could watch the match only after the lesson. Most certainly they thought I was being unfair because other students were allowed to watch the match and they were not.

Phase 3:

When I consider the questions, I notice that the answers are largely related to me and my own experience. Students' perception and everyday's life are hardly given any thought.

There were also some few teachers who wanted to watch the football match. Yet, the school management team had not made any arrangements for watching the game in a centrally situated room.

For me this meant that I had to try and keep my students quite in a way or another. Much to my regret I did not succeed.

The main problem was that I had not given enough thought to students' everyday's life. This situation has taught me that I must try to empathize more with my students, but also that I don't need to change my mind completely if similar situations would occur in the future.

Phase 4:

During the discussion of this school incident at the teachers college, several ways of handling this kind of situation were brought forward, namely:

- Let the students watch the game and reschedule the lesson;
- Allow the students to follow the game on the radio (low volume) during the lesson.

- Allow the students to watch the game if they are willing to participate fully in the lesson.

The advantage of these solutions is that the students can watch the game. A great disadvantage however is that in this kind of situation one does not have enough time to go through the whole material. So, it could be very painful if one is forced to insert one or more extra lessons.

This lesson has taught me that in situations like this, I must pay more attention to my students' needs and desires. Moreover, I realize that I must also consider my own situation and that I must never ever give in to my students' whims. Furthermore, I have to consider the requirements set by our school management.

If we compare the two logbook entries, we see a shift in the way the situation is analyzed and framed, which leads John to different conclusions. In particular, he has become more aware of the interpersonal and circular processes going on between him and the students, which seems to shape the direction into which he wants to develop his teaching behavior. This means that John has acquired a certain growth competence.

11.7. INDIVIDUAL SUPERVISION ON LOGBOOK WRITING

It will be clear that individual guidance is indispensable in learning to reflect, but also that it is possible to integrate that guidance into other aspects of the program. In the previous section, I showed how learning to reflect can be integrated with developing adequate interpersonal classroom behavior. There is indeed very little point in organizing a separate training in learning to reflect. Research into metacognition has shown that a training in metacognitive skills that is divorced from the domain in which those skills are to be used will have very little effect. A process of coaching, linked directly to actual teaching practice, is needed to ensure the desired integration.

I now want to bring up the question of whether the student's logbook should be available to the teacher educator, or if it should be considered the private property of the student teacher. I have always found the latter solution somewhat strange, if we assume that learning to reflect is an important goal of teacher education. As a teacher educator, you must be able to obtain insight into the manner in which the student reflects in order to guide him or her, as well as to judge his or her work. For this you must have the necessary "material" at hand, for example, if you are to identify difficulties such as those described in section 11.2. Surely, we would not say to a student teacher after a practice lesson that the follow-up discussion might give rise to such personal matters that it would be better for the student to discuss the lesson with a good friend and then let us know later about the outcome of the discussion.

Obviously, it must be clear to the students from the beginning that the logbook will, or at any rate may, be read by the supervisor. One can always suggest to students that they are free to keep a separate diary for things they consider too personal to show to others.

Brief written comments on the logbook are an important way of giving the individual student teacher concrete help and promoting the willingness and ability to reflect (cf. Paterson, 1995). As Bain et al. (1999, p. 70) report:

> Students indicated that the provision of constructive feedback, which challenges their naive assertions and helps them discover alternative perspectives, may be a major contributor to the encouragement of growth in reflective writing.

Needless to say, this requires some time on the part of the teacher educator; it is, however, possible to do this on a limited scale. Each week the teacher educator can comment on the logbooks of a few student teachers.

Teacher educators should keep in mind that a written commentary on a logbook focuses either on the contents of the recorded reflections (so that the intervention has an aim other than learning to reflect), or on the actual manner of reflection (i.e., the meta-level). In the latter case, through individual attention, the teacher educator can often help the student to see the potential advantages of keeping a logbook.

As in all forms of supervision, certain principles are of crucial importance, such as rewarding good results, acceptance of the student, empathy, and so on (see chapter 7). Here are some examples of written comments. All of these are examples at the meta-level, that is, they focus on the way the student reflects in the logbook, and not on the content of the reflections:

1. It's good that you keep such a precise record of what takes place during the course. Next time you might try to make clear what *you* thought was most important.
2. I see a definite change in your reports: they're much more personal now, and you write down what *you* think and feel.

3. I'm pleased that you really stop and think about how you can use the course theme to improve the way you teach! Try to keep this up in future reports.
4. I understand your aversion to "all the writing." What do you think would help *you* to improve your teaching?
5. I can see that you are careful to follow all the steps in the reflection model! What happened to your point of attention from last time? Can you see how it might be connected with the above?

11.8. INTERMEZZO: TWO MODES OF REFLECTION

The logbook, especially when used in a structured way, makes use of an important potential of the human mind: the ability to logically and rationally analyze experiences. This is, however, also a limitation: By rational, logical thinking, we sometimes distance ourselves from our concrete experiences, and by rationalizing our experiences, we often create something of an irrealistic world: Our behavior in practice will certainly not always stem from the sources that we like to believe are important. Needs, feelings, values, or internal images about the external situations that student teachers encounter may play a crucial role in shaping their behavior and experiences. Because they may hardly be aware of such sources, analyzing their experiences by means of logbook writing will perhaps draw their attention to their rational thinking about the situation, instead of less conscious aspects. Even when writing about the feelings involved, both their own feelings and those of the students in their classrooms, the limitation is that they will reflect on what they think these feelings are. As we have seen before (in section 3.4), all kinds of filtering mechanisms may play a role and create a distance between this thinking about feelings and the reality of the here-and-now in the classroom.

In section 3.5, this led to a distinction between two kinds of information processing: a rational or logical way, which is used in logbook writing, and a less rational way, which takes into account the less conscious gestalts that shape experiences in the here-and-now. This then leads to the question of how we can supplement logbook writing with other techniques, which through their nature stay closer to less conscious but important needs, concerns, values, meanings, preferences, feelings, and behavioral tendencies influencing experiences. The next section is devoted to such techniques.

11.9. TECHNIQUES AND INSTRUMENTS FOR HOLISTIC REFLECTION

In this section, I will describe techniques and instruments helpful in promoting awareness in teachers of the less rational processes guiding their actions. In chapter 12, the concept of reflection will be broadened so that these can be considered as reflection techniques. In contrast to the rational analysis of logbook writing, these techniques aim at a more holistic type of reflection.

Elaboration of Spontaneously Used Metaphors

In recent years, several authors (e.g., Marshall, 1988; Tobin, Kahle, & Fraser, 1990) have promoted the use of metaphors in teacher education and supervision. Among these is a group of teacher educators and researchers from Queen's University in Canada (Munby & Russell, 1989; T. Russell, Munby, Stafford, & Johnston, 1988). Their line of thinking on professional knowledge of teaching has much in common with the theoretical framework described earlier. They maintain that "(1) professional knowledge consists of more than that which can be told or written on paper and (2) professional learning is something more than a process of using 'rules' to make decisions about how to behave in a classroom situation" (T. Russell et al., 1988, p. 67). They refer to Lakoff and Johnson (1980, p. 5), who state that "the essence of a metaphor is understanding and experiencing one kind of thing in terms of another."

An example will illustrate the power of metaphors, and their significance for supervision. It was taken from a Dutch research project focusing on discipline problems encountered by beginning teachers, in which a beginning mother-tongue teacher, called Heleen, was supervised by an experienced teacher educator. (For more details of this study, see Créton, Wubbels, & Hooymayers, 1989.)

In the first few months of her teaching, Heleen had serious discipline problems. In the description of her situation, she said that she felt like a "lion-tamer," a metaphor suggested by a colleague. The supervisor discussed the use of this metaphor with her, which brought to light a number of implicit connotations. These were concerned not only with external things like giving her students detention work, which she interpreted as "using the whip," but also Heleen's inner reality (fears, hopes, etc.). For instance, she felt that the "cage" in which she was shut up with the "lions" was locked; she could not get out and had to cope with the situation as best she could. Moreover, she felt that, above all, she had to hide her fear, because showing that you are afraid is extremely dangerous with lions. As a lion-tamer, you must be constantly aware of the fact that the lions are stronger than you are; Heleen felt that if they ever jumped her, she would be torn to pieces.

Heleen and the supervisor could have used many words in rational analyses of all aspects of the classroom situation without ever grasping the essence of Heleen's interpretation of her situation, as it was possible to do through the use of the metaphor. I agree with Schön (1987) when he says that *reframing* is often a means of changing a situation like Heleen's. The first step in such a process is establishing the essence of a person's frame of reference. Heleen's story is an example of such a first step. Awareness of one's guiding gestalts (see chapter 10) is a prerequisite for entering a phase in which the teacher can ask him- or herself whether to explore other possible interpretations of the situation.

This may seem a rather serious example, but in many supervisory sessions small instances of metaphorical language can be recognized, and they can be taken seriously as a basis for further exploration. Examples are "the situation washed over me like a wave," "I sometimes feel like a police officer," "it was like a warm bath," and "I need something like a first-aid kit."

Drawing and Painting

In the previous example, the metaphor of the lion-tamer was expressed in words. In the case of a highly visual gestalt such as this, the translation into words may be a problem, although this can be avoided through the use of visual language. Alternatively, the teacher can make a drawing or a painting in order to express his or her experiences. I know a teacher educator who often asks a new group of student teachers to draw a picture of "education." This invariably produces a wide variety of pictures, ranging from jail-like buildings to a group of friendly looking people sitting happily together in the grass. The next step might be to ask student teachers to draw their picture of an "ideal educational setting," and then have them compare the two pictures.

In the same way, the drawing or painting of concrete teaching situations can be used in supervision sessions to help teachers to become aware of gestalts that direct their actions, or to get into conscious contact with their ideals. The details of these pictures can be very enlightening. For example, when a teacher draws a picture of a classroom, it is interesting to see which students are portrayed and in what positions. Certain messages are sent out by colors or objects that at first sight seem to be there by chance (cf. Weber & Mitchell, 1995).

Photographs

There are also teacher educators who use photographs as an instrument for promoting the expression of personal meaning. Weade and Ernst (1989), for example, asked their student teachers at the University of Florida to take photographs of their field experiences. For student teachers who feel a certain resistance to drawing or painting, this more technical approach may be an advantage; the disadvantage, however, is that photographs objectify more than drawings or paintings. In any case, one must realize that the significance of a photograph taken by a student teacher lies not in what is objectively portrayed, but rather in the answer to such questions as what made this student teacher take this picture of this situation involving these students (or perhaps without students) at this stage in his or her development.

The Presentation of Pictures

Yet another approach is one in which pictures are presented to the teacher or student teacher with the aim of promoting associations. Several alternatives are possible, such as drawing one postcard at random from a stack, or choosing one picture from a collection that is shown. I sometimes use cards that consist of two stacks, a smaller stack with pictures and a bigger one with words (hope, hate, game, success, child, dependent, etc.). When a small card is placed in the middle of a bigger one, this usually promotes awareness of a gestalt. It is not necessary to use such an advanced tool: Even a pile of postcards can be effective. If this technique is used in supervision, it can be a powerful tool, bringing the teacher into contact with very personal attitudes, fears, hopes, and so on. Supervision in teacher education, however, is not a therapy, and the teacher educator should, in my view, help the teachers to link their associations to concrete teaching situations.

I will now describe the way we elaborated this idea into a concrete instrument, applicable both in teacher education and in research (Dolk, Korthagen, & Wubbels, 1995). If used with teachers, they first form pairs, say A and B. Then A gets an envelope containing a number of metaphorical pictures (see Fig. 11.5 for some examples of these pictures).[5] B gets a paper with the following instructions:

Metaphorical pictures

Most educators have an image of their teaching, but not one they form with words. It is a "picture." This image is often based on feeling (like feeling comfortable with something) rather than on theoretical considerations. It is generally intuitive. This technique is intended to bring this image to light.

Step One: choosing the metaphor

Get together with someone else and form a pair. Together you decide on the subject: "images of education" or "images of educating teachers."

The envelop contains pictures. B takes out half of the pictures and chooses one that appeals to him/her. If this causes a problem at first, it might help to start by putting aside those pictures that are meaningless or unattractive. B should choose the most appealing picture from those remaining.

B takes care not to show the picture to A.

Step Two: developing the metaphor

A now asks B as many questions as possible in order to develop the metaphor. We want to stress that you should *stay within the confines of the metaphor/the image* and not speak explicitly about education/teaching. A should encourage B to use everyday words that he/she associates with the image. Try to draw upon as many senses as possible. For this, some creativity is required. It is helpful to let your imagination go and "drift" along with the flow of associations. It does not need to be "reasonable"!

Don't worry whether it is right for a little while. Nothing is silly!

Try not to allow B to think about the situation.

FIG. 11.5. Metaphorical pictures (drawings: Jan van Tartwijk; source: Wubbels, 1992a).

Questions A could use to help B along:

If I were to travel to the situation this picture illustrates, what would I see? (What does B make up, what does he/she imagine to be in the background, for instance? Suggestion to A: pay attention to details, make notes of them.)

who are you in this situation?

what do you hear?

what do you smell?

what do you feel?

what are you doing?

what do you want?

what is the other person doing/are others doing/are the objects doing?

what does that mean/do to you?

what happens next?

does the image change?

how does it change?

what is happening now?

Step Three: translating

After that you talk about how the metaphor "translates" into B's conception of education (teaching). A will get B to talk about the details he/she mentioned in step two and the contradictions (if any) in his/her metaphor. When you have finished translating, it may be interesting to explore whether B recognizes examples of his/her former teachers in the translation.

Finally, let B review the translation and reformulate in one sentence the part that was essential to him or her.

Step Four: Switch roles and repeat steps one, two and three.

Step Five: Discussion by the pair

a. what did you learn from this activity?

b. did this activity offer any new insights?

For teacher educators an extra question is:

c. how could you make use of this activity in teacher education?

Kelly's Repertory Grid

This technique is based on Kelly's (1955) technique for inquiry into the personal constructs people use when dealing with their environment, a technique widely used by researchers (e.g., Bonarius, Holland, & Rosenberg, 1981; Munby, 1984; Olson, 1982; Yinger & Villar, 1986; Yorke, 1985). It is described in section 9.4 as a technique that can easily be used in groups of student teachers.

Guided Fantasies

Allender (1982) uses the "Fourth-Grade Fantasy Activity" to help teachers to become aware of experiences that inhibit or promote learning:

> I tell everyone to find a comfortable spot, to close their eyes and I then turn off the lights. (This always produces a lot of stirrings and giggling. Remember that most of these students are used to a traditional lecture series.) I then proceed to have them quietly breathe deeply for 2-3 minutes, listening to the air flowing in and out of their bodies, and then 2-3 minutes tensing and untensing each part of their bodies beginning from the feet up to the head. When I feel they are relaxed I begin the activity. (pp. 37–38)

In their imagination, Allender takes the teachers back to their elementary school building. They are told that they are fourth graders and that it is time for their classes to begin. The teachers spend 10 minutes in their fourth-grade fantasy classrooms; Allender asks them to look at the desk arrangements, the walls, the atmosphere in the classroom, and so on. After these 10 minutes, they return to the here-and-now, and draw a diagram or picture of their classroom. They exchange their pictures and stories in small groups. Finally, the whole class gets together, sharing with each other what was discussed in the smaller groups.

I believe that Allender's method is a useful way of promoting teachers' reflection on their own experiences with learning (cf. Hunt, 1987), experiences that on the whole appear to be rather negative. As Rogers (1983, p. 107) notes in his comment on Allender's approach, many of these teachers' experiences were characterized by fear, failure, humiliation, resentment, and constraint. He emphasizes that the content of their courses, what they were supposed to have learned, does not even come to mind. It is important for teachers to take note of this point, especially in the light of the fact that often "teachers teach the way they have been taught, and not as they have been taught to teach" (Blume, 1971; cf. J. G. Knowles, 1991).

Another way in which guided fantasies can be used is to help student teachers to address their own ideals with respect to education. Visualizing one's ideal classroom situation can promote awareness of the directions that one wants to take. Another application of this technique may be to help student teachers visualize a former teacher, which in retrospect they regard as their ideal teacher. In the guided fantasy, the student teachers can be asked to "become" this ideal teacher, to step into his or her skin, and to feel what this ideal teacher does, how he or she perceives things, how he or she moves, how he or she sounds, and so on. Just like in the metaphorical pictures exercise already described, the use of a variety of "submodalities" (i.e., seeing, listening, feeling) may be important to create the complete gestalt.

11.10. LEARNING ORIENTATIONS

In this chapter, several techniques and instruments for promoting reflection were listed. Much emphasis was put on a structured approach toward logbook writing, but other, more holistic techniques have been introduced. However, this chapter cannot be concluded without reference to a basic problem teacher educators meet whenever they try to encourage reflection using specific techniques: Often certain student teachers will have severe difficulties with the actual use of reflection techniques or do not grasp what could be the benefit to them of such techniques. This has to do with what in chapter 6 we called *learning orientations*. *Internally oriented* student teachers want to learn by reflecting on their experiences, and *externally oriented* student teachers want instructions and guidelines from the teacher educator. If students of the latter type are forced to learn in a manner that is not theirs, then they may feel they are putting a lot of time into something they do not consider useful.

This points up the need for a careful strategy designed to make externally oriented students more internally oriented. The *gradualness* with which this takes place is important. Too much pressure toward intensive use of reflection techniques can be counterproductive in the case of externally oriented student teachers. It is also vital to offer sufficient *structure* and *safety*, for example, by initially giving this type of student teacher the directions and instructions that he or she desires. This is in line with the conclusion drawn by Reiman (1999, p. 607) from seven studies focusing on facilitating cognitive structural growth in the conceptual and ethical/moral domains for teachers:

> Some interns will prefer detailed instructions and high structure, be low on self-direction, and will follow curriculum or program guidelines as if they were "carved in stone." In the studies, the matching response was to offer detailed instructions and di-

> rections when appropriate. Only later would the teacher educator mismatch by providing less structure, thus encouraging more intern self-direction.

In addition, it may be useful to make the phenomenon of learning orientations explicit in discussions with the students. Various authors believe that stimulating reflection on one's own learning orientation is an excellent way of promoting a change in learning orientation (e.g., A. L. Brown, Campione, & Day, 1981). This issue has been elaborated in section 6.6.

It is also important to match techniques to student teachers' preferences. Often those students who seem to show resistance to reflection when asked to write a logbook do appreciate the more holistic techniques introduced in the previous section.

In collaboration with the students, unexpected alternatives for logbook writing are often devised: I remember one group of student teachers who decided that after each meeting they would get together for a discussion of their own, after which they wrote down their conclusions. In any case, I always try to allow students to decide for themselves exactly how much they actually write down. I do, however, suggest that when something happens that occupies them in some special way, they write down more than they are accustomed to doing. And, of course, now and then I stimulate meta-reflection on the question of how effective the student's ways of reflecting and logbook writing are, in the light of his or her professional development as a teacher.

SUMMARY

This chapter was devoted to techniques and instruments for promoting reflection. A gradual approach to the development of logbook writing was presented in which learning to reflect is integrated with learning in the field of interpersonal classroom behavior. Some difficulties in promoting the desired growth competence were discussed, such as the external orientation, self-centeredness, and focus on solutions of some student teachers. Essential ingredients of an approach taking such difficulties into account are a strategy of gradualness that starts even before student teaching, the use of standard reflection questions, moments of meta-reflection, emphasis on the analysis of circular processes, and individual guidance and feedback from the teacher educator.

Also, more holistic techniques for the promotion of reflection were introduced, which have the advantage of stimulating the surfacing of the less rational sources of teacher behavior. There was also discussion of the elaboration of spontaneously used metaphors, drawing and painting, photographs, the presentation of pictures, Kelly's repertory grid, and guided fantasies.

Once again it was emphasized that student teachers' learning orientations should be taken into account and room must be provided for individual preferences. The issue of learning orientations can be discussed with student teachers, as it is also important for the teaching of students in the schools.

BASIC CONCEPTS

Logbook

Strategy of gradualness

Meta-reflection

Circular processes

Holistic reflection

Metaphorical language

12 A Broader View of Reflection

Fred Korthagen

> The ideal role of the right hemisphere is to provide access to the deepest levels of one's true experience and to serve as a reality check against the left hemisphere's tendency to make up stories when it doesn't really know the answers.
>
> —*Betty Edwards, cited in Tony Schwartz* (1995).

Most conceptualizations of reflection and reflective teaching are based on logical and analytical ways of information processing during teaching. However, there are other ways of interpreting data and making decisions in the classroom that make use of "gestalts" and seem to be located in the right hemisphere. A broader view on reflection and reflective teaching is proposed that includes the mental "mirroring" of these nonrational processes. Technical, psychological, and philosophical reasons for the underestimation of the latter type of reflection are discussed.

12.1. INTRODUCTION

During the 1980s, the concepts of reflection and reflective teaching became quite popular among teacher educators and researchers in the field of teacher education. This development was related to the call for the professionalization of teaching and teacher education. The idea that teachers can learn to subject their own behavior to a critical analysis and to take responsibility for their actions met the long felt need for a kind of teacher education that transcends mere training in the use of specific behavioral competencies. Systematic and rational decision making lies at the very heart of professionalism (Kinchleoe, 1990; Yinger, 1986), and this explains not only the popularity of reflection but also the way in which the term has been interpreted by various authors. Although there are many different conceptualizations of reflection and reflective teaching (see chapter 4), most seem to share the underlying assumption that teachers should use logical, rational, step-by-step analyses of their own teaching and the contexts in which that teaching takes place. Language, whether spoken or written, plays a central role in these analyses. It is the vehicle by means of which teachers can express their observations or analyses to another person (often their supervisor) or to themselves.

As explained in chapter 4, this common core of the concept of reflection goes back to Dewey (1933), to whom many authors in the field refer. Indeed, it was Dewey who stated that "reflection involves not simply a sequence of ideas, but a *con*-sequence—a consecutive ordering in such a way that each determines the next as its proper outcome, while each outcome in turn leans back on, or refers to, its predecessors" (p. 4). Although this conceptualization of reflection is important and has undoubtedly proved useful in promoting the professional development of teachers, it describes only one way in which the human mind can process information and direct decision making. The present chapter builds on the alternative view of the relation between the mental processes going on inside the teacher and his or her behavior developed in chapter 10. The three-level model developed in that chapter will be used for broadening the concept of reflection as a means to promote professional development. This provides us with a theoretical background for more holistic techniques and instruments for promoting reflection, such as those introduced in section 11.9.

12.2. TWO WAYS OF INFORMATION PROCESSING

Authors working in different areas have made a distinction between one type of information processing that is logical and analytical and another that is not. This has produced a number of different concepts and terms, all of which seem to revolve around the theme of the duality of human consciousness. It is almost impossible to include everything that has been written about this issue, and the fast developments in brain research constantly create new insights. Later I will indicate some general lines.

Ornstein (1972) uses the terms "analytic" and "holistic," and speaks of the dichotomy between "rational" and "a-rational," whereas Levy-Agresti and Sperry (1968) refer to "analytic" and "gestalt." Polanyi (1961) distinguishes between "explicit knowledge" and "tacit knowledge," the latter being "a-critical." Bateson and Jackson (1964) make a distinction between "digital" and "analogic," and Milner (cited in Bogen, 1973) differentiates between "verbal" and "perceptual," which is reminiscent of Spearman's verbal factor and spatial factor in intelligence. Bogen (1973) points out that these distinctions are to be found in eastern psychologies as well; he cites Akhilananda who, in a work on Hindu psychology, uses terms that can be translated as "rational thought" and "integral thought," and he relates this "potpourri of dichotomies" to the lateralization of the brain. As Bogen points out, it was around 1960 that researchers started to tentatively characterize the left and right hemisphere as "symbolic" and "visuo-spatial." Levi-Agresti and Sperry (1968, p. 1151) suggested that

> the data indicate that the mute, minor hemisphere is specialized for Gestalt perception, being primarily a synthesist in dealing with information input. The speaking, major hemisphere, in contrast, seems to operate in a more logical, analytic, computer-like fashion.

The organization of the brain was later shown to be more complicated; it cannot be completely characterized as a hemispheric functional asymmetry (Bryden, 1982). There is, however, general agreement on the conclusion that, roughly speaking, the two sides of the human brain are capable of two different modes of information processing (see also B. Milner, 1989).

The dichotomies presented by the authors cited here are not exactly the same, but there is a common distinction. In this chapter I will refer to this distinction by means of the relatively broad terms *rational* and *non-rational* or *left-hemisphere* and *right-hemisphere* information processing. My assumption is that the process of sensory perception, interpretation of the information, and action or reaction can take place through two different "channels," roughly corresponding to the two sides of the brain (cf. Wubbels, 1992b). Whereas in the left hemisphere the interpretation of incoming information is mediated by logically structured cognitive schemata, the right hemisphere makes use of *gestalts*, the principal function of which is to integrate separate stimuli (see chaps. 3 and 10). A well-known example from gestalt psychology is the field process nature of vision, which means that the place and function of each part of a visual structure is determined by the structure as a whole (Kohler, 1947; Kubovy & Pomerantz, 1981). This principle has been broadened in gestalt therapy to include human information processing in other fields of life. For example, our interpretation of our relationships with other people is determined by gestalts, formed in earlier experiences with other important persons in our lives. In short, in the right hemisphere, the principle of the integration of experiences is dominant over the principle of logical ordering, whereas in the left hemisphere the reverse is the case.

As I explained in chapter 10, I believe that nonrational, right hemisphere information processing plays a central role in everyday teaching, and this is the psychological explanation for the existence of "teaching routines" (Clark & Yinger, 1979). In other words, the hypothesis is that during teaching certain cues from the environment often activate a gestalt, triggering an immediate interpretation and reaction. In this way, logical analysis can be circumvented, making it possible for teachers to deal with different stimuli at the same time (Day, 1984; Doyle, 1979).

Other researchers in the field of teaching and teacher education describe the same notions in other words. Connelly and Clandinin (1985), for example, emphasize the role of patterns (practical rules and principles, routines, habits) in the teacher's reactions to classroom situations. Narrative accounts of practitioners show that everything the person has been and undergone in the past creates meaningful unions in his or her present experience of classroom situations (Connelly & Clandinin, 1984, p. 147; Kelchtermans, 1993). What I call a gestalt is called "image" by Connelly and Clandinin, and is considered to be a type of knowledge that "draws both the past and the future into a personally meaningful nexus of experience focused on the immediate situation that called it forth" (Connelly & Clandinin, 1984, p. 147). I prefer the term *gestalt*, because as used in gestalt therapy, it refers not so much to a mental picture as to the whole of a person's experiences with regard to a certain situation.

Talking about "personal knowledge" of teachers, Connelly and Clandinin (1984, p. 137) state that "knowledge is that body of convictions and meanings, conscious or unconscious, which have arisen from experience, intimate, social and traditional, and which are expressed in a person's actions." Cole (1988) also emphasizes that personal meaning is embedded in the actions of the teacher in the immediacy of the moment in the classroom. Tom and Valli (1990) note that values and facts blend together in the meanings that practitioners construct out of educational and other social encounters.

Zeichner and Gore (1990, pp. 333–334) state that "deeply ingrained and partly unconscious feelings and dispositions developed as a pupil, exert a continuing influence on teacher activity." They present an overview of various life history methodologies used for capturing the socializing influence of the life experiences or "architecture of self" (Pinar, 1986) that student teachers bring to teacher education programs and teaching. They conclude that "a variety of biographical, autobiographical and life history methodologies ... have begun to provide us with rich information about the ways in which teachers' perspectives are rooted in the variety of personal, familial, religious, political and cultural experiences they bring to teaching." Hollingsworth (1989) points to the same phenomenon when she describes the role of "preprogram beliefs" on the professional development of teachers. Crow (1987) and J. G. Knowles (1988) propose a Biographical Transformation Model to explain the relations between early childhood experiences with significant others, teacher role identity, and classroom actions. The influence of life experiences on teacher's actions and reactions is also visible in the way social structure is often taken for granted (Britzman, 1986; Ginsburg & Clift, 1990). In section 10.8, I already discussed the close links between gestalts and social context.

Yinger is another researcher whose line of thinking has much in common with the framework presented earlier. Yinger introduced the notion of interactive teaching (e.g., Yinger & Villar, 1986). Carter (1990) summarizes this notion by stating that it is framed around the idea of improvisation: "Yinger argues that teachers have a rich store of knowledge that enables them to make sense of immediate scenes and bring past experiences to bear on these scenes to invent, virtually on the spot, actions that fit these circumstances" (p. 304). In line with this view, Clark (1986) notes that we should distinguish between knowledge of a discipline in the forms commonly represented in textbooks and the teacher's knowledge, which takes the form of images of cases (cf. Shulman, 1992), vivid experiences, and good examples. In an article on "the language of practice," Yinger (1987, p. 309) states that the teacher relies on a set of meanings and patterns for thought and action:

> In the pattern language, each pattern describes a problem that occurs repeatedly in the environment and then describes the core of the solution to that problem.... Each pattern expresses a relationship between a context, a problem, and a solution.

This comes very close to the notion of a gestalt, especially because Yinger emphasizes that the language of practice is not primarily a verbal matter, but that it includes embodied structures of meaning that are part of orientation, movement, and manipulation. In a gestalt as I conceive it, the person's needs, values, meanings, feelings, and behavioral tendencies are all united into one inseparable whole.

12.3. ONE-SIDEDNESS IN THE USE OF REFLECTION AS A MEANS FOR PROFESSIONAL DEVELOPMENT

One may well ask why the nonrational aspect of a teacher's functioning receives so little attention in the literature on interventions in teacher education. The main reason seems to be that nonrational processes cannot easily be analyzed and influenced, and rational processes lend themselves to analysis and can be communicated to a supervisor. Teacher educators need such communications in order to clarify concepts, ideas, and alternative courses of action, and in order to provide feedback to teachers. Although I am not critical of this assumption, I do question whether communication in supervision should always be logical, rational, analytic, and digital.

A second reason is of a philosophical nature, and draws on the influence of Plato on our western culture. Plato was convinced of the existence of "the Good," and he believed that its nature can be ascertained by intellectual analysis (B. Russell, 1974, p. 133). He applied this conviction to the case of "proving" that his ideal Republic was good. Proof, for Plato, consisted of a sequence of logical, causal relationships. We must not underestimate the influence of this stance on our view of the world, our scientific tradition, and more specifically, the way we customarily objectify "good teaching." A comparison with the standpoint of Thrasymachus, a Sophist and a contemporary of Plato, may help to clarify this influence. For Thrasymachus there is no question of proving or disproving; the only question is whether you like the kind of Republic Plato envisions (B. Russell, 1974, p. 134). One can see how Thrasymachus' view, applied to teaching, would focus more on subjective, aesthetic appreciation than on objective analysis. Such a view has been promoted by Eisner (see, e.g., Eisner, 1985a). He also points to the influence of Plato on our culture in his discussion of the high status of school subjects like mathematics as compared to the arts. He states that there is also an "aesthetic mode of knowing" and promotes the notion of *connoisseurship* as a counterbalance to the primacy of knowledge acquired by rationality. He defines connoisseurship as the art of appreciation, which here means "an awareness and an understanding of what one has experienced" (Eisner, 1985b, p. 92).

A third reason for the underestimation of nonrational information processing is a psychological one that is likewise deeply embedded in our culture. The nonrational parts of ourselves are often regarded as "dark and dirty," and certainly irrational. They are associated with our instincts and drives, and with the idea that these must be overcome, at least in a scientific approach of teaching. In this respect, the work of Freud still has considerable influence (cf. Maslow, 1971, p. 310).

Although there is a great deal to be said for each of the three reasons described, the emphasis on rational thinking in teacher education has a number of disadvantages. In the first place, it gives student teachers a one-sided view of teaching and this may create the impression that good teaching is determined by rationality. During their actual teaching, they will discover that there is not enough time to reflect on all their decisions—often not even after the lesson is over—and this may leave them with a feeling of inadequacy. In this respect, the emphasis on rationality and analysis in teacher education could be especially disadvantageous to student teachers who are already inclined to be worriers.

Another outcome may be that student teachers regard the approach of the teacher educators as theory and the field experiences as practice, whereby the latter is equated with reality. There is a grain of truth here, in that it is unrealistic to present rational analysis as the only way of dealing with practice; this may well be one of the reasons for the well-known gap between theory and practice.

Moreover, it is not only because of time limitations that teachers cannot or should not always analyze their own teaching. As Maslow (1971, p. 63) points out, rationality can interfere with spontaneity and creativity. According to Ornstein (1972, p. 33), our rational consciousness has evolved for the primary purpose of ensuring biological survival. I believe there is more to life and to teaching than mere survival. Elaborating on the aspect of spontaneity, one might conclude that too much rational and analytic inquiry on the part of the teacher into his or her own way of teaching can create a gap between the teacher and the here-and-now. I appreciate the metaphor of the dance: In its most inspiring and creative moments, the dance and the dancer become one. In the most beautiful educational examples, there seems to be a one-ness of the teacher, the students, teaching, and learning. Then the internal process in the teacher can be characterized by what Csikszentmihalyi (1991, p. 41) calls *flow*, or a state of inner harmony in which the teacher's "thoughts, intentions, feelings and all the senses are focused on the same goal." Would it not have been a pity if in such situations the teacher had mentally stepped backward for a moment of analysis?

12.4. CONSEQUENCES

What I am aiming at is not a complete shift from one paradigm in teacher education to another. I am convinced that rational analysis of one's own behavior as a teacher is an important tool in one's professional development. However, I do want to counter a certain one-sidedness in the approach to teacher education. Nonrational processes play an important and often positive role in teaching, and I believe that it can be helpful to teachers to realize this. Moreover, reflection on these processes, after they have taken place, is also important; not only does it make the teacher aware of them, but it may help him or her to change the way information is being processed by the right hemisphere. This requires approaches in teacher education other than those based on rational analysis. Examples of possible techniques and instruments have been presented in section 11.9. Many of these instruments can also be used for research purposes. A well-known study by Weber and Mitchell (1995) asks children to draw pictures of teachers. These pictures appeared to show a "visual vocabulary" (Weber & Mitchell, 1995, p. 18). Swennen, Jörg and Korthagen (1999) describe a research study into student teachers' drawings depicting their views of themselves as teachers. This study appeared to reveal student teacher concerns that had not been found using another, more traditional research instrument (a card sort procedure).

However, I think we should not just reduce this theoretical analysis to the application of a fixed set of new instruments. Most important is an openness to the fact that if we look at the reality of teaching, there is more than rational decision making involved. It may help teacher educators to recognize instances of nonrational processes in teaching, including the beautiful ones in which flow occurs and the more problematic situations in which ineffective gestalts seem to direct the teacher's behavior. We need willingness to look for creative ways to make teachers aware of their gestalts. My personal experience is that as soon as one looks at teaching and listens to teachers' reflections in this way, one recognizes many new possibilities. For example, small words revealing gestalts can get more significance. When one of my student teachers said that a certain classroom situation washed over her like a wave, I asked her to describe the wave in terms of substance and color, instead of using more rational questions such as "what did you think?", "what did you do?", and so on. This revealed the close mingling of her image of the situation, her feelings and actions, and opened the door to a rational analysis quite different from the one we would have had if we had started right away with a rational analysis of the situation. This example also illustrates that right hemisphere techniques such as the elaboration of metaphors can be used with the purpose of promoting awareness of the nonrational processes in teachers in combination with more rational-analytic reflection (cf. Olson, 1984). However, I have to stress that it is not always simple to grasp right hemisphere processes. The situation can be compared to the problem of trying to express the essence of a piece of art in simple language: Often, it is as if there are no suitable words, or as if words detract from the essence of the meaning that the work has for us.

In sum, the analysis presented in this chapter implies that I attach a broader meaning to the term *reflection* than is usually done, reverting to the original meaning of the word: the mirroring of something (e.g., an image, heat, etc.). The idea of a mirror is helpful, because it makes clear that there are different mirrors: a rational one, which is often used in teacher education, and other mirrors, which may be more suitable for reflecting nonrational processes. Any mirror is imperfect in itself, because it cannot reflect every aspect of an internal process. This is why the use of more than one mirror can help teachers to become aware of the relations between their actions and their inner processes. This broader view of reflection is in accordance with the definition of reflection used in this book (see section 4.5). The essence of this definition is the mental process of structuring or restructuring, which can also take place in a nonlinguistic and holistic way. I believe that especially the integration of both types of reflection (the mirroring of nonrational processes and rational analysis) would be beneficial, because they are directly related to the two different ways in which the teacher's consciousness operates. The integration of the two modes of reflection can be illustrated by means of Ornstein's (1972, p. 84) metaphor of building a house: "At first, there may be a sudden inspiration of the gestalt of the finished house, but this image must be brought to completion, slowly, by linear methods, by plans and contracts, and then by the actual construction, sequentially, piece by piece."

Reflection, conceived as the integration of rational analysis and the process of becoming aware of one's guiding gestalts, seems to focus more on the individuality of the teacher than such conceptions of reflection as that proposed by Zeichner (1983). The latter emphasizes the need for inquiry into the contexts in which teaching takes place, and the ethical, moral, and political issues that influence one's teaching. On the other hand, I see no fundamental antithesis between the approach presented and that of Zeichner. When it comes to contextual influences on one's teaching, reflection on right hemisphere information processing is no less important. It can help teachers to become aware of the values that they have incorporated during their socialization into the profession, and the origins of their guiding gestalts. Reflection, thus conceived, can enhance the power of each individual teacher to make a personal, creative, and innovative contribution to education.

SUMMARY

The brain makes use of two different ways of information processing, a rational and nonrational way, roughly corresponding to the two hemispheres. Nonrational information processing plays a central role in teaching, as the language of practice shows, but the common view of reflection, grounded in Dewey's idea of a consecutive ordering, is one-sided and does not pay attention to teachers' less conscious gestalts, their "connoisseurship," and instances of "flow." This one-sidedness is due to cultural influences and the fact that rational analyses of teaching situations can more easily be communicated by common language.

A broader view of reflection can be characterized by the concept of mirroring, and the observation that different types of mirrors can be used: rational and holistic. The integration of different modes of reflection is most productive.

BASIC CONCEPTS

Rational and nonrational information processing

The right and left hemisphere

The language of practice

Connoisseurship

Flow

Mirroring

13 Training Teacher Educators for the Realistic Approach

Bob Koster and Fred Korthagen

> Universities generally, and university-based teacher educators particularly, have no right to recommend to teachers any teaching practices that they have not themselves used successfully at the university.
>
> —*T. Russell (1999).*

The introduction of the realistic approach into teacher education requires specific teacher educator competencies. In this chapter we will focus on the importance of professional development of teacher education staff. We will discuss the structure and program content of a training course for teacher educators, aimed at developing a number of necessary competencies for the supervision of student teachers. Descriptions of several parts of the course are included. On that basis, we will focus on the pedagogical principles underlying the training. We will conclude the chapter with recommendations on the professional development of teacher educators.

13.1. INTRODUCTION

By now it may have become clear that the realistic approach to teacher education requires specific knowledge and skills in the teacher educators. That is why we cannot ignore the question of how teacher educators can learn to use the principles outlined in this book. This means that we go from the level of student teachers' learning to teach, to the level of teacher educators' learning to teach teachers. This may seem a remarkable step, because in the literature on teacher education there are almost no references to the need for professional development of teacher education staff. In the next section (13.2), we will dive into this issue of the professional development of teacher educators from a broad, international perspective. In section 13.3, we will focus on the situation in our own teacher education program at the IVLOS Institute of Education at Utrecht University. There we were very much confronted with the need for professional development of the IVLOS staff when the realistic approach started to take shape. We will describe this situation and the consequences that we observed (e.g., the need for a training course for cooperative teachers and teacher educators). Soon after, we started to offer such a course to teacher educators from other institutes. In section 13.4, a closer look at the aims, structure, and content of these training courses is presented. In 13.5, several parts of the courses will be illustrated with real-life examples from exercises, whereupon we will also highlight several pedagogical principles strongly influencing the course approach (in section 13.6). Finally, it is our turn to reflect on our experiences with giving the course, and we will make recommendations for the professional development of teacher educators (section 13.7).

13.2. THE PROFESSIONAL DEVELOPMENT OF TEACHER EDUCATORS

The professional development of teacher educators has rarely been discussed (Wilson, 1990). In most places, becoming a teacher educator without a specific education for this profession is still a reality. A research study into the selection and training of educators in the European Union (EU) countries, published in a special issue of the *European Journal of Teacher Education* (Wilson, 1990), shows that the position of teacher educators is obtained on the basis of extensive and successful teaching experience, and/or an academic education (e.g., in educational science). They receive no specific training to become professional teacher educators. As Korthagen and Russell (1995) state, the general picture is that after an often informal recruitment procedure, teacher educators are given the responsibility for a group of student teachers and are left alone. The idea seems to be that one learns the profession through trial and error. This situation is similar to that in the United States (Ducharme, 1993; Guilfoyle et al., 1995). As Wilson (1990) notes, this is highly remarkable in an area where professional development is the operative word.

A thorough literature research showed an almost complete lack of studies on the subject of the education of institute-based teacher educators, although in many places training programs are offered to cooperating teachers. The only known exceptions are a program of more than one year, which took place in the mid-1970s on a teacher education institute in Utrecht (Korthagen, 1982, pp. 190–195), a program given at national level in Austria (by Buchberger), and basic training courses for teacher educators organized by the Israeli MOFET institute and by the Dutch Pedagogical Centers (which support schools and teacher education institutes). In places, specific courses for teacher educators exist on themes such as "Extending special needs provision in schools." Since 1996, there is a development in the Netherlands whereby both the ministry of education and the union of teacher educators have started to view the competencies of teacher educators as conditional to the development of the quality of teacher education. A nationwide structure for describing these competencies has been developed (Koster & Dengerink, 2000), and will be linked to an official certification and registration procedure of teacher educators. Around the same time, a similar U.S. task force was created to formulate the competencies required for master teacher educators (Task Force on the Certification of Teacher Educators, 1996).

13.3. THE NEED FOR STAFF DEVELOPMENT IN A REALISTIC PROGRAM

Around 1990, we at the IVLOS Institute of Education started thinking about the development of training courses for teacher educators and cooperating teachers based on the principles of the realistic approach. It became clear that practicing realistic teacher education requires competencies that teacher educators often do not possess or that need further development. Working within a realistic approach means, for example, being able to build on student teachers' concerns, to create the safety needed for reflection, to organize reflective interactions between student teachers, to teach student teachers how they can develop themselves in a systematic way, to look at human development in a holistic way, and so on. Last but not least, teacher educators who wish to work in a realistic way should be experts in working from practice to theory, which requires completely different skills from those available in teachers in schools or staff in most other departments within the university. This is even more the case as the integration of practice and theory has to take place within the person of the student teacher, which means that teacher educators require knowledge, skills, and attitudes in the field of human development (adult development, social psychology, and the like).

Most of all, we considered it important to develop the teacher educator skills necessary for supervising student teachers according to the ALACT model (see sections 3.7 and 4.8). Consequently, the skills described in chapter 7 as important in helping student teachers go through the phases of this model form the heart of a course for teacher educators developed at the IVLOS Institute of Education.

The rest of this chapter will focus on this training course. After we started to organize courses for our own teacher educators and cooperating teachers, teacher educators from other institutes soon became interested. Since 1994, five IVLOS trainers have trained dozens of teams at teacher education institutes for both primary and secondary education. Our training courses have been offered to Belgian, Canadian, Danish, Finnish, German, Swedish, and Norwegian teacher education staff.

13.4. A CLOSER LOOK AT THE COURSE FOR TEACHER EDUCATORS

In this section, we will take a closer look at the aims, structure, and content of the course for teacher educators.

Aims and Structure of the Course

When supervising a student teacher, it is important to help him or her go through the phases of the ALACT model. However, this does not yet mean that the student also learns to reflect independently (i.e., without the help of the supervisor). To achieve that, the student will also have to reflect regularly on his or her own way of reflecting, and on the strengths and weaknesses in doing so. This can then lead to new learning points related to the student teacher's way of learning and reflecting. This *meta-reflection* is fundamental to learning to reflect without the help of a supervisor. Thus, the course for teacher educators that we developed has a twofold aim: to develop in teacher educators the skills necessary for facilitating reflection and the skills needed for facilitating learning to reflect independently. As noted in chapter 7, to a large degree, these skills can be taken from the literature on (training in) supervision and therapy (Brammer, 1973; Carkhuff, 1969a, 1969b; Egan, 1975; Rogers, 1969).

A basic assumption underlying our choice of skills is that supervision should build on the student teacher's gestalts and the problems they encounter. That means the starting point of the supervisory process should always lie in the student's experiences, the questions he or she asks him- or herself, and the problems he or she meets. Before the supervisor can confront the student, a safe environment between supervisor and student is an important precondition. After all, the student has to show his or her real concerns and feelings. The skills of acceptance, genuineness, and empathy can be seen as a group of skills that are important to that safety (see section 7.6), and thus crucial in Phase 2 of the ALACT model. Safety also plays a key role in the important third phase of this model. In this phase, the supervisor sometimes has to confront the student, for example, when there is a discrepancy between the student teacher's way of thinking and his or her actual actions. Again and again, the crux of good supervision appears to be in combining confronting with offering safety.

For most supervisors of prospective teachers, it is quite a revolutionary change to abandon the notion that they do have to tell students what they are doing right and wrong, and how to do it differently the next time. As a supervisor, you cannot just adopt the principle of connecting with the student's position, offer safety, and help the student reflect independently on a given lesson. It is a change of attitude and the mastery of different skills for which extensive practice and application are needed, in training situations as well as in daily educational practice.

The most important principle underlying our course for teacher educators is that the courses themselves should demonstrate a realistic approach. In our view, it is impossible to adequately develop the notions of building on students' concerns and promoting reflection without at the same time building on the concerns of the course participants and promoting their reflection on concrete experiences. This is the *congruence principle* (see also section 5.8). It also implies that we pay much attention to creating a safe atmosphere within the courses, and the theory offered in our staff development programs for teacher educators is always connected to concrete experiences of the participants (e.g., in recent supervisory conferences or in here-and-now experiences within the course). In fact, the design of our courses is based on the five-step structure described in section 9.2 and the kind of theory presented is generally what was called *phronesis* in chapter 2. As a consequence, participants can learn much through observation of the trainer's behavior, which models the behavior of a teacher educator in a realistic program. This trainer must be rather flexible, adapting the course content to the needs and experiences that arise in the here-and-now.

This may sound as if there is no clear framework underpinning the course, but there is. The course follows the phases of the ALACT model in the sense that the skills important in these phases always receive proper attention. Just like we described in the case of a realistic program for student teachers, it is possible to combine building on the needs and experiences of participants with a standard framework, as long as this framework is not used as a straitjacket. Moreover, by creating suitable experiences and putting the right questions, the trainer can promote the surfacing of specific concerns and needs. During a course, there are also numerous opportunities to make the participants aware of the importance of issues such as safety, obstacles to reflection, possibilities to overcome them, learning orientations, and so forth. In that respect, here-and-now examples are often the most powerful. We will now discuss some general issues that always come up in the course.

The Phases of the Spiral Model

In the first part of the training course, building on one or more concrete examples of supervision sessions (that take place in front of the group or in small groups), the ALACT model is introduced. The different phases of this model (Phase 2: looking back; Phase 3: awareness; and Phase 4: creating alternatives) are translated into three basic questions that the supervisor can use: What has happened? What is important in that? To what intentions does that lead? The supervisor helps the student to analyze his or her own actions and, on that basis, guide his or her own development by setting personal goals, by working toward these goals, and by being conscious of the ways that lead to these goals. In section 3.9, we called this the development of the student's *growth competence*. It is important that supervisors are able to recognize the different phases in the reflection process and to help the student pass through these systematically.

Safety

During the first training sessions, much elaborate attention is given to the skills of acceptance, empathy, and genuineness, through which a sound basis is formed for the view of supervision as the promotion of reflection. By accepting the student's contribution, by being able to put themselves in the other's position and at the same time focusing on their own feelings while facilitating, supervisors enable themselves to build an atmosphere of safety and trust. This enables an open relationship to arise, within which much can be discussed. It forms the basis for a helping relationship in which the student's reflections can be taken as a starting point and will become its focus.

Nine Aspects

The next step is the attention to *concretizing*, the fourth important skill in Phase 2. We clarify that when reviewing a teaching situation, four aspects play a central role:

wanting, thinking, feeling, and acting (see section 7.6). If dealing with a student teacher's lesson, the important questions will be: What did the student teacher want his or her students to achieve through this lesson? What were the student teacher's thoughts during the lesson? What were the student teacher's feelings, for instance, when a few students were sitting with their backs turned? And, how did the student teacher react to this behavior?

By asking students to answer these questions, the supervisor will help them to concretize the action and shape the experiences. A global answer (e.g., "It did not go well at all today") can be made more specific with questions (e.g., "What exactly did not go well?" "What did?" "What did you do during the first 5 minutes of the lesson?" "What did you feel when the majority started to work?").

Concretizing next involves helping the student teacher to answer the same four aspects for the students: What did the students want during the lesson? What did they do at different moments of the lesson? What did they feel and think while doing it?

During the training course, much attention is devoted to the four skills in Phase 2, and these are practiced in different ways. Phase 2 holds the key to the fundamental change in attitude we talked about earlier: All the supervisor's skills are aimed at eventually letting the students themselves do all the work, but they will have to be directed to that effect. Much practice (and reflection on that practice by the supervisor) is necessary for this to slowly become common practice. Examples of the exercises are given in section 13.5.

Toward the Essence

Eventually, the purpose of supervision is that student teachers will come to see the relationship between the left and the right side of Fig. 13.1. They discover that their own feelings influence their behavior, which in turn influences the feelings and actions of the students in their classrooms. In short, the aim is for the student teacher to realize that classroom communication is often of a circular character (see sections 7.6 and 11.5). This is an important way to reach the aim of Phase 3 of the ALACT model: awareness of essential aspects.

Discrepancies

The essence of a problem often appears to lie in a discrepancy between, for example, the feeling of the student teacher and his or her acting. A theory in which discrepancies are central has been systematically formulated by De Bruin and Vulker (1984). De Bruin points out that the supervisor confronts the student with inconsistent statements that can be in different areas: between thinking and feeling (e.g., "I think I prepared the lesson well, but I felt uncertain about the subject matter"), between saying and acting (e.g., "I warned the students that I would not accept any further disturbances, but as the lesson went on, I did not dare to evict Paul from the classroom"), and so on. Evidently, possible contradictions between the different aspects of the concretizing grid (Fig. 13.1) are important examples of such inconsistent statements.

Creating Alternatives

When the student, with the help of the supervisor, has become aware of strong points and essential weaknesses, and is capable of formulating these points at a concrete level, then the moment has arrived to move to the next stage: the brainstorming of alternatives (Phase 4).

During training sessions we often see that after practicing supervisors are capable of systematically placing the initiative with the student teacher in Phases 2 and 3, letting him or her review the lesson, and letting the student name the weaknesses. However, often the initiative is taken away from the student in the last stage of the conversation. Thus, when creating alternatives, the following questions count as important points of attention: "Is the student teacher involved in formulating the alternatives?" "Who draws the conclusions?" These are a few of the 7 points of attention in Phase 4 that we use in the training course (see Fig. 7.3 for the complete list).

Independent Learning by Reflection

The aforementioned training process intends to give supervisors of students a wide range of skills: the ability to react empathetically, to help in concretizing, to confront, to help in developing alternatives, and so on. All these skills enable the students to go through the reflection phases. Once these skills have been mastered, the next step is taken: What can you as a supervisor subsequently do to see to it that the students learn to go through the reflection process independently? First of all, it is important that the students become aware of the system that underlies the supervision. Consequently, it is the task of the supervisor to explain that system to the student by referring to the ALACT model, the phases within this model, and its principles. Here, an important condition is that the students have been informed about this model before the supervision period and, for example, during their teacher education course have been taught to work with it. The students are now encouraged to consider their own way of reflecting (meta-reflection; see sections 7.10 and 11.3). This can lead to specific learning points in regard to their own way of

0. Context	
1. What did I want?	5. What did the students want?
2. What did I do?	6. What did the students do?
3. What did I think?	7. What did the students think?
4. What did I feel?	8. What did the students feel?

FIG. 13.1 Concretizing on the basis of nine aspects.

learning. The questions formulated in Fig. 13.2 can be of help in this area. In fact, these are the translations of the three basic reflection questions to the situation in which one's own learning is the action phase (Phase 1 of the ALACT model) to be reflected on.

A Curriculum Aimed at Reflection

Up to this point, the focus has been on helping the students reflect on their teaching experiences. Generally, during the training courses, a more general question of teacher education pedagogy emerges, namely, "How can the principles of reflection be translated into every element of the teacher education curriculum?"

The course deals with this question in two different ways. First, it monitors which ways participants are already or have been handling successfully promoting reflection in groups or individual students. And second, it suggests a number of alternatives.

We have at our disposal a wide range of ways in which educators can find concrete answers to the question of how reflection and learning from experience can be encouraged in different contexts (i.e., different subjects, different group sizes, etc.). Many of the relevant techniques and instruments have been described in the previous chapters. First of all, we emphasize the central part played by the logbook, and its implementation in the course (for a more detailed elaboration, see chapter 11). We also stress the importance of instruction of the systematic use of the ALACT model within the teacher education program. To improve reflecting in large groups, a choice can be made from a wide range of methods, for example, the wall, the columns, the rep-grid, and the arrows technique (for a detailed description, see chapter 9). Each of these techniques aims at a different reflection domain. The columns technique, for example, encourages reflection on the students' goals for their teaching practice, which makes them aware of how easy it is to forget these goals, how unrealistic they often are, how they can be concretized, and which strategies are effective or ineffective for achieving these goals. The rep-grid is a technique alerting teachers to the often unconscious constructs that pilot their actions toward students. The fact that such reflection techniques are used in a group adds a dimension to the process of reflecting ("collaborative reflection"). In a training course for teacher educators, we use these techniques at the level of the participants so that they can experience the techniques themselves. For example, if the wall is used, we offer them bricks with statements about teacher education and/or supervision.

Questions promoting reflection on the process of learning itself

1. **How did I learn?**
2. **What strikes me in the way I learn? (strengths/weaknesses)**
3. **Intentions, alternatives, learning needs in regard to my own learning**

Fig. 13.2 Reflection on the process of learning itself.

13.5. SOME TRAINING ACTIVITIES AND EXERCISES

The aims, structure, and contents of the training course have now been discussed. As already mentioned, different activities and exercises are being offered on which theory and the various skills are built. Next, we will give several examples of exercises used during the training course.

Question Time

In our courses, one of the first questions asked is: "Which are the specific questions with which you as a teacher educator have come to this training course?" It is an example of promoting reflection in the participants themselves.

In answer to this question, a group of educators from a secondary teacher education program mentioned, for example:

- How can I supervise students "at a distance" (without attending their lessons), without falling in the trap of giving advice too soon, and have them solve their own problems more often?
- I want to be less directive, and learn how to keep quiet.
- I am supervising my students intuitively; am I doing it the right way?
- What models are there that are more effective in the practice of supervising and that are time-saving?
- What skills do you need to help students to reflect?
- How can you incorporate a systematic structure in reflection?

Such issues then determine the kind of activities used and the content of the specific course.

Exercises in the Skill of Concretizing

To train the skill of concretizing, we use real problematic situations encountered by the participants in their everyday work and several short video fragments showing one of our student teachers talking with a supervisor about an experience from teaching practice. These short fragments start with the supervisor asking a question. One of these fragments is as follows:

> Supervisor: "Edith, how was it today?"
>
> Edith: "It didn't work at all, it was really terrible. That group was terribly turbulent throughout the whole lesson. Well, I thought: I will get through somehow or other, and I started talking louder and louder and so on. And at one stage I thought oh well, let's not, and then I just started talking softly. But the noise and the racket continued.... At one stage I threw Linda out, and after the lesson she returned, to-

gether with Claire, and they were sitting in front of me and I just couldn't come between them. It was really awful! You're talking loudly during the whole lesson and you're doing your best to gain people's attention and then you have to throw out Linda again. And then you're talking to her and then you notice that you don't come through ..., that they're accusing *me* of several things. Really, I thought it was terrible."

The participants' assignment is to screen this fragment using the nine fields of Fig. 13.1 (which fields does Edith talk about?). Subsequently, they are asked to formulate one concretizing question in one of the fields not yet mentioned by the student. This is combined with an empathizing response. After everyone has finished, the various responses are read out loud and discussed (a possible response agreeing with the theory is to be found in Fig. 13.3). This often leads to a deeper insight into the meaning of empathy and concretizing.

Exercise in Using the Spiral Model

As training material, much originates from the supervision experiences of the participants themselves. The following conversation took place as a result of the question put forward by the trainer: "Who has something he or she has been confronted with during supervision, and who wants to discuss this here?" A participant, whom we call "A" reacted by saying he had such a problematic situation. The trainer asked another participant (B) to act as A's supervisor. This led to the following conversation:

B: "Can you tell me something about the context?"

A: "Yesterday I paid a school visit. During the discussion after the lesson, I asked the student if the lesson went as planned. All he came up with were positive points. During my observation, I had noticed that he had lost sight of a group of students. I could-

Possible responses agreeing with the "theory"

As a result of the exercise "concretizing":
"This class is really making life difficult for you, ... Where did you want to end up with them?"
This response agrees with the "theory" because it starts off naming the feelings of the student (making life difficult, i.e., reacting empathetically), followed by asking for something not yet mentioned by the student (i.e. the wanting).

As a result of the exercise "spiral model":
1 *phase 2 (looking back on an experience), 3 (awareness of essential aspects, although this is touched on very shortly), and 4 (developing alternatives).*
2 *context ("can you tell me something about the context"), A's actions ("what exactly did you say or do?"), A's feelings ("I'm wondering, what is it that irritates you? What exactly is it?"), the student's feelings ("Let's look at the situation, he felt . . .").*
3 *concretizing, summarizing: "What exactly did you do?" (concretizing), "So you did two things . . ." (summarizing).*

As a result of the exercise "discrepancies":
"You really want to do something, but you feel powerless."
(This is an example of focusing on the discrepancy between feeling and wanting, but there are more discrepancies hidden in this fragment).

FIG. 13.3 Possible responses agreeing with the "theory."

n't get him to volunteer it of his own. That was very unsatisfactory. Finally, I took over the conversation. But then he backed off."

B: "What exactly did you say or do?"

A: "First, I went over the outline of the lesson with him. Then I said: I noticed that group at the window started to talk …"

B: "You yourself mentioned that point and did not give a value judgment?"

A: "He immediately went on the defensive. Then I said: It isn't that bad, is it? I just wanted to bring it up. But I feel I failed to get through."

B: "Let's look at the situation, he felt …"

A: "That's right, he smelled a rat."

B: "So you did two things: you went over the lesson with him, and you mentioned an observation. Did you let him bring forward things of his own accord at the beginning?"

A: (thinks, pause) "No."

B: "I'm wondering, what is it that irritates you? What exactly is that?"

A: "It's not irritation, I want to handle it differently, I can't get through, that's my problem."

B: "What could you possibly do?"

A: (Silence) "I don't know."

B: "Have you tried it with other people? Did it work then?"

A: "It has to do with the student's attitude. Perhaps I should try and offer him a feeling of greater safety at the start of the discussion."

B: "How in concrete terms can you do that?"

At this point, the conversation was interrupted by the course trainer.
The assignment to the course participants was as follows:

1. Which are the phases that can be recognized in this conversation?
2. Which areas were used in B's concretizing questions?

3. Which skills did B use well in this conversation?

(A potential reaction agreeing with the "theory" is to be found in Fig. 13.3).

Discrepancies

Another video fragment is as follows:

> Supervisor: "And, how was it today?"
>
> Edith: "Oh well, it went all right. I think the students were enjoying themselves all right. It was quite a nice lesson, they really had a very good time together. This lesson was a reading comprehension lesson, so I could well imagine they didn't feel like it, but after a while it did escalate a bit. I was at the back of the class and I got a sweeper thrown at me. I just didn't know what to do, so I thought ..., well, I just didn't know. I walked to the front and just looked at them, but, well, you can just ..., this can't be, I thought. I myself could also imagine pretty well that they didn't feel like paying attention to that lesson any more and seriously work at that text."

The assignment for this fragment is to name a discrepancy mentioned by the student in this fragment. During the ensuing discussion, these discrepancies are placed in a general framework (again a potential reaction agreeing with the theory is to be found in Fig. 13.3).

Structures Aimed at Reflection

A question often asked of the participants of our training courses is: "Who wants to show ways, already used by you in your present training course, urging students to reflect?" During a training session at a teacher education college for primary education, this caused the training group to look at logbook writing as an instrument for promoting reflection. In the next training session, the participating teacher educators brought one or two logbooks of their own students, in which their students described how they had experienced their first practice teaching. In the training session, we practiced how to discuss the logbooks in a group of student teachers, with the teacher educators playing the students whose logbooks were being discussed, and with one other course participant presiding over the session.

First, an educator supervised the group in a structured way. She asked which questions the students had, gave turns, summarized, and so forth. After this example, the course trainer asked if there was somebody who wanted to show another way to discuss the logbooks in a group of students. Another course participant volunteered and showed a very different way. She started by saying: "The purpose of today's session is to find out together how your teaching goes, but also to get to know each other better because of that, and to learn to trust each other. Therefore, we will take turns and tell each other where you do your practice teaching and what in particular has struck you in that practice." This introduction was given in front of the group by the teacher educator. Then she sat down among the group and during the conversation saw to it, especially in a nonverbal way, that the "students" were really exchanging experiences and were communicating.

Because of this exercise, two principles in the encouragement of reflection became crystal clear to each teacher educator in the training session: As a teacher educator, you have to take a guiding, supporting role and not a central role, and precisely because of that, you have to leave the initiative to the students and let them do the work. It also became clear that it is the teacher's job to structure the discussion.

(Homework) Assignments

In almost all cases, the course session ends with an assignment meant to link the training to the daily educational practice. At the end of the fist session, the participants of the training course are asked: "What has been important to you in this first session; what do you think you will use next week? If necessary, write this down in your logbook." (Note that these questions are related to Phases 3 and 4 of the ALACT model, this time applied to the participants' own learning processes.)

At the start of the second session, this assignment is the starting point of a pair exercise: A supervises B on the intentions of the previous session. What have been the results? What has been attempted? How did it go? What were the bottlenecks in the implementation? What new questions have come up because of this?

At the end of the second session (in which responding empathetically has been a focus), the following question is submitted to the participants: During the next week, find three situations in which you are having a conversation, and deliberately try to react more empathetically than you normally do; then try to reflect: What happened to you and what happened to the other person? Write that down as concretely as possible.

13.6. PRINCIPLES OF COURSE PEDAGOGY IN THE TRAINING COURSE

The previously described parts of the training course already show something of its underlying principles:

1. In the training itself, an important principle is that a connection is established with the individual questions of the participants.
2. The skills and theory offered are linked to concrete experiences and the participants practice the skills in between training sessions. This means that there is an alternation between the contribution of practical experiences, reflection on them, connecting them to relevant theory, and their application to fresh situations. In so doing, the structure and the

contents of the course are an illustration of using the spiral model in teacher education.

3. By starting from the experiences of the people themselves, two things go hand in hand: The contents of the exercises are relevant to all participants, because the contributed problems have to do with their questions of supervision, and the exercises deal with real problems in the analysis of which the actual reaction of the supervisor and supervisee can be used. In fact, little role playing is necessary.
4. A safe learning environment has to be created so that the participants will not be afraid to experiment with different behaviors, both in and outside the training sessions. In that respect, the trainers fulfill a model function, for example, by seeing to it that in the beginning positive feedback is given both by the participants together and by the trainer.
5. The principle of a constant and self-directed professional development comes to life by systematically paying attention to the learning questions of the participants themselves, and by systematically having the participants record their own progress.
6. Most importantly, by applying the previous five principles, the training course is congruent with the principles of the realistic approach and the trainer serves as a role model.

13.7. A REFLECTION ON THE COURSE AND RECOMMENDATIONS

The training courses in supervision skills clearly fill a need. The evaluations show that the training yields so much mainly (a) because of its practical nature, (b) because supervision is put within a structural framework, (c) because many of the skills that were learned "could be used the following day" (a quote from a participant), (d) because reflection took place on one's own role as a supervisor, and (e) because it is pleasant to work on everyday problems together with colleagues. Participants also report that they develop more insight into the question of how reflection can be structurally included in their teacher education program. However, a point of attention is the final translation of the course content into an organizational framework in the participants' "home situation." A training course should not be a once only activity. The course should be linked to supervision and reflection in all different parts of the teacher education curriculum.

In sum, we want to kick off several changes with the training course: developing a different view on supervision, offering supervisory skills to give shape to this changed view, and also developing knowledge and skills through which educators are capable of promoting reflection with their students across the whole of the teacher education program.

The skills teacher educators, in our view, need to have are indicated in Fig. 7.5. However, promoting reflection and supervising student teachers during their teaching practice is only one of the many areas in which teacher educators need to be competent. In that respect, this chapter describes only part of a program for the professional development of teacher education staff. We also give training courses on how to deal with groups of student teachers such that school experiences and theory become connected (based on the five-step structure described in section 9.2), courses in both promoting independent learning in groups of student teachers and preparing student teachers for promoting independent and reflective learning in their students, as well as other courses tailored to the questions and concerns of the teacher educators or institute with which we are working. We have also started to give train-the-trainer courses for teacher educators who wish to train colleagues or cooperating teachers in the realistic approach.

Our work with teacher educators has made it clear that what is needed is a broadly accepted occupational profile of the teacher educator. It is at least remarkable that, in many countries, people develop occupational profiles for teachers in primary and in secondary schools, but seldom for teacher educators themselves. In our view, this is a task for governments and for professional associations of teacher educators. An occupational profile for teacher educators would specify necessary competencies. That could lead to the development of training programs for teacher educators, which would guide their professional development (Koster & Dengerink, 2000).

SUMMARY

In the available literature, the professional development of teacher educators receives little attention. It is, however, an important issue when implementing the realistic approach. We described the aims, structure, and content of a training course for teacher education staff and our experiences in giving this course. The course, which first of all focuses on supervision skills and the ALACT model, is in itself an example of the realistic approach (the congruence principle). This means that a safe learning climate is created and the course builds on the needs and concerns of the participants and their practical experiences, both from without and within the course. There is an alternation of action in practical experiences, reflection, and theory. The participants are also stimulated to monitor their own professional development. This course fills a need, but should be complemented with other courses for teacher educators, ideally based on a framework describing the necessary competencies of teacher education staff.

BASIC CONCEPTS

Professional development of teacher educators

Competencies of teacher education staff

Congruence principle

14 The Realistic Approach: Its Tenets, Philosophical Background, and Future

Fred Korthagen

> Along with education, which generally deals only with academic accomplishments, we need to develop more altruism and a sense of caring and responsibility for others in the minds of the younger generation studying in various educational institutions. This can be done without necessarily involving religion. One could therefore call this "secular ethics," as it in fact consists of basic human qualities such as kindness, compassion, sincerity and honesty.
>
> —The Dalai Lama: Millennium message

In this final chapter, the realistic approach is summarized. This leads to an analysis of the question of to what extent this approach is new. Realistic teacher education appears to constitute a synthesis of valuable theories and practices developed in the past. Its justification not only lies in psychological considerations about professional learning, but also in a philosophy of education aiming to contribute to a better world in two respects: through the development of realistic education in schools and the development of self-understanding and a sense of interconnectedness in teachers and students. Finally, a look into the future of teacher education points toward the need of realistic research to support the implementation of the ideas developed throughout this book.

14.1. INTRODUCTION

In the previous 13 chapters, the realistic approach to teacher education has been described. Practical examples have been given, and theoretical foundations elaborated. The idea of this chapter is to look backward and forward. I will summarize the essential features of realistic teacher education and look ahead to ways in which it may possibly influence teacher education in the future.

But I wish to go one step further. I will also discuss the question of what's new about the realistic approach, which will lead to a reconsideration of its theoretical foundations. I will also pay attention to the philosophy of education behind the whole framework introduced in this book. In doing so, I hope to clarify a sociopedagogical view that goes much further than just teacher education and is rooted in serious concerns about society as a whole. In fact, here I return to the concerns and struggles mentioned in the preface. The problems in my own classes when I started teaching have, 25 years later, evolved into a view of the role of education in society that I will outline in this chapter. In fact, many of the ideas that I will put forward in this chapter are an important justification of the realistic approach, or better, the driving force behind my work in teacher education and research.

In section 14.2 I will start with a brief summary of the realistic approach in teacher education, and its five basic tenets. In section 14.3, the realistic approach will be reconsidered, with attention to what is new about this approach. I will show that the realistic approach is both grounded in earlier theoretical approaches and constitutes a new synthesis. Section 14.4 will be devoted to a discussion of the philosophy of education behind the approach. I will analyze the huge problems education is currently being confronted with and I will indicate possible directions in the search for solutions. This will contribute to a deeper understanding of the term *realistic education*. Finally, in section 14.5, I will discuss the future of teacher education, especially the question of the prospects for realistic teacher education. In this section, I will emphasize the need for practice-relevant research and propose the term *realistic research*.

14.2. REALISTIC TEACHER EDUCATION: A SUMMARY

The realistic approach has its roots in a wish to bridge the gap between theory and practice, a problem that has dominated teacher education for a long time. We saw that the theory–practice gap is a result of the view that the goal of teacher education is to teach expert knowledge (resulting from psychological, sociological, and educational research) to student teachers, who can then use this expertise in their practice (the technical-rationality approach). This view leads teacher educators to make a priori choices about the theory that should be transmitted to student teachers. Research shows that this approach has a very limited effect on practice. The main causes of the failure to transfer theory to practice are the socializing influences of the school context, student teachers' own preconceptions about learning and teaching, the feed-forward problem (theory always comes too early or too late), and the nature of theory relevant to practice. The latter issue is clarified by the distinction between episteme (Theory with a big T) and phronesis (theory with a small t). Episteme is generalized scientific knowledge, based on a broad empirical basis. What teachers use, in practice, is phronesis: situation-specific principles, context-dependent, that help them to rapidly arrive at decisions that solve practical problems. The latter kind of theory is much more perceptual than conceptual: What is important is that it helps the teacher, within the practical situation, to quickly perceive what is relevant in the situation and to base his or her actions on that perception.

We also saw that the emphasis on scientific knowledge results in a certain one-sidedness in the approaches used in teacher education. They tend to focus more on rational, logical, analytical thinking, whereas behavior in practice is much more based on gestalts: personal conglomerates of needs, concerns, values, meanings, preferences, feelings, and behavioral tendencies. In order to take such gestalts seriously in teacher education, the realistic approach builds on concrete experiences, and the concerns and gestalts elicited by these situations. The approach aims at an ongoing process of learning by reflection, defined as the mental process of trying to (re)structure an experience, a problem, or existing knowledge or insights.

The ideal reflection process is described by the ALACT model in terms of five phases: (1) action; (2) looking back on the action; (3) awareness of essential aspects; (4) creating alternative methods of action; and (5) trial, which itself is a new action and therefore the starting point of a new cycle. Student teachers should not only be stimulated to reflect, but most of all to learn how to reflect: They have to develop the ability to go through the phases of the ALACT model, both on their own and by means of peer-supported learning, thus acquiring a *growth competence*.

A realistic teacher education program should help student teachers to become aware of their learning needs, to find useful experiences, and to reflect on these experiences. This requires a balance between safety and challenge, a careful adjustment of individual long-term learning processes and programmatic lines, close cooperation between the teacher education institute and the schools, integration of theory and practice and of the various disciplines tied to teacher education, and systematic attention for the professional development of teacher educators and cooperating teachers. For this professional development of those responsible for teacher education, a framework was presented describing the skills necessary to help individual student teachers reflect and develop their growth competence. We also looked at approaches and techniques to promote reflective learning in groups, for example, the five-step procedure summarized in Fig. 9.1 that leads to a fusion of theory and practice.

As far as the cognitive psychological basis for the realistic approach is concerned, chapter 10 is a key chapter in this book, because it describes the process of learning about teaching in terms of three stages: gestalt formation, schematization, and theory building. The fundamental idea behind this model is that much so-called immediate behavior takes place in an unconscious and unintentional way, but that professional learning implies reflection on the functioning of one's gestalts. The three-level model connects several notions about teacher behavior and teacher education into one coherent framework, and leads to tangible consequences for the work of teacher educators. As the model clarifies the discrepancy between the sources of immediate teaching behavior, on the one hand, and theory, on the other, it explains why the traditional technical-rationality approach in teacher education is not successful. The model also helps to develop an alternative pedagogy of teacher education based on the need to create suitable experiences as a starting point for learning.

In chapters 11 through 13, some practical issues related to the implementation of the realistic approach have been elaborated, such as techniques and instruments for promoting reflection. Theoretical support was gained from a more holistic view of reflection. The necessity of professional development programs for teacher educators has been discussed, and courses on supervision skills have been described.

Emphasis has been put on the *congruence principle*: Training courses for teacher educators aiming to help them to work in a realistic way should themselves be organized according to the principles of the realistic approach in order to be successful.

Realistic teacher education can be condensed into five basic tenets:

- Realistic teacher education starts from concrete practical problems and the concerns experienced by (student) teachers in real contexts.
- It aims at the promotion of systematic reflection of (student) teachers on their own and their students' wanting, feeling, thinking, and acting, on the role of context, and on the relations between those aspects.
- It builds on the personal interaction between the teacher educator and the (student) teacher and on the interaction among the (student) teachers.
- It takes the three levels of professional learning (gestalt, schema, and theory level) into account, as well as the consequences of the three-level model for the kind of theory that is offered (episteme vs, phronesis).
- It has a strongly integrated character. Two types of integration are involved: integration of theory and practice and integration of several disciplines.

14.3. WHAT'S NEW?

Having arrived at this point in the book, the reader may wonder what aspects of the realistic approach are really new. This question may come up because many characteristics of the approach seem to build on older foundations. For example, the whole idea of learning-by-doing is in fact an old one, as is the notion of gestalts, which goes back to early gestalt psychology (see, e.g., Köhler, 1947). In the places where I emphasized that these gestalts are linked to early experiences in life, one might even sense influences from a psychoanalytical perspective. The realistic approach also shows a strong emphasis on a holistic view of the individual development of the student teacher and the personal factors involved. This holistic view brings back memories of humanistic psychology (Maslow, 1971; Rogers, 1969) or its educational branch, confluent education (G. I. Brown, 1971). Humanistic psychologists included the development of the *self* as a central aspect of teacher education (see, e.g., Combs et al., 1974) and the realistic approach is in line with their view of the teacher as "a unique human being who has learned to use himself effectively and efficiently to carry out his own and society's purposes in the education of others" (Combs, 1965, p. 9). Even a behavioristic view comes to the fore where the rewarding of strong points is emphasized or the importance of skills training. Finally, more recent developments in learning psychology play an important role, such as the attention to the role of mental structures and the way in which these structures are grounded in the social contexts in which they developed (Cobb & Bowers, 1999).

Perhaps the fact that the realistic approach has its roots in many other important theoretical frameworks is precisely its most striking feature. What is new about realistic teacher education is that it represents a synthesis of those elements from a variety of theoretical frameworks that appear to be beneficial to practices in teacher education. One important aspect of the realistic approach is that it builds on a specific three-level model of professional learning, which has been described in chapter 10. Although at first sight it may seem unfamiliar, this framework too can be considered a synthesis of other, more well-known perspectives on learning.

Basic in the three-level model is the idea that much teacher behavior is guided by unconscious or only partly conscious gestalts and that professional learning involves the development of more awareness of and changes in these gestalts. This idea is certainly not completely new, but it builds on research on teachers' images, implicit theories, tacit knowledge, and so forth. It is also strongly connected to a view of knowledge as "situated" (J. S. Brown et al., 1989; Lave & Wenger, 1991). This view seems to represent a break with traditional perspectives characteristic of mainstream cognitive psychology, in which professional learning generally means the acquisition of theories about learning and teaching and the development of the capacity to apply these theories to practice. However, this more traditional view of learning also finds its place in the three-level model described in chapter 10. During the process of professional learning, the teacher may reflect on his or her gestalts and develop a conscious schema about a class of situations or even a theory that is logically consistent.

The connection between the gestalt view of knowledge as "situated" and the classical cognitive psychological view of knowledge can not only be found in the notion that conscious schemata and theories can develop from unconscious gestalts through reflection. In section 10.7, the principle of level reduction was discussed, which implies that schemata or theories can also develop into gestalts that, in a more unconscious way, guide teacher behavior. The level model can thus be considered as a synthesis of the perspective of situated learning, which views knowledge as embedded in contexts (Cobb & Bowers, 1999), and classical cognitive psychology, which views knowledge development as a process of abstraction from concrete situations. My point of view, elaborated in the three-level model, is that both views are valid, but which one best describes the process of learning about teaching or the kind of knowledge involved in this process depends on the stage the teacher is in.

In conclusion, both in its approach of teacher education and in its psychological foundations, this book presents a perspective that is not so much at odds with more traditional approaches, but a new synthesis of many helpful theories and practices developed in the past. However, by stating this conclusion in this way, the danger may be that the practical consequences for teacher educators of the realistic approach remain somewhat concealed. My experiences with teacher education staff in many different institutions show that they often have to pass through an intensive change process to become able to work in a realistic manner. Most teacher educators are used to and happy with one particular view of teacher development, either a behavioristic, a cognitive psychological, or yet another view. Over the years, they have developed their personal way of working and feel comfortable with it. For example, in the training courses for teacher educators described in chapter 13, we often witness supervisors of teaching practice telling student teachers as quickly as possible what they should improve on in their next lessons, generally in the most friendly wordings. It is not exceptional for teacher educators to explain to student teachers not to rely too much on explaining. As Russell (1999) puts it:

> The image of "teaching as telling" permeates every move we make as teachers, far more deeply than we would ever care to admit to others or ourselves.

We also come across lecturers who keep believing that even if there is no short-term effect of their lectures in teacher education, the theories they present will in the long run really influence practice. It can then be a giant step for such educators to work from basic principles such as listening to the perceptions of the student teacher, to really connect with his or her needs and concerns, to stimulate reflection within a safe atmosphere, and to a joint search for theory with a small t. As we apply these very same principles in our guidance of these teacher educators, the process of professional development necessary for the implementation of the realistic approach often takes time. I believe there is no shortcut to fundamental attitudinal change.

A final problem to mention is that, as soon as teacher educators start to change and become willing to adopt the realistic approach, they are confronted with institutional barriers that are sometimes hard to overcome. This is why we seldom give training courses for individual teacher educators from separate institutions, but instead try to involve the entire staff of departments of teacher education, often including deans or program coordinators.

14.4. THE MORAL BASIS OF THE REALISTIC APPROACH

So far, the presented justification for the realistic approach has been based mainly on psychological considerations, such as the characteristics of learning from practice, an analysis of the relation between teacher cognition and teacher behavior, and the effectiveness of certain techniques and instruments in terms of learning outcomes with student teachers. However, the choice to emphasize the promotion of reflection and to focus on the development of a growth competence is not only based on psychological considerations. The realistic approach is also rooted in a view of the goals of education that I want to discuss now. This discussion brings us into a field that in Europe is referred to as *pedagogy*, which literally means the domain dealing with the guiding of children. An important issue in this domain is the goal of preparing children to take responsibility for the position they will occupy in society. Many European educationalists have published about this and about the consequences for education, especially for the role of the teacher. In this section I will lean heavily on this European tradition. In a North American context, the term *pedagogy* has a different meaning, and in this situation it would be better to use the term *sociopedagogy* or to say that I will now describe my philosophy of education or the moral basis of the realistic approach.

Society and Education

The British educationalist Michael Barber is one of the many people who emphasize that our society is currently in a crisis. Barber (1997, pp. 15–17) states that the problems facing people across the globe are of a staggering magnitude. He mentions the sharp contrast to be found in most big cities between the luxury of economically successful people and the homeless people sleeping in shop doorways, the immense problem of war refugees and economic refugees from many different countries, the rapid population growth in the world's most poverty-stricken regions, the fact that some of the poorest societies on earth possess large stocks of the most effective instruments of destruction mankind has been able to devise, the bewildering changes caused by information technology, and environmental problems such as the holes in the ozone layer, and the destruction of rainforests. Barber states (p. 17):

> Taken together, these problems present a set of challenges more profound than any in human history.... This generation and its successors cannot pass the buck. It is their destiny to inherit a unique combination of unparalleled power and terrible responsibility.
>
> A well-balanced, thoughtful society would surely give the highest imaginable priority to ensuring that its young people were well-prepared for this awesome destiny. It would examine the upbringing and education provided for its young, and ask whether the arrangements were equal to the task.

In this respect small numbers can tell impressive stories:

> A black male child who was born in California in 1988 is three times more likely to be murdered as he is to be admitted to the University of California. (Zeichner, 1993, p. 213)

Barber also discusses the crisis in education, caused by the discrepancy between the global challenge and the progress in education, and by the moral state of affairs. I will consider both these issues next.

The Global Challenge

The first issue, the discrepancy between the global challenge and the progress in education, is a problem of both content and form. I agree with Barber that much of the content taught in schools is far removed from the realities of the actual problems of modern society. Moreover, in schools there is still a strong tendency to teach this content in traditional ways.

Preparing children for the responsibility of using knowledge for the benefit of society means helping them to become reflective thinkers, able to use subject matter in real situations, and confident that their actions can make a difference. This is what is meant by realistic education. In section 1.7, I started the discussion of the realistic approach in teacher education with the example of realistic mathematics education. I consider realistic mathematics education, as developed by the Freudenthal Institute, an impressive breakthrough in education. It stresses the ability to use mathematics in real situations, instead of the acquisition of isolated concepts. It focuses on the capacity of children to structure situations themselves and develop their own strategies for solving real problems arising from real contexts. As such, realistic mathematics education connects practice and theory. It implies a shift in both content (i.e., the kind of subject matter that is considered as relevant) and form (i.e., the subject matter changes from a created subject to a subject to be created). This leads to a fundamental change in the role of the teacher, who becomes more of a guide in a joint search process. Most importantly, this can completely change students' ideas of the role of scientific knowledge. They learn, or better they experience, that science does not provide us with the fixed answers to our problems, but that every new challenge we are faced with requires a process of reflection and creation. They can also experience that in the search process, the exchange of ideas and approaches between people is essential in order to finally arrive at an acceptable approximation of the nonexistent ideal solution.

Realistic mathematics education may be considered a model for other school subjects, and certainly not only for subjects like science. I believe the very same principles that I mentioned in the previous paragraph are also important in subjects like geography, history, the social sciences, and even native and foreign language teaching. We live in a world in which it is more urgent than ever that children learn to deal with many different challenges, ranging from environmental problems to problems of human communication, from confrontation with violence to engaging in contacts with humans from completely different backgrounds. Children should, in my view, be helped to take responsibility for the immense challenges we are faced with and be supported to take pride in fulfilling their roles in dealing with these challenges. This should influence all school subjects. Don't we need realistic science education, realistic geography education, realistic education in communication, and so forth?

This line of thinking has strong implications for teacher education. An old adage tells us that "teachers teach as they are taught and not as they are taught to teach" (Blume, 1971). If we wish education in schools to become more realistic and for students to become self-confident enough to take more responsibility for the world in which they live, then teacher educators must serve as a role model in the ways they work with student teachers. Where else could teachers learn to look at education differently and experience both the strengths and the problems of a realistic approach? Only if they themselves have struggled with problem-solving processes in which they knew no fixed solution existed can they develop the necessary empathy for children who feel uncertain when, instead of receiving cut-and-dried answers, they have to work out problems for themselves. Teacher educators can show future teachers how to build on the present state of development of students, how to create safety, how to promote reflection, how to stimulate peer interaction, how to develop a growth competence in students, and most of all, how to accept students as they are.

As T. Russell (1999, p. 234) puts it provocatively, in a discussion of the challenges of change in schools and universities:

> If genuine change is to occur in schools, then those changes may have to occur FIRST in teacher education. It is certainly not enough for teacher educators to advocate changes that they have not achieved in their own practices.

One of my main reasons for advocating the realistic approach in teacher education is that it may help to change education in schools. This is an example of the congruence principle: Teacher education should be congruent with the view of education that it aims to develop in teachers (Northfield & Gunstone, 1997, pp. 49, 54). As T. Russell (1997) puts it, reflecting on the way he teaches teachers: "How I teach IS the message." The congruence principle should also have consequences for the subject matter component of teacher education programs. As Tom (1997, p. 97) states:

> Among the many possible ways of conceiving of subject matter, the teacher education faculty must make its own view explicit and embed that view in professional instruction.

If we want to prepare future teachers for more realistic forms of education in schools, then we should teach them the subject matter in a realistic way. This is a great challenge, because in many institutions the responsibility for the subject matter component of teacher preparation does not lie with those responsible for teacher education. This is a problem at my own university, too. Moreover, attempts to influence the way subject matter is being taught at universities often fail, because there are no separate programs in university faculties for those going on to teacher education and others. Generally, students studying an academic discipline do not even know until the end of their studies whether or not they wish to enter teacher education.

A real integration of the professional component of teacher education and the subject matter component only seems to have a fairly good chance of success in institutions where the teaching of subject matter falls under the responsibility of teacher educators. This was, for example, the case in the SOL program described in section 6.5. In that section, I explained the existence of one coherent view of teacher preparation, guiding both the professional and the subject matter preparation of the student teachers. Still, in institutions where the professional preparation of teachers is more separated from the subject matter component, it is important to stimulate teacher education students to reexamine their subject matter courses. They may reflect on how they learned during these courses, on what helped and hindered them in how these courses were taught, on the significance of the content of these courses for school teaching, and so forth. Reflection on the differences between the educational approaches in the subject matter component and those in their professional preparation can be important to clarify the essence of the realistic approach. It is my experience that without such reflection, the impact of the congruence principle on students may be limited. Teacher educators should, in my view, deliberately reap the fruits of their consistent application of the realistic approach by making students aware of the pedagogical principles guiding the teacher education program they follow.

The Moral Basis of Education: Self-Understanding and Interconnectedness

I will now focus on the second problem put forward by Barber, namely, the moral state of affairs in education. Many people within education—faced with the problems of inner-city schools, the lack of motivation in students, and the changes in the norms and values students bring in, and most of all, recent examples of lethal violence within schools—point toward the need to pay more attention to the moral basis of education.

It is clear that in the Western world, we live in a complex and rapidly changing society, where for many people traditional bonds (e.g., those of family and church) have fallen away. If people not only want to survive in such a world, but also wish to create a meaningful life with a sense of contributing to the world, they have to stay in contact with their own personal *identity*. I believe that it is of paramount importance that they acquire a sense of *self-understanding* (Heschel, 1965) as a basis for developing their own unique potential, to direct themselves in realizing that potential and to relate to other people. For example, modern technology makes it easy to find information on the world wide web in a matter of seconds. It is important that children learn how to get access to this information and develop the necessary problem-solving skills. Most important, however, is the ability to keep in contact with the question of for what purpose one should gather this information, especially what the relationship is with one's own being and acting in the world.

For me, this means that the search for a moral basis in education should start with helping students to develop a sense of identity. As Buber (1983) helped us see, one's own identity is formed and experienced in meeting other people. Moreover, the encounters with other people help us realize that we are not merely individuals, but that our lives are connected with others, in fact that we could not survive without them. In other words, in the I–you relationship, self-understanding becomes possible, as well as the awareness of one's *interconnectedness* with other humans. My philosophy of education implies that it is a teacher's task to guide children in this essential aspect of life, the development of self-understanding and a sense of interconnectedness.

This can start very early, for example in kindergarten. Two children, fighting about the same toy, can be helped by an empathetic teacher to become more aware of their wish to play with the toy and of the fact that the other child has the same wish. Even at that age, they can be stimulated to find a solution satisfactory to both.

In many kindergarten classes, one can frequently see beautiful examples of teacher interventions successfully leading to such solutions, invented by the children themselves. The role of the teacher is crucial in this: A merely technical way of intervening is generally not adequate. The children must feel the personal commitment of the teacher, his or her personal expression of the conviction that people need to strive for a way of living in which they take care of each other. Also of crucial importance is empathetic understanding from the part of the teacher, which this teacher can only offer if sufficiently aware of the processes going on inside him or her when confronted with conflicting needs.

Such a pedagogical approach requires much more from a teacher than the mere teaching of norms and values. I believe that for a healthy society, a technical-rational model of "transmission of values" is insufficient. I follow Kohnstamm (1929), who stated that many durable learning experiences are rooted in the I–you relationship between teacher and student, in genuine personal encounters in which both are, within the here-and-now, in contact with their inner selves. The previous example illustrates what Kohnstamm means by this and illustrates that this view can also take shape in relatively simple situations. As Bullough and Gitlin (1994, p. 72) put it:

> Teaching is a relationship, a way of being with and relating to others, and not merely an expression of having mastered a set of delivery skills.

This view requires from teachers courage, enthusiasm, and commitment (to students and to their own values), but also a respectful way of communicating.[1] These requirements are not easy to fulfill in crowded classrooms, or with students from different cultural backgrounds. The reality will be that teachers and students will, in their encounters, also meet the limits inherent in their personalities and the conditions determined by the circumstances. For example, in a situation in kindergarten like the one described earlier, it will not always be possible to arrive at a solution acceptable to each child and the teacher. Still, through such experiences, awareness of values and norms is promoted and self-understanding and respect for the uniqueness of every human being can gradually grow, especially if conflicts as well as pleasant interpersonal experiences are regularly reflected on afterward. This points toward the fundamental role of reflection in developing moral consciousness in children.

Personal encounters not only bring teachers and students into contact with limits, values, and norms, but also create the necessity to look for new possibilities of cooperation, accepted by all the participants. This means that I am talking about a creative process, of course within the limits of the school context and society at large. Biesta (1995) stresses that in such encounters the strictly singular and idiosyncratic worlds of the participants undergo a transformation, pushed by the need to arrive at joint action (compare the kindergarten example). In this respect, Biesta follows the work of Dewey, who considered socialization, viewed as a permanent process, in terms of a continuous reconstruction of experience.

The view on the goals of education outlined in the previous paragraphs implies that reflection by teachers should also be aimed at the question of to what degree their own identity and the identity of each student are allowed to play a role in the educational encounter, and what this brings to both. For example, a student teacher confronted with a situation like that in the kindergarten example can be stimulated to reflect on the question of whether or not she is willing to show the children something of her personal norms and values and how she can help the children to develop their own. This means that an important aim of reflection by teachers should be the development of students' self-understanding, but also the development of these teachers' own self-understanding. This part of teachers' professional development has attracted little attention in the literature. As Gore and Zeichner (1991, p. 120) note,

> In some extreme cases, the impression is given that as long as teachers reflect about something, in some manner, whatever they decide to do is acceptable since they have reflected about it.

The view presented has strong implications for what we wish student teachers to reflect about:

> In order to be able to do all this, student teachers can learn a great deal about themselves. They must learn to reflect on their own personal characteristics, actions and identity. Being a teacher means that one is engaged in a very 'interactive' profession. Many student teachers experience teacher education as a social and emotional process that influences self-understanding quite dramatically. Teacher educators have the task of stimulating self-analysis and helping student teachers develop their own professional identity as a pre-requisite for pedagogical sensitivity. This is the awareness of and ability to reflect on the pedagogical aspects of teaching and learning situations and problems of interaction. (Korthagen, Klaassen, & T. Russell, 2000, p.251)

Or, as Bullough (1997, p. 21) states it:

> Teacher identity—what beginning teachers believe about teaching and learning and self-as-a-teacher—is of vital concern to teacher education; it is the basis for meaning making and decision making.... Teacher education must begin, then, by exploring the teaching self.

This points toward the need to have student teachers reflect on their life histories and the way these histories have shaped their beliefs and view of themselves as teachers (cf. Kelchtermans, 1993). Bullough (1997, p. 23) describes the assignment he gives to his student teachers:

> Write an "education-related" life history. In the life history describe how you came to your current decision to become a teacher. Especially identify important people or "critical incidents" that significantly influenced your decision and your thinking about the aims of education, the proper role of teachers, and about yourself as teacher. Con-

sider your "experience of school," how school felt, and how you best learned and when you felt most valued, connected, and at peace—or least valued, most disconnected and at war with yourself and with school.

Such a self-analysis alone is not enough: Teachers must also be able to use their personal identity in their teaching. In this book, in which both theory and practice get a place, I do not want to end this section without giving a concrete example of how we bring such ideas into practice in the 1-year postgraduate teacher education program at Utrecht University:

Near the end of this program we worked with a group of student teachers in a voluntary workshop of four afternoons, entitled "Did you encounter your students or yourself?" I gave this workshop together with a colleague.[2] In the announcement of this workshop, we indicated that we would like to work with student teachers who had the feeling that their practice teaching period confronted them with a personal struggle. That could vary from discipline problems to problems with their own motivation for the profession or other struggles. One of the first exercises we did in this workshop was as follows.

From their experiences during teaching practice, we asked the student teachers to choose two instances, one positive and one negative. The idea was to choose an example of a situation in which they felt fine, in which they had the idea: "yes, this is how I want to work!", and a situation that they disliked. We indicated that in the follow-up structure, they would work in pairs on analyzing the difference between these two contrasting experiences. We also clarified that they would not have to share these situations, but that they could keep them to themselves (and that this would even be better than sharing them, as that would deflect the attention from the aim of the exercise). In front of the group, we modeled the procedure to be followed in the pairs. My colleague had chosen two situations from her own recent experiences as a teacher educator and I helped her reflect on the difference between these situations, using interventions such as acceptance, concretizing, empathy and summarizing (see 7.6). These are interventions the student teachers had been trained in during the program, within the context of helping each other during teaching practice periods. We demonstrated that the result of our conversation was that, without making the situations explicit, my colleague could formulate what to her was the difference between the two experiences. It appeared that this difference had to do with the question whether or not she felt she could be herself in a group. The next step was that I helped her finish one or more of the following sentences:

I am a person who finds it important that

I am a person who needs to

I am a person who strives for

The aim of this part of the procedure is to formulate a personal value or goal, important in one's work as a teacher.

After the work on this exercise in the pairs, we asked each pair to try and situate the resulting value statements on one of the levels of "Bateson's model of logical levels"[3] (see Fig. 14.1).

Going upwards (and at the same time to the more inward layers of the personality), the questions are:

What do I come across? (environment)

What do I do? (behavior)

What am I able to do? (competencies)

What do I believe in? (convictions/beliefs)

Who am I? (identity)

To what purpose do I exist? What am I part of? (spiritual level, transpersonal level or level of interconnectedness)

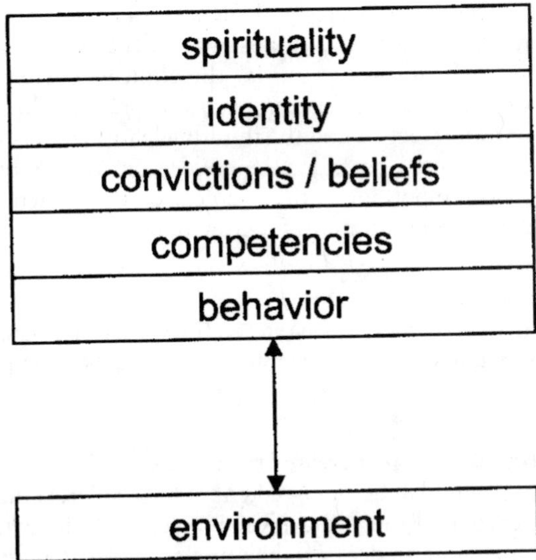

FIG. 14.1. Bateson's model.

> We explained that everyone has his or her own struggle in the profession and that the model is helpful in becoming aware of the level on which this struggle takes place. Connecting the sentences resulting from the first part of the exercise (one's value-statements) with the levels, helps to clarify this. It also shows how the levels influence each other. For example, one student's convictions ("it must be possible to teach without behaving as a police officer") appeared to determine the competencies this student teacher wished to develop. This in turn determined his behavior and thus the environment (his classes). In reverse order, the confrontation with an unmotivated class made a student teacher aware of the fact that she lacked the competency to use the kind of teaching behavior she would have liked to show, leading to a wish to develop that competency. This could possibly also lead to a change in her convictions. That, in turn, could stimulate to ask the question to what degree one can be oneself in teaching, and what that "self" stands for. Ultimately, starting from the confrontation with the environment, the process can proceed to the highest level, raising questions about one's professional calling or even one's purpose in life. In other words, it is precisely in difficult encounters with the environment, that opportunities for professional growth are concealed.
>
> This became clear when the student teachers, in pairs, analyzed the value-statements resulting from the first part of the exercise with the model, and through a follow-up discussion in the whole group. The student teachers reported that the exercise contributed to a better understanding of their own developmental process. They were often a bit surprised to realize that this process will in fact never stop, but that struggles and dilemmas will keep presenting themselves.

I believe that such exercises are fundamental sources of professional growth. Through such processes of personal professional reflection, teachers develop more self-understanding and a stronger basis for the choices they make, both in their classroom behavior and in their learning goals. Moreover, through the growing awareness of their own struggles and the resulting learning processes, they can develop more insight into the struggles the children in their schools experience.[4] What is perhaps most important, is that we noticed the student teachers start to frame their problems as opportunities for growth.[5]

As one of our student teachers put it:

> I think you learn to be a teacher by trial and error, and that stumbling is important in proceeding. Everything cannot go smoothly right from the beginning. It is not necessary to get into a kind of identity crisis as soon as you don't perform well.

Personally, I believe that an increased tolerance of problems, if grounded in personal experience, is a fundamental ingredient of a sound preparation for the pedagogical task of a teacher. Through the development of self-understanding, teachers develop a basis for guiding students in their process of developing self-understanding. This is necessary if in children we wish to stimulate a healthy development toward adulthood, and wish them to contribute to a world in which there is less violence, more understanding between people of diverse cultural backgrounds, and more willingness to take responsibility for the environment. The ideas discussed in this section may be an incentive to understand the term *realistic* (teacher) *education* also in the sense that it refers to the education of real human beings, having personal convictions, beliefs, feelings, needs and values, and a unique identity and calling. Moreover, realistic education tries to take into account the reality of the world in which we live.

14.5. LOOKING AHEAD

Finally, I want to look ahead toward the future of teacher education. What is to be expected from the realistic approach? Will it soon influence teacher education? To answer these questions, I will first look at teacher education practices, and second, I will discuss the role of research.

Teacher Education Practices

I cannot help thinking back to my own experiences in the 1970s, working at the SOL teacher education program in Holland, where the staff had developed strong ideas about the promotion of reflection, and succeeded in implanting these ideas into the curriculum. I published a book and many articles about this work based on the evaluative research studies summarized in chapter 6, only to discover later that teacher educators do not read much of the professional literature. This finding was also reported by Ducharme (1993). As Zeichner (1999, p. 12) puts it:

> It is ironic how unscholarly the process of teacher education reform has often been even in institutions that pride themselves on their scholarship and research.... There are only relatively few people who work in teacher education programs who actually read the research literature and think about it in relation to their own teacher education programs.

Of course, a major problem is that most teacher educators simply do not have the time to keep up with the enormous amount of publications in their field. As Ducharme (1993) also reports, they prefer to put their limited time into caring for their student teachers, a choice that I fully support.

However, at the end of the 1980s and in the early 1990s, the notion of the reflective teacher suddenly became popular and it was then that people started to become interested in our experiences with the promotion of reflection. I discovered that even then very few teacher educators read about such things. What did seem to work for them were the courses we started to give at the IVLOS Institute of Education at Utrecht University. These courses attracted many teacher educators. Gradually, the emphasis shifted toward institution-based training courses that we gave on site. Through that work, our experiences and the principles of the realistic approach became more known in the Netherlands and at other institutions elsewhere.

I believe that all this is not so much the result of the quality of our work, but more of the fact that our ideas matched a popular trend. The same story is true for many other developments in education. I am afraid it is not only the quality of the work of innovators and researchers that makes the difference for educational developments, but also the coming and going of trends and hypes.

Thus, the question of whether or not the realistic approach will really influence teacher education in the future mainly depends on the degree to which there will be a more general interest among teacher educators in the idea of integrating theory and practice. There are many indications that this interest is growing. The pressure in many countries toward more school-based programs is a sign that not only teachers, but also parents and politicians are dissatisfied with the traditional approaches in teacher education (Ashton, 1996; Barone et al., 1996, pp. 1108–1109). In Great Britain, for example, a major part of preservice teacher education has now become the responsibility of the schools, creating a situation in which (to a large degree) teacher education takes the form of on the job training. The argument for this practice points out that traditional teacher education programs fail in preparing prospective teachers for the realities of the classroom (Goodlad, 1990).

Many teacher educators think that a professional teacher should acquire more than just practical tools for managing classroom situations and that it is their job to present student teachers with a broader view on education and to offer them a proper grounding in psychology, sociology, and so on. This is what Clandinin (1995) calls "the sacred theory-practice story" (see also section 1.2): teacher education conceived as the translation of theory on good teaching into practice. The resulting type of discussion is dangerous because it focuses on the question of whether teacher education should start with theory or practice instead of how to integrate the two within the teacher. If we do not address this more fundamental question, then it is uncertain whether institutions for teacher education may survive in the future.

On the other hand, we should not close our eyes to the fact that more realistic approaches in teacher education ask a lot from individual teacher educators and from institutional structures. I think the realistic approach will only gain ground if there is a willingness among those responsible for teacher preparation to accept that traditional teacher education has lost its legitimacy in a society where change is the central notion. What is needed is a general commitment to Barber's view that education is faced with an immense responsibility. This may lead to a willingness to invest in curriculum development in teacher education, in close connection with staff development programs. Such a willingness should also be expected from the very same politicians who criticize the present state of affairs. Program chairs should create the climate necessary for staff development in teacher education, bearing in mind Sarason's (1996) view that teachers cannot create and sustain contexts for productive learning unless those conditions exist for them. A couple of principles, important in creating supportive conditions for staff development in teacher education, are summarized in section 13.6.

Even if all requirements are met for a sound developmental process within institutions for teacher education, we should not expect this process to proceed rapidly. One of the requirements is to provide room for trying new arrangements and interventions, to reflect on the results, to change the arrangements or interventions a little, and so forth. Such a process of ongoing development should be a joint effort of closely cooperating teacher educators who regularly discuss their ideas and stay in contact with teachers in the schools and with school administrators. I wish to emphasize that such a development toward a realistic program in my own university has taken more than a decade. As T. Russell (1999) warns us:

> It is far too easy to propose early changes that fail to give the innovation a clear chance.

The Role of Research

Earlier, I showed a slight disappointment about the lack of influence of research reports that could offer a basis for development. However, this does not imply that I think research is not important. It certainly is, in at least three respects. First, if teacher educators finally start to become interested in a new approach, they then pose the question of whether there is any proof of the value of that approach. We must be ready to provide them with such proof. Second, I have learned that the most important side effects of my research on teacher education and that of my colleagues has been that one starts to better understand where the holes are in one's framework, and where the problems are when implementing a new approach. Finally, the most important contribution of research is that it saves you from staying with views based more on beliefs than on reality.

I have also learned that this requires a type of research that is closely connected to practice, and carried out from an *insider perspective* (cf. G. L. Anderson & Herr, 1999). To ensure relevance to our teacher education program, research studies in my own university are often conducted by teams in which researchers and teacher educators work together or by people who are experienced in both fields. Different from traditional forms of research in which the relation between two or more variables is assessed in a quantitative way, much of our research tries to grasp the learning processes of student teachers and the influences on these processes of certain characteristics of the educational arrangements in our program. At first it was not easy to publish this kind of research, as many other teacher educators with an eye for the practical relevance of their research have experienced:

> In their practices, teacher educators often went through a paradigm shift by conquering the sacred theory-practice story and developing views in which knowledge was considered much more context-bound, personal and dynamic. In their research work, however, teacher educators had to show that they believed in traditional views of knowledge growth. A failure to live with this split-personality syndrome was, and still is, punished by expulsion from academia—tenure positions generally open only to staff members with a sufficiently long list of publications in the field's traditional journals, which generally support the old research paradigm. Moreover, the academic world has other means to safeguard its dominant paradigms: publications that are re-

> garded as out of the mainstream are often just not cited by the veterans in teacher education. (Korthagen & T. Russell, 1995, pp. 188–189)

At the 1993 annual meeting of the American Educational Research Association (AERA), a first sign of a breakthrough was visible when more than a few teacher educators were presenting reflective accounts and narratives about their own work in teacher education. What made this development striking was that among these presenters were some well-known teacher educators and researchers. This was also the AERA meeting at which a new special interest group was founded consisting of people interested in reflection on and action research into their own practice in teacher education. The group, called Self-Study of Teacher Education Practices (S-STEP), was in full operation at the 1994 AERA meeting and saw a rapid growth to more than 200 members from all over the world. By now, it is one of the largest groups in AERA. Every 2 years, the special interest group has a conference in the United Kingdom[6] and its research is increasingly appearing in well-reputed academic journals. Zeichner (1999, p. 11) concludes:

> Contrary to the frequent image of the writings of teacher educators in the wider educational research community as shallow, under-theorized, self-promotional, and inconsequential, much of this work has provided a deep and critical look at practices and structures in teacher education. This work can both inform the practices of the teacher educators who conduct it and contribute to knowledge and understanding of teacher education for the larger community of scholars and educators.

Perhaps the term *realistic research* can be introduced. It can be an incentive to more explicitly formulate its own specific goals and methodological foundations. Realistic research on teacher education is research grounded in the real practice of teaching teachers, taking into account the real people involved—the students and teacher educators. As indicated in section 6.6, the teacher education community can benefit from studies describing what is really happening in programs all over the world. Such studies should link program goals with careful analyses of the behavior of teacher educators or cooperative teachers, and effects on student teachers' learning processes, with special attention for the contextual influences of practicum schools. The columns technique described in section 9.4 could be a helpful framework in designing such studies (see Fig. 9.3) if applied to the level of the teacher educator's work: What are the program goals; how are these translated into a specific program component; what is the concrete thinking, feeling, and behavior of the teacher educator or cooperative teacher in that component; and what is happening at the level of the student teachers (i.e., What are the effects on their thinking, feeling, wanting, and doing)? It is my experience that such approaches to research can reveal issues one would never have thought of before and that are fundamental to the improvement of teacher education. It also makes one more realistic in setting program goals or designing future developments within teacher education institutes or departments.

A real integration between theory and practice is also possible in research: We need not separate fundamental theoretical research from applied research. I agree with Schoenfeld (1999, p. 14) that

> it is possible and desirable to think of research and applications in education as synergistic rather than as points at opposite ends of a spectrum, or as discrete phases of a "research leads to applications" model. We can choose to explore theoretical issues in contexts that really matter; and, when we work on important problems we can try to frame them so that our work helps us make progress on fundamental issues.

To me it is clear that not everything written by teacher educators about their own practices is of equal value to others, either from a practical perspective or from a scholarly point of view. If we want to further develop the realistic approach to teacher education as a means to improve all education, we must not only put more effort into improving the practical work of teacher educators, but we will also have to invest in the quality of our research on teacher education. And finally, we must connect these two pillars for educational development. In this respect, I hope that this book has suggested some valuable and inspirational directions.

SUMMARY

This final chapter started with a summary of the book. In brief, the following are the basic tenets of the realistic approach:

1. Realistic teacher education starts from concrete practical problems and the concerns experienced by (student) teachers in real contexts.
2. It aims at the promotion of systematic reflection of (student) teachers on their own and their students' wanting, feeling, thinking, and acting, on the role of context, and on the relationships between those aspects.
3. It builds on the personal interaction between the teacher educator and the (student) teacher and on the interaction among the (student) teachers.
4. It takes the three levels of professional learning (gestalt, schema, and theory level) into account, as well as the consequences of the three-level model for the kind of theory that is offered (episteme vs. phronesis).
5. It has a strongly integrated character. Two types of integration are involved: integration of theory and practice and integration of several disciplines.

The realistic approach builds on older, well-known foundations and approaches, but offers a new synthesis that does not concur with most common practices in teacher education. The realistic approach to teacher education is also rooted in a philosophy that emphasizes the need to come to terms with the immense problems and challenges of our world and the wish to make education in schools more realistic. The term *realistic* can also be understood in the sense that it aims at taking the unique identity of each individual (real) person into account. Part of the underlying view of education is the need to help children develop their self-understanding and a sense of interconnectedness. As a consequence, these aspects need to be developed in teachers, thus supporting them to use personal encounters and the I–you relationship for stimulating moral consciousness and personal growth in students in school.

Finally, a look into the past and the future clarified that the realistic approach can only gain ground if there is a general commitment to the immense responsibility of education and the goal of linking practice and theory in teacher education. Staff development in teacher education is a basic prerequisite. Realistic research into the practices of teacher educators and long-term effects on teachers, from an insider perspective, can help to facilitate this development.

BASIC CONCEPTS

The global challenge
Realistic education in schools
(Teacher) identity
Self-understanding
Interconnectedness
The I–you relationship
Moral consciousness
Realistic research

NOTES

Chapter 1

1. This is a question Willis Copeland from the University of California in Santa Barbara posed to me in 1990. It appeared to be a very helpful question stimulating me to further develop my thinking about reflection.

Chapter 2

1. This chapter is a revision of an article published in the *Educational Researcher* 25(3), 17–22.
2. For instance, Wubbels and Levy (1993) describe a model for interpersonal behavior in the classroom, offering concrete guidelines for teachers.
3. An excellent introduction to Plato is Irwin (1995).
4. Here we follow Jonsen and Toulmin (1988, pp. 65ff), stressing the Aristotelian conception of knowledge. For a summary of the Platonic conception, see Irwin (1995, chap. 16). The distinction between episteme and phronesis is paralleled in Russell's well-known distinction between knowledge by description and knowledge by acquaintance (B. Russell, 1912, chaps. 5 & 13).
5. Marton and Booth (1997) arrive at a similar view. They, too, strongly emphasize the role of perception and awareness in learning and state that after the intended learning process "the learner has become capable of discerning aspects of the phenomenon other than those she had been capable of discerning before" (p. 142). In previous work, Marton, Dahlgren, Svensson, and Saljö (1977, p. 23) referred to this kind of learning as "a change in the eyes through which we see the world." Marton and Booth (1997, p. 142) add that, through the changed awareness of the phenomenon, the relation between the person and the phenomenon has changed.

Chapter 3

1. For this section, we thankfully made use of texts by Cor Koetsier describing the IVLOS program.
2. In fact, we describe one of the programs, because now there is also an inservice program that is rather different in nature and a special bilingual, international program.

3. I would like to mention my colleague Louis Galesloot, who developed this approach, also with an eye on developments in Dutch secondary education, where high school students are stimulated to take more responsibility for their own learning.
4. The process of learning how to reflect, for instance, is started on the basis of the learning processes during group seminars at the beginning of the preparation program (see chap. 11 for details).
5. We will use the words *supervision* and *mentoring* as synonyms. For us, they refer to activities of cooperating teachers, clinical faculty, mentors, or university professors to help student teachers or novice teachers to learn from their experiences. They do not refer to evaluation for licensing or graduation or to activities to guarantee the quality of the (student) teacher's teaching.
6. Use of cases in teacher education has been advocated as a way to integrate insights from different disciplines to apply to practical teaching problems (Shulman, 1992). This can also be an example of an inductive approach: Student teachers' thinking about practical problems can be taken as a starting point for theoretical input. Cases can, however, also be used in a deductive approach when student teachers are asked to apply their knowledge from disciplinary classes to practical problems presented in cases.
7. At Utrecht University, much attention is paid to the development of adequate interpersonal behavior, based on the work of Créton and Wubbels (1984). See, for an extensive description in English, Wubbels and Levy (1993).

Chapter 4

1. As we noted earlier, Miller, Galanter, and Pribram use the word *image* to refer to such a mental structure. In chapter 10, we will look more closely at the nature of mental structures and refine the confusing terminology in this field. There we will formulate a coherent theory in which the different types of mental structures find their place.

Chapter 5

1. This chapter is strongly based on the work of many of my colleagues at the IVLOS Institute of Education, and informal and formal documents on the IVLOS teacher education program. I used parts of a description of the IVLOS program previously published in Koetsier, Wubbels, and Korthagen (1997).
2. The consequences described in this section are, to a large degree, taken from Wubbels, Korthagen, and Brekelmans (1997).

3. In order to help them bear this responsibility, we organize meetings of cooperating teachers under the guidance of a teacher educator in order to clarify the criteria for assessment of student teaching and to discuss worries and questions of cooperating teachers concerning this part of their task.

Chapter 7

1. This does not imply that this independent learning is the ideal situation to be strived for in education. The availability of a skilled supervisor—for example, for beginning teachers and for teachers who suffer from burn-out—can greatly enhance the quality of teachers' work, as well as their job satisfaction. Moreover, intensive contacts between colleagues and forms of structured *peer-supported learning* (see section 9.6) are essential to the way teachers function in their profession. However, the capacity for independent learning is always important and complements these forms of learning under supervision or together with colleagues.
2. In the next chapter, we will be more precise with regard to the question of in which respect a reflective teacher may be considered to be a better teacher.
3. In fact, we should say: to meta-reflect on, as it is reflection on one's way of learning by reflection that we aim for here.
4. The distinction between the different dimensions can, of course, never be made strictly; it will always be a matter of more emphasis on a particular dimension.
5. In terms of chapter 4, the thought behind that is that the student teacher's relevant delta-one systems must come into action and potential failings can become clear. (Those failings can relate to knowledge, skills, and/or attitudes.)
6. Sometimes supervisors decide right away that the learning process should begin with the simplest situation. They are convinced that the learning process will then proceed more efficiently. However, the opposite is often true, because a student teacher may not be enabled to discover any real problems.
7. In terms of chapter 4, the student teacher should dare to risk changing existing director systems.
8. Rogers uses the terms *genuineness* and *realness* interchangeably.
9. Compare the concepts of internal and external feedback discussed in section 4.8. When I am helping a student teacher, these considerations motivate me to not only mirror the student teacher's feelings, but also his or her thoughts, opinions, and behavior. However, I do hold the

opinion that the helper should emphasize "giving back" feelings: I regard feelings as signals from director systems (chap. 4) and it is exactly the awareness of those feelings that can stimulate the individual to correct him- or herself.

10. Thus, the supervisor must try to find suitable occasions to discuss the learning process with the student teacher and try to build on positive learning experiences. This is the translation of the Phase 1 skill of "giving help in finding useful experiences" to the level of learning to learn. The other skills discussed in this chapter can be applied to this level in the same way. For example, *acceptance* of the student's specific learning orientation, the expression of *empathy* for the student's struggles during the learning process, and so on, are all important for stimulating a process of learning to learn.
    For a more theoretical analysis of the relations between the levels of action, learning, and learning to learn, I refer to De Jong, Korthagen, and Wubbels (1998).

Chapter 8

1. We thank Petra van de Broek, Rob Houwen, and Hildelien Verkuyl for their contributions to this chapter.
2. From other research it is known which scales of the QTI are positively related to cognitive and affective learning outcomes (see Wubbels & Levy, 1993). By adding the scores on these scales, they were combined into one measure on which we compared the two groups.

Chapter 9

1. Large parts of this section have been derived from a Dutch publication (Wubbels, Korthagen, & Tigchelaar, 1999). The portions of text describing the discourse are based on literal transcripts of tapes recorded during the session. Thanks go to Thom Somers, who made the transcripts. The text has been abridged and transposed from spoken to written language, while retaining the meaning of the contents. Where portions of text have been deleted, this is indicated by " ... ".
2. After two such sessions, the student teachers were asked to write down for themselves what they had learned, and which points they thought they should give particular attention to during such talks. The session was concluded with a number of short practice talks in which the guest teacher educator took the role of a high school student. In each role play, he tried to create a specific learning experience for each individual student teacher by first playing the student's role in such a way that the student teacher was confronted with his or her own problem or learn-

ing issue, and then providing coaching to help the teacher to find the appropriate behavior.

3. The wall is based on an idea of Hans Pouw of the Dutch APS Institute.
4. Kelly made use of this fact in developing the repertory grid technique as a research method designed to describe people's subjective perceptions of their environment. He showed that people have no trouble scoring others on the basis of the constructs they have formulated themselves, as opposed to those offered to them by others (e.g., a researcher). Using this same principle, at the end of the exercise the student teachers can score all students from the class under consideration on a 5-point scale for each of the constructs from their personal list. The resulting matrix illustrates the role of the personal constructs in the student teachers' perception of the students.
5. To get an idea of how this training in supervision skills is being carried out, see chapter 13, where a training course for teacher educators is described. In the training of student teachers preparing them for peer-supported learning, we use similar procedures and structures. We also makes this congruence explicit to student teachers. That also makes them more aware of the way their teacher educators and cooperating teachers supervise them.

Chapter 10

1. One of the most interesting aspects of the Van Hiele theory was that it contradicted the classical interpretation of Piaget's theory, which assumes the existence of general stages of cognitive development that are directly related to age. One consequence of Van Hiele's theory is that the stages (known as levels) are not so much age dependent as domain specific. In this respect, the Van Hiele theory was neo-Piagetian before the term even existed.
2. Van Hiele (1986, pp. 229–230) indicated that the level model could also be used in the fields of psychology and pedagogy. However, until now, the work of Van Hiele has received little attention outside the field of mathematics education.
3. The term *subjective theory* is more common in Europe, whereas in North America the term *implicit theory* is widely used (Carter, 1990). However, the latter term has a connotation of "tacit knowledge," which seems to refer to what we call gestalts. That is why we prefer the term *subjective theory*.
4. Compare the three pedagogical principles presented in section 5.4. Lauriala (1998, p. 61) states that "authentic experiences in new, deviating classroom contexts may challenge teachers' cognitions and lead to changes in them."

5. The one-to-one arrangement has been the object of intensive study. See Vedder and Bannink (1987).

Chapter 11

1. Gipe and Richards (1992) note that—at least at that time—there was no reported research that examines prospective teachers' reflective thoughts in relation to improvement in teaching.
2. In any case, it is important that students themselves should decide which situations they want to reflect on. People learn the most from situations in which they are personally involved, and that occupy them. A prime aspect of learning from one's work as a teacher is the ability to step back and observe one's own feelings of irritation, impatience, happiness, and so forth, to take them seriously and to use them as an occasion for reflection.
3. In section 6.5, research findings were presented showing a decline in teachers' reflection during their first period in the teaching profession.
4. My thanks go to Paul Hennissen for providing this case.
5. These drawings are made by Jan van Tartwijk and published in Wubbels (1992a).

Chapter 14

1. I believe *respect* is a keyword: Respect for others and their needs, as well as respect for one's own identity and needs, is in my view the foundation of a healthy society and a necessary requirement for classroom or school environments supporting learning and development. The notion of respect refers to a thoughtful, accepting way of caring for what is present in the encounter between human beings, and a willingness to critically examine and adjust one's own prejudices, in contrast to a preoccupation with the wish to change the other.
2. This is Hildelien Verkuyl, who has contributed much to the ideas described in this chapter.
3. Especially in the literature of neuro-linguistic programming (NLP) this model is referred to as Bateson's model (e.g., in Dilts, 1990), although Gregory Bateson (1904–1980) never formulated this model in this way, not even in the publications by Bateson often referred to.
4. This reminds me of Jung's principle of the *wounded healer* (Read, Fordham, & Adler, 1966, para. 239; Sharp, 1998, pp. 104–107).

5. In this context, I explained to them that the Chinese represent crisis with two pictographs—one meaning "danger," the other "opportunity" (Rosen, 1996).
6. For a collection of contributions to this conference, see Hamilton (1998).

References

Abdal-Haqq, I. (1997). *Professional development schools: weighing the evidence.* Washington, DC: American Association of Colleges for Teacher Education.

Admiraal, W. F., Lockhorst, D., Wubbels, T., Korthagen, F.A.J., & Veen, W. (1998). Computer-mediated communication environments in teacher education: Computer conferencing and the supervision of student teachers. *Learning Environments Research, 1,* 59–74.

Allender, J. A. (1982). Fourth grade fantasy. *Journal of Humanistic Education,* 6, 37–38.

Anderson, G. L., & Herr, K. (1999). The new paradigm wars: Is there room for rigorous practitioner knowledge in schools and universities? *Educational Researcher, 28*(5), 12–21, 40.

Anderson, J. R. (1980). *Cognitive psychology and its implications.* San Francisco: Freeman.

Argyris, C., & Schön, D. A. (1974). *Theory in practice: Increasing professional effectiveness.* New York: Jossey-Bass.

Ashton, P. (1996). Improving the preparation of teachers. *Educational Researcher, 25*(9), 21–22, 35.

Ashton, P., Comas, J., & Ross, D. (1989, March). *Examining the relationship between perceptions of efficacy and reflection.* Paper presented at the annual meeting of the American Educational Research Association, San Francisco.

Bain, J. D., Ballantyne, R., Packer, J., & Mills, C. (1999). Using journal writing to enhance student teachers' reflectivity during field experience placements. *Teachers and Teaching: Theory and Practice,* 5(1), 51–73.

Bandura, A. (1978). *Social learning theory.* Englewood Cliffs, NJ: Prentice Hall.

Bandura, A. (1982). Self-efficacy mechanism in human agency. *American Psychologist, 33,* 344–358.

Barber, M. (1997). *The learning game: Arguments for an educational revolution.* London: Indigo/Cassell.

Barlow, H. (1990). What does the brain see? How does it understand? In H. Barlow, C. Blakemore, & M. Weston-Smith (Eds.), *Images and understanding* (pp. 5–25). Cambridge, England: Cambridge University Press.

Barone, T., Berliner, D. C., Blanchard, J., Casanova, U., & McGowan, T. (1996). A future for teacher education. In J. Siluka (Ed.), *Handbook of research on teacher education* (2nd ed., pp. 1108–1149). New York: Macmillan.

Bateson, G., & Jackson, D. D. (1964). Some varieties of pathogenic organization. *Research Publications of the Association for Research in Nervous and Mental Disease,* 42, 270–283.

Beckman, D. R. (1957). Student teachers learn by doing action research. *Journal of Teacher Education,* 8(4), 369–375.

Bell, B., & Gilbert, J. (1996). *Teacher development: A model from science education.* London: Falmer Press.

Bennett, N., & Carré, C. (1993). *Learning to teach.* London: Routledge.

Ben-Peretz, M. (1995). Curriculum of teacher education programs. In L. W. Anderson (Ed.), *International encyclopedia of teaching and teacher education* (pp. 543–547). Oxford: Elsevier-Science/Pergamon.

Berlak, H., & Berlak, A. (1981). *Dilemmas of schooling.* London: Methuen.

Berliner, D. C. (1986). In pursuit of the expert pedagogue. *Educational Researcher, 15*(7), 5–13.

Berliner, D. C. (1987). Ways of thinking about students and classrooms by more and less experienced teachers. In J. Calderhead (Ed.), *Exploring teachers' thinking* (pp. 60–83). London: Cassell.

Berry, D. C., & Dienes, Z. (1993). *Implicit learning, theoretical and empirical issues.* Hillsdale, NJ: Lawrence Erlbaum Associates.

Biesta, G. (1995). Pragmatism as a pedagogy of communicative action. *Studies in Philosophy and Education, 13,* 273–290.

Blume, R. (1971). Humanizing teacher education. *Phi Delta Kappan,* 53, 411–415.

Bogen, J. E. (1969). The other side of the brain: II. An appositional mind. *Bulletin of the Los Angeles Neurological Society, 34,* 135–162.

Bogen, J. E. (1973). The other side of the brain: An appositional mind. In R.E. Ornstein (Ed.), *The nature of human consciousness* (pp. 101–125). San Francisco: Freeman.

Bonarius, H., Holland, R., & Rosenberg, S. (Eds.). (1981). *Personal construct psychology: recent advances in theory and practice.* London: Macmillan.

Borko, H., & Putnam, R. T. (1996). Learning to teach. In D. C. Berliner & R. C. Calfee (Eds.), *Handbook of educational psychology* (pp. 673–708). New York: Macmillan.

Borrowman, M. L. (1965). Liberal education and the professional education of teachers. In M. L. Borrowman (Ed.), *Teacher education in America: A documentary history* (pp. 1–53). New York: Teacher's College Press.

Boud, D., Keogh, R., & Walker, D. (Eds.). (1985). *Reflection: Turning experience into learning.* London: Kogan Page.

Brammer, L. M. (1973). *The helping relationship: Process and skills.* Englewood Cliffs, NJ: Prentice-Hall.

Brekelmans, J.M.G. (1989). *Interpersoonlijk gedrag van docenten in de klas* [Interpersonal teacher behavior in the classroom]. Utrecht: WCC.

Britzman, D. (1986). Cultural myths in the making of a teacher: Biography and social structure in teacher education. *Harvard Educational Review,* 56(4), 442–456.

Brouwer, C. N. (1989). *Geïntegreerde lerarenopleiding, principes en effecten* [Integrative teacher education, principles and effects]. Amsterdam: Brouwer.

Brown, A. L., Campione, J. C., & Day, J. D. (1981). Learning to learn: On training students to learn from texts. *Educational Researcher, 10*(2), 14–21.

Brown, G. I. (1971). *Human teaching for human learning: An introduction to confluent education.* New York: Viking.

Brown, J. S., Collins, A., & Duguid, P. (1989). Situated cognition and the culture of learning. *Educational Researcher, 18*(1), 32–42.

Bruner, J. S. (1960). *The process of education.* Cambridge, MA: Harvard University Press.

Bruner, J. S. (1964). The course of cognitive growth. *American Psychologist, 19,* 1–5.

Bryden, M. P. (1982). *Laterality: Functional asymmetry in the intact brain.* New York: Academic Press.

Buber, M. (1983). *Ich und Du* [I and you]. Heidelberg: Schneider.

Bullough, R. V. (1997). Practicing theory and theorizing practice in teacher education. In J. Loughran & T. Russell (Eds.), *Purpose, passion and pedagogy in teacher education* (pp. 13–31). London: Falmer Press.

Bullough, R. V., & Gitlin, A. D. (1994). Challenging teacher education as training: Four propositions. *Journal of Education for Teaching, 20*(1), 67–81.

Bullough, R. V., Hobbs, S. F., Kauchak, D. P., Crow, N. A., & Stokes, D. (1997). Long-term PDS development in research universities and the clinicalization of teacher education. *Teaching and Teacher Education, 7*(5–6), 531–535.

Bullough, R. V., & Kauchak, D. (1997). Partnerships between higher education and secondary schools: Some problems. *Journal of Education for Teaching, 23*(3), 215–233.

Bullough, R.V.J. (1989). *First year teacher: A case study*. New York: Teacher's College Press.

Bullough, R.V.J., Knowles, J. G., & Crow, N. A. (1991). *Emerging as a teacher.* London: Routledge.

Burden, P. (1990). Teacher development. In W. R. Houston (Ed.), *Handbook of research on teacher education* (pp. 311–328). New York: Macmillan.

Calderhead, J. (1988). Introduction. In J. Calderhead (Ed.), *Teachers' professional learning* (pp. 1–11). Philadelphia: Falmer Press.

Calderhead, J. (1989). Reflective teaching and teacher education. *Teaching and Teacher Education*, 5, 43–51.

Calderhead, J. (1991). The nature and growth of knowledge in student teaching. *Teaching and Teacher Education, 7*(5–6), 531–535.

Calderhead, J., & Gates, P. (1993). *Conceptualizing reflection in teacher development.* London: Falmer Press.

Calderhead, J., & Robson, M. (1991). Images of teaching: Student teachers' early conceptions of classroom practice. *Teaching and Teacher Education, 7*(1), 1–8.

Cantor, N. (1972). *Dynamics of learning.* Mannheim: Agathon Press.

Carkhuff, R. R. (1969a). *Helping & human relations* (Vol. 1). New York: Holt, Rinehart & Winston.

Carkhuff, R. R. (1969b). *Helping & human relations* (Vol. 2). New York: Holt, Rinehart & Winston.

Carlson, H. L. (1999). From practice to theory: A social constructivist approach to teacher education. *Teachers and Teaching: Theory and Practice, 5*(2), 203–218.

Carr, W., & Kemmis, S. (1986). *Becoming critical: Education, knowledge and action research.* London: Falmer Press.

Carter, K. (1990). Teachers' knowledge and learning to teach. In W. R. Houston (Ed.), *Handbook of research on teacher education* (pp. 291–310). New York: Macmillan.

Carter, K., Cushing, K., Sabers, D., Stein, P., & Berliner, D. (1988). Expert–novice differences in perceiving and processing visual classroom information. *Journal of Teacher Education, 39*(3), 25–31.

Carter, K., & Doyle, W. (1996). Narrative and life history in learning to teach. In J. Sikula (Ed.), *Handbook of research on teacher education* (2nd ed., pp. 120–142). New York: Macmillan.

Castle, J. B. (1997). Toward understanding professional development: Exploring views across a professional development school. *Teachers and Teaching: Theory and Practice, 3*(2), 221–242.

Chadbourne, R. (1997). Teacher education in Australia: What difference does a new government make? *Journal of Education for Teaching, 23*(1), 7–27.

Clandinin, D. J. (1985). Personal practical knowledge: A study of teachers' classroom images. *Curriculum Inquiry, 15*(4), 361–385.

Clandinin, D. J. (1995). Still learning to teach. In T. Russell & F. Korthagen (Eds.), *Teachers who teach teachers* (pp. 25–31). London: Falmer Press.

Clark, C. M. (1986). Ten years of conceptual development in research on teacher thinking. In M. Ben-Peretz, R. Bromme, & R. Halkes (Eds.), *Advances of research on teacher thinking* (pp. 7–20). Lisse: Swets & Zeitlinger.

Clark, C. M., & Lampert, M. (1985, April). *What knowledge is of most worth to teachers? Insights from studies of teacher thinking.* Paper presented at the annual meeting of the American Educational Research Association, Chicago.

Clark, C. M., & Yinger, R. J. (1979). Teachers' thinking. In P. L. Peterson & H. J. Walberg (Eds.), *Research on teaching: Concepts, findings and implications* (pp. 231–263). Berkeley, CA: McCutchan.

Cloetta, B., & Hedinger, U. K. (1981). *Die Berufssituation junger Lehrer* [The professional situation of beginning teachers]. Bern: Haupt.

Cobb, P. & Bowers, J. (1999). Cognitive and situated learning perspectives in theory and practice. *Educational Researcher, 28*(2), 4–15

Cogan, M. L. (1973). *Clinical supervision,* Boston: Houghton Mifflin.

Cole, A. L. (1988, April). *Personal knowing in spontaneous teaching practice.* Paper presented at the annual meeting of the American Educational Research Association, New Orleans.

Cole, A. L. (1997). Impediments to reflective practice. *Teachers and Teaching: Theory and Practice, 3*(1), 7–27.

Cole, A. L., & Knowles, J. G. (1993). Teacher development partnership research: A focus on methods and issues. *American Educational Research Journal, 30*(3), 473–495.

Combs, A. W. (1965). *The professional education of teachers: A perceptual view of teacher preparation.* Boston: Allyn & Bacon.

Combs, A. W., Blume, R. A., Newman, A. J., & Wass, H. L. (1974). *The professional education of teachers: A humanistic approach to teacher preparation.* Boston: Allyn & Bacon.

Connelly, F. M., & Clandinin, D. J. (1984). Personal practical knowledge at Bay Street School: Ritual, personal philosophy and image. In R. Halkes & J. H. Olson (Eds.), *Teachers thinking: A new perspective on persisting problems in education* (pp. 134–148). Lisse: Swets & Zeitlinger.

Connelly, F. M., & Clandinin, D. J. (1985). Personal practical knowledge and the modes of knowing: Relevance for teaching and learning. In E. Eisner (Ed.), *Learning and teaching the ways of knowing, 84th yearbook of the National Society for the Study of Education, part II* (pp. 174–198). Chicago: University of Chicago Press.

Copeland, W. D., Birmingham, C., DeMeulle, L., D'Emidio-Caston, M., & Natal, D. (1994). Making meaning in classrooms: An investigation of cognitive processes in aspiring teachers, experienced teachers, and their peers. *American Educational Research Journal, 31*(1), 166–196.

Corcoran, E. (1981). Transition shock: The beginning teacher's paradox. *Journal of Teacher Education, 32*(3), 19–23.

Corey, S. (1953). *Action research to improve school practices.* New York: Teacher's College Press.

Cornbleth, C., & Ellsworth, J. (1994). Teachers in teacher education: Clinical faculty roles and relationships. *American Educational Research Journal, 31*(1), 49–70.

Corporaal, B. (1988). *Bouwstenen voor een opleidingsdidactiek* [Building blocks for a pedagogy of teacher education]. De Lier: Academisch Boeken Centrum.

Créton, H. A., & Wubbels, T. (1984). *Ordeproblemen bij beginnende leraren* [Discipline problems of beginning teachers]. Utrecht: WCC.

Créton, H. A., Wubbels, T., & Hooymayers, H. P. (1989). Escalated disorderly situations in the classroom and the improvement of these situations. *Teaching and Teacher Education, 5*(3), 205–215.

Crow, N. (1987, April). *Preservice teacher's biography: A case study*. Paper presented at the annual meeting of the American Educational Research Association, New Orleans.

Cruickshank, D. R., Holton, J., Fay, D., Williams, J., Kennedy, J., Myers, B., & Hough, J. (1981). *Reflective teaching*. Bloomington, IN: Phi Delta Kappa.

Csikszentmikalyi, M. (1991). *Flow: The psychology of optimal experience*. New York: Harper Perennial.

Damasio, A. R. (1994). *Descartes' error: Emotion, reason and the human brain*. New York: Grosset Putman.

Dann, H. D., Cloetta, B., Müller-Fohrbrodt, G., & Helmreich, R. (1978). *Umweltbedingungen innovativer Kompetenz* [Contextual conditions of innovation competence]. Stuttgart: Klett-Cotta.

Dann, H. D., Müller-Forhbrodt, G., & Cloetta, B. (1981). Sozialization junger Lehrer im Beruf. Praxisschock drei Jahre später [Professional socialization of young teachers. The transition shock three years later]. *Zeitschrift für Entwicklungspsychologie und Pädagogische Psychologie, 13*, 251–262.

Darling-Hammond, L. (1994). *Professional development schools: Schools for developing a profession*. New York: Teacher's College Press.

Day, C. (1984). Teachers' thinking—intentions and practice: An action research perspective. In R. Halkes & J. K. Olson (Eds.), *Teacher thinking, a new perspective on persisting problems in education* (pp. 134–148). Lisse: Swets & Zeitlinger.

Day, C. (1999). *Developing teachers: The challenges of lifelong learning*. London: Falmer Press.

De Bruin, B., & Vulker, N. (1984). *Counselingstraining: Theorie en methodiek voor hulpverlening en begeleiding* [Counseling training: Theory and methods for helping and supervision]. Baarn: Nelissen.

De Jong, J., Korthagen, F., & Wubbels, T. (1998). Learning from practice in teacher education. *Teachers and Teaching: Theory and Practice, 4*(1), 47–64.

Denis, M. (1991). *Image & cognition*. Herefordshire: Harvester Wheatsheaf.

Dennett, D. C. (1991). *Consciousness explained*. Boston: Little, Brown.

Desforges, C. (1995). How does experience affect theoretical knowledge for teaching? *Learning and Instruction, 5*, 385–400.

Desforges, C., & McNamara, D. (1979). Theory and practice: Methodological procedures for the objectification of craft knowledge. *British Journal of Teacher Education, 5*(2), 139–152.

Dewey, J. (1910). *How we think*. Boston: Heath.

Dewey, J. (1933). *How we think: A restatement of the relation of reflective thinking to the educative process*. Boston: Heath.

Dilts, R. (1990). *Changing belief systems with NLP.* Cupertino: Meta Publications.

Dirkx, J. M. (1989, March). *Self-reflection in the clinical experience: Using group processes to improve practitioner–client relationships*. Paper presented at the annual meeting of the American Educational Research Association, San Francisco.

Dolk, M. (1997). *Onmiddellijk onderwijsgedrag: Over denken en handelen van leraren in onmiddellijke onderwijssituaties* [Immediate teaching behavior: On teacher knowledge and behavior in immediate teaching situations]. Utrecht: WCC.

Dolk, M., Korthagen, F.A.J., & Wubbels, T. (1995, August). *What makes teachers teach the way they teach? Instruments to investigate aspects of teachers' gestalts.* Paper presented at the 6th European Conference for Research on Learning and Instruction (EARLI), Nijmegen.

Donaldson, G. A., & Marnik, G. F. (1995). *Becoming better leaders: The challenge of improving student learning.* Thousand Oaks, CA: Corwin Press.

Doyle, W. (1979). Making managerial decisions in classrooms. In D. L. Duke (Ed.), *Classroom management* (pp. 42–74). Chicago: University of Chicago Press.

Doyle, W. (1990). Themes in teacher education research. In W. R. Houston (Ed.), *Handbook of research on teacher education* (pp. 392–431). New York: Macmillan.

Ducharme, E. R. (1993). *The lives of teacher educators.* New York: Teacher's College Press.

Duffy, T. M., & Jonassen, D. H. (Eds.). (1992). *Constructivism and the technology of instruction: A conversation.* Hillsdale, NJ: Lawrence Erlbaum Associates.

Eccles, J. (1985). Self-perceptions, task perceptions, socializing influences, and the decision to enroll in mathematics. In S. F. Chipman, L. R. Brush, & D. M. Wilson (Eds.), *Women and mathematics: Balancing the equation* (pp. 95–121). Hillsdale, NJ: Lawrence Erlbaum Associates.

Edelman, G. M. (1987). *Neural Darwinism: The theory of neuronal group selection.* New York: Basic Books.

Egan, G. (1975). *The skilled helper: A model for systematic helping and interpersonal relating.* Pacific Grove, CA: Brooks/Cole.

Eisner, E. (1985a). Aesthetic modes of knowing. In E. Eisner (Ed.), *Learning and teaching the ways of knowing* (pp. 23–36). Chicago: University of Chicago Press.

Eisner, E. (1985b). *The art of educational evaluation.* London: Falmer Press.

Eisner, E. W. (1979). *The educational imagination.* New York: Macmillan.

Elbaz, F. (1983). *Teacher thinking: A study of practical knowledge.* New York: Nichols.

Elbaz, F. (1991). Research on teachers' knowledge: The evolution of a discourse. *Journal of Curriculum Studies, 23*(1), 1–19.

Elliot, J. (1978). What is action research in schools? *Journal of Curriculum Studies, 10*(4), 355–357.

Elliot, J. (1991). *Action research for educational change.* Buckingham: Open University Press.

Ellis, W. D. (1950). *A source book of gestalt psychology.* New York: Humanities Press.

Epstein, S. (1994). Integration of the cognitive and the psychodynamic unconscious. *American Psychologist,* 49(8), 709–724.

Eraut, M. (1994). *Developing professional knowledge and competence.* London: Falmer Press.

Eraut, M. (1995). Schön shock: A case for reframing reflection-in-action? *Teachers and Teaching: Theory and Practice, 1*(1), 9–22.

Erkamp, A. (1981). *Ervaringsleren* [Experiential learning]. Amersfoort: De Horstink.

Feiman, S. (1979). Technique and inquiry in teacher education: A curricular case study. *Curriculum Inquiry,* 9, 63–79.

Feiman-Nemser, S. (1983). Learning to teach. In L. Shulman & G. Sykes (Eds.), *Handbook of teaching and policy* (pp. 150–170). New York: Longman.

Feiman-Nemser, S., & Buchman, M. (1986). Pitfalls of experience in teacher preparation. In J. D. Raths & L. G. Katz (Eds.), *Advances in teacher education* (Vol. 2, pp. 61–67). Norwood, NJ: Ablex.

Feiman-Nemser, S., & Floden, R. (1986). The cultures of teaching. In M. Wittrock (Ed.), *Handbook of research on teaching* (pp. 505–526). New York: Macmillan.

Fenstermacher, G. D. (1994). The knower and the known: The nature of knowledge in research on teaching. *Review of Research in Education, 20*, 3–56.

Fischer, K. W., & Bullock, D. (1984). Cognitive development in school-aged children: Conclusions and directions. In W. A. Collins (Ed.), *Development during middle childhood: The years from six to twelve* (pp. 70–146). Washington, DC: National Academy Press.

Fiske, S. T., & Taylor, S. E. (1984). *Social cognition*. New York: Random House.

Flaherty, J. F., & Dusek, J. B. (1980). An investigation of the relationship between psychological androgyny and components of self-concept. *Journal of Personality and Social Psychology, 39*, 921–929.

Fosnot, C. T. (1996). *Constructivism: Theory, perspectives, and practice*. New York: Teacher's College Press.

Freudenthal, H. (1978). *Weeding and sowing: Preface to a science of mathematical education*. Dordrecht: Reidel.

Freudenthal, H. (1991). *Revisiting mathematics education*. Dordrecht: Kluwer.

Fullan, M. (1991). *The new meaning of educational change*. London: Cassell.

Fullan, M. (1998). The meaning of educational change: A quarter of a century of learning. In A. Hargreaves, A. Lieberman, M. Fullan, & D. Hopkins (Eds.), *International handbook of educational change* (pp. 242–260). Dordrecht: Kluwer.

Fullan, M., & Hargreaves, A. (1992). *Teacher development and educational change*. London: Falmer.

Fuller, F. (1969). Concerns of teachers: A developmental conceptualization. *American Educational Research Journal*, 6(2), 207–226.

Fuller, F. F., & Bown, O. H. (1975). Becoming a teacher. In K. Ryan (Ed.), *Teacher education, the 74th yearbook of the National Society for the Study of Education* (pp. 25–52). Chicago: University of Chicago Press.

Furlong, J., Whitty, G., Whiting, C., Miles, S., Barton, L., & Barrett, E. (1996). Re-defining partnership: Revolution or reform in initial teacher education? *Journal of Education for Teaching, 22*(1), 39–55.

Gazzaniga, M. S. (1970). *The bisected brain*. New York: Appleton-Century-Crofts.

Gazzaniga, M. S. (1999). *The mind's past*. Los Angeles: University of California Press.

Gibbons, M., & Philips, G. (1979). Teaching for self-evaluation: Promising new professional role. *Journal of Teacher Education, 30*(5), 26–28.

Gibbs, G. (1983). Changing students approached to study through classroom exercises. In R. M. Smith (Ed.), *Helping adults how to learn* (pp. 83–96). San Francisco: Jossey Bass.

Giddens, A. (1984). *The constitution of society*. Cambridge, England: Polity Press.

Gilroy, P., Price, C., Stones, E., & Thornton, M. (1994). Teacher education in Britain: A JET symposium with politicians. *Journal of Education for Teaching, 20*(3), 261–300.

Ginsburg, M. (1988). *Contradictions in teacher education and society: A critical analysis*. New York: Falmer Press.

Ginsburg, M. B., & Clift, R. T. (1990). The hidden curriculum of preservice teacher education. In W. R. Houston (Ed.), *Handbook of research on teacher education* (pp. 450–465). New York: Macmillan.

Gipe, J. P., & Richards, J. C. (1992). Reflective thinking and growth in novices' teaching abilities. *Journal of Educational Research, 86*(1), 52–57.

Goodlad, J. I. (1990). *Places where teachers are taught.* San Francisco: Jossey-Bass.

Goodman, J. (1985, April). *Making early field experience meaningful: An alternative approach.* Paper presented at the American Educational Research Association, Chicago, IL.

Gore, J. M. (1987). Reflecting on reflective teaching. *Journal of Teacher Education, 38*(2), 33–39.

Gore, J. M., & Zeichner, K. M. (1991). Action research and reflective teaching in preservice teacher education: A case study from the United States. *Teaching and Teacher Education, 7*(2), 119–136.

Graber, K. C. (1996). Influencing students beliefs: The design of a "high impact" teacher education program. *Teaching and Teacher Education, 12*(5), 451–466.

Grimmett, P. P. (1988). The nature of reflection and Schön's conception in perspective. In P. P. Grimmett & G. L. Erickson (Eds.), *Reflection in teacher education* (pp. 5–15). Vancouver: Pacific Educational Press/Teacher's College Press.

Groeben, N. (1981). Die Handlungsperspective als Theorierahmen für Forschung im pädagogogischen Feld [The action perspective as a theoretical framework for research in the pedagogical domain]. In M. Hofer (Ed.), *Informationsverarbeitung und Entscheidungsverhalten von Lehrern* [Information processing and decision behavior] (pp. 17–49). München: Urban und Schwartzenberg.

Groeben, N., & Scheele, B. (1977). *Argumente für eine Psychologie des reflexiven Subjekts* [Arguments for a psychology of the reflective subject]. Darmstadt: Steinkopff.

Grundy, S. (1987). *Curriculum: Product or praxis?* London: Falmer Press.

Guilfoyle, K., Hamilton, M. L., Pinnegar, S., & Placier, M. (1995). Becoming teachers of teachers: The paths of four beginners. In T. Russell & F. Korthagen (Eds.), *Teachers who teach teachers, reflections on teacher education* (pp. 35–55). London: Falmer Press.

Haan, P. H. (1975). Supervisie als leermiddel in de scholing van supervisoren [Supervision as a learning aid in the education of supervisors]. In F.M.J. Siegers, P. M. Haan, & A.M.P. Knoers (Eds.), *Supervisie 1, Theorie en begrippen* [Supervision 1: Theory and concepts] (pp. 249–275). Alphen a/d Rijn, The Netherlands: Samsom.

Habermas, J. (1973). *Knowledge and human interests.* London: Heinemann.

Halkes, R., & Olson, J. K. (1984). Introduction. In R. Halkes & J. K. Olson (Eds.), *Teacher thinking: A new perspective on persisting problems in education* (pp. 1–6). Lisse: Swets & Zeitlinger.

Hamilton, M. L. (Ed.). (1998). *Reconceptualizing teaching practice: Self-study in teacher education.* London: Falmer Press.

Hargreaves, A. (1994). *Changing teachers, changing times: Teachers' work and culture in the postmodern age.* Toronto: OISE Press.

Hargreaves, A. (1998a). The emotional practice of teaching. *Teaching and Teacher Education, 14*(8), 835–854.

Hargreaves, A. (1998b). The emotions of teaching and educational change. In A. Hargreaves, A. Lieberman, M. Fullan, & D. Hopkins (Eds.), *International handbook of educational change* (pp. 558–575). Dordrecht: Kluwer.

Harrington, H. L., Quin-Leering, K., & Hodson, L. (1996). Written case analyses and critical reflection. *Teaching and Teacher Education, 12*(1), 25–37.

Harvard, G. R. (1994). An integrated model of how student teachers learn how to teach, and its implications for mentors. In G. Harvard & P. Hodkinson, *Action and reflection in teacher education* (pp. 125–157). Norwood, NJ: Ablex.

Hatton, N., & Smith, D. (1995). Reflection in teacher education: Towards definition and implementation. *Teaching and Teacher Education, 11*(1), 33–49.

Hawkey, K. (1995). Learning from peers: The experience of student teachers in school-based teacher education. *Journal of Teacher Education,* 46(3), 175–183.

Hermans, J. J., Créton, H. A., & Korthagen, F. A. J. (1993). Reducing the gap between theory and practice in teacher education. In J. T. Voorbach (Ed.), *Teacher Education 9, Research and developments on teacher education in the Netherlands* (pp. 111–120). De Lier: Academisch Boeken Centrum.

Heschel, A. J. (1965). *Who is man?* Stanford, CA: Stanford University Press.

Hewson, P. W., & Hewson, M. G. (1989). Analysis and use of a task for identifying conceptions of teaching science. *Journal of Education for Teaching, 15*, 191–209.

Hewson, P. W., Zeichner, K. M., Tabachnick, B. R., Blomker, K. B., & Toolin, R. (1992, April). *A conceptual change approach to science teacher education at the University of Wisconsin-Madison.* Paper presented at the annual meeting of the American Education Research Association, San Francisco.

Hilgard, E. R., Atkinson, R. C., & Atkinson, R. L. (1975). *Introduction to psychology.* New York: Harcourt Brace.

Hinsch, R. (1979). *Einstellungswandel und Praxisschock bei jungen Lehrern, eine empirsche Längsschnittuntersuchung* [Attitudinal change and transition shock in beginning teachers, an empirical longitudinal study]. Weinheim: Beltz.

Hollingworth, S. (1989). Prior beliefs and cognitive change in learning to teach. *American Educational Research Journal, 26*, 160–169.

Holmes, M. (1998). Change and tradition in education: The loss of community. In A. Hargreaves, A. Lieberman, M. Fulland, & D. Hopkins (Eds.), *International handbook of educational change* (pp. 558–575). Dordrecht: Kluwer.

Hoy, W., & Rees, R. (1977). The bureaucratic socialization of student teachers. *Journal of Teacher Education, 28*(1), 23–26.

Hoy, W. H., & Woolfolk, A. E. (1989). Supervising student teachers. In A. E. Woolfolk (Ed.), *Research perspectives on the graduate preparation of teachers* (pp. 108–131). Englewood Cliffs, NJ: Prentice-Hall.

Hoyle, E. (1980). Professionalization and deprofessionalization in education. In E. Hoyle & J. Megarry (Eds.), *World yearbook of education 1980: Professional development of teachers* (pp. 42–56). London: Kogan Page.

Hoyle, E., & John, P. D. (1995). *Professional knowledge and professional practice.* London: Cassell.

Huibregtse, I., Korthagen, F., & Wubbels, T. (1994). Physics teachers' conceptions of learning, teaching and professional development. *International Journal of Science Education, 16*(5), 539–561.

Hunt, D. E. (1987). *Beginning with ourselves: Practice, theory and human affairs.* Toronto: OISE Press.

Imig, D. G., & Switzer, T. J. (1996). Changing teacher education programs. In J. Sikula (Ed.), *Handbook of research on teacher education* (2nd ed., pp. 213–226). New York: Macmillan.

Irwin, T. (1995). *Plato's ethics.* New York: Oxford University Press.

Jamieson, I. (1994). Experimental learning in the context of teacher education. In G. Harvard & P. Hodkinson, *Action and reflection in teacher education* (pp 35–54). Norwood, NJ: Ablex.

Johnson, M. (1987). *The body in the mind.* Chicago: University of Chicago Press.

Jonsen, A. R., & Toulmin, S. (1988). *The abuse of casuistry: A history of moral reasoning.* Berkeley, CA: University of California Press.

Joyce, B. R. (1975). Conceptions of man and their implications for teacher education. In K. Ryan (Ed.), *Teacher education, 74th yearbook of the National Society for the Study of Education* (pp. 111–145). Chicago: University of Chicago Press.

Katz, L. G. (1972). Developmental stage of preschool teachers. *Elementary School Journal, 73*(1), 50–54.

Kaufmann, G. (1985). A theory of symbolic representation in problem solving. *Journal of Mental Imagery,* 9, 51–69.

Kelchtermans, G. (1993). Getting the story and understanding the lives: From career stories to teachers' professional development. *Teaching and Teacher Education,* 9, 443–456.

Kelly, G. A. (1955). *The psychology of personal constructs, vols. 1 & 2.* New York: Norton.

Kemmis, S., & McTaggart, R. (1981). *The action research planner.* Victoria: Deakin University.

Kennedy, M. M. (1990). Choosing a goal for professional education. In W. R. Houston (Ed.), *Handbook of research on teacher education* (pp. 813–857). New York: Macmillan.

Kilgore, K., Zbikowski, J., & Ross, D. (1989, March). *Changes in teachers' perspectives about teaching: From preservice to inservice.* Paper presented at the annual meeting of the American Educational Research Association, San Francisco.

Kinchleoe, J. L. (1990). *Teachers as researchers: Qualitative inquiry as a path to empowerment.* London: Falmer Press.

Kjersdam, F., & Enemark, S. (1994). *The Aalborg experiment: Project innovation in university education.* Aalborg, Denmark: Aalborg University Press.

Knowles, J. G. (1988, April). *Models for understanding preservice and beginning teachers' biographies: illustrations from case studies.* Paper presented at the annual meeting of the American Educational Research Association, New Orleans.

Knowles, J. G. (1991). Shaping pedagogies through personal histories in preservice teacher education. *Teachers College Record, 93*(1), 87–113.

Knowles, M. (1975). *Self-directed learning: A guide for learners and teachers.* Englewood Cliffs, NJ: Prentice-Hall.

Koetsier, C. P., & Wubbels, T. (1995). Bridging the gap between teacher training and teacher induction. *Journal of Education for Teaching, 21*(3), 333–345.

Koetsier, C. P., Wubbels, T., & Korthagen, F.A.J. (1997). Learning from practice: The case of a Dutch post-graduate teacher education programme. In M. I. Fuller & A. J. Rosie (Eds.), *Teacher education and school partnerships* (pp. 113–132). New York: Edwin Mellen Press.

Koetsier, C. P., Wubbels, T., & Van Driel, C. (1992). An investigation into careful supervision of student teaching. In J.H.C. Vonk, J.H.G.I. Giesbers, J. J. Peters, & T. Wubbels (Eds.), *New prospects for teacher education in Europe II* (pp. 245–254). Amsterdam/Utrecht: Vrije Universiteit/WCC.

Köhler, W. (1947). *Gestalt psychology.* New York: Liveright.

Kohnstamm, P. A. (1929). *De psychiater als opvoeder* [The psychiatrist as a pedagogue]. Mededeelingen van het Nutsseminarium voor Paedagogiek aan de Universiteit van Amsterdam, 6 [Booklet].

Kolb, D. A., & Fry, R. (1975). Towards an applied theory of experiential learning. In C. L. Cooper (Ed.), *Theories of group processes* (pp. 33–58). New York: Wiley.

Korb, M. P., Gorrell, J., & Van de Riet, V. (1989). *Gestalt therapy, practice and theory* (2nd ed.). New York: Pergamon Press.

Korthagen, F.A.J. (1982). *Leren reflecteren als basis van de lerarenopleiding* [Learning how to reflect as a basis for teacher education]. 's-Gravenhage: Stichting voor Onderzoek van het Onderwijs.

Korthagen, F.A.J. (1985). Reflective teaching and preservice teacher education in the Netherlands. *Journal of Teacher Education,* 9(3), 317–326.

Korthagen, F.A.J. (1988). The influence of learning orientations on the development of reflective teaching. In J. Calderhead (Ed.), *Teachers' professional learning* (pp. 35–50). London: Falmer Press.

Korthagen, F.A.J. (1992). Techniques for stimulating reflection in teacher education seminars. *Teaching and Teacher Education,* 8(3), 265–274.

Korthagen, F.A.J. (1993a). Measuring the reflective attitude of prospective mathematics teachers in the Netherlands. *European Journal of Teacher Education,* 16(3), 225–236.

Korthagen, F.A.J. (1993b). The role of reflection in teachers' professional development. In L. Kremer-Hayon, H. C. Vonk, & R. Fessler (Eds.), *Teacher professional development: A multiple perspective approach* (pp. 133–145). Lisse: Swets & Zeitlinger.

Korthagen, F.A.J. (1993c). Two modes of reflection. *Teaching and Teacher Education,* 9(3), 317–326.

Korthagen, F.A.J., & Kessels, J.P.A.M. (1999). Linking theory and practice: Changing the pedagogy of teacher education. *Educational Researcher,* 28(4), 4–17.

Korthagen, F.A.J., Klaassen, C., & Russell, T. (2000). New learning in teacher education. In R.J. Simons, J. van der Linden, & T. Duffy (Eds.), *New learning* (pp. 243–259). Dordrecht: Kluwers Academic.

Korthagen, F.A.J., & Russell, T. (1995). Teacher who teach teachers: Some final considerations. In T. Russell & F. Korthagen (Eds.), *Teachers who teach teachers* (pp. 187–192). London: Falmer Press.

Korthagen, F.A.J., & Verkuyl, H. S. (1987, April). *Supply and demand: towards differentiation in teacher education, based on differences in learning orientations.* Paper presented at the annual meeting of the American Educational Research Association, Washington, DC.

Korthagen, F.A.J., & Wubbels, T. (1995). Characteristics of reflective practitioners: Towards an operationalization of the concept of reflection. *Teachers and Teaching: Theory and Practice,* 1(1), 51–72.

Koskela, R. (1985). *A search for reflective thought in the student teaching seminar: A case study.* Madison, WI: University of Wisconsin Press.

Kosslyn, S. A., Van Kleeck, M. H., & Kirby, K. N. (1990). A neurological plausible model of individual difference in visual mental imagery. In P. J. Hampson, D. F. Marks, & J.T.E. Richardson (Eds.), *Imagery: Current development* (pp. 39–77). London: Routledge.

Koster, B., & Dengerink, J. (2000, February). *Towards a professional standard for Dutch teacher educators.* Paper presented at the ATE conference, Orlando, FL.

Koster, B., Korthagen, F.A.J., & Schrijnemakers, H. G. M. (1995). Between entry and exit: How student teachers change their educational values under the influence of teacher education. In F. Buffet & J. A. Tschoumy (Eds.), *Choc démocratique et formation des enseignants en Europe* [Democratic shock and the education of students in Europe] (pp. 156–168). Lyon: Presses Universitaires de Lyon.

Kremer-Hayon, L., & Zuzovsky, R. (1995). Themes, processes and trends in the professional development of teacher educators. In T. Russell & F. Korthagen (Eds.), *Teachers who teach teachers: Reflections on teacher education* (pp. 155–171). London: Falmer Press.

Krogh, S., & Crews, R. (1989, March). *Do guidelines help students demonstrate reflective ability?* Paper presented at the annual meeting of the American Educational Research Association, San Francisco.

Kubler LaBoskey, V. (1997). Teaching to teach with purpose and passion: Pedagogy for reflective practice. In J. Loughran & T. Russell (Eds.), *Purpose, passion and pedagogy in teacher education* (pp. 150–163). London: Falmer Press.

Kubovy, M., & Pomerantz, J. R. (Eds.). (1981). *Perceptual organization.* Hillsdale, NJ: Lawrence Erlbaum Associates.

Kuhn, T. S. (1977). *The essential tension: Selected studies in scientific tradition and change.* Chicago: University of Chicago Press.

LaBoskey, V. K. (1990, April). *Reflectivity in preservice teachers: Alert novices vs. commonsense thinkers.* Paper presented at the annual meeting of the American Educational Research Association, Boston.

Lacey, C. (1977). *The socialization of teachers.* London: Methuen.

Lacey, C. (1985). Professional socialization of teachers. In T. Husén & T. N. Postlethwaite (Eds.), *The international encyclopedia of education* (pp. 6122–6127). Oxford, England: Pergamon.

Lakoff, G., & Johnson, M. (1980). *Metaphors we live by.* Chicago: University of Chicago Press

Lasley, T. J. (1980). Preservice teacher beliefs about teaching. *Journal of Teacher Education, 31*, 38–41.

Lauriala, A. (1998). Reformative in-service education for teachers (RINSET) as a collaborative action and learning enterprise: Experiences from a Finnish context. *Teaching and Teacher Education, 14*(1), 53–66.

Lave, J., & Wenger, E. (1991). *Situated learning: Legitimate peripheral participation.* Cambridge, England: Cambridge University Press.

Lawson, D. I., & Lawson, A. E. (1993). Neural principles of memory and a neural theory of analogical insight. *Journal of Research in Science Teaching, 30*, 1327–1348.

Levine, M., & Trachtman, R. (1997). *Making professional development schools work: Politics, practices, and policy.* New York: Teacher's College Press.

Levy-Agresti, J., & Sperry, R. W. (1968). Differential perceptual capacities in major and minor hemispheres. *Proceedings of the National Academy of Sciences of the U.S. of America, 61*, 11–51.

Lewin, K. (1947a). Group decision and social change. In T. Newcomb & E. Hartley (Eds.), *Readings in social psychology* (pp. 330–344). New York: Henry Holt.

Lewin, K. (1947b). Frontiers in group dynamics: II. Channels of group life: Social planning and action research. *Human Relations, 2*, 142–153.

Lieberman, A. (1998). The growth of educational change as a field of study: Understanding its roots and branches. In A. Hargreaves, A. Lieberman, M. Fullan, & D. Hopkins (Eds.), *International handbook of educational change* (pp. 13–20). Dordrecht: Kluwer.

Liston, D. P., & Zeichner, K. M. (1989, March). *Action research and reflective teaching in preservice teacher education.* Paper presented at the annual meeting of the American Educational Research Association, San Francisco.

Little, J. W. (1982). Norms of collegiality and experimentation: Conditions of school success. *American Educational Research Journal, 19*(3), 325–346.

Lortie, S. (1975). *Schoolteacher: A sociological study.* Chicago: University of Chicago Press.

Loska, R. (1995). *Lehren ohne Belehrung: Leonard Nelsons neosokratische Methode der Gesprächsfürung* [Learning without indoctrination: Leonard Nelson's neo-socratic conversation method]. Bad Heilbronn: Klinkhardt.

Louden, W. (1991). *Understanding teaching: Continuity and change in teachers' knowledge.* New York: Teacher's College Press.

Loughran, J. (1997). An introduction to purpose, passion and pedagogy. In J. Loughran & T. Russell (Eds.), *Purpose, passion and pedagogy in teacher education* (pp. 3–9). London: Falmer Press.

Lucas, P. (1996). Coming to terms with reflection. *Teachers and Teaching: Theory and Practice, 2*(1), 23–40.

Luijten, M.C.G., Marinus, J. E., & Bal, J. M. (1995). *Wie gaat er in het onderwijs werken?* [Who is going to work in education?] Leiden, The Netherlands: Research voor Beleid.

Maccoby, E. E., & Jacklin, C. N. (1975). *The psychology of sex differences.* London: Oxford University Press.

Magoon, A. J. (1977). Constructivist approaches in educational research. *Review of Educational Research, 47*, 651–693.

Mandl, H., & Huber, G. L. (1983). Subjektive Theorien von Lehrern [Teachers' subjective theories]. *Psychologie in Erziehung und Unterricht, 30*, 98–112.

Marshall, H. H. (1988). Work or learning, implications of classroom metaphors. *Educational Researcher, 17*(11), 9–16.

Marton, F., & Booth, S. (1997). *Learning and awareness.* Mahwah, NJ: Lawrence Erlbaum Associates.

Marton, F., Dahlgren, L. O., Svensson, L., & Saljö, R. (1977). *Inlärning och omvärldsuppfattning* [Learning and conceptions of reality]. Stockholm: Almqvist & Wiksell.

Maslow, A. H. (1968). *Towards a psychology of being* (2nd ed.). New York: Harper & Row.

Maslow, A. H. (1971). *The further reaches of human nature.* New York: Pinguin.

Mayer, R. E. (1981). *The promise of cognitive psychology.* San Francisco: Freeman.

McCombs, B. L. (1988). Motivation skills training: Combining metacognitive, cognitive and affective learning strategies. In C. E. Weinstein, E. T. Goets, & P. A. Alexander (Eds.), *Learning and study strategies, issues in assessment, instruction and evaluation* (pp. 141–169). San Diego: Academic Press.

McCullough, R. C. (1987). Professional development. In R. L. Craig (Ed.), *Training & development handbook* (pp. 35–65). New York: McGraw-Hill.

McEvoy, B. (1986, April). *She is still with me: Influences of former teachers on teacher practice.* Paper presented at the annual meeting of the American Educational Research Association, San Francisco.

McIntyre, D. (1995). Initial teacher education as practical theorizing: A response to Paul Hirst. *British Journal of Educational Studies, 43*(4), 365–383.

McInyre, D., & Hagger, H. (1992). Professional development through the Oxford Internship Model. *British Journal of Educational Studies, 40*(3), 264–283.

McKernan, J. (1991). *Curriculum action research: A handbook of methods and resources for the reflective practitioner.* London: Kogan Page.

McLaughlin, M. (1998). Listening and learning form the field: Tales of policy implementation and situated practice. In A. Hargreaves, A. Lieberman, M. Fullan, & D. Hopkins (Eds.), *International handbook of educational change* (pp. 70–84). Dordrecht: Kluwer.

Miller, G. A., Galanter, E., & Pribram, K. H. (1960). *Plans and the structure of behaviour.* New York: Holt, Rinehart & Winston.

Miller, J. B. (1976). *Toward a new psychology of women.* Boston, MA: Beacon Press.

Milner, B. (Ed.). (1989). Memory: Dedicated in memoriam to professor O.L. Zangwill (1913–1987). Theme issue of *Neuropsychologia, 27*(1).

Müller-Fohrbrodt, G., Cloetta, B., & Dann, H. D. (1978). *Der Praxisschock bei jungen Lehrern* [The transition shock in beginning teachers]. Stuttgart: Klett.

Munby, H. (1984). A qualitative approach to the study of a teacher's beliefs. *Journal of Research in Science Teaching, 21*(1), 27–38.

Munby, H., & Russell, T. (1989, March). *Metaphor in the study of teachers' professional knowledge.* Paper presented at the annual meeting of the American Educational Research Association, San Francisco.

Munby, H., Russell, T., & Martin, A.K. (in press). Teachers' knowledge and how it develops. In V. Richardson (Ed.), *Handbook of research on teaching, 4th ed.*

Nelson, L. (1973). Die Unmöglichkeit der Erkenntnistheorie [The impossibility of the theory of knowledge]. In L. Nelson (Ed.), *Gesammelte Schriften* [Collected writings] (Vol. 2, pp. 459–483). Hamburg: Felix Meiner Verlag.

Nias, J. (1996). Thinking about feeling: The emotions in teaching. *Cambridge Journal of Education, 26*(3), 293–306.

Noffke, S., & Brennan, M. (1991). Action research and reflective student teaching at the University of Winconsin-Madison: Issues and examples. In B. R. Tabachnick & K. Zeichner (Eds.), *Issues and practices in inquiry-oriented teacher education* (pp. 186–201). London: Falmer Press.

Northfield, J., & Gunstone, R. (1997). Teacher education as a process of developing teacher knowledge. In J. Loughran & T. Russell (Eds.), *Purpose, passion and pedagogy in teacher education* (pp. 48–56). London: Falmer Press.

Nussbaum, M. C. (1986). *The fragility of goodness: Luck and ethics in Greek tragedy and philosophy.* Cambridge, MA: Cambridge University Press.

Ochanine, D. (1978). Le role des images operatives dans la regulation des activités de travail [The role of operative images in the regulation of working activities]. *Psychologie et Education, 2*(2), 63–72.

O'Hanlon, C. (Ed.) (1996). *Professional development through action research in educational settings*. London: Falmer Press.

Oldfather, P., Bonds, S., & Bray, T. (1994). Stalking the "fuzzy sunshine seeds": Constructivist processes for teaching about constructivism in teacher education. *Teacher Education Quarterly, 21*(5), 5–14.

Olson, J. (1982). Constructivism and education: A productive alliance. *Interchange, 13*(4), 70–75.

Olson, J. (1984). What makes teachers tick? Considering the routes of teaching. In R. Halkes & J. K. Olson (Eds.), *Teacher thinking* (pp. 35–42). Lisse: Swets & Zeitlinger.

Ornstein, R. E. (1972). *The psychology of human consciousness*. San Francisco: Freeman.

Paterson, B. L. (1995). Developing and maintaining reflection in clinical journals. *Nurse Education Today, 15*, 211–220.

Perrodin, A. (1959). Student teachers try action research. *Journal of Teacher Education, 10*(4), 471–474.

Peterson, P., & Comeaux, M. (1989). Assessing the teacher as a reflective professional: New perspectives on teacher evaluation. In A. Woolfolk (Ed.), *Research perspectives on the graduate preparation of teachers* (pp. 132–152). Englewood Cliffs NJ: Prentice-Hall.

Piaget, J. (1970). Piaget's theory. In P. H. Mussen (Ed.), *Carmichael's manual of child-psychology* (pp. 703–732). New York: Wiley.

Piaget, J. (1977). *Recherches sur l'abstraction réflechissante 1: L'abstraction des relations logico-aritmétiques* [Research on the reflective abstraction 1: The abstraction of logical-mathematical relationships]. Paris: Presses Universitaires de France.

Pinar, W. (1986). *Autobiography and the architecture of self.* Paper presented at the annual meeting of the American Educational Research Association, Washington, DC.

Pinnegar, S. (1995). (Re)experiencing student teaching. In T. Russell & F. Korthagen (Eds.), *Teachers who teach teachers; reflections on teacher education* (pp. 56–67). London: Falmer Press.

Pintrich, P. R. (1990). Implications of psychological research on student learning and college teaching for teacher education. In W. R. Houston (Ed.), *Handbook for research on teacher education* (pp. 826–857). New York: Macmillan.

Polanyi, M. (1961). *The study of man.* Chicago: University of Chicago Press.

Polanyi, M. (1967). *The tacit dimension.* New York: Doubleday.

Polanyi, M. (1978). *Personal knowledge: Towards a post-critical philosophy.* London: Routledge & Kegan Paul.

Pollard, A., & Tann, S. (1995). *Reflective teaching in the primary school: A handbook for the classroom* (2nd ed.). London: Cassell.

Posner, G. J., Strike, K. A., Hewson, P. W., & Gertzog, W. A. (1982). Accommodation of a scientific conception: towards a theory of conceptual change. *Science Education, 66*, 211–227.

Putnam, R. T., & Borko, H. (1997). Teacher learning: Implications of new views of cognition. In B. J. Biddle, T. L. Good, & I. F. Goodson (Eds.), *International handbook of teachers and teaching* (Vol. 2, pp. 1223–1296). Dordrecht: Kluwer Academic.

Read, H. Fordham, M., & Adler, G. (Eds.). (1966). *The collected works of* C.G. *Jung* (Vol. 16). London: Routledge.

Reiman, A. J. (1999). The evolution of the social roletaking and guided reflection framework in teacher education: Recent theory and quantitative synthesis of research. *Teaching and Teacher Education, 15*, 597–612.

Resnik, L. B. (1983). Mathematics and science learning: A new conception. *Science, 220*, 477–478.

Reynolds, A. (1992). What is competent beginning teaching? A review of the literature. *Review of Educational Research, 62*(1), 1–35.

Rickers-Ovsiankina, M. (1928). Die Wiederaufname von unterbrochenen Handlungen [The resumption of interrupted actions]. *Psycholigische Forschung, 2*, 302–389.

Roberts, T., & Nolen-Hoeksema, S. (1989). Sex differences in reactions to evaluative feedback. *Sex Roles, 21*(11/12), 725–747.

Rogers, C. R. (1969). *Freedom to learn.* Columbus, OH: Merrill.

Rogers, C. R. (1983). *Freedom to learn for the 80's.* Columbus, OH: Merrill.

Rosen, D. (1996). *The tao of Jung.* New York: Viking Penguin.

Ross, D. D. (1987, April). *Teaching teacher effectiveness research to students: First steps in developing a reflective approach to teaching.* Paper presented at the annual meeting of the American Educational Research Association, Washington, DC.

Ross, J. A. (1995). Professional development schools: Prospects for institutionalization. *Teaching and Teacher Education, 11*(2), 195–201.

Rumelhart, D. E., & Norman, D. A. (1981). Accretion, tuning, and restructuring: Three modes of learning. In J. W. Cotton & R. Klatzky (Eds.), *Semantic factors in cognition* (pp. 37–60). Hillsdale NJ: Lawrence Erlbaum Associates.

Russell, B. (1912). *Problems of philosophy.* London: Oxford University Press.

Russell, B. (1974). *History of western philosophy.* London: Allen & Unwin.

Russell, T. (1997). How I teach IS the message. In J. Loughran & T. Russell (Eds.), *Purpose, passion and pedagogy in teacher education* (pp. 32–47). London: Falmer Press.

Russell, T. (1999). The challenge of change in teaching and teacher education. In J. R. Baird (Ed.), *Reflecting, teaching, learning: Perspectives on educational improvement* (pp. 219–238). Cheltenham, Victoria: Hawker Brownlow Education.

Russell, T., & Korthagen, F. (Eds.). (1995). *Teachers who teach teachers.* London: Falmer Press.

Russell, T., Munby, H., Stafford, C., & Johnston, P. (1988). Learning the professional knowledge of teaching: Metaphors, puzzles and the theory–practice relationship. In P. P. Grimmett & G. L. Erikson (Eds.), *Reflection in teacher education* (pp. 67–89). Vancouver/New York: Pacific Educational Press/Teacher's College Press.

Samson, L., & Luijten, R. (1996). *Wie gaat er in het onderwijs werken?* [Who is going to work in education?]. *Part of the research dealing with the teacher education program at Utrecht University.* Leiden, The Netherlands: Research voor Beleid.

Sandlin, R. A., Young, B. L., & Karge, B. D. (1992). Regularly and alternatively credentialed beginning teachers: Comparison and contrast of their development. *Action in Teacher Education, 14*(4), 16–23.

Sarason, S. B. (1996). *Revisiting "The culture of the school and the problem of change."* New York: Teacher's College Press.

Schoenfeld, A. H. (1987). *Cognitive science and mathematics education.* Hillsdale, NJ: Lawrence Erlbaum Associates.

Schoenfeld, A. H. (1999). Looking towards the 21st century: Challenges of educational theory and practice. *Educational Researcher, 28*(7), 4–14.

Schön, D. (1995). The new scholarship requires a new epistemology. *Change: The Magazine of higher learning, 27*(6), 27–34.

Schön, D. A. (1983). *The reflective practitioner, how professionals think in action.* New York: Basic Books.

Schön, D. A. (1987). *Educating the reflective practitioner.* San Francisco: Jossey-Bass.

Schwartz, T. (1995). *What really matters, searching for wisdom in America.* New York: Bantam Books.

Scott, A. (1995). *A stairway to the mind: The controversial new science of consciousness.* New York: Copernicus/Springer-Verlag.

Sharp, D. (1998). *Jungian psychology unplugged: My life is an elephant.* Toronto: Inner City Books.

Shavelson, R. J., Webb, N. M., & Burstein, L. (1986). Measurement of teaching. In M. C. Wittrock (Ed.), *Research on teaching* (3rd ed., pp. 50–91). New York: Macmillan.

Shulman, J.H. (Ed.). (1992). *Case methods in teacher education.* New York: Teacher's College Press.

Sigel, I., & Cocking, R. (1977). *Cognitive development from birth to adolescence: A constructivist perspective.* New York: Holt, Rinehart & Winston.

Silcock, P. (1994). The process of reflective teaching. *British Journal of Educational Studies, 42*(3), 273–285.

Skemp, R. R. (1979). *Intelligence, learning and action.* Chichester, England: Wiley.

Sprinthall, N. A., Reiman, A. J., & Thies-Sprinthall, L. (1996). Teacher professional development. In J. Sikula (Ed.), *Handbook of research on teacher education* (2nd ed., pp. 666–703). New York: Macmillan.

Stenhouse, L. (1975). *An introduction to curriculum research and development.* London: Heineman.

Sternberg, R. J., & Caruso, D. R. (1985). Practical modes of knowing. In E. Eisner (Ed.), *Learning and teaching the ways of knowing* (pp. 133–158). Chicago: University of Chicago Press.

Stofflett, R., & Stoddart, T. (1994). The ability to understand and use conceptual change pedagogy as a function of prior content learning experience. *Journal of Research in Science Teaching, 31*(1), 31–51.

Swennen, A., Jörg, T., & Korthagen, F. (1999, April). *Assessing the development of concerns of student teachers in pre-service teacher education.* Paper presented at the annual meeting of the American Educational Research Association, Montreal.

Task force on the certification of teacher educators (1996). *Certification of master teacher educators (final report).* Reston, VA: Association of Teacher Educators.

Tigchelaar, A., & Melief, K. (2000). Peer supported learning for students on paid practice: Student teachers learn to supervise one another. In G. M. Willems, J.H.J. Stakenborg, & W. Veugelers (Eds.), *Trends in Dutch teacher education* (pp. 185–195). Leuven (Belgium)/Apeldoorn (The Netherlands): Garant/VELON.

Tobin, K., Kahle, J. B., & Fraser, B. J. (1990). *Windows into science classrooms: Problems associated with higher-level cognitive learning.* London: Falmer Press.

Tom, A. (1985). Inquiring into inquiry-orientated teacher education. *Journal of Teacher Education, 36*(5), 35–44.

Tom, A. (1997). *Redesigning teacher education.* Albany, NY: State University of New York.

Tom, A. R., & Valli, L. (1990). Professional knowledge for teachers. In W.R. Houston (Ed.), *Handbook of research on teacher education* (pp. 373–392). New York: Macmillan.

Toulmin, S. (1990). *Cosmopolis: The hidden agenda of modernity.* Chicago: University of Chicago Press.

Treffers, A. (1987). *Three dimensions: A model of goals and theory description in mathematics instruction—The Wiskobas Project.* Dordrecht: Reidel.

Turk, D. C., & Speers, M. A. (1983). Cognitive schemata and cognitive processes in cognitive-behavioral interventions: Going beyond the information given. In P. Kendall (Ed.), *Advances in cognitive-behavioral research and therapy* (pp. 1–31). New York: Academic Press.

Unwin, D., & McAleese, R. (Eds.). (1978). *Encyclopaedia of educational media, communication and technology.* London: Macmillan.

Valli, L. (1990). Moral approaches to reflective practice. In R. T. Clift, W. R. Houston, & M. C. Pugach (Eds.), *Encouraging reflective practice in education* (pp. 39–56). New York: Teacher's College Press.

Van der Meulen, M. (1987). *Self-concept, self-esteem and language: Sex-differences in childhood and adolescence.* Providence, RI: Floris Publications.

Van der Valk, T., Somers, T., Wubbels, T., & Korthagen, F. (1996, April). *Commuting between practice and theory in an immersion teacher program.* Paper presented at the annual meeting of the American Educational Research Association, New York.

Van Hiele, P. M. (1973). *Begrip en inzicht* [Understanding and insight]. Purmerend, The Netherlands: Muusses.

Van Hiele, P. M. (1986). *Structure and insight, a theory of mathematics education.* Orlando, FL: Academic Press.

Van Manen, M. (1977). Linking ways of knowing with ways of being practical. *Curriculum Inquiry,* 6, 205–228.

Van Manen, M. (1990). *Researching lived experience: Human science for an action sensitive pedagogy.* Albany, NY: State University of New York Press.

Vedder, J. (1984). *Oriëntatie op het beroep van leraar* [Orientation toward the teaching profession]. Lisse: Swets & Zeitlinger.

Vedder, J., & Bannink, P. (1987, August). *The development of practical skills and reflection at the beginning of teacher training.* Paper presented at the conference of the Association of Teacher Education in Europe (ATEE), Berlin.

Veenman, S. (1984). Perceived problems of beginning teachers. *Review of Educational Research,* 54(2), 143–178.

Von Glasersfeld, E. (1990). Constructivism: Some like it radical. In R. Davis, C. Maher, & N. Noddings (Eds.), *Constructivist views on the teaching and learning of mathematics, Journal of Research in Mathematics Education monograph 4, vol. 4* (pp. 19–29). Reston, VA: National Council of Teachers of Mathematics.

Vosniadou, S., & Brewer, F. (1987). Theories of knowledge restructuring in development. *Review of Educational Research,* 57(1), 51–67.

Vygotsky, L. (1978). *Mind in society: The development of higher psychological processes.* Cambridge, MA: Harvard University Press.

Vygotsky, L. (1986). *Thought and language.* Cambridge, MA: MIT Press.

Wade, R. C., & Yarbrough, D. B. (1996). Portfolios: A tool for reflective thinking in teacher education. *Teaching and Teacher Education,* 12, 63–79.

Wahl, D., Weinert, F. E., & Huber, G. L. (1984). *Psychologie für die Schulpraxis* [Psychology for school practice]. München: Kösel Verlag.

Watzlawick, P. (1978). *The language of change.* New York: Basic Books.
Watzlawick, P., Beavin, J. H., & Jackson, D. D. (1967). *Pragmatics of human communication.* New York: Norton.
Watzlawick, P., Weakland, J. H., & Fisch, R. (1974). *Change: Principles of problem formation and problem resolution.* New York: Norton.
Weade, R., & Ernst, G. (1989, March). *Through the camera's lens: Pictures of classroom life and the search for metaphors to frame them.* Paper presented at the annual meeting of the American Educational Research Association, San Francisco.
Weber, S., & Mitchell, C. (1995). *"That's funny, you don't look like a teacher!"* London: Falmer Press.
Weinstein, C. S. (1989). Teacher education students' preconceptions of teaching. *Journal of Teacher Education, 39,* 53–60.
Wideen, M., Mayer-Smith, J., & Moon, B. (1998). A critical analysis of the research on learning to teach: Making the case for an ecological perspective on inquiry. *Review of Educational Research, 68*(2), 130–178.
Wideen, M. F., Mayer-Smith, J. A., & Moon, B. J. (1993, April). *The research on learning to teach: Prospects and problems.* Paper presented at the annual meeting of the American Educational Research Association, Atlanta.
Wildman, T. M., & Niles, J. A. (1987). Essentials of professional growth. *Educational Leadership, 44*(5), 4–10.
Wilson, J. D. (1990). The selection and professional development of trainers for initial teacher training. *European Journal of Teacher Education, 13*(1/2), 7–24.
Wubbels, T. (1992a). *Leraren tellen* [Teachers count] (Inaugural lecture). Utrecht: Universiteit Utrecht.
Wubbels, T. (1992b). Taking account of student teachers' preconceptions. *Teaching and Teacher Education, 8*(2), 137–149.
Wubbels, T., Créton, H. A., & Holvast, A.J.C.D. (1988). Undesirable classroom situations. *Interchange, 19*(2), 25–40.
Wubbels, T., & Korthagen, F.A.J. (1990). The effects of a pre-service teacher education program for the preparation of reflective teachers. *Journal of Education for Teaching, 16*(1), 29–43.
Wubbels, T., Korthagen, F.A.J., & Brekelmans, M. (1997). Developing theory from practice in teacher education. *Teacher Education Quarterly, 24*(3), 75–90.
Wubbels, T., Korthagen, F., & Broekman, H. (1997). Preparing teachers for realistic mathematics education. *Educational Studies in Mathematics, 32,* 1–28.
Wubbels, T., Korthagen, F., & Dolk, M. (1992, April). *Conceptual change approaches in teacher education: Cognition and action.* Paper presented at the annual meeting of the American Educational Research Association, San Francisco.
Wubbels, T., Korthagen, F., & Tigchelaar, A. (1999). Aansluiten bij dio's: Op zoek naar de plek waar de energie zit [Linking up with student teachers: in search of where the energy is located]. *VELON-Tijdschrift voor lerarenopleiders, 20*(3), 12–18.
Wubbels, T., & Levy, J. (1993). *Do you know what you look like?* London: Falmer Press.
Yinger, R. J. (1986). Examining thought in action: A theoretical and methodological critique of research on interactive teaching. *Teaching and Teacher Education, 2*(3), 263–282.
Yinger, R. J. (1987). Learning the language of practice. *Curriculum Inquiry, 17*(3), 293–318.

Yinger, R. J., & Villar, R. M. (1986, June). *Studies of teachers' thought-in-action: A progress report.* Paper presented at the conference of the International Study Association on Teacher Thinking (ISATT), Leuven, Belgium.

Yorke, D. M. (1985). *Constructing classrooms and curricula: A framework for research.* Paper presented at the conference of the International Study Association for Teacher Thinking (ISATT), Tilburg, The Netherlands.

Zeichner, K. (1987). Preparing reflective teachers: An overview of instructional strategies in preservice teacher education. *International Journal of Educational Research, 11*(5), 565–575.

Zeichner, K. (1993). Action research: Personal renewal and social reconstruction. *Educational Action Research, 1*(2), 199–220.

Zeichner, K. (1995). Reflections of a teacher educator working for social change. In T. Russell & F. Korthagen (Eds.), *Teachers who teach teachers: Reflections on teacher education* (pp. 11–24). London: Falmer Press.

Zeichner, K. (1999). The new scholarship in teacher education. *Educational Researcher, 28*(9), 4–15

Zeichner, K., & Liston, D. (1985). Varieties of discourse in supervisory conferences. *Teaching and Teacher Education, 1*, 155–174.

Zeichner, K. M. (1983). Alternative paradigms of teacher education. *Journal of Teacher Education, 34*(3), 3–9.

Zeichner, K. M., & Gore, J. M. (1990). Teacher socialization. In W. R. Houston (Ed.), *Handbook of research on teacher education* (pp. 329–348). New York: Macmillan.

Zeichner, K. M., & Liston, D. P. (1987). Teaching student teachers to reflect. *Harvard Educational Review, 57*(1), 23–48.

Zeichner, K., & Tabachnik, B. R. (1981). Are the effects of university teacher education washed out by school experiences? *Journal of Teacher Education, 32*, 7–11.

Zeichner, K., & Tabachnick, B.R. (1982). The belief systems of university supervisors in an elementary student teaching program. *Journal of Education for Teaching, 8*, 34–54.

Zeichner, K., Tabachnick, B., & Densmore, K. (1987). Individual, institutional and cultural influences on the development of teacher's craft knowledge. In J. Calderhead (Ed.), *Exploring teachers' thinking* (pp. 21–59). London: Cassell.

Zeigarnik, B. (1927). Das Behalten erledigter und unerledigter Handlungen [The conservation of finished and unfinished actions]. *Psychologische Forschung, 9*, 1–85.

Author Index

Subject Index